William Sachs explores the process by which Anglicanism was transformed from being primarily an "establishment" to becoming a missionary church in diverse contexts. He shows how modern circumstances gave the Church both challenges to overcome and opportunities for expansion, and seeks to understand the nature of Anglicanism's adaptation to modern culture. Not simply a narrative history of an institution, this is the story of various persons who sought a new vision of what it meant to be Anglican, and in so doing fundamentally changed the character of the Church.

THE TRANSFORMATION OF ANGLICANISM

William L. Sachs

THE TRANSFORMATION
OF ANGLICANISM

*From state Church
to global communion*

WILLIAM L. SACHS

*Assistant Rector, St. Stephen's Church, Richmond
Visiting Professor, Union Theological Seminary in Virginia*

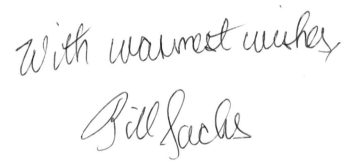

With warmest wishes

Bill Sachs

CAMBRIDGE
UNIVERSITY PRESS

Published by the Press Syndicate of the University of Cambridge
The Pitt Building, Trumpington Street, Cambridge CB2 1RP
40 West 20th Street, New York, NY 10011-4211, USA
10 Stamford Road, Oakleigh, Victoria 3166, Australia

First published 1993

Printed in Great Britain at the University Press, Cambridge

A catalogue record for this book is available from the British Library

Library of Congress cataloguing in publication data

Sachs, William L., 1947–
The transformation of Anglicanism : from state Church to global
communion / William L. Sachs.
p.   cm.
Includes bibliographical references and index.
ISBN 0 521 39143 1
1. Anglican Communion – History.   1. Title.
BX5005.S23   1993
283'.09 – dc20   92–11486 CIP

ISBN 0 521 39143 1 hardback

To
D. Raby Edwards and Martin E. Marty
Mentors and friends

Contents

Preface   page xi

1   The dawn of modernity   1

2   New visions of establishment   32

3   The adjustment of Church and state   75

4   The struggle to define the Church and its belief   120

5   The Church and empire   164

6   Anglicanism confronts cultural diversity   208

7   The crisis of Church and culture   255

8   The search for the authentic Church   303

Notes   337
Index   375

Preface

This book began in a series of conversations about the nature of Anglicanism with Peter Gorday of the Cathedral of St. Philip, Atlanta, Georgia. We realized that Anglicanism has been profoundly influenced by the modern world and attempted exploratory essays whose influence can be seen in the sections of this book dealing with eighteenth-century Church life and with the Oxford movement. I am indebted to Peter's expertise in crafting this work.

I appreciate the criticisms offered by various readers, including C. Coleman McGehee, Thomas Naylor, Joseph W. Trigg, and James P. Wind. Bishop Peter James Lee of Virginia encouraged the typescript's progress. I appreciate the suggestions made by Bishop Stephen Sykes of Ely, whose writings have structured the debate on Anglican identity. I also express gratitude for the interest shown by Paul Clasper, Archbishop Yona Okoth of Uganda, and Archbishop Desmond Tutu of Cape Town. William F. Honaman, Robert Nishimura, and David Tsukada introduced me to Church life in Japan. In Hong Kong, Ian Lam, Philip Shen, and David Yue impressed upon me the dynamism of Anglicanism. Bishop Armando Guerra of Guatemala has been a genial host with a nuanced understanding of Anglicanism.

Joseph M. Kitagawa urged me to consider the international character of Anglicanism. Janet Hodgson raised the issue of the indigenous Church in South Africa and introduced me to Andrew Walls of Edinburgh, who broadened my understanding of Christian mission. Denys Whitehead in Livingston, Zambia, helped me to understand the Church's response to the end of colonialism. A variety of persons also supplied research materials and offered guidance, notably Professor K. Ugawa of Tokyo, Anna Cunningham of Johannesburg, K. H. George Seow in Singapore, Matthew Cho in Kuching, Malaysia, John Weller in Harare, Zimbabwe, Archbishop

Timothy Olofusoye of Nigeria, J. F. Ade Ajayi of Ibadan, Nigeria, and Bishop John Savarimuthu of Kuala Lumpur, Malaysia.

I appreciate the assistance of various libraries where I labored to deduce the modern Anglican essence, including the British Library, the Alderman Library at the University of Virginia, the Day Missions Collection at Yale Divinity School, and the libraries of Duke University, Virginia Theological Seminary, Episcopal Divinity School, and General Theological Seminary. Union Theological Seminary in Virginia, provided a rich library and warm friendships. Charles Maxfield, a doctoral student at Union, compiled the book's index.

Alex Wright of Cambridge University Press has warmly and capably guided this project to completion. Friends at St. Stephen's Church, Richmond, Virginia, where I serve, encouraged this book and tolerated the author's preoccupation with it. Austin Tucker, my wife, and Sloan Smith, my step-daughter, graciously supported this work. I appreciate their confidence in the book and its author. The work is dedicated to two men whose examples have shaped my ministry and scholarship. The shortcomings of this book reflect not the quality of their guidance, but the limitations of my ability to heed it.

CHAPTER ONE

The dawn of modernity

THE PROBLEM OF ANGLICAN IDENTITY

The modern dilemma

"The real truth about the Church," Frank Weston wrote in 1916, "is that she is the human race as God meant it to be." An Anglican bishop in Zanzibar, Weston believed that Europe's war clarified the Church's task. "She is a society . . . for the accomplishing of a work that must be done unless Europe is to be permanently at the mercy of brute force. That work is the enshrining in an international society of the Christ-idea."[1] Without realizing it, Weston expressed both the Church of England's historic self-conception and the modern dilemma which beset it. In the modern world the Church of England has become an international communion of Anglican churches attempting to be both a human society and a valid expression of apostolic Christianity.

Anglicans prize the ideals of Church life which Weston set out. But modern circumstances have complicated the task of being both human and divine. A decade after Weston wrote the above words, A. E. J. Rawlinson, an English theologian, repeated the Bishop of Zanzibar's thesis in four lectures before London clergy. Rawlinson declared that the Church "originates in the creative activity and the redemptive purpose of God." The Church of England retained this conception of its nature when it became a national Church at the Protestant Reformation. Moreover, "even under modern conditions," the Church valued "close national associations and national ties." Rawlinson observed, however, that "the Anglican Church is no longer specifically English," but was, rather, global, free of state control, "shaking off limitations," and thinking of itself "in relation not to Englishmen merely, but to mankind."[2]

Weston and Rawlinson sensed the emergence of a confusion which

I

has permeated modern Anglican life. By the late twentieth century the Anglican communion has acquired global scope while uncertainty about the Church's identity has reached crisis proportions. Issues such as revision of the Church's Prayer Book, the Church's relation to the state, the ordination of women, and challenges to traditional sexual mores strain the Church's ability to uphold historic Christian forms and convictions while affirming an array of human experiences. Anglicans lack a definitive means of mediating between their deposit and their contemporary settings. Thus English theologian Paul Avis asks "what is distinctive about Anglicanism? What is its peculiar contribution to world Christianity?" What binds the Church of England and "the sister churches of the Anglican communion together?"[3]

These nagging questions have produced a variety of proposals for defining Anglicanism. Avis suggests that Anglicanism is "sociological Catholicism," a Church of universal scope which reveres traditional structures of ministry and worship while expressing "a deep, unquestioned, implicit integration of life and faith, world and church, nature and spirit." Anglicans, he believes, cherish their ability to adapt a Catholic form of Church to the authority and life of a "secure, territorial, social basis in a culture and life of a people." Identity, from this Anglican view, suggests "*continuity*" and "*tradition and structure*," as well as the "*idea of the group*" and "*interaction with similar but not identical groups*."[4] The question of identity, and the terms of Avis' answer, reveal the influence of Stephen Sykes' *The Integrity of Anglicanism*, which in the late 1970s framed the debate's contours. Sykes, a Cambridge theologian and English bishop, has elicited widespread agreement that the churches in communion with the Church of England lack assurance of their identity and mission. Certain common features, such as English descent, structures of global scope, Catholic forms, cultural malleability, and Reformation heritage pervade this family of churches. Yet Anglicans have no coherent sense of identity and no apparent means to resolve their uncertainty. An uncertainty over the Church's nature has arisen under the impact of modern circumstances.

The idea of Anglicanism itself is a product of modern times. The Tractarian movement in England, which began in the 1830s and whose legacy I shall discuss in detail subsequently, criticized control of the Church by the state and insisted upon the Catholic nature of the Church of England's worship and ministry. John Henry Newman, a leader of that movement, suggested that the Church was Anglican, and not merely English, because its ancient offices transcended a purely English heritage. Newman awakened the idea of an Anglican identity that was broader than its English heritage and which he attempted to ground in apostolic precedent. This work recalled the High Church movement of the late seventeenth and early eighteenth century. However, Newman converted to Roman Catholicism in 1845, for he concluded that Anglicanism was not truly apostolic, but based in national life. An influential segment of Tractarian opinion, associated with Edward Bouverie Pusey, remained within Anglican boundaries and has found Newman's idea of Anglicanism alluring. Yet his fear that the Church's nature was confused anticipated subsequent controversies. A succession of figures have sought secure rootage for Anglicanism in antiquity, the Reformation, or the sixteenth century, as well as in modern life.[5] The search for rootage illustrates the problem Newman encountered, namely, the uncertain basis of Anglican identity.

By the late twentieth century the integrity of Anglicanism had become the Church's central concern. Why did this challenge arise? How did Anglicans succeed in expanding globally yet ultimately doubt their resolve? This book has two objectives in response to these questions. It offers a broad, chronological narrative of Anglican history from 1800 to 1978, a compendium of major figures and movements. Such a synthesis draws on myriads of contemporary studies to present within one volume a broad overview of the Church's modern life. The book risks being unwieldy because I want to illustrate the variety of forms of Anglicanism and the abundance of persons who have spoken to the issue of Anglican identity. I use both familiar and unfamiliar primary and secondary sources to construe the Church's diversity in terms of a succession of persons and movements which have attempted to adjust the Church to modern life and to resolve its nature. The Anglican response to modernity has included both social and intellectual movements within which various ideas of Anglicanism have prevailed. Thus, this is neither purely social nor purely intellectual history. It is the story of a search for a clear idea of the Church's nature under the impact of modern social and intellectual life.

That story assumes a coherent pattern in repeated attempts by Anglican clergy and laity to apply historic ideals of Church life to rapidly changing conditions. The problem of Anglican identity has concerned the uncertainty of standards of Church life from the past as normative models for modern Church identity. Anglicans, for instance, have historically been England's established Church, rooted in equal appreciation of Scripture, Tradition, and Reason. How these ideals translate into a modern Church in non-English circumstances is not clear. A cacophony of voices with equal claim to being normatively Anglican has arisen without a means to mediate among them. Thus the history of modern Anglican life reveals a bewildering profusion of claims to be Anglican and a pervasive tension between order and community. That is, in manifold ways, Anglicans have sought a definitive way to be both grounded in diverse cultures and genuinely apostolic. The profusion of modern Anglican forms points to a common search for coherent identity. But coherence, as I shall show, has proven elusive.

Words such as "modern," "modernity," and "modernization" risk analytical bankruptcy, as historian Martin Marty acknowledges. The terms have become sufficiently imprecise to become banal. A secondary concern of this book is to contribute to discussion of the meaning of the modern world for religious life. Although, as Marty explains, "modern" simply demarcates a general category of time, as opposed to ancient or medieval, the modern world is generally presumed to have been unhealthy for religious beliefs and institutions. Marty uses the metaphor of a hurricane to describe the impact of modernity. Modernity has bred anxiety and dislocation among religious people. Modern life is generally equated with skepticism and the loss of traditional systems of belief.[6]

The harmful effects of modern circumstances upon revered traditions are acknowledged by respected observers. Jaroslav Pelikan's *The Vindication of Tradition* cites the decline of the Church and other social repositories of tradition. He hopes that historical-critical scholarship might inspire a recovery of appreciation for tradition. Edward Shils agrees that "traditions as normative models of action and belief are regarded as useless and burdensome." Tradition has been equated with dogma, superstition, autocracy, and resistance to change. Traditions seem the antithesis of progress and enlightenment, individuality and spontaneity, affect and experience. The idea of received wisdom, accepted uncritically as authoritative from the past, goes against all that modern sensibility values. Religion stands first and foremost among those inheritances which modernity seems to have demolished.[7]

Religious life necessitates an appropriation of tradition; belief "exists in a faith-world" of received meaning. A communal identity, belief requires "vehicles of duration," structures to perpetuate the contents of religious belief and life. Tradition encompasses "theology's comprehensive, material reference, that religious determinacy which makes theology's setting and symbol system a specific historic faith and not just general ontology." It demands a particular, historic set of actions, places, and objects. Beliefs must be perpetuated with specific references, traditions which encapsulate the content of revelation.[8] Yet modern life has seen the progressive application of rational analysis to tradition, suggesting alternative forms of legitimation for social institutions and criteria for truth. Christianity, dependent upon a focal set of historic events and an institution designed to vivify them, has been challenged in the modern world by critical historical scholarship. Miracles and even the resurrection have been challenged by modern thought.[9]

The appeal of liberalism

For religious life modernity's bane has been the historical consciousness which subjects inherited interpretations to rigorous scrutiny. Some observers have argued, however, that modernity's effects have not always been destructive of religious life. Max Weber's classic thesis that the "Protestant ethic" contributed to the process of modernization illustrates the complexity of modernity's meaning for religion. Religious institutions encouraged the rise of modern life in various ways and have benefitted from modern circumstances. The rise of modernity transformed the Church of England from a state Church to a global communion, shifting the nature of its identity from English to Anglican. As Newman first envisioned, the possibility arose that a Church intended for English civilization alone might uncover within its deposit a religious essence of ancient origin which could encompass all civilizations. When the Church of England began to spread beyond English circumstances, implicit features of its nature were rendered in explicit form. Sociologist S. N. Eisenstadt argues that the modern world compels the explication of cultural assumptions. That necessity encouraged the Church to use modern experience to realize the universal possibility of Anglican identity.

As the established Church of the British throne, the Church of England presumed its identity as the religious expression of a particular culture. Eisenstadt adds, however, that modernity has been characterized by the autonomy of religious life which had formerly been integrated with social institutions of a given culture.[10] As the Church of England's established status became problematic, many Anglicans retained the ideal of a Church expressing the values of a host culture, yet drawing that culture closer to the divine society enshrined in Catholic forms. For Anglicans the concept of "unity" has reflected the vision of a confluence of all Christians, and of a union of these earthly societies with the heavenly one, with the Anglican tradition as the means to that end. Many Anglicans believe that modern life makes possible such an historic union. If the Church adapted itself to the modern world, these figures maintained, the intentions of its tradition would be fulfilled.

There have also been repeated Anglican protests against modern life. The Tractarian movement, out of which the idea of Anglicanism arose, resisted alignment of the Church with the modern world, and the spiritual legacy of this protest has remained powerful among Anglicans. The notion that the Church takes its identity from its cultural locus has troubled a succession of groups within the Church producing a fundamental tension between those concerned to defend its apostolic order and those anxious to extend its understanding of community. The fear that Anglicans might abandon apostolic order arises from a belief that modern life abrogates, rather than fulfills, Catholic tradition. Nevertheless, the preponderance of the Anglican world adopted the values of liberalism. A diffuse concept, liberalism connoted such personal qualities as generosity and breadth of vision until the American and French Revolutions, when it also meant freedom from autocratic rule. In the nineteenth and twentieth centuries, when liberalism became the source of social philosophy, its meaning expanded to include an emphasis upon scrutiny of inherited ideas. Religious liberals have believed that modern techniques must reconstruct Christian dogmas and institutions to suit present experience.

Modernization has meant that a new social order could emerge by the development of new forms of political consensus. Liberalism suspects that each culture possesses an inherent goodness which uncritically accepted traditions have obscured. As Adolf Harnack – a foremost liberal Christian – believed in his historic studies of early Christianity, a religious essence, freed of doctrinal overlays, could be revealed. That conviction inspired numerous Anglicans to search for an inherent unity between Anglican Christianity and non-English cultures. As liberalism has become problematic, however, a crisis of

Anglican identity has arisen. I am mindful of Stephen Sykes' conviction that liberalism has challenged inherited beliefs without providing a definitive new center of authority.[11] Tolerating diversity without reconciling it, liberalism has proven a tenuous modern foothold for Anglicans. The lack of a definitive way to relate to culture has stranded the Church between its ideal of apostolic order and a search for modern religious community.

Though intentionally broad in scope, this book does not offer a comprehensive history of modern Anglicanism as previous works have done.[12] These works were blemished by an uncritical confusion of the Church's ideals with its experiences, of Anglicanism in theory and the multiplicity of forms of Anglican life. In what follows I risk a diffuse narrative for the sake of illustrating modern Anglicanism's many faces. The Church's struggle for identity cannot be grasped until the bewildering variety of its responses to modern life are traced. Although the forms of Anglicanism multiplied, common convictions emerged among Anglicans about the Church's nature and mission. As the Church entered the twentieth century, however, this confidence in its identity would soon be dashed by social disintegration.

Each chapter of the book assesses a set of themes as the Church's search for secure identity unfolded. Thus, the book's flow is both chronological and topical. Chapter 2 addresses the revision of the meaning of English religious establishment which began early in the nineteenth century and signaled the onset of modernity for Anglicans. Ending with a section on the American shift from colonial to national circumstances, I cite the impact of social and intellectual circumstances upon the historic idea of the Church of England. Chapter 3 considers new Anglican initiatives in mission in response to changing social conditions. As the formal nature of religious establishment was eroded, the Church initiated programs to extend its ministry in hopes of functioning as an established Church in a changing world. Chapter 4 shows that while the Church was adapting the idea of establishment, fundamental theological changes were underway. The idea of Anglicanism emerged out of Tractarianism and blossomed into a sense that the Church was Liberal Catholic in nature. The idea of Liberal Catholicism afforded Anglicans a coherent sense of identity which seemed to secure the Church's adaptation to modern life.

By the early twentieth century Anglicanism referred to a Church that had absorbed modern life without apparent compromise of its heritage. Despite challenges to this Anglican synthesis from more

rigorous modernists and traditionalists, the Church seemed to have
found an effective pattern of adaptation. Thanks to its proximity to
empire, as chapter 5 discusses, the Church spread globally and turned
to a synodical form of government. The modern Anglican achievement seemed to be a definitive theological posture of global scope. As
chapter 6 suggests, this modern identity was incomplete. The Church's
increasing cultural diversity revealed its dependence upon Anglo-
Saxon, male leadership and uncomfortably close tie to empire.

Modern Anglicanism's frustration is that its apparently coherent
identity has been steadily eroded during the twentieth century. The
Church's alliance with Western, liberal values was undermined by
social crisis. Following the First World War a palpable disarray in
society was accompanied by an Anglican search for stability. In
chapter 7, however, I show that the magisterial efforts of William
Temple embodied a last burst of assurance in the Church's nature and
social role. Temple inspired a sense of balance between the Church's
locus in society and distinctiveness from it. Resolute through the
Second World War, such conviction began to disintegrate in the
1960s under the weight of social stresses. By the last quarter of the
twentieth century the Anglican Church had become both influential
globally and pervasively uncertain about its identity. Modern life has
fostered the Church's growth to an astonishing but unwieldy
profusion of forms.

Thus this book is the history of the modern idea of being Anglican.
It poses that identity as a conversation between an ecclesiastical
inheritance and social and intellectual forces. Throughout this
dialogue Anglicans have idealized a balance between respect for
tradition and alignment with culture. The achievement of such a
balance, of the Church's reliance upon its English locus yet search for
an apostolic nature, occurred in the religious settlement which
developed in England between 1660 and 1760. The origins of this
ideal of balance, however, lay in the Protestant Reformation of the
sixteenth century. The importance of the Reformation for Anglicans
must be noted before the emergence of an English establishment can
be understood.

The Reformation heritage

"Anglicans everywhere love to appropriate the phrase 'the *via media*' –
the middle way. It is a phrase that characterizes Anglicanism as an

institution that is at once Catholic, episcopal and Protestant," a
"middle ground between the extremes of medieval Roman Catholicism and Anabaptism" in the Reformation context. African theologian John Pobee further explains that Anglicans now must translate
Church principles from their Reformation origins into modern, non-
Western, settings. The Reformation remains the origin of the Church
of England but not the realization of its historic intention of being
England's established Church.

Histories of Anglicanism characterize the Reformation era as the
creation of a definitive Anglicanism. In fact the Reformation
outlined a set of Church principles without a definitive exposition
of them.[13] Those principles were refined over more than half a
century of disparate attempts to formulate a religious settlement.
Henry VIII's Act of Supremacy in 1534 installed the sovereign
rather than the Pope as head of the English Church. Under
Edward VI the Prayer Books of 1549 and 1552 compiled by
Thomas Cranmer took the first steps toward codifying the religious
standards of this national Church. Cranmer also influenced the
Forty-two Articles in 1553, which became the basis of the Thirty-
nine Articles in 1571, the clearest hint of an Anglican doctrinal
framework. Collectively these articles reveal Cranmer's hope for
breadth of doctrine and practice. Comprehension became the
Church's earliest ideal as it aspired to be a means of encompassing
England's Catholic and Protestant factions. From 1558 to 1603 the
reign of Elizabeth I lent stability to efforts at a comprehensive
settlement and Parliament enforced the sovereign's role as the
Church's governor.

During Elizabeth's reign a cluster of articulate Anglican defenders
suggested the nature of a lasting religious settlement. John Jewel's *An
Apology of the Church of England* in 1562 identified the Church with
Protestantism but included appeals to ancient Church leaders as valid
interpreters of Scripture. The Reformation ideal of Scripture alone,
Henry Chadwick comments, "is not, after all, a principle that can be
derived from Scripture alone." Jewel argued that the English Church
preserved the trinitarian and christological formulas of the early
Church councils which were embodied in the Nicene and Athanasian
creeds.[14] Anglicans blended scriptural and patristic sources to ground
the Church's authority. As continental reformers grew selective in
their usage of early Christianity, Anglicans stressed early Christian
forms of exegesis and ecclesiology. Jewel "insisted that the Church of

England had departed not from the Catholic Church but from the errors of Rome."[15]

The characteristic figure of this era was Richard Hooker, who endowed Anglicans with a number of marks by which they might identify their Church. His *Laws of Ecclesiastical Polity* suggested that Scripture–Reason–Tradition together guaranteed the Church's authority. Hooker stressed the idea of the unity of the Body of Christ, seeing in Baptism a manifestation of God's Kingdom. Unlike Roman Catholic ecclesiology or Protestant "marks of word, sacrament and discipline," the Anglican Church finds its identity in its "outward profession of faith," that is, its proclamation of Christian unity in an earthly society.[16] That affirmation grew after Elizabeth's accession as hope for greater reformed influence upon the Church rose in England. Hooker opposed Walter Travers, an articulate Puritan, who hoped to replace episcopacy and Catholic ceremonial with Presbyterian usages. Unity of Church and nation, the linchpin of Hooker's system, was an impossible ideal.

From the Reformation through the Puritan Commonwealth of the seventeenth century (c. 1529 to 1660) the Church of England emerged as a series of efforts at a comprehensive, religious settlement. The idea of a distinctive, English view of the Christian life appeared at the same time from Richard Hooker through the Caroline divines. Perceiving Romans and Puritans alike as enemies, figures such as William Laud and Henry Hammond enhanced the idea that this Church was a Catholic form of Christianity which had been reformed. Jeremy Taylor upheld the Church as a moderate Catholicism which married an ancient spiritual tradition to Reformation tenets and national circumstances. His protégés, who included Laud and Joseph Hall, accepted this framework but insisted upon the primacy of its Catholic aspects. This early High Church party prized the authority of Scripture but urged that a Catholic context was necessary for its proper exposition.

Thus the English Church included a variety of disparate measures of its authenticity including such principles as comprehensiveness, unity, the national Church, and the *via media*. Because Puritanism marked the failure to achieve a religious establishment, however, the Church's first century must be treated cautiously as a reference point for Anglican identity. Early Anglican principles failed to find definitive expression but served as ideals for the achievement of establishment during the century from the Restoration of 1660 to the accession of George III in 1760. The basis of modern Anglicanism, I argue, must be found in the eighteenth-century religious establishment. Here the Church of England approached the realization of its aspiration to be a comprehensive, English Church, blending Protestant and Catholic forms, grounded in Scripture, Reason, and Tradition. Understanding the nature of Anglicanism and the Church's modern transformation requires an assessment of the eighteenth-century achievement.

THE SEARCH FOR COMPREHENSION, 1660–1714

The reality of Dissent

The Restoration

The arrival of Charles II in England to assume the throne ended the Puritan Commonwealth, but did not eradicate Puritans as a force to be reckoned with. In 1660 they hoped for a Church of England that offered a comprehensive religious establishment acknowledging their sensibilities. Their hopes rose as Charles II, in his Declaration of Breda and in successive Declarations of Indulgence, called for compromise with those who were not Anglicans. A broad religious consensus seemed distinctly possible and could have produced a Church virtually coextensive with moderate, reformed Christianity in England.

The Act of Uniformity, which appeared in 1662 with a new Book of Common Prayer, made comprehensiveness on such a scale impossible and led to the Great Ejection, in which as many as one thousand Puritan clergy vacated positions in the Church of England. Even notable moderates such as Richard Baxter felt compelled to become religious Dissenters rather than be bound against conscience. Dissent hardened into denominations as non-Anglicans created religious structures outside the Church of England. As late as 1667 a proposal for comprehensiveness in Parliament failed and the image of a Church unifying the nation remained an unrealized ideal. The form of Anglicanism which triumphed placed greater emphasis upon Church structure than upon its social breadth.

The reason for this lack of conciliation was bound up in the circumstances surrounding the Savoy Conference in 1661, when Puritans and Anglicans attempted a resolution. Moderate Anglicans such as Gilbert Sheldon (a future Archbishop of Canterbury) did not deliberately scheme to force Puritans out; but they did hold to a "prescribed common worship and a minimum standard of ceremonial" as "indispensable safeguards of the Church's unity." Episcopal ordination became the crucial issue because the office of bishop seemed a visible link with the past and an embodiment of the unity Anglicans looked for within the nation. Episcopacy's reestablishment seemed to Sheldon the natural complement to the reappearance of parish and diocesan structures and the return to monarchy.[17]

However, the character of the restored Church of England stemmed less from the opinions of clergy than from the influence wielded by politicians. Robert Bosher holds that a few laity sympathetic to the views of William Laud from two decades previously swung the Church decisively toward episcopacy, vestments, and liturgy; and while doubting that a coherent Laudian group existed, I. M. Green acknowledges that the return of Anglicanism was orchestrated in political circles. Edward Hyde, the Earl of Clarendon, argued that the Church should be an extension of the political structure which antedated the Puritan Commonwealth. Clarendon opposed Charles II's interest in maintaining a Puritan–Anglican balance and won over influential country gentry to his point of view in Parliament.[18] The "Clarendon Code" gradually put the seal upon refurbished Anglicanism. The Code consisted of a series of Acts in Parliament, including the Corporation Act of 1661, the Act of Uniformity of 1662, the first Conventicle Act of 1664, and the Five Mile Act of 1665. Taken as a whole, this body of legislation defined unity in the nation in terms of adherence to a form of religious establishment comparable to the times of Elizabeth I and James I.

The Code gave credence to the idea that establishment required an historical precedent by which the Church was bound. But the Church also played a synthetic role in the social fabric and fell under the influence of political forces. Modern Western sensibilities, accustomed to secularization, might wonder if parliamentary control compromised the Church's identity; however, the Church's integrity lay in its ability to unite religious and social life. The fundamental question concerned the form that such unity should take and, consequently, the shape of ecclesiastical order. The Restoration settlement was not able to proscribe non-Anglican forms, but cast them into disadvantaged political straits. The Clarendon Code required that officeholders participate minimally in the Church of

England, and that Dissenting places of worship register with public authority.

Despite its exclusive tendency, the restored Church of England reflected a broad national consensus and displayed impressive variety and vitality. An important element in the Church became the Latitudinarians, whose principal figures included Edward Stillingfleet and John Tillotson. This group emerged at Cambridge under the influence of the Cambridge Platonists, who called for rationalism and breadth in philosophical inquiry. Descended intellectually from the sixteenth-century Anglican distinction between *diaphora* and *adiaphora* – things essential and nonessential – the group also drew on earlier seventeenth-century figures such as John Hales and William Chillingworth. Devoted to a spirit of inquiry rather than a particular program, the Latitudinarian group believed doctrine and Church life should be construed broadly, since the essentials of the faith were few, but the possibilities for expressing them were manifold.

Latitudinarians also believed that the Church's form should be left to royal authority. Insisting on the necessity of the Church's subjection to government, Stillingfleet "ascribed to the magistrate the power to define the religion to protect in the nation even if he judged wrongly." Members of the Church were also subjects of the realm who "were obliged to obey the civil magistrate in ecclesiastical affairs." The Church possessed no separate power but must cooperate with government to create public order. Public consensus mattered more than protection of individual opinion and expression.[19] This curious blend of breadth and narrowness, latitude and Erastianism (a belief in the Church's subordination to the state) reflected Anglican fear of the excesses which appeared to characterize Puritanism. Diversity of belief seemed appealing so long as public order prevailed. Stillingfleet believed that individual conscience must curb its impulses to preserve a national consensus. Thus he stressed the need for a comprehensive Church, not one which was tolerant of all religions. The Church's historical example could become coextensive with national life, uniting the English people in the profession of apostolic faith. Latitudinarians saw no conflict between apostolic precedent and the Church's national role.

This perspective proved compatible for the time being with a new High Church group which gained strength after the Restoration. In 1678 William Sancroft became Archbishop of Canterbury, an appointment implicitly acknowledging the influence of this new group. Unlike the Erastianism of the Latitudinarians, the High Church element stressed the priority of ancient Church example to a greater degree than the demands of national life. High Church polemicists found a fresh vision of Anglicanism in patristic studies and in talks with French Roman Catholics. The Gallican Church suggested a model for a Church seeking to be both apostolic and national in the late seventeenth century. Accordingly, Sancroft and his colleagues emphasized the Church's independence and its order, characteristics guaranteed by its sacraments and by the authority of its bishops. In the Restoration era, Anglican episcopacy gained lasting significance and the office's monarchical air seemed an assurance of its apostolic freedom from subservience to the state. Nevertheless bishops cooperated with the sovereign as joint rulers of the divine and earthly manifestations of God's Kingdom. Hopeful of a comprehensive Church, they agreed with the "Latitude-men" that the Church must honor the King and order English life.

Richard Hooker had theorized that the Church and the commonwealth were two compatible spheres of influence that were organized comprehensively, with minimal differences over nonessentials, and that preserved distinctive roles for monarchy and episcopacy, Parliament and the clergy. The exclusion of Nonconformists from the Restoration Church, however, prevented it from being truly comprehensive, and the appearance of diverse subgroups within the Church foreshadowed the rise of Church parties. Nevertheless the Church achieved a consensus about its identity and its national role, and the idea of a national establishment of the Christian religion neared achievement.

The Glorious Revolution
The unprecedented events of the Glorious Revolution shattered the Restoration consensus. The ideal of a national Church had rested upon the concerted authority of monarchy and episcopacy. Erastians and High Churchmen agreed on the divine right of kings to rule and on the symbolic role of monarchy in uniting the nation. In the late 1680s the unquestioned right of a king to rule, and hence to lead the Church, became problematic, shattering the Restoration consensus within the Church and forcing it to seek a new center of identity. In 1685 James II succeeded his brother Charles II as king and, in 1686, converted to Roman Catholicism and made no secret of his religious preference. He reassured nervous advisers that he would uphold the

Church of England; however, his support for greater religious toleration sounded like a plea on behalf of the Roman Church. Harboring no democratic intentions, he wished to remove the disadvantages against the English Catholic Church so that it could proselytize.[20]

Concern that James would persecute Anglicans seemed justified when, in the case of the Seven Bishops, leading Anglicans who spoke out against James' advocacy of Catholicism were imprisoned in the Tower of London. Tried for libel, the Seven Bishops were acquitted and received great public acclaim. The specter of monarchical intrigue against the Church on behalf of a foreign power set in motion a peaceful, parliamentary revolution. Late in 1688 and early in 1689 James II was forced from the throne in favor of his sister Mary and her Dutch, Protestant husband, William. The Glorious Revolution secured a Protestant monarchy for England and confirmed Parliament as the seat of political power. It turned the Church toward Parliament as the link between its religious and civil functions, the locus of hope for a national religious establishment. However, Parliament seemed a poor source of religious unity. Late in Charles II's reign, divergent views between parliamentary factions gave rise to the first modern political parties, Tories and Whigs.[21] Although the distinction proves too simple, historians habitually align Whigs with the country gentry who dominated the House of Commons and the Tories with defenders of royal prerogative. The Church of England also displayed party lines by 1680, with Latitudinarians and Erastians following Whig inclination as a Low Church party, and the High Church party coincident with Tories.

When the accession of William and Mary hardened the divisions between parties, the idea of a comprehensive Church of England receded in the face of political reality and gave way to limited toleration. The nation required a religious framework which balanced breadth with the need for order. The possibility of comprehension fueled fears of Roman Catholic intrigue or of Puritan resurgence because it suggested the religious equality toward which James had pointed. Though non-Anglicans must be acknowledged, because of the new, Protestant king, religious establishment was legally secured. Following the precedent of the Clarendon Code and John Locke's idea of toleration, non-Anglicans assumed a second-class status which was not relieved until the age of reform began in the late 1820s.

The Glorious Revolution created a legacy of Anglican Dissent because High Church Anglicans were stung by James' deposition and William and Mary's accession. Although James had turned to Rome, Sancroft believed the King ruled by divine right and should not be driven from the throne. He joined over five hundred other Anglican clergy who resigned their positions and refused the oath of allegiance to William and Mary. These Non-Jurors believed the Church of England had invalidated itself, and they created a religious underground rather than compromise their scruples. The Non-Juring spirituality of such figures as Thomas Ken and Charles Leslie endured as reference points for Anglicans who feared that the Church's apostolic order had been compromised by worldly influence. The irony of this view is that the Non-Jurors protested not against the Church's political role, but against the rearrangement of traditional political architecture.[22]

Defining the Church, 1689–1714

Despite widespread sympathy for the Non-Jurors, the majority of clergy and laity stayed within the Church of England to search for a new understanding of the Church as the nation's religious framework. Between 1689 and 1714 that process advanced as part of a general political realignment in England. A contest between Whig and Tory, Low and High Church parties proceeded uncertainly for a generation. Unable to control the Church, the monarch could influence it through appointments to the episcopate. Thus William III tended to favor moderates and Anne, when she assumed power in 1702, leaned toward Tory, High Church figures.[23]

One of William's appointments was Gilbert Burnet, an example of Latitudinarianism at its best. Burnet belied the assumption that latitude meant laxity, or that Erastianism meant inattention to the Church's character. A prolific author and conscientious bishop, Burnet defended the Church of England as a broad national settlement which preserved the essence of apostolic Christianity. Hoping to reconcile Anglicans with the Lutheran and reformed traditions, he based the Church's authority not in episcopacy alone but in a synodical authority. He intended to enlarge Anglican doctrine to the point where the High Church party feared surrender of the Church's distinctiveness. Burnet continued the perspective of Stillingfleet, who believed that no one form of Church governance was of divine origin and that the Church should be adaptable to social circumstance.[24] Burnet in 1702 noticed the rigidity of divisions between Church parties and coined the terms "High" and "Low," which have endured as characterizations. The Low Church party seemed sympathetic to Nonconformists and cooperative with parliamentary authority while the High Church party held out for royal prerogative and the right of Convocation to direct the Church's life parallel to the role of Parliament in governing the nation.[25] Convocation became the arena in which High Church spokesmen could protest Low Church influence as that party became ascendant.

Circumstances favored the Low Church's advance as, following the Glorious Revolution, England felt the influence of reason throughout its intellectual and social life. Encouraged by the work of Locke and Newton, the theological impact of reason emerged in the movement called Deism. Figures such as John Toland depicted a world which could be deciphered and stripped of mystery. God no longer superintended the creation, if God ever had at all. Deism opened the door to outright atheism, and blasphemy became common in public expression. For a generation from the 1690s, a variety of antireligious groups appeared in England. They reinforced the perception that reason removed restraints and that the established Church still lacked a conclusive character.

The stature of Burnet and a few other bishops of William's choosing notwithstanding, Church life was undistinguished during his reign. The general standard of clerical practice was lax, and the Church functioned largely as an arm of the state. Worse, the practice of Occasional Conformity, which permitted Protestant Dissenters to worship in the Church annually in order to hold public office while remaining Nonconformists, confirmed the public image that the Church's rites had political overtones. In response High Church dissatisfaction spawned a variety of voluntary groups designed to compensate for work the Church seemed unable to do. Late in the 1690s, especially in London, several societies appeared to promote religious devotion and to strengthen public morality. Though their example later influenced the Evangelical agenda, these societies expressed a High Church emphasis upon cultivation of religious devotion rather than conversion to it. The idea of education in the faith spread to the Society for the Promotion of Christian Knowledge (SPCK), organized in 1698 to publish popular Christian literature, and the Society for the Propagation of the Gospel (SPG), which from

1701 created colonial chaplaincies in the Americas and India. Anglicans could not yet envision massive missionary work; but they nevertheless perceived a need for the Church's ministry in British colonies and occasionally attempted to convert non-English persons in these territories.[26]

The appearance of voluntary efforts to extend the Church's influence was representative of anti-Erastianism among the High Church party. Driven from its former theological locus of divine kingship by James II's apostasy and William III's accession, the High Church party relocated the Church's authority in its patristic sources, especially episcopal office, and in its possibility for self-governance in imitation of ancient Church councils, Convocation. This was no effort to distinguish the Church from the state, as Tractarians inspired in the nineteenth century. Rather the High Church position was that the Church should be coequal with the state, not an arm of it as the Low Church party tended to believe. During the reign of Queen Anne, from 1702 to 1714, the Tory and High Church groups gained ground impressively. When Anne appointed High Churchmen such as George Hooper, George Bull, and Francis Atterbury to the episcopate, she encouraged the High Church hope of a national religious establishment which honored the Church's apostolic character. In this atmosphere Henry Sacheverell preached a virulently Tory sermon proscribing religious Dissent. The sermon sparked popular fears and mobs assaulted Nonconformists and their meeting houses. Sacheverell's trial in 1710 ended inconclusively but gave evidence of the appeal of the Tory slogan, the "Church in Danger."[27]

The contest between Whig and Tory, Low Church and High Church, reached its climax during Anne's reign. This struggle should not be interpreted in modern terms as a tension between those who would disengage the Anglican Church from the culture surrounding it and those who valued its locus in that culture. Both parties presumed the connection between political and religious life, the alignment of Low Church and Whig sentiment, and High Church with the Tories. Low and High concurred that the Church ensured the state's legitimacy. In the "first age of party," Tories and Whigs accepted the basic political framework and, in general terms, the Church's role in it.[28] Instead the party contest centered on the High Church contention that the Church should oversee its own matters through Convocation and uphold the prerogatives of episcopacy versus Low Church insistence that Parliament was the Church's proper forum and episcopacy functioned as an arm of the state. This tension between insistence on proper Church order and defense of the Church's alignment with the political community frustrated the hope of religious establishment and anticipated the modern Anglican dilemma.

The struggle between Church parties came to a head over the nature of Convocation. This ecclesiastical forum did not meet from 1664 to 1689. After the Glorious Revolution, Convocation failed to address such pressing issues as revision of liturgy and revamping of canons and ecclesiastical courts, a reticence to act which Norman Sykes believes hindered subsequent efforts to upgrade its role.[29] Despite such unimpressive precedents, Convocation became the center of High Church claims from 1697, when Francis Atterbury published *A Letter to a Convocation Man concerning the Rights, Powers, and Privileges of that Body*. This work offered the classic High Church position that Convocation was the highest spiritual forum, and, as with Parliament, the King's power to summon Convocation was restricted. Thus, for the High Church party after the Non-Juror Schism, the royal supremacy mattered less than the Church's right to be equal to other arms of national governance, a delicate balancing act between the Church's national and apostolic roles.[30]

William Wake (later Archbishop of Canterbury) replied to Atterbury with *The Authority of Christian Princes over their Ecclesiastical Synods Asserted*. His text illustrated the sway of Erastianism over Low Church opinion. Wake urged that the claim of parallel status for Convocation was historically new, contravening ancient precedent. Historically he perceived that Church councils met with permission of the civil magistrate. Kings often led Church councils with respect to matters discussed and the manner of discussing them. The medieval contest for control of the Church distanced it from civil oversight but enhanced papal prerogative, leading to abuses of power and requiring Protestant reforms. Any effort to distinguish ecclesiastical from civil power would fracture a vital alliance. Convocation should exist subsidiary to Parliament, not equal to it.[31]

Wake maintained this view in his *Appeal to all true members of the Church of England* in 1698, where he condemned " 'the new sort of disciplinarians' who repudiated the historic Anglican position in regard to the royal authority." Refusing to back down, Atterbury published *The Rights, Powers and Privileges of an English Convocation Stated and Vindicated* in 1700. Dismissing Wake, Atterbury insisted upon the right of clergy to gather in convocations in order to resolve Church business and the right of archbishops to summon such meetings. This time Atterbury was engaged by White Kennett, who published *Ecclesiastical Synods and Parliamentary Convocations in the Church of England* early in 1701, a few days before Convocation convened. Bishop of Peterborough, Kennett argued that Atterbury confused civil and ecclesiastical assemblies, to the Church's discredit. Convocations could not be equated with ancient Church synods because English bishops had cooperated with lords since the Anglo-Saxon era for mutual governance of the realm. Clergy possessed rights through their ability to assent to taxation, and should not consider a separate forum the appropriate means to preserve their legitimacy.[32] Wake's *The State of the Church and Clergy of England* of 1703 reiterated Kennett's argument through an expanded historical study. Wake also held that Atterbury's depiction of Convocation as equal to, but distinguished from, Parliament lacked precedent and altered the Church's nature. English experience legitimately blended the Church's apostolic offices with civil functions.

This complex debate illustrated the shifting fortunes of Church parties. Once defenders of royal prerogative, the High Church party now upheld the clergy's right to decide Church matters through Convocation and criticized the alliance of the Church with the throne and Parliament. Historically supporters of the Glorious Revolution, Whigs and the Low Church party now endorsed the monarchy and embraced Parliament as the Church's forum. Parliament embodied the Low Church sense of balance between the Church's distinctive, religious order and its role in civil society. Wake and Kennett cited Anglo-Saxon example against Atterbury's assertion that the Church's actual precedent lay in ancient councils distanced from civil influence.

In fact both images were historical constructs designed to serve ideological purposes in the political circumstances of the moment. High and Low alike claimed decisive precedent, using the past to create images of religious establishment in the present. By the early eighteenth century this contest over how the Church would relate to the state favored the Low Church and Whig parties, and the High Church and Tory fortunes faded. Religion and politics had "merged to feed the rage of party in this period"; but by 1710, when Sacheverell was tried for inciting public disorder, Tory and High Church fears could alarm the nation, but not determine political settlement.[33] By the later years of Anne's reign High Church sentiment appealed primarily to lower, parochial clergy, not to Church leaders. Although the fall of the Tories from influence after the accession of George I in 1714 cannot be explained easily, clearly the Tories had become factionalized and marginalized, and skillful Whig organization allowed that party to ascend. Tory and High Church sentiments influenced only a grassroots minority as Convocation was prorogued from 1717 to 1741, and then for over a century. Episcopal appointments came to Low Church figures and, from 1714 to 1760, the Church adapted its life to the Whig political oligarchy.

In such circumstances the Church approached the reality of being England's religious establishment. Ironically the nature of that establishment proved both incomplete and distasteful. Furthermore the Church could find neither a comprehensive form of establishment, nor one which ensured its distinctiveness from social influence. Nevertheless religious establishment has been Anglicanism's foremost ideal, and its eighteenth-century form became the backdrop for Anglicanism's modern development.

WHIG OLIGARCHY AND RELIGIOUS ESTABLISHMENT, 1714–60

The nature of establishment

How did political oligarchy function for nearly half a century, and what role did the Church play in this form of political stability? The answers lie in the coincidence of economic and social circumstances with Whig doctrine. Political channels carved by Whig supremacy sufficed to contain popular aspirations. For instance, expansion of the professions during this period lent credence to hopes of social mobility and dispersed a sense of having a personal stake in the social structure regardless of one's political loyalty.[34]

Social stability also came about as a result of the Whig ability to articulate an ideology which solidified social consensus. Whig beliefs endowed England with a sense of political identity and a method of political function. Whiggism enhanced the role of the property-owning classes and argued for the consent of the governed, including the right of resistance to the throne, but it hesitated at the thought of popular sovereignty. More optimistic about human nature than the Tory emphasis upon original sin, Whiggism stopped short of uncritical idealism about human capacity for good. As wary of human intentions as it was of government restraint upon human freedom, Whiggism idealized a balance between order and liberty, deference and freedom, the authority of tradition and social hierarchy versus the consent of property-owners. Government must have authority because God endorses restraint of human passion; however, government's precise form derives from human participation in executing the divine will. Good government manifests a consensus throughout society on authority's nature and its appropriate form.[35] More than a consensus, the eighteenth-century Whig achievement, historian J. C. D. Clark has argued persuasively, represented an *ancien régime*, a fusion of political and social elements into a sense of unity. Whig oligarchy accommodated diverse political views into generally acceptable values and means of order. Its notions of aristocracy, property, patriarchy, and deference satisfied political and social aspiration for half a century.[36]

The religion of the Church of England was right at the heart of this order. The Church infused Whig political doctrine with a rationalist theology that reflected basic social assumptions. The Church became the embodiment of that balance toward which Whig constitutionalists aspired. The pivotal religious doctrine consisted in the idea of Providence. Consonant with reason and social necessity, God ordered and sustained the world. Theologians generally stopped short of Deist implications that perhaps God had retired to allow nature self-governance, or that God's ways could be discerned by reason alone, without the need for revelation. Attuned to the Whig fear of unchecked liberty, theologians of the age sought a balance between reason and revelation, science and Scripture, in determining God's nature and intention.

The Church of England became central to society's operation as well as its thought. Through its parish structure and its voluntary societies, the Church extended the Whig oligarchy throughout all social classes. It offered schools, especially charity schools, for poor children. Here the emphasis lay upon duty and deference, not social mobility. Children learned to read the Bible and prepared to be servants to higher social classes. Parishes also took on care of the local poor, although there was often a fear of rewarding the idle. Clergy frequently managed hospitals and charity funds, reprimanding those whose behavior lapsed but caring for those in genuine need, especially poor children, providing them with clothing and food. At times of economic distress, many parishes appear to have been generous in providing poor relief. Thus, the Church offered the only network of relief and health care that was available at the time.[37]

The Church's parish network was an important feature of its eighteenth-century establishment, and it offered proof that the establishment generally attempted to alleviate social ills. However, its function as a public relief agency meant that the Church appears to have acted as an extension of political oligarchy, not the source of religiously motivated charity. Other features of the Church's life also suggest the abuses which befell the political establishment. Preferment in the Church was in many respects synonymous with the political patronage system. The Duke of Newcastle, reputedly the great "borough-monger" on account of his influence over a significant number of seats in Parliament, dabbled with equal skill in Church appointments. The Church has been accused, furthermore, of widespread clerical laxity. Wealthy clergy sometimes lived outside the parishes they served, leaving poor curates to undertake most duties there. Many cathedral canons resided far from the close, and even bishops preferred London and the House of Lords to visitations in their dioceses. A few bishops, especially Benjamin Hoadly of Bangor, became notorious for depicting the Church as an arm of the state, and theology as a branch of public policy. The Hanoverian Church appeared to surrender Christianity's apostolic deposit to lax, worldly standards.

Norman Sykes' *Church and State in England in XVIIIth Century* examined the charge of widespread laxity. Sykes replied that within the boundaries of its self-understanding as the religious establishment the Church functioned responsibly if not admirably. He acknowledged the Church's ties to political life through the patronage network. Bishops were often absent in London on business, and class distinctions among the clergy, together with the Church's archaic financial arrangements, created enormous variations between clerical incomes. This meant that a few clergy enjoyed great comfort while others scrambled to live decently. Clerical preferment resulted more from whom one knew than from one's gifts and energies. In this respect the Church succumbed to many of the failings of the age.[38]

The Church, however, did manage to rise above those failings in notable ways. Hanoverian bishops were usually conscientious pastors as well as active politicians. Poor curates exhibited great dedication, and the Church attracted talented and committed people at all levels of its ministry. Often characterized as the age when social graces mattered more than devotion, and reason triumphed over affect, the eighteenth century paradoxically featured a profound spirituality. The prevailing style frowned upon mysticism or dogma; instead, it called for a virtuous, practical piety which was reliant upon the guidance of the Holy Spirit. Sermons encouraged believers to uplift the community, for the Church promotes virtue and godliness, aid to those in distress, and reliance upon God for guidance. The religious establishment emphasized perfecting society's bonds by aiming to extend Christian devotion throughout the nation. Yet the eighteenth-century Church of England's social role did not obscure the distinctiveness of its piety. Adaptation to the age of reason did not mean that the Church surrendered its sacramental theology. The Church's spirit of moderation welcomed vesture and ceremonial left over from the days of William Laud, especially on occasions of great significance (such as George II's coronation, when bishops wore miters). A few parishes celebrated the Holy Communion weekly, and inspiring preaching and sound exposition of the Bible were demanded. Within its alliance with the state, the Church took care to ensure its traditions were not compromised.[39]

Recurrent suspicion that participation in a social alliance did compromise the Church's apostolic nature reflects the bitterness of those such as Non-Jurors and Tories who felt excluded by the establishment. Latter-day exponents include Evangelicals, who delight in reciting the age's failings, and Marxists, who identify social corruption and religion.[40] This tradition overlooks the Church's ability to adopt the temper of the age without capitulating to it. Abuses and incompetencies naturally afflict all ages and churches, and it must not be overlooked that the Hanoverian Church successfully blended the religious and social aspects of its age. Integrated into the *ancien régime*, the Church joined a social sense of whole to a responsible conviction of God's order and sustenance.

The diversity and integrity of establishment religion can be seen in the works of Joseph Butler and George Berkeley. Butler's *The Analogy of Religion* expresses the balance between reason and revelation, and the grounding in society and in the Gospel, which the Church upheld. Butler respected the authority of conscience in the individual, yet challenged the expression of self-interest. He stressed the role of reason, not sentiment, but repudiated the Deist depiction of a disengaged divinity. Berkeley refuted Deism by denying the absolute reality of the visible world. Reality lay in the mind through which images of reality passed. God produces impressions upon the mind which offer each person a means of advancing toward divine knowledge. Berkeley applied this conclusion to plans for education, notably his attempt to establish a college on Bermuda. Similarly Butler supported charities and hospitals, and "insisted on the need for a more vital spirit in the church, partly by means of decent and reverent ceremonial, but above all by prayers and visitations and by the education of children in the love of God."[41]

The spirituality of this creative age included a theological view of the relation between Church and state. Edmund Gibson, Bishop of London, published in 1713 the *Codex Juris Ecclesiastici Anglicani*. Here Gibson compiled the statutes, constitutions, and canons of the Church of England systematically, with a commentary on their sources and development. He intended this volume to establish the Church's independence from Parliament by securing the prerogatives of ecclesiastical courts and procedures over religious issues. Gibson respected the Church's integrity, but he favored lessening the disabilities against Dissent in the hope of a broader, national Church, though never at the expense of Anglican distinctiveness. With his tolerant inclinations went a love of Anglican ways and a devotion to his episcopal duties. Later in life Gibson despaired because the alliance of the Church with the state seemed tenuous, threatening to disadvantage the Church with an inappropriate political influence. At heart Gibson was a devout churchman who prized established religion even while he defended the Church's integrity.[42]

For William Warburton, by contrast, the establishment of the Church secured its identity. In 1736 Warburton published *The Alliance Between Church and State*, the great statement of the meaning of religious establishment. He argued that the Church must assert authority over the sphere of religious life including those who spurned its offices. Warburton acknowledged the need to define the Church's distinctiveness as part of the defense of revealed religion. His major premise concerned not the Church's particular functions but those of society generally. Believing that God governed political as well as ecclesiastical life, Warburton stressed that Church and state were meant to complement one another. Human activity demonstrates the necessity of their union and seeks the appropriate form for that. In true Whig fashion Warburton maintained that form must acknowledge precedent but also adapt to present circumstance. A state Church finds validity because it attracts the majority of the population to its worship. As the union of state and religion, the Church of England would endure so long as it remained the dominant religion. Its future security required an effective restraint of vice and the promotion of virtue. An established Church produced knowledge necessary to salvation and married the temporal realm to the eternal.[43]

The alliance of Church and state results from "*free convention and mutual compact,*" since both are independent and sovereign. From mutual wants and benefits there emerges a "Church by law established." The union is freely sought but mutually required, because neither Church nor state completes itself without the other. Truth and utility coincide, Warburton asserted, in what represents an Anglican axiom. Thus the established Church does not submit to the state, but finds in its political alliance the most appropriate expression of its earthly mission to bring God's Kingdom about. The form of the alliance must vary from age to age, because it was circumstance that defined form. Furthermore, he commended the Church of England because it met his criteria for establishment, which he derived from examining its eighteenth-century form.[44] The established Church rested upon a balance between divine order and earthly form which consciously reflected the balance between order and liberty which was prized by Whig ideology. Thus Warburton deserves recognition as the exponent of eighteenth-century ideals which have an enduring force in Anglican self-understanding. These values include belief in the coincidence of truth and utility and in the virtue of a balanced social constitution.

Its social niche, Church leaders presumed, was to be found among the propertied classes, where resources to restrain vice and promote piety throughout society could be found. Among the influential classes, the Church could promote a sense of unity throughout the social organism. Thus the achievement of religious establishment in the eighteenth century strengthened the Anglican ideal of unity. Similarly other attitudes which characterized the Hanoverian religious establishment had existed prior to the eighteenth century, but found definitive form between 1714 and 1760. The Hanoverian experience stamped the Church of England with an ineradicable sense of its nature.

Warburton failed to see that the "alliance of Church and state in England was in fact not one, but many. An immensely variegated mosaic of customary accommodations between squire and parson, between cleric and patron, between bishops and ministers of state, between all of these and the Crown, sometimes in harmony with one another, sometimes quarrelling."[45] He presumed a seamless garment when in fact its stresses were beginning to rend it asunder.

The erosion of oligarchy

Integration of the Church of England into the Whig oligarchy resulted in an Anglican identity characterized by a fusion of apostolic precedent and present English experience. The period of Whig oligarchy comprised that moment in Anglican history when the Church secured the role of established Church. However, the achievement was incomplete and, after 1760, began to unravel. The major strains on establishment brought to light important limitations in its conception and pointed to the forces which would overwhelm it in the nineteenth century. Religious Dissent had been subdued but not eradicated by the oligarchy, and the various forms of Dissent after 1760 represented political power blocs of increasing importance. Though hindered by limited toleration, Protestant Dissenting groups such as the Presbyterians, Baptists, and Congregationalists formed an important set of religious subcultures. Their theologies concurred on the idea of being a gathered people, called out of the nation at large as paradigms of holiness. They sustained alternative forms of piety, church discipline, and even charity among their own. Protestant Dissenters frequently became merchants and skilled artisans, strengthening the identity they felt they had as a distinctive people.[46]

In the "Dissenting academies" the Protestant communities offered their own kind of education and produced a distinguished literary tradition. The notable spiritual writer Philip Doddridge served as a tutor at Northampton's academy, where he led his students through the works of Isaac Newton and rigorous historical study including the history of Dissent. This course of study was representative of the general excellence of Dissenting education. Conscious of providing an alternative system, the academies based their validity on the demonstrable excellence of their work.[47]

Philip Doddridge brought together two of the aspects of the Dissenting life in his work as a tutor and a spiritual writer. When the eighteenth century began, the Dissenting churches understood their task to be the perpetuation of a spiritual culture. The poetry and hymnody of Isaac Watts early in the century revealed a Calvinist aesthetic sense prizing "*simplicity, sobriety,* and *measure,*" a "tribal sentiment" that disputed the Anglican claim to cultural hegemony.[48] However, oligarchy could function because Dissenting groups found for themselves social niches which facilitated their subjugation. As the century progressed Protestant Dissenters thought of themselves less in spiritual than in rational and sociological ways. Their academies encouraged the rise of a rational theology, while the growth of English trade opened up opportunities for merchants. Dissent adapted itself to the Whig social order until the last quarter of the century.

The Tory party and its High Church wing proved less compliant in political exile. Their social niche solidified their sense of exclusion and their "capacity for concerted political action." Like Dissenters, the Tories sustained a pattern of friendships, marriages, and affiliations which served to solidify a common identity. Characteristically their sons went to Oxford and read a body of literature refuting Whig political and historical views. Tories supported charity schools on account of their religious sympathies rather than for their social utility. Tory sensibility valued the Church in regard to its spiritual nature, not because it was the religious establishment.[49] Although Tories had been excluded from the higher ranks of the Church of England, they attracted widespread sympathy among the lower, parochial clergy, who felt that Tory doctrine dignified their office. Tories encouraged the religious and moral rectitude of the clergy. The Church's integrity, Tories suspected, had been compromised by collaboration in Whig control. Instead the national Church should recover its spiritual heritage. Through influential writers such as William Law, Toryism became an exiled religious philosophy, sustaining an alternative vision of Church and society until such time as they could be rebuilt. That opportunity approached as modern circumstances required a rearticulation of the Church's nature.

Tory religious conviction stressed the duty of the individual to advance in the spiritual life, a conviction finding expression in the success of Evangelicalism. Commonly associated with the experience and career of John Wesley, which began in the 1730s, Evangelicalism actually included a plethora of figures, theologies, and groups which spread across Britain and British North America. Wesley, however, came to be the symbol of the movement because he embodied its sources, forms, and intentions. Nurtured in a High Church, Tory parsonage, he studied at Oxford, often joining a few pious students known as the Holy Club for prayer. His frustration in serving the

Church of England as a Georgia missionary, and envy of the faith of the Moravians he met, drove Wesley into a profound spiritual crisis. In May, 1738 he emerged suddenly, unexpectedly, at a sense of resolution. Wesley experienced conversion, a dramatic, personal reorientation, which brought with it both an inner assurance and a profound drive toward a life of mission. He became the founder of Methodism, which emerged as small groups connected to one another by his discipline and charisma.

This pattern of conversion, mission, and organization pervaded Evangelicalism. High Church piety and Dissenting rationality supplied theological content to the movement and the appearance of forceful leadership encouraged it to take coherent form. Inevitably this expansive movement collided with establishment religion. George Whitefield, the first transatlantic revivalist, was a popular phenomenon who treated large crowds to his fervent oratory. Despite his ordination to serve within the Church, Whitefield was denied permission to preach in Charleston, South Carolina by the local Church commissary, Alexander Garden. Anglican authorities fervently condemned the new movement as "enthusiasm," the unchecked passion from which the age of reason recoiled. Evangelicalism awakened fears of the political upheaval that had been triggered by religious fervor in the seventeenth century. The movement was a grassroots phenomenon whose common features lent credence to fears of a united, passionate opposition which challenged reason and oligarchy. In fact the Evangelical movement proved fissiparous in various ways. For example, Wesley and Whitefield assumed opposing theological views. Wesley inclined toward the Arminian emphasis on human initiative in the religious life, and considered the possibility that a believer could achieve spiritual perfection. Whitefield retained a Calvinistic theology, stressing the priority of God's grace in achieving personal righteousness.

Evangelicals, moreover, differed over the nature of the Church of England. Many Evangelicals moved rapidly away from what they believed was a bankrupt institution, while others, in apparent continuity with Tory example, established a network of sympathetic parish clergy. Figures such as Henry Venn, John Fletcher, and William Romaine articulated a new, dynamic spirituality which they hoped would suffuse the Church. They reinterpreted the idea of God's Providence from an impersonal sense of cosmic design to a personal sense of moral accountability. Events in the natural world, such as the

Lisbon earthquake of 1751, revealed moral causes and encouraged personal repentance. Evangelicals encouraged a form of personal reintegration which aligned oneself with God's design, not the order of the political establishment.

The task of rebuilding the self suggested the possibility of rebuilding the world and, after 1760 (when George III became king), attempts at social reform multiplied. At first the sources were not apparently religious. There is evidence of a coffee-house political world in London where active discussions focused discontent and encouraged new political platforms. In the 1760s the celebrated case of John Wilkes, excluded from Parliament for controversial statements, increased public calls for free speech and political reform. By the 1780s religious Dissent called for a repeal of the Test and Corporation Acts which restricted their civil liberties. By the 1790s the appearance of Methodism as a distinctive religious organization signaled the end of the age of oligarchy and the emergence of the age of denominationalism. Religious pluralism, a symptom of modern circumstances, rendered the Church of England's self-understanding obsolete.

The Church could not avoid these new conditions and responded by attempting to preserve a sense of itself as the religious establishment. William Paley defended the Church as socially expedient for its ability to inspire moral commitment. Implicitly, however, this arrangement shifted the basis of the Church's identity. Before 1760, establishment had been defended on the basis of political obligation. The Church derived its legitimacy from the warrant of Scripture and from the fact of the Glorious Revolution. In the age of oligarchy the religious establishment successfully derived a theory of political obligation from a balanced view of biblical injunction and English experience. That balance concealed incongruities which, after 1760, could no longer be denied. Paley's stress on the Church's social utility concealed the loss of balance and the emergence of tensions in Anglican identity.[50]

Political disarray increased the uncertainty of the Church's nature. Although a few figures, such as the quixotic commentator Soame Jenyns, viewed Christianity as inherently apolitical, an intimate bond to political life was the Church's legacy. Radicals such as Tom Paine accused religion of being antithetical to reform, and the Church of England's instincts convicted it of the charge. As the age of the American and French Revolutions unfolded, leading Anglicans called for public loyalty and social order. Given the Anglican emphasis upon establishment this stance was not surprising. Revolution threatened the Church's assumptions, notably its belief in a balanced constitution.

As Parliament became the locus of political reform the Church's social nature became problematic. The Church's Whig leadership had viewed the political forum as its governing body, where the bonds linking Church and state were forged. Calls for parliamentary reform which began in the 1760s outside parliamentary channels had by the 1820s begun to reshape the political structure and challenged the Church's alliance with the political nation. As a result the Church could no longer assume that a given political order supplied an appropriate center of ecclesiastical identity, and the search began for a new way to consider the Church of England and its social role. The Church required a new vision of unity between the religious and civil orders, a reintegration of apostolic forms with social function. The rise of the modern world precipitated a search for the basis of Anglican integrity. That search extended far beyond England and gave rise to unanticipated possibilities for Anglican expression. The modern search for the Church's essence resulted in opportunities for its ideals to transcend English expression. Modernity also burdened the Church with a tension between protection of its distinctiveness and adaptation to its cultural locus. Anglicans have found that both opportunity and threat are endemic to their modern experience.

CHAPTER TWO

New visions of establishment

THE CHALLENGE TO ESTABLISHMENT

"It has been the misfortune . . . of this age, that everything is to be discussed, as if the constitution of our country were to be always a subject rather of altercation than enjoyment."[1] Edmund Burke wrote these words in 1790 because he feared that a French-style revolution would afflict Britain. He cautioned that Britain needed monarchy and the Church which France had swept away. The specter of revolution demonstrated the necessity of established institutions for freedom and order. Britain's religious establishment, Burke believed, preserved the nation from ruin, imbued those who administer the government with a high sense of calling, and diffused its principles throughout society. The religious establishment secured the freedom of its citizenry and impressed upon them their accountability to the author of society. By educating the people in their common interests with government, the Church promoted national harmony.

The significance of Burke's defense of establishments lay not in his particular construal, but in the fact that he felt compelled to construct a defense at all. In the age of revolution Britain's established institutions experienced severe challenges. The causes were complex and the diversity of opinions assessing society's plight were multifarious; nevertheless there was broad consensus that British life had entered an age in which public institutions must be reassessed. A broad swath of opinion outside the aristocracy scrutinized historic institutions, compelled them to respond to public scrutiny, and created a new kind of public discourse legitimating their roles in public life.

Burke could not perceive that a parliamentary revolution was ahead and an industrial one had begun. New urban areas blossomed in Britain's North from dramatic population shifts and from impressive population growth. New economic power appeared among the middle classes, and combinations of laborers foreshadowed a different kind of political influence. Most apparent to Burke was a new style of extra-parliamentary politics which hinted at the nature of political change. A few years before Burke wrote, religious Dissenters had failed to secure repeal of the Test and Corporation Acts which burdened them for not affiliating with the established Church, but few abandoned the goal of religious equality. Fearing the ascendancy of radicalism in Britain, Burke would not have been relieved because bloodless economic and social changes compelled traditional institutions to accommodate political opinions which previously had been excluded. Alteration of the political fabric meant that institutions had to reassess historic assumptions about their authority and their place in society.

Integral to the fabric of political establishment, the established Church shared in the general scrutiny of British institutions. As Burke affirmed in 1792, "in a Christian Commonwealth the church and the state are one and the same thing, being different integral parts of the same whole."[2] The Church had pegged its self-understanding on a particular political order and, until that framework encountered substantial challenge, the Church had no incentive to overhaul its self-image. The erosion of the eighteenth-century constitution compelled the Church to reconsider its role as the religious establishment. In this chapter I show the various ways in which the reconsideration proceeded. I argue that the Church was subjected to unprecedented social forces, as key thinkers sensed. However, intellectual activity alone did not suffice, for the age required activism of the sort generated by Evangelicals.

Evangelicals forged a new, moral basis for religion in the social framework by seeking to remake the nation in their image of God's Kingdom. Their commitment to mission extended the Church of England's sphere beyond that of English civilization. In America, on the other hand, disengagement of the Church from the Crown intensified the need for a new image of religious establishment. The modern Anglican ideal of establishment derives from F. D. Maurice, one of the Church's major figures. He grasped that the triumph of a new vision required extension of the Church's ministry, as the next chapter discusses.

The Church was compelled to adjust its form to new social forces. Like the political framework generally, the Church's place was eroded because increasing numbers of persons sought alternative channels of influence. As the numbers of Dissenters and Evangelicals grew, especially in new urban, industrial areas, they became impatient with political exclusion; reform found significant sources in British religious life. Unable to modify the establishment from within, reformers achieved influence through mobilization of an extra-parliamentary power. They united a variety of social and religious discontents into a powerful movement, compelling the political order to acknowledge their aspirations.

An early reformer was Anglican cleric Christopher Wyvill of Yorkshire, who inspired a surge of activism in the late eighteenth century. Wyvill called for the elimination of political abuses and the addition of county members to the House of Commons. His style rather than his platform influenced a variety of reformist, extra-parliamentary groups. A new political form emerged in British politics; groups perceiving themselves to be dispossessed brought pressure upon Parliament from without by amassing public opinion. Wyvill's model presumed the centrality of Parliament, but resisted being bound by traditional channels of influence. Instead this new form viewed politics as a public matter and brought discussion into the public arena where opinion could be mobilized. This new political style had important ramifications for reconsideration of the meaning of religious establishment because sufficient public pressure focused upon constitutional flaws could compel a new understanding of establishment.

Religious interests characterized a crucial segment of the groups demanding an expanded sense of establishment. Both Protestant Dissenters and Roman Catholics adopted the model of extra-parliamentary politics, and Dissenters and Evangelicals contributed significantly to the mobilization of antislavery sentiment. In turn, opposition to slavery nurtured aspirations of future political reform, and effectively linked political and religious causes.[3] Protestant reformers hoped for political support from influential establishment politicians while Roman Catholics drew heavily upon their Irish base. Daniel O'Connell's Catholic Association rivaled the antislavery committee as a potent extra-parliamentary force and, like Protestant Dissenters, the Catholic Association labored to repeal disabilities. Despite the fears of reactionaries such reformers did not intend to challenge the principle of establishment. They wished a stake in the political framework, for they held it accountable for its claim to be representative of the variety of interests in the nation.

Resolution of the sense of inequity was postponed by war and economic hardship. By 1827, however, there was general agreement that the Test and Corporation Acts represented an Anglican supremacy over Protestant Dissent which could no longer be maintained. Articulate Dissenters cited the increase of their numbers, the growth of reform sentiment, and the anachronism of legal disabilities. Dissenters had acquired respectability and could mobilize political influence. The conditions which once justified Anglican privilege no longer prevailed, and the political framework changed to admit Protestant Dissent. Catholic Emancipation was a more bitter battle, because Catholics bore the hint of allegiance to an alien power. Opposition to Catholicism seemed integral to British conceptions of monarchy, aristocracy, and establishment since the Reformation. It was one thing to acknowledge Protestant Dissent; many Dissenters nurtured fervent anti-Catholicism. Catholic Emancipation had extensive ramifications including the hint of a revised form of Irish policy. Catholic Emancipation was the hard test of political reform whose achievement confirmed the need for a new understanding of the political and religious establishments.[4]

Despite virulent anti-Catholic feeling, Catholic Emancipation carried Parliament in 1828. Catholics gained participation in the political apparatus, and their political leader, Daniel O'Connell, assumed a parliamentary seat. He joined a growing number of reformers, moving from without to within, calling for general reform. There was a sense that Parliament itself remained unrepresentative of the nation which was emerging, and harbored an establishment that no longer embodied the mind of the political nation. Thus religious reform foreshadowed the Reform Bill of 1832 which adjusted parliamentary representation to accommodate the new middle classes and the burgeoning cities of England's industrial North. Promising to curb corruptions and privileges, reform intended to forestall radical solutions.[5] This reform was modest when measured by subsequent reform, and by the political conditions which would exist later in the century. It could be viewed as the triumph of the old aristocracy, successfully adapting and preserving a modicum of prerogative. Nevertheless to contemporaries the Reform Bill of 1832 seemed a transformation of the political framework, a dismantling of the establishment. At the time it was difficult to perceive the future shape of politics or the Church's prospects. But it was clear that the Reform Bill did not conclude reform but inaugurated a revision of the political fabric.

Further reform emerged not only from extra-parliamentary

interests but from a new, reformist kind of Whig. Epitomized by Henry Brougham, Lord John Russell, and the second Earl Grey, these Whigs sensed the political capital latent in extra-parliamentary groups such as antislavery sentiment. However, though a Whig cabinet carried reform in 1832, the stage for reform was set by Tories such as the Duke of Wellington and Robert Peel. Theoretically committed to a traditional sense of establishment, the Tories grasped the nature of the political moment. Wellington, as Prime Minister, and Peel, as Home Secretary, in Tory ministries of the late 1820s acknowledged the legitimacy of the Dissenting and Catholic causes and felt compelled to grant concessions. To the horror of reactionary voices, a Tory government participated in striking blows at the established Church.

If Tories accepted the necessity of reform, clearly the time had come. Significantly reform did not overturn an old political order; rather, it expanded the franchise and advanced a new political style with profound implications for the Church's life. The Reform Bill acknowledged the political power inherent in public opinion and legitimated the idea that government required popular assent. Establishment's role became the accommodation of diverse interests, a task requiring flexible forms and functions in order to retain legitimacy. This change required the Church to reconsider its identity as the religious establishment. The Church lost the assurance of its proximity to government. Rather than favor one Church, government had to encompass diverse interests in order to be representative. Government could no longer vindicate itself upon its faithfulness to habitual form, or upon its divinely appointed character. Public approbation legitimated new forms of political authority.

Liberal philosophy dictated the terms by which the Church of England responded to its age. Unsurprisingly Liberal ideals attracted suspicion from defenders of the Church of England. Conservatives such as Sydney Smith dismissed the idea that the Church should undertake special measures to attract the new middle and lower classes. They rejected notions of rights and representation as the doctrines of dangerous malcontents. The Church's bishops constituted reform's most determined opponents, delaying the Reform Bill's passage for several parliamentary sessions. Nevertheless calls for reform of the Church began to come from within in 1800, when Bishop Richard Watson expressed fear for the established Church if nonresidence of the clergy and plurality of livings were not corrected.

Until it amended its ways, Watson observed, the Church could not check the spread of irreligion. Most of Watson's episcopal colleagues feared the concern smacked of Dissenters' complaints.

Nevertheless, Watson's Whig sentiment spread. In 1815 cleric Richard Yates published *The Church in Danger*, later expanding his convictions in *The Basis of National Welfare* (1817) and *The Patronage of the Church of England* (1823). Yates argued that the Church's great threat came from the new populous areas, where there was little establishment presence. Rather than tighten discipline the Church needed to restructure its machinery; without such readjustment the Church's claim to be the religious establishment was jeopardized. Yates' opinions attracted public support soon after the first book's publication, for Lord Sidmouth, a Tory, and Christopher Words-worth, a High Churchman, discussed ways of conveying his ideas to a wider public. An impetus to reform the Church was building without a clear sense of how to proceed.[6]

To be in favor of reform was not to be a Liberal, for Yates would have rejected the label. In a sense he defended the Church's traditional prerogatives with no new conception of establishment, or expansion of the Church's sphere. Other figures sought new norms of religious establishment derived from social experience. They sensed possibilities for ecclesiastical order amid the currents of change and thus grasped that new ideals of religious establishment would be formulated outside official channels. In England such figures included Samuel Taylor Coleridge and Thomas Arnold, the Clapham Sect and the members of the Hackney Phalanx. In America, the organization of the Episcopal Church incorporated colonial experience with the contrasting views of church order of William White and Samuel Seabury. Subsequently John Henry Hobart offered a corrective to the influence of Evangelical Protestant culture in order to guard the Church's integrity. American experience foreshadowed the global transformation of Anglicanism, for the Church repeatedly encountered environments where any notion of the Church as a religious establishment could not be based upon an historic recognition by the political nation. Instead, the Church redefined establishment to mean a sense of identification with a host culture.

Such persons believed the Anglican tradition must respond to the Liberal spirit in order to adapt its self-conception as an established religion. They advanced the idea that the Church must embody the culture by embracing its essence. Because it must participate in a divine remaking of society, the Church required more than minor adjustment or spirited defense. These figures feared the Church's irrelevance to social change and incorporated Liberal ideals to search for a new understanding of religious establishment. They also perceived opportunities for the Church to realize its integrity in a global, rather than simply an English, context. These persons attempted to think about religious establishment in ways which have endured in Anglican discussion. Their example encouraged Anglicans to value articulate persons outside the Church's hierarchy for, in the age of political reform, new images of establishment came from without. A new ideal of public authority inaugurated the transformation of Anglicanism.

IDEALS OF RELIGIOUS ESTABLISHMENT

New understandings of the Church came from thinkers whose theories helped to clarify the transition from historic ideals of establishment to modern ones. There also were activists whose practical influence secured new concepts of establishment and, in America, the Church confronted the full implications of a modern environment. For the first time the Church struggled to articulate its identity with neither precedent nor advantage. Each of these strands of experience suggested new norms of ecclestical identity.

Coleridge

Samuel Taylor Coleridge was a series of contradictions. A romantic poet who wrote theologically, he was a Unitarian who returned to the Church of England. Enamored of the French Revolution, he later embraced conservative views of social order. Imbued with German insights into Scripture, he staunchly defended revealed Christianity. Thus Coleridge embodied the major impulses of his age in his search for new forms of social order. His personal transformations mirrored the drift of his society from the fragmentation of the eighteenth-century framework, through a phase of daring experimentation, to a hope of new forms that would mediate between past and present. The personal significance of Coleridge's vision of the Church as the nation's religious establishment was that it came near the end of his life when he desperately sought a lasting, synthetic vision.[7]

A notable tension which recurred throughout Coleridge's thought became the basis for his vision of a religious establishment. This was the dichotomy between Reason and Understanding as Coleridge used these terms. Understanding, he commented, is a direct human response to experience; Reason, in this scheme, accounts for the supersensuous, or religious knowledge. Understanding permits conception of objects in the sensible world. Apprehending a higher order, Reason relies upon analogies from the objective world to express subjective experience.[8] Because of the necessity of both forms of knowledge, they maintain a tension between faith and its object, which resists attempts to resolve it. Eighteenth-century thought grounded theological truth in certain objective evidences which the mind can know directly. From such a method, an objectively verifiable form of the Church could be demonstrated. For Coleridge, moving beyond eighteenth-century assumptions, Christianity was a way of life. Not a set of postulates which could be demonstrated by proper argument, the faith required assent by participation. Not solely affect as Evangelicals suggested, faith encompassed affect and Reason, and the modern task was mediation between them. Religion, as Coleridge posed it otherwise, encompasses the particular and the universal, the individual and the general.[9]

Coleridge viewed religion as the manifestation of an inner essence; however, he was not content with Idealism. Unless God was intelligible, personal, there could be no genuinely religious experience. There must be some identity between the divine and the mind, between nature and the person. Religion as knowledge must be balanced by emotional assurance in a single, immortal reality, which forms the source of hope.[10] Coleridge acknowledged Christianity as the highest form of human religion. It offers the supreme possibility of restoring the harmony between the individual and the absolute which had been disrupted by sin. Christianity's virtue is its attentiveness to social and natural realities. Each generation of Christians face the demand of basing their faith upon accurate perceptions of nature and of history. Accordingly, Coleridge incorporated insights from German trends in biblical criticism. He learned to appreciate history as a process of development and to read the Bible as any book would be read, with proper attention to the social context of its writing.[11] It is a heterogeneous body of literature revealing a process of social development, of a growing sense of shared human experience. The Bible is distinguished from other literature by its impact upon the reader, who can grasp its uniqueness and import. More than any other source, the Bible speaks to human spiritual hunger. It conveys a sense of the eternal to the individual because it assumes guises appropriate to particular times and places.

Thus, when Coleridge addressed the idea of a religious establishment, and the proper relationship between Church and state, he did so with novel understanding of the nature of Christian faith and sensitivity to the social dimensions of belief. For Coleridge there could be no social experience without religious reference, and no religion without recourse to social forms and political questions. Refocusing his pervasive sense of tension, he intended to clarify the relations between Church and state. That is, in his terms, he sought to specify their ideas as regulative forms of social experience. Ideas denoted fundamental human categories which correspond to the objects which they imply and point an institution toward its ultimate aim.[12] For example, the British Constitution is "an idea arising out of the idea of a state."[13] The Constitution exists as a continuing principle, a criterion by which particular forms of government must be tried, distinguishing false from genuine progression. In Britain, the Constitution derives from concrete social needs and interests. The British Constitution's particular principle is balance, which must be preserved under changing circumstances. In every society, the state must resolve the tension of competing interests, which Coleridge termed permanence and progression. The one Coleridge linked to agriculture, to hereditary titles and possession; the other he identified with manufacture and commerce, with diffusion of knowledge and extension of science. The social Constitution intends to balance permanence and progression.[14]

Every people requires the third estate in order to be a nation. Its task is to

guard the treasures of past civilization, and thus to bind the present with the past; to perfect and add to the same, and thus to connect the present with the future; but especially to diffuse through the whole community, and to every native entitled to its laws and rights, that quantity and quality of knowledge which was indispensable both for the understanding of those rights, and for the performance of the duties correspondent.[15]

Finally the national Church maintains for the nation a place in the character of general civilization, balancing permanence and progression so that the civilization of the nation might be secured.[16] These ideals reflected the realities of Coleridge's time and place. He intended to awaken the Church of England to embrace its proper role in the nation. He desired to defend continued Anglican prerogative, yet realized the Church's basis required clarification.[17] No longer assured, its role as establishment required affirmation by a collective act of will.

An intellectual establishment and the source of the nation's identity, the national Church is led by a class whom Coleridge termed the clerisy. Learned persons, such cultural experts have been maintained by states from primitive times to the present. Coleridge did not presume the identity of a national Church with Anglicanism or with any particular body in a given society. His argument was utilitarian, as well as historical. In order to sustain national identity a Church led by a clerisy will arise. It has no necessary connection to any religious tradition, although, for Coleridge, Christianity and the Church of England were supreme. Social need prompts the appearance of a national Church whose clerisy serve as the repository of national experience. The clerisy must "preserve the accepted forms of the nation's cultural knowledge and transmit to each new generation those aspects of this knowledge by which the individual becomes a full-fledged member of the group."[18] In scholastic fashion Coleridge arranged knowledge, capping off his edifice with theology, which included "national education," for theology teaches the duties appropriate both to the gods and to one another in a civil state. Theology serves as the source of cultural thought, the basis of that which the clerisy impart, which Coleridge called "civility," i.e., "the qualities essential to a citizen, and devoid of which no people or class of the people can be called on by the rulers and leaders of the state for the conservation or promotion of its essential interests." Here Coleridge quietly upheld one of Liberalism's dearest tenets. The clerisy, he argued, educated the nation for rule by popular consent.[19]

The essence of the clerisy's task, education includes a progressive quality, advancing the life of the nation through the pursuit of new knowledge. Moreover the clerisy direct public opinion toward hope of social betterment. Less privileged persons can aspire to improve themselves and their children through education. Here Coleridge anticipated the Victorian emphasis upon education for self-help. He envisioned that a national Church's influence would foster social

progress, democratization, fluidity of class lines. The clerisy bind
together society's classes into a living organism, directing national
adaptation to a new age: a view of the clerisy's role based upon liberal
values. Coleridge presumed the necessity of the middle classes as
"essential to the stability and well-being of society. They provide an
essential safety valve by offering the lower classes the possibility of
social advancement, but at the same time they are linked to the
landowning classes."[20] Coleridge expected the continued dominance
of traditional land-owners, but extended the possibility that the upper
echelons of the middle classes might amalgamate with them.
Embodying middle-class ideals, the clerisy could diffuse a new sense of
unity throughout all social levels.

The clerisy must grasp the state of the nation, and the importance of
public opinion to the modern age. In the conditions dawning in
Coleridge's day, historical change required national education,
cultivation of public opinion, what Coleridge called "the critical
spirit of the nation." That group which effectively performed the role
of mobilizing public opinion would constitute the clerisy. No
particular body, however historic its claim, could assume such status;
there was no necessary connection between the national Church and
the Church of Christ, which is an Idea, a principle grounded in the
Gospel. A kingdom not of this world, it stands in tension with worldly
kingdoms and resists easy identification with a particular nationality.
Yet Christ's Church is challenged to exist in "every kingdom and state
of the world, in the form of public communities . . . to exist as a real
and ostensible power."[21] Ultimately mystical and universal, the
Church of Christ becomes visible in the conduct of its mission. There is
a perpetual tension between the eternal, universal Church and a
national Church which strives to approximate it.

Coleridge sensed the outline of a new Anglican understanding of
the Church as religious establishment. He balanced the Church's
ability to foster national development with the need for faithfulness to
the ideal Church of Christ. Mediating between the two, the
establishment is challenged to realize the God-given natures of both
the nation and the Church, and thus to fulfill their potential
compatibility. Coleridge offered no defense of the distinctiveness of
the Church of England, although he suggested criteria for being in
fact what it claimed to be in theory. These criteria presumed the
appropriateness of social change in Britain and the necessity of

preserving the Church's distinctiveness. It remained for others to pick up where Coleridge left off.

Arnold

Coleridge's ideal of the national Church informed one of the early nineteenth century's most influential clergy, Thomas Arnold, an educator and social commentator. He shared the convictions of a group of liberal Anglican clergy identified with Oriel College, Oxford, and with a comparable group at Trinity College, Cambridge, who shared certain presuppositions and belonged to the same philosophical and scientific societies. Clustered around Edward Copleston and his successor at Oriel, Edward Hawkins, these "Noetics" produced some of the nineteenth century's great liberal Church figures – notably Richard Whately and Renn Hampden.[22] The Noetics saw themselves in continuity with William Paley and Joseph Butler, who viewed nature as a primary means of communicating further revelation. Whately and Hampden echoed Butler's conclusions, and attempted simply to clarify the idea that God could be known only by analogy with human experience. It was possible to achieve knowledge of God through a method of induction, derived from the Scriptures, which should be studied as nature would. In turn, the inductive mind presumed a certain outlook. The Noetic school was an openness of mind, a breadth of spirit, a pursuit of comprehensive truth, not a dogmatic method.

Whately urged that the Scriptures were communicated historically, accumulating diverse cultural guises. Knowledge of Scripture presumed understanding of the human condition, an appreciation of human historicity which would establish the basic truths of Christianity as the basis of a comprehensive Church. Yet, like Coleridge, the Noetics prized Anglicanism as the best hope for their vision of the Church and tried to reassure High Churchmen with stress upon ecclesiastical form and tradition. Eventually Archbishop of Ireland, Whately believed the Church to be a visible, historical institution possessing authority identified in such external marks as episcopacy. Yet, in liberal fashion, he grounded the Church's authenticity not in its sacramental character, but in its historical continuity and its adaptability to the demands of the present.[23]

Thomas Arnold helped to convey the liberal theological spirit to a new generation of Whig politicians, notably Lord John Russell. Concerned with accommodating the Bible to a scientific age, Arnold understood revelation as progressive and resonant with scientific discovery. For Arnold all of life was intimately related to Christian truth which readily adapts its form to different historical contexts. Though society ought to be Christian, the manner depends upon social circumstances.[24] Restating a principle derived from Richard Hooker, Arnold argued that the Church is the religious aspect of the state. Both "have the same essential function and would ideally merge with one another." The Church should not insist upon episcopacy, or any other external feature, as essential to its identity, which derives from its function in the life of the nation. The Church embodies a way of life, not a structure or a speculative system. The Church's task is to christianize the life of a nation. Through education it conveys a sense that the nation is a whole.

The presence of social corruption can be stemmed only by the Church's system of practical truth. Of course, with Christ as its head, the Church is also "a society, all of whose members [are] to be active in promoting the society's objectives." The supreme objective is to be a moral force, extinguish moral evil from God's creation. However, few Christians appreciate their responsibility and the Church bears faint resemblance to the society Christ intended. Its self-understanding has become mistaken, compromising its integrity. The Body of Christ is divided into factions, its social nature is neglected, and its ministry "corrupted into a priesthood."[25] If the Church embodied Scripture's standards, it would manifest a healthful social spirit characterized by fewer divisions "hindering the Church from becoming national and effective"; there would be "a true zeal for the welfare of Christ's Church established in this kingdom." Anglican liturgy and articles could be understood in their proper perspective, and the Church's piety and truth could be perfected.[26] Christianity's distortions arose from viewing its doctrines as abstract truths, not as the moral lessons which the Church should embody. Thus Christians erred in distinguishing between the Church and the state, in "lowering and limiting the duty and business of the State." Warburton mistakenly held that the state's duty was the protection of liberty and property. Instead the state should "imitate God's government wherever the imperfections of humanity do not render such imitation impossible," for human happiness is the proper object of the state.[27]

Arnold revealed the liberal conception that government should actively seek the fulfillment of its members. To that end, he argued for the triumph of function over form in ecclesiastical identity. He believed that primitive Christianity, as well as the English Church of the Reformation, understood the social utility of Christianity's mission. Governments which have fulfilled their intentions have required the superior wisdom which derives from true religion. Though the state absorbs the message of the Church, yet the Church does not lose its outward form and organization. The Church does not "become so lost in the State as to become . . . secularized. The spirit of the Church is transfused into a more perfect body, and its former external organization dies away. The form is that of the State, the spirit is that of the Church; what was a kingdom of the world is become a kingdom of Christ, a portion of the Church in the high and spiritual sense of the term." Outwardly a Church has become a Christian kingdom.[28]

Arnold dismissed the accusation that his view would interfere with the rights of individuals who, "in a political sense, are necessarily members; as distinct from the body they are nothing. Against society, they have no political rights whatever." Against the charge that a state could be Christian only in a general sense he vacillated, seeing this argument as a reference to religious minorities fearful of losing their own identity. Ultimately, unsatisfactorily, he defined Dissenting groups as private yet able to influence the state's religious establishment.[29] Like Dissent, moreover, wasn't the established Church's integrity dependent upon its distinctiveness from the state? Indeed, wasn't the question acute for the religious establishment? Here Arnold acknowledged the influence of an outlook which he traced to Warburton, an assertion that the Church necessarily is distinct, and must preserve the purity of its ministrations. Arnold countered that in practice the object of the Church virtually matched that of the state, namely, the happiness of society, consisting of moral and physical good. He stressed that the state was capable of being directed by the Church and able to achieve religious ends through proper use of state power.[30]

Since Arnold did not fear that the Church might dissolve itself in the state, he doubted the need for a distinctive ecclesiastical identity. Instead he feared pluralism, wondering how the state and the Church could be identical when there were various churches, and when one form was established in England and another in Scotland. Arnold insisted that Christians should emphasize social mission as the basis of

their integrity, regarding church forms and rites as local conveniences
not worth causing divisions. Upholding differences caused confusion
and frustrated the Church's intent. Unmoved by appeals to the
apostolic episcopate, Arnold countered that "I am maintaining the
self-same argument against the High Church superstition of the
present day, which Hooker upheld, in his time, against the
superstition of the Puritans, namely, the sovereignty of the Christian
State over all its subordinate offices, whether ecclesiastical or civil."[31]
He insisted that the ministry was not legitimate apart from its social
character. Rather "the Church can never exist in its perfection
without an Establishment, if men will but consider what an
Establishment properly is, and what principles it involves."[32] In its
highest form the Church exists as a Christian commonwealth, which
educates its people and provides for everything which relates to their
moral good.

Religious Dissent's existence revealed the establishment's failure,
notably its inefficient ministrations in poor, populous areas. Reform of
the establishment would mitigate the necessity of Dissent, which
could be extinguished by absorption. An effective religious establishment was noted for its comprehensiveness, for differences among
Christians could be sublimated to the Church's broad, social mission.
Though Hooker articulated this principle, Laud and Whitgift had
sacrificed it, forcing multitudes outside the Church and threatening
the principle of establishment. Arnold believed that if comprehension
could triumph, the ideal of establishment could be fulfilled.[33] To
achieve comprehension, the Church's dioceses must be restructured
and lay authority enhanced. The form of the episcopate could be
retained as an ancient usage, but its authority could not be
monarchical. The Church's ritual should be sufficiently broad to
satisfy the religious feelings of all. Clearly there were abuses, such as
clerical lassitude and nonresidence; however, abuses only heightened
the necessity of an effective establishment.[34] America's moral
weakness evinced the danger of no religious establishment in a nation,
and an ineffectual establishment was almost as bad. England's
established Church must encompass the increasing variety of English
life.

Like Coleridge, his mentor, Arnold understood that the Church of
Christ as a mystical body could not be congruent with any established
Church. However, Arnold could not think in such terms for long.
Principles derive from social experience and ancient example must

bend to the realities of the present. Ancient forms derive their truth from perennial influence, not from a tradition of blind allegiance. The Church cannot be authentic on the basis of distinctive forms, for comprehension is the mark of ecclesiastical authenticity. Though criticized for his handling of episcopacy, and dismissing the question of the Church's distinctiveness, Arnold achieved lasting influence. His ideal of comprehension permeates Anglican assumptions. To be authentic, the Church must adapt its understanding of establishment to the essence of its culture.

CHURCH PARTIES AND THE ORIGINS OF MISSION

Evangelicalism

Stimulated by Liberal ideals, Coleridge and Arnold encouraged the Church of England's acknowledgement of the presuppositions of reform. To be the religious establishment, the Church must be shaped by new social forces, otherwise it lacked a basis for guiding the nation. Moreover, Coleridge and Arnold suggested new conceptions of authority in Church matters. In the new social age neither the Church's hierarchy nor its lay patrons possessed decisive religious authority. In the era of Liberal reform, the Church could be influenced by articulate figures of various ranks, who were able to disseminate their ideas and to rally discernible support. Religious life, like political life, had to incorporate sentiments generated by the sway of a particular platform, by a sense of shared cause, and by the mobilization of a sympathetic public. It was the ecclesiastical parallel to the rise of Britain's middle class in national politics. Finally, the views of Coleridge and Arnold became the basis of a new Anglican view of mission, of the Church's adaptability to new cultural settings, not just the Church's adjustment to new British circumstances.

The reality of the Church's new situation was apparent in the rise of Church parties. Though in previous centuries there had been several ecclesiastical styles and groupings, in the era of reform Church parties acquired new positions and elaborate means of exerting influence. Such subgroups epitomized a transformation within the Church. Clusters of persons formed subuniverses within the Church for the sake of particular expressions of the faith and specific revisions of Church life. The most pervasive social and religious force in British life, a primary source of Liberalism, appeared within the Church of England as such a party.

By the time of the Reform Bill of 1832 Evangelicalism in Britain had become the "pre-eminent source of religious activity in the nation." Evangelicals accounted for "nearly every fresh departure, nearly every new organisation which grew up in the religious world."[35] In a century Evangelicalism had moved from humble beginnings to pervade Anglo-American religion. It had produced magisterial figures such as John Wesley, George Whitefield, Jonathan Edwards, and John Newton. Evangelical language and categories had generated a new, personal style of being religious. Novel religious institutions and styles of leadership had appeared. Although its locus remained among the lower and middle classes, Evangelicalism had begun to influence the upper classes.

Evangelicals differed among themselves over the mechanism of conversion and the nature of the Church. Nevertheless all Evangelicals insisted upon the need for sanctification, visible growth in the Christian life. Thomas Haweis called sanctification a fruit of the Spirit. It marked conversion as the inception of purification. George Whitefield expected the Christian to perform charitable acts as evidence of grace. Thomas Scott sensed great potential for worldly endeavor in the pursuit of holiness. The redeemed soul was capable of acting to better the world. John Wesley posed a scheme of Christian perfection which stressed an active, charitable life. Evangelicals expected the convert to continue in grace, to give evidence of zeal for good works, to redeem God's creation.[36]

Evangelicalism represented a broad spectrum of groups united by a common paradigm of religious experience and an urgent sense of social mission. These groups epitomized the social challenge of the age to the nature and function of establishment. Convinced that established institutions were failing to express the divine mind, Evangelicals created alternative channels at the margins of establishment, not unlike the reform-minded political associations which were emerging. I view Evangelicalism as illustrative both of the fissiparous nature of modern conditions upon inherited social forms and of the possibility for adapting religious institutions to modernity. The Evangelical premise for adaptation lay in an emphasis upon extending one's faith into worldly zeal which inspired Evangelicals to generate a massive number of voluntary associations for the purpose of morally improving the nation. Evangelicals identified numerous social cancers and mobilized to excise them from British life, in the process exerting a powerful reformist impulse.

For most Evangelicals zeal was directed toward eradication of personal vices, such as drinking, gaming, debauchery, and Sabbath-breaking. For a few Evangelicals, including Wesley and some of his followers, Christian activism extended to social problems. Wesley's energetic example inspired nineteenth-century Evangelicals to carry their faith into worldly endeavors. For example, as historian Boyd Hilton has recently shown, Evangelical categories proved influential in economic debates in the first half of the century. The idea of Providence encouraged a public sense of moral accountability which meshed with the rise of free-trade policies. Going further, some Evangelicals linked their moral zeal to the hopes of nascent Liberals. The triumph of political reform included the supreme Evangelical legislative victory when, in 1833, Parliament abolished British slavery.

Roger Anstey's scholarship has demonstrated the importance of Evangelical beliefs and activism for the antislavery movement and enhanced the idea of a connection between Evangelicalism and Liberalism. The antislavery campaign was directed by a group of Anglican, Evangelical politicans and philanthropists known as the Clapham Sect, or the Saints. Bound to one another by Evangelical experience and by moral outrage, the Saints dedicated their careers to the purification of public policy, slavery being the most flagrant abuse. William Wilberforce was the group's convenor and chief parliamentary spokesman. He viewed slavery as the paradigmatic national evil and, using Christopher Wyvill's model of voluntary association, mobilized public pressure for abolition. His turn to public opinion stemmed from a religious vision, as Anstey has shown. Wilberforce believed that Britian bore great responsibility for bringing God's Kingdom into history. Britain could fulfill her destiny if her people would reject moral abuse and purify public policy. He viewed the nation not as established institutions, but as a people, a living organism. The locus of establishment lay in the religious life of the nation.[37]

The other Saints shared Wilberforce's perspective. The group included economist and politician Henry Thornton, authors Zachary Macaulay and Hannah More, barrister James Stephen, India experts Charles Grant and John Shore (Lord Teignmouth), politician Thomas Buxton, and philanthropists Granville Sharp and Thomas Clarkson. They advocated a religious vision for what the nation ought to be. They pursued political goals which they believed would advance their hopes. Such conviction was the result of Evangelical experience. Conversion led them to schemes of social betterment and bound them to each other. In pursuit of their goals, they cooperated with anyone who could assist them, including Dissenters and reformers. The loss of ecclesiastical distinctiveness or the modification of tradition did not disturb the Saints. They feared that the nation's institutions might fail the test of moral accountability. Form was a lesser priority than moral substance. Yet, loyal to the Church of England, they were determined not to jettison it. Established institutions could be renewed to serve as moral beacons for the life of the nation. Institutions could grasp their responsibility for achieving God's Kingdom upon earth.

The Saints' attack on slavery was their focal effort, and this campaign came in three phases. In 1807 Parliament proscribed the slave trade in a measure sponsored by the Saints. Hoping that slavery would be eroded, the Saints used their diplomatic influence to pressure European powers to end their own slave trades. In the 1820s the Saints joined a British groundswell for the abolition of slavery in Britain's West Indies. Here the Saints merged with the chorus calling for political reform. This campaign was a training ground for political reformers as the Saints' use of voluntary associations to mobilize public opinion became a key feature of Liberal politics.[38]

The abolition of slavery was only one expression of the Saints' hope that Britain might fulfill its national destiny. British institutions could inaugurate a process of moral improvement for the world. Their Evangelical sense of the urgency of the Christian offer of redemption meshed with their dynamic image of the nation as an organism which could be redeemed. They believed Britain was responsible for awakening the world to the Gospel, bringing a process of cultural redemption inspired by Britain's institutions. Reform was the first step in the Saints' scheme. Cleansed of slavery's stain, Britain's established institutions should conduct a global mission.

Mission

There was little basis for global mission within the Church of England. Before 1800 only the SPG and SPCK existed for mission work, and their spheres were limited to North America and India, where they worked with British subjects. There was little thought about evangelism among non-British persons, and no basis for transplanting Anglicanism to other cultures. Despite occasional attempts to preach to slaves and to American Indians, there was no systematic, sustained program of Anglican mission. Outside Britain the Church concentrated its work upon its own nationals. Indeed, in India, there was fear that evangelizing other cultures would provoke hostility, disrupting economic and military ententes.

However, by 1800 a new sense of the Church's mission emerged from some of the same sources which inspired new conceptions of political and economic empire. At the onset of the nineteenth century a new enthusiasm for global discovery was apparent in Britain. There was great curiosity about India and Africa which took the form either of romanticism or of cultural superiority. The British public was intrigued by perceptions of both elaborate cultural traditions and primitive savagery, and debated broader definitions of human nature.[39] Opposition to slavery encouraged Evangelicals to consider human nature and its development. William Wilberforce was curious about the "natural man," and the Saints believed that through education and social influence any race or individual could live as civilized British people would. Wilberforce saw no inherent superiority in any race or culture; slavery had degraded Africans, who awaited Britain's beneficial influences.

Wilberforce expounded a popular theory of cultural diffusion. Human history revealed stages of progression from primitive forms of hunting to farming and commerce through encounters with other civilizations. The pace of progress could be quickened by proper social example or slowed by exploitation. Thus Wilberforce and his colleagues presumed both their nation's superiority and its responsibility. Blessed with prosperity, Britain was bound by commercial and religious obligations. Through the extension of proper British example, Africans could be bettered from tribal life to nationhood and assume responsibility for themselves in a modern way.[40] Underlying their social metamorphosis was their conversion to Christianity. Evangelicals joined philanthropists in new forms of African endeavor to supplant the slave trade. In 1783 naturalist Henry Smeathman and Evangelical Granville Sharp completed plans to relocate poor, free blacks from London to an African site where a model society could develop. Though Smeathman died, Sharp continued the plan. In 1787 over four hundred settlers landed on Africa's Sierra Leone peninsula. But by 1789 disease and attacks from a nearby tribe caused the experiment to fail.[41]

Interest in a model community in Sierra Leone persisted under the

Saints' auspices. Sharp's committee reconstituted itself as the Sierra Leone Company in 1790 and sought to create a legitimate commerce for Africa. Its initial contingent of settlers came from black refugees from the American colonies who had fled to Nova Scotia. In 1792 more than a thousand black Nova Scotians sailed aboard a fleet chartered by the Company to Sierra Leone. There one hundred English met them and began a permanent settlement.[42] Sierra Leone became the first British colony in a new pattern of empire and the locus of a new kind of Anglican mission under Clapham's Evangelicals. The idea came from participants in the Eclectic Society, a fortnightly gathering of Evangelical clergy and laity which included some of the Saints. The group addressed topics of mutual interest with a commitment to breathing fresh life into the Church of England.

During the 1790s the question of foreign mission surfaced often at Eclectic meetings. On February 8, 1796 Cambridge cleric Charles Simeon posed the question of a "mission to the heathen." Simeon became a tireless worker for mission, but on this occasion his question received no mandate. Some Eclectic members expressed enthusiasm, but most were fearful of usurping the Church's prerogative. At issue was the rectitude of an unofficial group speaking on behalf of the Church in a bold, new manner. There was concern that bishops, as well as the SPG and SPCK, would object.[43] However, on March 18, 1799 the Society addressed the subject again. By this time its members had determined to go ahead. On April 12, 1799 a public meeting heralded the creation of the Society for Missions to Africa and the East, subsequently known as the Church Missionary Society.

It is difficult to pinpoint the shift in attitude which made foreign mission possible. The new society represented an initiative outside the bounds of existing conceptions of institutional prerogative. Most of the Society's Evangelical clergy feared affronting the Church's bishops, and only a few members, such as Charles Simeon, were wholehearted advocates of mission. Support for mission came from Evangelical laity who possessed political and financial resources to be assertive. Several such Eclectic members were Saints, and their perspective was decisive in achieving commitment to a mission program. It was natural, therefore, that the Eclectic Society should consider Sierra Leone as the site of its initial endeavor. Different from a chaplaincy to British subjects abroad, this was a new conception of the Church of England as a missionary body. More than Britain's establishment, the Church was a way of being the religious establishment in a developing culture. More than an English form of faith, it was a society of believers determined to relate the faith to a given culture in an affirmative way. Sierra Leone could vindicate all that the Saints and the Eclectic Society believed about the Church's role in God's plan of redemption.

However, the new society's founders hesitated to organize their mission while they sought approval from the Church hierarchy. The CMS founders intended to convert the Church to their new philosophy of mission. William Wilberforce spent more than a year seeking approval for the new society from Beilby Porteus, Bishop of London, and John Moore, Archbishop of Canterbury, in 1801.[44] British society, however, generally remained indifferent. At first no British missionaries could be found. Instead the Society's first representatives were recent graduates of a Lutheran seminary near Berlin. Melchior Renner and Peter Hartwig began work in Sierra Leone in 1804, and three other Lutherans arrived in 1806.[45] For a decade the CMS relied upon Germans citing as precedent India, where there had been informal British support for Lutheran work. British Evangelicals viewed Lutherans as Evangelicals who like them came from a state-supported Church. Lack of Anglican orders did not trouble the Society's leaders. Anglican Evangelicans prized mission zeal more than fear of compromising ecclesiastical identity.

In 1810, however, a discordant note came from Claudius Buchanan when he delivered the Society's annual sermon. A veteran chaplain to the East India Company, Buchanan had earlier proposed creation of a bishop for India. He believed the CMS must consider the Church of England's distinctive features as resources for disseminating the Gospel. Human institutions, Buchanan argued, are blessings from God which are the means of persuading people to believe.[46] Buchanan agreed with Evangelical sentiment that education was the foremost means to proclaiming the Gospel. Missionaries must be teachers converting more through pedagogy than exhortation, as experience in Sierra Leone had shown. In 1810 thirty-five children participated in a mission school for a tribe adjoining the Sierra Leone colony. One hundred and fifty children of Nova Scotian emigrants also attended schools at Freetown, the colony's capital. By 1814 Henry Ryder, Dean of Wells and later Bishop of Gloucester, could highlight the significance of education for the new conception of mission. In Africa, Ryder observed, "we seem to have found at last the accessible point of these people, in the instruction of their children . . .

Minds enlightened by education, and having free access to the Bible, will gladly welcome him, who comes to impress those truths which are ever the more acceptable, the more the heart is enlarged and the understanding informed."[47]

As the Society expanded its educational programs it began to train and to rely upon local teachers. From its inception the Society envisioned indigenous leadership as crucial to missionary success. The Society's *Proceedings* in 1822 boasted of training "Native Teachers." The report cited William Davis, a tailor, "who has useful gifts in prayer and explaining the Scripture, and reads," and mentioned that other converts had assumed the duty of instructing their own people. While it desired a more systematic approach to education, the Society was pleased that its educational program taught reading, writing, and basic biblical themes to a growing number of African children.[48] Early in its experience the Society assumed that education fostered the advance both of the Gospel and of civilization. From 1816 the Sierra Leone colony's governor forged a cooperative scheme of public education with the Society. Government subsidy of mission schools became an important precedent for other new British territories.[49] At the same time a systematic plan of mission education emerged. It encompassed the Society's interest in encouraging local leadership. In India Andrew Bell had devised a novel system of instruction using advanced students as instructors. Bell's method attracted the interest of Zachary Macaulay, a Saint and former governor of the Sierra Leone colony, who helped to create Britain's National Society for the Education of the Poor in the Principles of the Church of England, and appointed Bell as its director. Bell's plan became the CMS model for mission instruction. As with British poor, it emphasized hard work and self-help, as well as literacy and biblical understanding.[50]

An increasing number of English missionaries conducted the CMS program. A notable one was W. A. B. Johnson, active in Sierra Leone from 1816. Johnson spent much of his time instructing children and adults, establishing schools, and training teachers. He also preached and reported congregations swelling with converts. When Johnson's London superiors, Josiah Pratt and Edward Bickersteth, concluded that if Johnson were ordained he could baptize converts and extend his influence, the lack of a bishop in Sierra Leone was no deterrent. Pratt and Bickersteth advised Johnson to seek ordination by the Society's Lutheran missionaries and, on March 31, 1817, Johnson received Lutheran orders.[51] Thus the Church Missionary Society's new conception of mission initially did not emphasize transference of the Church of England into new locales. The Society advocated a broadly Evangelical style of church life for which insistence upon ecclesiastical allegiance seemed an encumbrance upon the Gospel.

Nevertheless CMS work inevitably reflected an Anglican style and relied upon establishment perquisites such as government support for education programs and responsibility for directing civil affairs in some villages. Baptist and Methodist missionaries, growing in numbers, cited the CMS entente with colonial government as evidence of a compromised commitment to the Gospel. Non-Anglican groups focused upon revival fervor rather than education and mission strategy, and shunned the hope for social development which the CMS espoused in favor of stressing immediate, personal conversion. This style of mission appealed in a way which CMS evangelism could not.[52] Nevertheless Sierra Leone served as a laboratory for a new kind of Anglican mission. It remained to integrate a conception of Anglican distinctiveness into the Church's adaptation to a new culture.

The Eclectic Society also expressed interest in Australia, a penal colony founded in 1788 at Botany Bay. Richard Johnson, the first chaplain, conducted his ministry without considering the needs of native peoples, did not establish schools, and shunned an evangelistic approach. Johnson faithfully performed the Church's offices solely for the British populace.[53] The new vision of mission arrived in the south Pacific with Evangelical clergyman Samuel Marsden, appointed assistant chaplain in 1794, and Johnson's successor in 1800. A protégé of William Wilberforce, Marsden built new churches, orphanages, and schools. With money Wilberforce helped to raise, Marsden recruited other clergy and hired schoolmasters. Suspicious of the Church's dependence upon the state, Marsden relinquished his appointment as a civil magistrate. He argued that the Church's work required that its integrity be protected. Unfortunately Marsden was a humorless and demanding person, thoroughly lacking Wilberforce's genial compassion. His evident prejudices about Roman Catholics and women among the convict population render him unattractive to modern sensibilities. Nevertheless the imprint of his work is significant. He not only expanded the range of the Church's mission, but was one of the first in the mission field to argue for ways to guard the Church's distinctiveness.[54] Traders arriving from New Zealand excited Marsden's interest with impressions of the Maori race, whom

Marsden became keen to evangelize. Eventually he met a chief named Ruatara and, in 1810, he sent two missionaries to New Zealand on the basis of this connection. The small missionary beginning there proved to be lasting.[55]

Hints of a new kind of mission began to reshape the Church's presence in India, where the challenge was to expand the work of the East India Company's chaplains beyond ministry to the small British contingent. In 1788 Evangelical David Browne, a protégé of Charles Simeon and an East India Company chaplain, joined several other chaplains in making a formal proposal to Lord Cornwallis, India's Governor-General. Convinced that Britain bore a special responsibility to India, Browne and his colleagues argued for a system of educating Indian people in the English language. This proposal suggested the nature of the Evangelical agenda and the future form of British influence.[56] Company chaplain Claudius Buchanan continued the Evangelical advocacy of expanding the Church's ministry to evangelize the Indian populace. Inspired by the examples of British Baptists, especially William Carey, Buchanan organized translations of Scripture and the Prayer Book into India's vernacular tongues. More importantly, in 1805 he published a *Memoir of the Expediency of an Ecclesiastical Establishment for British India*. Buchanan's publication represented an important turning point for Evangelicals and for advocacy of a new conception of the Church of England as a religious establishment in a mission field. Buchanan argued that only the provision of the Church as an institution could ensure its missionary success, a conviction he reiterated in *An Apology for Promoting Christianity in India*.[57]

Buchanan endorsed an aggressive style of mission among the Indian populace. He noted the success of Baptist and Lutheran missions and applauded the work of fellow chaplains such as Henry Martyn. But as a priest of the Church of England Buchanan thought in terms of religious establishment, which secured the identity of the Church's mission. Britain's duty was to transfer her established Church through a local religious establishment grounded in English tradition. The English ecclesiastical hierarchy, however, as well as the East India Company's directors, did not rush to embrace this proposal. They feared irritating Indian social and religious sensibilities, which would disrupt political and commercial bonds. Nevertheless, with support from political reformers and the antislavery coalition, a new kind of mission and of religious establishment secured parliamentary mandate. A new image of the Church's mission came from its fringe.

Charles Grant, a member of the Clapham Sect, was an MP, a Director of the East India Company, and a veteran of India service. In 1792 he published a critique of British presence in India which included a proposal for missionary work there. India's cultural degradation as he viewed it required the light of the Gospel. Grant timed his proposal to coincide with parliamentary renewal of the Company charter in 1793. He suggested the addition of a charter clause, popularly termed the "Pious Clause," acknowledging acceptance of missionary responsibility for India's people. This proposal caught Wilberforce's fancy and became a plank in the Saints' platform.[58]

The Saints mobilized to promote Grant's scheme much as they organized opposition to the slave trade and promoted the Church Missionary Society. In this case they waited twenty years, when the charter again faced renewal proceedings, and modified their strategy. In charter debates early in 1813 Wilberforce advocated the insertion of the clause into the Company charter and urged the creation of an Indian episcopate. For Christianity to be successful in a missionary context, England's religious establishment was necessary. The "Pious Clause" was not simply a sanction for mission; it committed Britain to a program of social transformation, of redeeming India.[59] The episcopate symbolized Britain's commitment to diffuse the beneficence of her institutions, especially the form of her Church. Having garnered sufficient support, this dual conception of English responsibility carried Parliament. India policy was remade and a new vision of religious establishment received legislative sanction.

Episcopacy

When Thomas Fanshawe Middleton arrived in Calcutta in 1814 as the first Bishop of India, the Saints were not the only group of activists to feel a sense of accomplishment. Support for the Indian episcopate also came from the Hackney Phalanx, which included Alexander Knox, Charles Daubeny, Christopher Wordsworth, and Joshua Watson. Its manual of arms was Daubeny's *Guide to the Church*, published in 1798. High Anglicanism of the Hackney sort aspired to preserve the Church's distinctive offices.[60] Daubeny insisted that genuine mission could occur only in the transmittal of the apostolic ministry which stamped the Church as a divine institution. The Church's ministry ensured the validity of its expansion, for there could be no legitimate faith where there was not apostolic Christianity as the Church of England preserved it.[61]

Daubeny noted sentiment throughout Britain for a charitable view of Dissenters and fear that insistence upon apostolic form seemed a sacrifice of breadth and toleration. He countered that the Church could not compromise on one principle without possibly sacrificing others. Though Christianity's primary object was the salvation of souls, this could not mean the distortion of the Church's character. Only through conformity to the tradition established by Christ could the Church be the bearer of God's promises. In continuity with ancient precedent the Church must continue as a visible society with Christ as its head.[62] Daubeny's colleague, Joshua Watson, who shared this view, left his successful accounting business in 1814 to become Hackney's Wilberforce, promoting Daubeny's ideals as the group's manifesto. Mistrusting Evangelical conversions and personal assurance as the supreme religious authority, Hackney's coterie upheld the Church's corporateness and tradition.[63]

This was not reactionary, because Watson understood the necessity of expanding the Church's compass. Active in the SPG and SPCK, he made overtures to the CMS, hoping to wed Evangelicals to the idea of episcopal oversight in the mission field. The consecration of Thomas Middleton thrilled Watson, who energetically raised funds for SPG work in India. He also wrote the Archbishop of Canterbury urging the creation of an indigenous ministry and discouraging reliance upon non-Anglicans in the mission field. Watson believed that conversion to Christianity must occur in an ecclesiastical context. Because it combined evangelizing zeal and apostolic tradition, Anglicanism was the ideal form for Christianity's missionary endeavor.

When Thomas Middleton died in 1822, Joshua Watson was disappointed that the successor was Reginald Heber, a firm Evangelical. Friendly to the Saints, Heber embarked on a vigorous mission program in India, giving education a high priority by founding schools and colleges and even drafting plans for educating Indian women. Believing that conversion was successful only in the context of social metamorphosis, Heber envisioned preparing Indians for Christianity by westernizing their society.[64] To that end Heber began an indigenous ministry in 1825 when he ordained Abdul Masih, a

Delhi Muslim, as deacon, admitting Theophilus Reichart, a Lutheran, to the diaconate in the same liturgy.[65] Like his Evangelical counterparts in Sierra Leone, Heber readily relied upon non-Anglicans, viewing broad cooperation as the basis of mission.

Nevertheless the episcopate in India symbolized the confluence of two streams of the Church's mission toward a new image of the Church as a religious establishment. On the one hand, the Evangelical priority was mission which entailed adaptation of the Gospel to a plethora of cultural forms in search of an indigenous Christianity. On the other hand, the High Church element stressed the Church's tradition as the guarantee of its purity. The goal of mission was neither individual conversions nor the transformation of culture but the transplantation of the Church. The apostolic society would serve as visible witness to the universality of the Gospel. The Church's distinctiveness, not its role as a religious establishment, ensured the integrity of its mission.

A later Bishop of India, Daniel Wilson, who served from 1832 to 1858, drew on both parties for an ideal of religious establishment in mission. He brought an Evangelical heritage to the office, having known such figures as Charles Simeon and supported the formation of a CMS seminary for missionaries. In office Wilson pursued Evangelical goals. He opposed perpetuation of caste distinctions among Indian converts; Evangelicals viewed caste as illustrative of India's social evils and a primary obstacle to its social improvement. Wilson admonished clergy and laity to renounce caste and directed that parishioners should not sit in caste groups in church or receive Communion only with members of their own caste. Clergy should visit parishioners without regard for caste, and even the choice of godparents must not be based upon caste distinctions.[66] This stance evoked renunciations of Christianity among higher-caste Christians at several mission stations. Two priests and two lay catechists at Tenjore refused to conform and were dismissed. Yet Wilson insisted that caste was idolatry and diluted the Church's distinctive social nature. The social gradations which Christianity acknowledged arose naturally, from equitable social processes, and lacked metaphysical sanction. The Church could not countenance cultural forms which conflicted with Christian principles.

While advancing an Evangelical priority, Wilson underscored a High Church emphasis. He argued that the controversy surrounding caste should not involve the government. Only the bishop, as embodiment of the Church, could define Christian belief and practice. Wilson welcomed the opportunity to draw a distinction between the Church and its host culture. He enhanced the vision of Anglicanism as distinct both from colonial and from a host culture. He also added to episcopal prerogative in other ways. Working with the CMS and SPG to place their workers under episcopal oversight, he emphasized that, while the societies' initiatives should be honored, the growth of Christianity must entail "Order, subordination, and discipline, or else the diffusion of Christianity is lost, and the confusion and discord of human passions succeeds."[67] He forged agreements with mission societies which enshrined the bishop's right to superintend missionaries. He also committed the societies to phasing out reliance upon non-Anglican missionaries. Wilson also made visitations to areas previously unreached by the episcopate. On the voyage to India from Britain Wilson paused at Cape Town to assess the Church's life there. In 1834 and in 1857 he sailed along the Malay peninsula with stops in Burma. He encouraged the first Anglican church at Singapore, and paused at Penang and Ceylon. Wilson encouraged a new pattern of episcopal oversight.

Wilson's episcopate revealed the tension between new visions of religious establishment. While Evangelicals spread the Gospel through adaptation, the High Church party defended the Church's indelible marks. One party feared loss of opportunities for evangelism; the other dreaded the Church's surrender of its integrity. Neither was able to surmount this tension. But in the expansion of the episcopate and in the adaptation of Anglicanism to new contexts, a missionary strategy emerged. In America that strategy received an extensive test which suggested the future shape of Anglicanism's ideal of religious establishment.

TOWARD AN AMERICAN IDENTITY

Colonial America

The adaptation of Anglicanism to new social circumstances required modifying historic Anglican features. Anglicanism's transformation was a process of distinguishing necessary aspects of the Church's nature from malleable ones. The tension which arose between what must be adapted and what must be maintained intact constitutes the fundamental impact of modernity upon Anglicanism. The central feature of traditional Anglican self-understanding was the Church's role as the nation's religious establishment. No modern environment tested this ideal's capacity for adjustment more than North America, where the legacy of establishment and the reality of revolution collided. There the Church was forced to resolve the tension between adaptation and perpetuation with no sense of precedent.

The Church of England's American form had been circumscribed by environmental factors, for the fabric of English establishment was difficult to replicate and the Church found itself among contending groups. In colonial America "establishment" meant, first, that the Church of England received "official recognition, certain privileges, and certain immunities" in colonies where such benefits could be legally sanctioned. Second, the Church was not merely "a voluntary body of people who contributed to the settled order of the good society; it is that order," summoning the public to lives of service and devotion.[68] Nevertheless the Anglican establishment only spread incompletely through colonial America. Anglican establishments were found partially in six of the thirteen colonies – from Virginia in 1619, to New York, North Carolina, Maryland, South Carolina, and, finally, Georgia in 1758. In Connecticut its growth afforded it *de facto* influence.[69] However, the Church never achieved its ideal of establishment, for it competed with other religious influences and, even within colonies where the Church was legally established, the meaning of establishment acquired coloration appropriate to the American environment. In America the ideal of religious establishment defied realization and the reality resisted consistent form.

Virginia was the most prominent establishment in America. From the first, Virginia's emphasis upon order and civility followed English example. Yet Virginia was far from the mother country, and by 1660 divergence in ecclesiastical life was apparent.[70] Virginia proceeded with its own theological blend of Calvinism and Platonism, unlike the character of the Restoration Church in England. Bereft of bishops, lacking clerical initiative, Virginia Anglicans relied upon local, lay control which became the indelible mark of the Church's life in Virginia.[71] There was English precedent for such a development, because vestries to superintend church property and finance had been a feature of parish life since the late Middle Ages; but this example acquired special import in the new world. Without ecclesiastical machinery control of Church life passed into the hands of Virginia's General Assembly and the parish vestries. Formal establishment of the Church in 1619 set the stage for an Act of Conformity to the Church's canons in 1632. Church wardens, not clergy, were charged to enforce regular public worship as well as to uphold public morality. Clergy were required to report their annual ministrations to the colony's court.[72] Until legislative efforts to secure clerical status in the eighteenth century, Virginia's clergy had no means to check arbitrary lay control.

Local magistrates annually met with vestries in a kind of oversight which left little to clerical initiative and, though vestries were elected, powerful individuals often dominated the process. In Virginia the Church was the religious arm of society to the extent of sacrificing its identity. In response to this colonial dilemma, examples of ecclesiastical assertiveness began in the late seventeenth century. In 1677 Henry Compton, Bishop of London, citing abuses in the colonial Church, gained authority to license colonial clergy. Though Compton and his successors relied upon good relations with colonial governors, this was an important step, which created awareness of the need for a resident delegate, someone accountable to him outside the framework of colonial government. In 1680 he proposed the appointment of a commissary to exercise ecclesiastical superintendence in a colony subject to the Governor. The commissary could not perform liturgical functions peculiar to the episcopate; however, he could make parish visits and conduct clergy conventions. Because of their access to the see of London, commissaries possessed considerable power.[73] Able figures such as Thomas Bray, who served briefly in Maryland in 1700, became commissaries. Bray, who founded the Society for the Propagation of the Gospel (SPG) on the basis of his North American exposure, and who also inspired the SPCK, encouraged the Church to sponsor new forms of education and sent SPG missionaries to spread the Church in New England. Between 1701 and 1783, more than three hundred such emissaries founded almost as many churches. One of these Anglican Jesuits, George Keith, compiled a study of the North American Church in 1702 which became a blueprint for Anglican growth in the eighteenth century.[74]

Other commissaries also spurred the Church's assertiveness. In Virginia James Blair aligned himself with local, lay control, championing the rights of vestries. He stood aloof from royal governors and clergy alike, preferring to identify with the gentry and to promote the authority of colonial assemblies. Alexander Garden's twenty years in office marked the consolidation of South Carolina's Anglican establishment. Unlike Virginia, South Carolina Anglicanism initially existed in a pluralistic religious environment, but by the beginning of the eighteenth century a spirit of Anglican expansion was apparent among influential laity. Governor Nathaniel Johnson led a series of legislative maneuvers which resulted in legal establishment for the Church in 1706.[75] Meanwhile Garden, who created an ecclesiastical court to maintain discipline among the clergy, habitually supported a parish's laity if a controversy erupted with their minister.[76] He also opposed what he viewed as religious excess and confronted George Whitefield when the great itinerant came to South Carolina in 1740. Garden refused him permission to preach in St. Philip's Church and Whitefield preached among Dissenters, where he blasted the state of established religion. A meeting with Garden ended in mutual recrimination, a portent of disruptions to come.

The office of commissary bespoke the Church's adaptation to its environment, and Virginia remained the paradigm. There a new church design appeared in the 1730s, a plain, brick, cruciform design which heightened the Church's Protestant feel. Places of honor awaited gentry; remote galleries remained for a few slaves. In architecture as in liturgy, the Church reinforced a hierarchical, lay-dominated society.[77] To a striking degree the Church's rites also centered on the home, where rites of passage occurred as family occasions rather than ecclesiastical ones. As the Church accommodated itself to the lives of the gentry, it left numerous others on the periphery, notably the lower social classes, slaves, and members of non-Anglican religious groups, whose social influence would eventually challenge the Church's role. The Church's social accommodation also moved its own clergy to seek greater security for themselves in the courts and by creating their own assemblies. The Church's social limitations and the strictures upon its clergy suggested the incompleteness of the American form of religious establishment.[78]

In colonial New England Anglicanism was not in a position to be the established Church, for it confronted the Puritan theocracy. By the late seventeenth century, however, deepening political and economic dependence upon the mother country opened the door to New England for the Church of England. When Edmund Andros arrived in 1686 as Massachusetts' new, royal governor, the Church of England was able to begin ministrations as a missionary religion on English soil. The Church adapted admirably, and its parishes grew steadily under impressive clerical leadership. Anglicans offered a biblical, rational, and liturgical faith which blended with the tenor of colonial life. Success in New England encouraged Anglicans to envision becoming a *de facto* establishment, the Church of literate people, for whom God appeared as loving and reasonable, rather than the impatient, jealous Puritan deity. The Anglican conception resonated with an age of assurance, with trade and gentrification expanding. However, social conditions alone did not ensure growth; the Church expanded through the assertiveness of their energetic SPG missionaries, who inspired an impressive pattern of Anglican growth in the first quarter of the eighteenth century.[79] The most celebrated evidence of Anglican muscularity came from Connecticut. At Yale College, a Puritan bastion, President Timothy Cutler, instructor Daniel Brown, and respected Congregationalist pastor Samuel Johnson announced their conversions to Anglicanism in 1722. They had concluded that episcopacy was necessary to valid ecclesiastical order.[80] New England Anglicanism acquired the stamp Cutler and his colleagues embodied. Literate, talented, and High Church, they enhanced the attraction Anglicanism had for New England's influential classes.

Education played an important role in this advance. In addition to William and Mary in Virginia, the Church supported the College of Philadelphia and King's College in New York. Philosopher and Bishop George Berkeley hoped to start a Bermuda college which would reform colonial manners and evangelize Indians. He shifted the site to Rhode Island, but by 1731 had to abandon the plan.[81] Nevertheless education became a primary means of Anglican advance in the northern colonies. That growth, however, had limits. Since the early eighteenth century SPG missionaries had attempted to convert American Indians. Charles Inglis of New York, later the first Bishop of Nova Scotia, doggedly attempted to envigorate a mission to the Mohawks in 1770. But Inglis was unable to generate much interest, and the onset of war precluded further efforts. With its emphasis upon education the Church had greatest appeal to the educated, or to those with such aspirations. The Anglican sense of establishment focused the Church's mission upon a particular stratum of colonial life.

The irony was that there was no resident bishop to oversee an episcopal Church. However, there was public controversy, for New Englanders feared the arrival of a bishop in the middle of the eighteenth century. The miter betokened tighter English control, an assault on freedom which even many Anglicans feared, and these fears fed on sufficient fact to be sustained.[82] In New Jersey in 1766 a group of Anglican clergy met to call for a resident bishop. Clergy from Connecticut to Pennsylvania attended, petitions went forth to England, and plans for galvanizing wider support advanced. Some Virginia and Maryland clergy voiced enthusiasm, and the campaign for the American episcopate progressed.[83] Yet, as Puritan opponents of episcopacy sensed, most Anglicans themselves resisted the imposition of episcopal oversight. The charge had abundant truth, for episcopacy was the priority of a regional church group; Anglican self-understanding differed across the colonies. However, circumstances would offer resolution of that issue.

In the South, Anglicans also faced the challenge of revivalism. In George Whitefield's wake came waves of revival, and by the 1760s Baptist growth had reached impressive dimensions and embodied a critique of colonial culture. The revival excoriated colonial gentry and their church in favor of community, equality, and democracy, catharsis, conversion, and fellowship. The revival was an elite of the common folk, an inversion of extant social norms. To those whom society had disregarded, including slaves and frontier dwellers, the revival offered new life, status, and immense hope. It was the religious version of the American Revolution.[84]

The new nation

Revolution intensified the difficulty of the Church's adaptation to the American environment. It culminated in the rise of Evangelicalism, which, in the American setting, created a civil religion which assaulted official religious establishments as it gained political weight. Baptists, Methodists, and Presbyterians adopted the new style and insisted upon voluntarism and the separation of Church and state as the basis of American religious life. Virginians, bolstered by James Madison's "Memorial and Remonstrance" and Thomas Jefferson's bill for religious freedom, disestablished the Anglican Church in Virginia in 1786 and became the model for rejecting colonial establishments in favor of religious freedom.[85]

The American Revolution was the triumph of a new kind of order which prized voluntary association. Americans valued adaptation to changing realities as the supreme test of truth, but the Anglican capacity for adaptation seemed pitifully small. The Church had lost the privileges of establishment, and large numbers of clergy and laity had either fled to Canada and Britain or rejected the Church of the King.[86] Anglicanism's survival in America entailed readjusting the meaning of religious establishment to the American way of seeking consensus. For Anglicans establishment came to mean engagement with society in order to transform it while guarding the Church's distinctiveness from dilution by American influence. In this respect, America represented a challenge which Anglicans were to experience repeatedly in the face of modernizing circumstances.

Two figures with divergent views of the Church's relation to society directed its adaptation to American life. In 1782 Philadelphia clergyman William White authored a pamphlet which thrust him into the discussion of the Church's reorganization. *The Case of the Protestant Episcopal Churches in the United States Considered* acknowledged that the Church had lost its historic basis of establishment within English political authority. The American Church had to incorporate the fact of voluntary association, to acknowledge that each congregation "was independent and free to decide whether to participate in any plan for organizing on the state and national levels." A national organization arose through the consolidation of local ideals.[87]

White's plan reflected the explication of Anglican ideals in American guise. Absorbing American political values into the Church, he insisted that, as in society, the people should be afforded full measures of authority and participation. White's proposal for Church polity absorbed the American style of state and national government. He emphasized the need for a national convention of clergy and laity in guiding the Church's affairs. He also proposed that assemblies of parish representatives should have power to elect a "superior order" of ministers. Here, White applied "the concepts of natural rights and contract theory of government to the practical problem of reorganizing the Episcopal churches,"[88] subordinating the episcopate to assemblies of clergy and laity. He avoided the office's traditional title, recalling the opposition which greeted suggestions of a colonial bishop, and emphasized the office's administrative, not its regal, character.

White believed that, in the absence of the episcopate, a Presbyterian style of ordination could be adopted if ordinations in England were unavailable and the Church had insufficient numbers of clergy. In defense of his position, White cited Hooker, Cranmer, Whitgift, Ussher, and Hoadly, who had allowed lapses from episcopacy in special circumstances. Of all White's points, the diminution of the episcopate elicited the most disagreement.[89] Most Episcopalians saw merit in White's plan of Church governance, but many sought protection of the Church's ministry. While, from 1783 to 1786, state conventions of Episcopalians in such places as Maryland, Pennsylvania, Massachusetts, and Virginia accepted the associative features of White's plan, in Connecticut there was a different priority for Church organization. There ten clergy met in 1783 and selected Samuel Seabury as their bishop. Moreover these clergy "had no intention of permitting the laity to sit with them in a convention where matters of organization, faith, and practice were decided."[90] Fearful that the triumph of White's perspective would sap the episcopacy's character, Seabury was consecrated by Non-Juror bishops in Scotland in 1784.

Though plans for a national Church went forward, disagreement on fundamental principles obstructed hope for effective union. When that Convention of 1785 endorsed lay authority, fear of permanent divergence in the Church increased. Nevertheless the hint of a comprehensive solution was perceptible, for the Convention of 1785 adopted a plan for securing bishops in the English line. Seabury's consecration stimulated discussion of episcopacy, and a consensus emerged that it was the necessary mark of Anglican life. In 1786 conventions in New York, Pennsylvania, and Virginia elected bishops, and Samuel Provoost of New York and William White of Pennsylvania were consecrated in England. On the other side Connecticut clergy were urged by John Skinner, one of Seabury's Scottish consecrators, to relent in their opposition to lay representation.[91] In the end the major divide among Episcopalians was the personality rift between White and Seabury. Compromise permitted incorporation of the dual principles of lay representation and episcopal oversight. The Episcopal Church created a national structure which mimicked that of America's new government. The General Convention was divided into houses, one for lay and clerical delegates, the other for bishops. Such an arrangement adapted the Church to the American setting.[92]

This compromise actually advanced a process of adaptation to American life which continued. Idealizing a creative tension with American life, the Church embarked upon the process of preserving this tension in a dynamic society. Because of diverse party influences within the Church, Episcopalians could embrace American life without fearing loss of ecclesiastical identity to social circumstances.

Thus, early in the nineteenth century, the Church assumed clear middle- and upper-class lines. Episcopalians perceived their identity as proximity to society's influential strata. Most clergy came from homes of means and refinement, and laity were likely to be professional persons, many of them city dwellers, who were at home with prosperity and education. The initial growth of the Episcopal Church resulted from attracting this sort of person. The Church sought its place among those who came to manage and to govern in the wake of frontier expansion.[93]

During the first decade of the nineteenth century the Church began a period of impressive expansion. Its aspiration of being an effective embodiment of American life required that it expand with America's westward growth, and between 1815 and 1835 new dioceses rapidly formed. The Episcopal Church took root when civilization was secure and emphasized the virtues of order and education. The Church entitled itself a "Domestic and Foreign Missionary Society," underscoring its commitment to mission, and soon signs of vitality abounded. Numerous new church buildings appeared from 1810 as a new generation of leaders and clarified Church structure injected energy and possibility into Church life.[94] Education became an important means of Church growth. The Episcopal Church sponsored an impressive number of new schools and colleges during this era, some of which, notably Hobart, Kenyon, and Trinity Colleges, survive admirably. An emphasis upon Sunday schools was also an aspect of its interest in education. Originally an English device for instructing poor children, the Sunday school became a primary means of American Protestant growth. It became the basis for a united Evangelical phalanx committed to taming America's cities and frontiers alike in the early nineteenth century.

Sunday schools blurred denominational peculiarities in order to teach basic biblical and moral themes. The Bible became a means to learn how to read and how to behave, not how to believe or how to organize the Church. Social unity was the recurrent theme, and charity and civility were the dominant values of American civil religion. Low Church Episcopalians believed that their tradition must embrace this civilizing agenda. These Episcopalians prized the Church's Protestant strands, such as the subjective features of religious life and an emphasis upon Bible study.[95] In 1814 two of Bishop William White's assistants at Christ Church, Philadelphia, Jackson Kemper and James Milnor, launched the first Episcopal Sunday school. Other schools began in Massachusetts, New York,

New Jersey, and Maryland. In 1817 Episcopal Sunday school societies began in New York and Philadelphia, and the Episcopal Sunday School Union appeared in 1826. National organization represented general acceptance of the Sunday school as an adjunct to Church life. Already, however, a shift in the school's nature was underway as Episcopal Sunday schools evolved into parish institutions for training children in the particular features of Episcopal Christianity.[96] The transition had its counterparts in other denominations; in the Episcopal Church, however, it bespoke a tension between identification with the culture and preservation of the Church's sense of its own unique mission.

The New York Episcopal Sunday School Society was the creation of John Henry Hobart, Bishop of New York from 1811, who mistrusted the Evangelical, interdenominational culture. Informed by reading the works of the Hackney Phalanx, Hobart stressed the Church's catholicity and the apostolic origins of its offices and rites, and feared loss of the Church's character. Unlike the English High Church tradition, Hobart did not idealize the Christian state; instead he prized the Church's integrity as a visible society, set apart from civil offices. Rather than seek points of commonality with other denominations, the Church must preserve its distinctiveness.[97] This ecclesiastical instinct inspired an admirable example of pastoral oversight. Hobart promoted societies for missions and for Bible study and lent the Church an image of grandeur as a liturgical society.[98] He depicted it as a pre-Constantinian Christianity which must stand aloof from the Evangelical hegemony for the sake of correct ecclesiastical order. Hobart and his theological heirs stressed the necessity of external channels of grace such as the sacraments and viewed philanthropy as an individual matter rather than as an interdenominational responsibility.[99] This tradition feared that the American values of voluntary assembly and individual opinion might threaten the Church's distinctiveness. High Church party spirit sharpened the tension between Episcopalians and Protestants and created an internal rivalry which immersed Episcopalians in issues of self-definition. How to make this a creative tension remained a basic dilemma.[100]

THE CHURCH AS SPIRITUAL KINGDOM

The age of revolution demanded reconsideration of the meaning of establishment. In the old order the Church of England presumed that its identity derived from its legal status in the English political framework. The tremors unsettling the social edifice threatened the idea of establishment which Anglicans had presumed to be the Church's center. Pervasive political and social change elicited from the Church a variety of responses which suggested the depth of Anglicanism's modern dilemma; however, until F. D. Maurice, no one response suggested how the Church might adapt its historic self-understanding to a comprehensive, modern sense of its place in the Christian tradition.

In 1838, Frederick Denison Maurice, a young theologian, suggested a vision of sufficient breadth when he published *The Kingdom of Christ*. Revised in 1842, this work and others of his writings pursued the idea that the Church was a kingdom both spiritual and worldly, doing justice both to the Gospel and to human experience.[101] A former Quaker, Maurice continued the notion of the inner light, that each person possessed an inherently spiritual nature which lay dormant until consciously affirmed. Knowledge of God is the basis of human experience, and the person who acknowledges this reality becomes a member of God's spiritual Kingdom as well as a member of natural social units.[102] Maurice glossed over the nature of this inner light for the sake of explaining the Church's nature as a kingdom in the context of investigating religion as a human phenomenon.

Maurice understood the changing nature of the social order as the context of his analysis. He concurred with those who sought to regenerate political arrangements; however, he contended that such change became genuine only by identifying God as the basis of all social harmony. In the Liberal age, human beings hungered for a form of order which prevented society "from being disturbed by the friction of individual sentiments and speculations." This passion for order in all the ordinary relations of life pointed to the existence of "some spiritual order, answering in universality to the order of nature, in and through which it has pleased God to manifest his perfections." Maurice set the stage for an analysis of human history in which the evolution of the Church offered the only possible fulfillment of human social hopes.[103]

Maurice highlighted "the old principle of the Church being a kingdom." The Gospel, he insisted, "is indeed the revelation of a kingdom within us, a kingdom, of which the heart and spirit of man can alone take cognizance, and yet of a kingdom which ruleth over all." This universal kingdom possesses outward marks, assuring its distinctiveness. Concomitantly it "is not the adversary of national order and family life, but is the sustainer and consummation of them both." It is "the appointed trainer" of human reason and will, endowing them with "a state and a knowledge which, without her, they could never acquire." The Church's commission is to bring all forms of human life to the "highest possible development of which they are capable."[104]

The emergence of the United States embodied the hope of political development as a product of spiritual unity. Because Protestantism ultimately fragmented in sectarian movements, national feeling must be preserved in a universal, spiritual society which is integral to the human constitution and promises to fulfill national aspirations.[105] Maurice saw the roots of this society in human family experience. The most historic of human social units, the family performed an educative, nurturing role. Maurice believed the biblical story of Abraham demonstrated the divine origin of this fundamental social unit, and he viewed marriage as the family's backbone.[106] In the union of husband and wife, the human and the divine intertwine, and produce family relationships which give rise to the spiritual perceptions that creep into human consciousness.[107]

Historically nations evolved from families. Maurice depicted the rise of ancient Israel as the exemplification of a universal, spiritual kingdom rooted in human social development. Thus, as Maurice commented, "a nation, then, like a family, would seem to possess some of the characteristics of a spiritual constitution."[108] Religious sensibilities arise out of national as well as family life. National life features particularity of ethos, and distinctiveness of cultural institutions such as law and language; however, national life reached its pinnacle in pointing beyond itself to a universal brotherhood. The most successful nations in history – Greece, Rome, Israel – advanced the vision of human unity, for these societies understood that family and national life would be fulfilled as human beings discovered the lineaments of a spiritual constitution in their midst.

Maurice refused a simple identification of this universal society, the Church, with the world. He devoted a considerable portion of *The Kingdom of Christ* to demarcating the Church from the world. The Church's catholicity, seen in its sacraments of Baptism and the Eucharist, and the apostolic ministry, centered in the episcopate, identified the universal, spiritual society. However, Maurice, influenced by Coleridge, stressed that Church and society must be linked for either to realize its aspirations. Scripture is puzzling unless one perceives within it the signs of a real, universal kingdom.[109] This kingdom must become "the foundation and upholder of all political institutions." In the Old Testament "a spiritual element was proved to be necessary to uphold a legal society, so now a legal element, a body expressing the sacredness and majesty of law, is shown to be necessary in order to fulfill the objects for which the spiritual and universal society exists."[110]

Through historic dispensations God began to restore the divine image in human life and Christ announced the universal dispensation. Now, in the modern world, it was possible that the redemption of national life could occur and might advance Christ's Kingdom. Under God's dominion, each nation could witness to "the true order and universal fellowship of the world . . . by using the society which embodies this fellowship as an instrument for cultivating the spirit of each nation, for awakening each to the perception of the object of its existence." This perception would extinguish bellicose, competitive sentiments and encourage the reign of peace. Thus, Maurice believed, it was "the will of God that the nations should come into being . . . not for the chastisement of the Church, but for its development."[111]

The Church's responsibility was to encourage national fulfillment by drawing its host culture toward the universal, spiritual society. Maurice delivered this message in a variety of ways. In *The Kingdom of Christ* he insisted that the Church could not mimic the power of civil rulers; but, the Church "may prove to them that she has another power entirely distinct from theirs, far higher than theirs, to which they must resort, or perish in their feebleness." In a collection of essays first published in 1853, Maurice commented similarly that the "world contains the elements of which the Church is composed. In the Church, these elements are penetrated by a uniting, reconciling power. The Church is, therefore, human society in its normal state; the World, that same society irregular and abnormal. The world is the Church without God; the Church is the world restored to its relation with God."[112]

The Church should promote national development by encouraging national education. Current religious bodies, Maurice claimed, promote sectarian education. By contrast, "a national Church, which believes that it exists for the purpose of cultivating the inward man, just as the civil power exists for the sake of the outward man, which believes that it has a commission and vocation for this end, must be a continual witness against all these notions of education."[113] Only through such a broad approach could the Church be the cultural catalyst for the universal society it is called to represent. Maurice boldly assessed how far contemporary religious systems embraced this ideal. He held that despite its various parties, the English Church gave the clearest witness to the universal and national spiritual society. Maurice explained that the French Revolution had "taught him the unspeakable importance of a distinct national life."[114] However, Coleridge taught him that French and other national aspirations pointed to the human desire for spiritual unity attainable only in a universal polity.

Maurice expected the Church of England to be revamped by international developments. I have indicated Maurice's conviction that the United States would demonstrate the form of a better integration of Church and state. He also expected Britain's colonies to teach the mother Church lessons it could not learn within. Overseas bishops "would feel the advantage of leaving the functions, jurisdiction, and formal legislation to the representatives of the State, and would recognize their own high calling as guides of a spiritual society ... indicating the relation of men to a more comprehensive fellowship, a family in heaven and earth." Writing to Australian clergy in 1868, Maurice stressed that Church and state are both divine; the Church "is not more exclusive than the State but is the all embracing Society, while the State's business is to assert the dignity and distinctness of each people and race."[115]

Convinced that social forms revealed divine purpose, Maurice became a pioneering student of comparative religions. Anticipating later scholarship he argued that all of the world's great religions were legitimate forms of human experience in particular places, and that Christianity is rooted "in the heart and intellect of man as much as any other system." Christianity is subject to the "same law of decay from the progress of knowledge and society with all the rest."[116] Upholding the Church's mission as culture's completion, Maurice argued that Christianity's superiority was its offer of universal, spiritual unity which glimpsed every culture as an expression of the divine personality awaiting completion.

A number of Maurice's emphases left their stamp on Anglicanism. As the Church disengaged from the old conception of establishment, Maurice stressed its nature as a family and the place of such distinctive marks as the sacraments in securing its integrity. He also sustained the cherished Anglican ideal of proximity to the levers of cultural influence. The Church's role in education suggested a niche for the Church as a *de facto* establishment, adjacent to a nation's policy-makers, and suggested an Anglican response to the age of revolution. Often vague, his parameters of Church life turned response to social crisis into a missionary strategy. Maurice sensed that the Church must evolve an identity rooted in *praxis* in mission. He anticipated the transformation of Anglicanism with a comprehension no other figure achieved.

CHAPTER THREE

The adjustment of Church and state

THE CHURCH AND THE POLITICIANS

In July, 1830, Charles James Blomfield delivered his first address to the clergy as Bishop of London. Blomfield observed that the

signs of the times are surely such, as to indicate, to him who attentively observes the movements of God's providence, the approach, if not the arrival, of a period pregnant with important consequences to the cause of religion. With respect to ourselves . . . the repeal of those laws, which were long considered to be indispensable to the safety of the Established Church . . . at least places us in a new position, compels us, for the future, to depend entirely upon our internal resources, and will be a test of their sufficiency.[1]

Blomfield understood that new social conditions required the Church not merely to reconsider its nature as the nation's religious establishment, but to function in a new way. Guided by this conviction Blomfield became a pivotal figure in reforming the Church of England's programs to develop vigorous domestic and foreign mission. As the Church lost many of the advantages of being established, it secured its own resources for mission and became a global, rather than an English, institution.

Blomfield believed that the Church's chief opponent was "the spirit of infidelity," making it easy to decry the new political schools, and the "active body of men, who are attempting to lay other foundations of the social virtues and duties than those which are everlastingly laid in the Gospel." However, Blomfield viewed the moment as an opportunity for mission. "The almost universal diffusion of elementary knowledge . . . also furnishes the friends of truth with the obvious means of counteracting the influence of erroneous doctrines, and of instilling sounder principles into the bulk of the community." Rather than combat "the spirit of inquiry," violate "the indefeasible liberty of the human mind," and interefere with "its natural constitution," the Church should adapt to the age in order to guide it. "To impart to that spirit a right direction, to sanctify it with holy motives, to temper it to righteous purposes, to shape it to ends which lie beyond the limits of this beginning of our existence, will be the endeavour of those, who desire to make the cultivation of intellect conducive to moral improvement, and to establish the kingdom of Christ at once in the understandings and affections of mankind."[2]

I cite Blomfield as a principal source of a new conception of the Church's mission by the middle of the nineteenth century. He understood that although the Church was being thrust upon its own resources, the age afforded opportunities for realizing itself in mission. Blomfield viewed the transformation of Anglicanism in terms of clerical initiative. However, I believe the role of lay persons and democratic process became the characteristic features of the adjustment of Church and state. A sense of Anglican mission arose from the influences of figures who pressed the Church to develop means of self-sufficiency. The dynamism of Liberalism afforded Anglicans a means of disengaging from the state in a way which enhanced the Church's integrity. As a result, the Church began to consider itself as a global, missionary institution.

The Church's readjustment to an age of political reform resulted not from abstract forces but from personal convictions. Prominent, Liberal politicians carried their faith into matters of policy and embodied the meaning of the age for the established Church. Although these figures have been accused of religious expediency, they emphasized the role of religion in the new social order and endowed the Church with a new sense of social role. The leader of the young reformers, Lord John Russell, and his colleagues were not willing to sacrifice the established Church for political advantage. These young Whigs held deep religious convictions, stressing a "sense of Christian duty, of a debt owed to God for the blessings of Providence, which obliged them to be worthy stewards of whatever earthly lot the Deity had bestowed on them."[3]

Whig humanitarianism absorbed the influence of Clapham's Evangelical conviction. Some Whigs, such as Althorp, believed their careers were religious vocations and wondered if the nation had a distinctive role in the divine plan of salvation. Their opinions were shaped by reading Wilberforce, Thornton, Simeon, and Daniel Wilson. The young Liberals joined religious and charitable voluntary associations in the hope of spreading public virtue and instilling

Christian belief in new urban areas. Liberals fretted about the souls of their children and urged them to attend religious lectures and practice personal devotions. Not indifferent, Liberals maintained a pious, public faith characterized by a search for socially inclusive forms of Christianity and by scorn for sectarian religious allegiance. Liberals such as Spring Rice criticized forms of Christianity which prized "peculiar tenets and distinct professions," instead of general formulations. Liberalism was a search for means of social cohesion in an age of upheaval.[4]

The writings of Thomas Arnold confirmed Liberals in their inclinations. Spring Rice called Arnold the one "in whose principles we place the greatest confidence and for whom we entertain the ultimate respect." Morpeth wrote of Arnold, "Oh, why was I not brought up under him or as that could not be, why could I have not known more of him?" Russell aligned himself with Arnold and afforded ecclesiastical preferment to Broad Church figures he believed fit the Arnold mold. Russell and Liberal Whigs moved comfortably among Broad Church clergy who shared their interest in an inclusive Christianity and in social and political reconstruction.[5] The essence of Liberalism was a concern with the moral character of the nation.

Liberal political philosophy acknowledged the need for a religious establishment which must maintain the affections of a majority of the people, and could be modified by the political mechanisms of the state in order to ensure that it did. The Church of Ireland seemed to reformers to be an anomaly, an established Church which attracted only one-tenth of Ireland's population. Similarly, Liberals intended to reform the operations of the Church of England. A broad swath of opinion concurred that the Church required examination, although the manner of ecclesiastical restructuring was disputed. The Liberal impact upon the Church can be gauged from two politicians who embodied the readjustment of religious faith to new circumstances.

Between December, 1834 and April, 1835, and then from 1841 to 1846, the Conservative Party held power under Robert Peel, a cautious man with a deep Christian faith who prized the Church of England's connection to the state. Nevertheless Peel sensed that non-Anglican opinion "was now so great that the Church of England could never again be singled out for support by the Government, even in a good cause." He accepted the necessity of the Reform Bill, declaring that "good government must include prudent but significant amendment of institutions, always excepting further reform of Parliament or reform tending towards the disendowment or disestablishment of the churches of England and of Ireland." Thus Peel attempted to secure the form of Britain's Constitution while adjusting its substance to match changing circumstances. This acknowledgement gave reform a general imprimatur, and Peel's attempt to balance preservation and change typified the state's new approach to the Church of England. Not disestablished, it was thrust upon its own resources while being favored as a *primus inter pares*.[6] While Whig clergy, High Churchmen, and extreme Evangelicals disliked him, Peel received the support of most clergy who perceived him as a Church defender concerned to increase establishment's efficiency. He endorsed Church schools and mission projects and consulted Church leaders on matters of government policy. Blomfield and Peel became close friends, and Peel frequently asked the Bishop of London about suitable persons for ecclesiastical preferment. Blomfield encouraged Peel's interest in mission, and Peel agreed that the Church required new parishes and dioceses. He was "ready for reform of tithe, for the reorganization of Church revenues, and for a full enquiry into the working of the Church Establishment, not with a view to its abolition but to improve its effectiveness."[7]

Unfortunately for Blomfield and for Conservatives Peel failed to be the champion they desired. Peel believed that Church extension should be left to voluntary contributions and improved methods of managing Church endowments. Peel opposed use of public funds for Church reform because he had grasped that publicly funded Church measures were not possible politically. Despite Blomfield's overtures Peel remained steadfast. The government would listen to the Church, but it could not defy public opinion. In one sense, though, Peel did not understand the age in which he lived. He believed that institutions required adjustment, but that reform had been "finally and irrevocably disposed of. He was now determined to look forward to the future alone, and considering the Constitution as it existed, to take his stand on main and essential matters." For Peel main matters included the Corn Laws, the repeal of which cost him office in 1846, and the social influence of religion.[8] A committed Anglican, Peel hoped to win all religious interests to his own moderate politics. He proposed raising government's annual grant to Maynooth, an Irish training college for Roman Catholic priests, in the hope of negating anti-British sentiment by generosity, and he won a majority early in 1845, carrying a broad swath of Anglican opinion with him.

Nevertheless the Maynooth Bill produced a significant casualty in

Conservative ranks when William Ewart Gladstone, President of the Board of Trade, tendered his resignation on February 4, 1845.[9] Gladstone embodied the political and religious transformation of the Liberal age. Initially a Conservative, he became "the epitome of Liberalism," a champion of minorities and an opponent of authority grounded in tradition alone. He sped Liberalism toward its logical conclusion by calling for further reform, including, later, Home Rule for Ireland. At the heart of his political pilgrimage were a brooding commitment to social justice, a lofty personal vocation, and passionate concern to defend the integrity of the Church of England. Gladstone intended for the Church to realize itself as the Catholic expression of God's Kingdom on earth. Defense of the Church was the fulcrum of his political swing.

As a young politician Gladstone was a persuasive defender of the Church establishment who believed that politics was an arena of religious responsibility.[10] Between 1833 and 1845, he articulated a quixotic brand of Conservatism informed by William Wilberforce and Joshua Watson. Gladstone felt the integration of religious and political issues required an explicit connection between the Church and the state. The national Church was not an expedient "means of christianizing the nation, it was the articulation of the nation's religious conscience."[11] Gladstone defended this position in *The State in its Relations with the Church*, which appeared in 1838, and represented the apogee of his Toryism. As Gladstone wrote his father, it was a discussion of "the *principles* which bind society together, direct the mutual conduct of governor and governed and determine their relations." The principal issue was "the grounds and reasons of the alliance, not . . . its terms."[12] Gladstone saw an historic compact whose terms were of secondary importance. "But the principle itself is an obligation antecedent to all verbal and determinate expression; and it is acknowledged by, not founded on, the assent of the contracting parties."[13]

Richard Hooker saw that the connection of Church and state resides in natural law and taught Gladstone to consider the "moral personality of the State." Like a family, which is natural and concerned with moral development, the state is the organ of a nation, which must make public profession of a religion. Religion takes the shape of an institution so that Christian belief can pervade human life. Church and state in England are coextensive bodies forming a social establishment without compromising the integrity of either body.[14]

The necessity of religion to the state was one feature of this argument. Gladstone noted that Burke and Coleridge taught the necessity of a national religion in order for government to realize its ends. On the other hand, Gladstone defended a Catholic form of establishment as the one most likely to be permanent. Scripture, sacraments, historic creeds, and apostolically ordained clergy ensured the Church's identity and preserved it from submergence in the state. Gladstone noted the presence of voluntary religious bodies apart from the establishment. He granted that no establishment could encompass a nation's religious diversity. But no sect could reach the masses of the people; only a national Church can bring "motives to bear upon mankind in favour of religion, with a power greater than that which would belong to it . . . when unestablished."[15]

Gladstone intended for *Church Principles Considered in their Results*, published in 1840, to be a companion volume to its predecessor, but this work elicited less response, for it reiterated a conservative defense of the establishment. Gladstone argued that "we look not to change . . . but to renovation; to a bringing back of that which our fathers once had . . . To remove from the face of that truth whatever may have sullied or obscured it, to repel assaults upon its purity and integrity, to illustrate and make it known, and to adapt and prepare the minds of men, by the means which itself supplies for its reception – these are the objects of religious reform."[16]

Gladstone proposed to examine "the specific and particular bearings which these principles are likely to have upon the religious interests and feelings of the day in our own country." He believed that opposition to the Church's alliance with the state relied "not so much upon the question of their theological truth or falsehood, as upon that of the inconveniences . . . supposed to follow logically from their recognition."[17] He contended for a visible ideal, namely, the apostolic, established Church, and initially responded to the ferment in Church–state relations with a conservative defense of the Church of England. Nevertheless Gladstone struck political Conservatives as unreliable; even Tractarians, who tried to win his allegiance, found him too independent to assist their cause. Gladstone's Conservatism resulted from idealism and offered little basis for political alliance. As his view of reform developed, however, Gladstone adopted the premises of Liberalism, a personal transformation which embodied the mind of the age.

Later in life Gladstone admitted that he had been blind to social realities in the first half of the century, viewing Dissent as bothersome without regard for its strength. Until the Religious Census of 1851 he did not realize that Dissent must be accommodated in a new political arrangement, a realization at the heart of the Liberal perception.[18] As he absorbed the Liberal agenda, he increasingly characterized the Church's spiritual independence, not its Erastian past, as its essence. In Peel's government Gladstone sensed that the modern task might be to secure the Church by private initiative, not by alliance with the state, in other words, to ensure the Church's integrity by securing its identity. The Church's role in national life required it to guard its catholicity and extend its sphere.

Colonial affairs increased Gladstone's suspicion that social change had eroded the Church's traditional form. In 1844, when Peel increased the government's grant to Maynooth, Gladstone's suspicions were confirmed. He glimpsed the frailty of historic notions of establishment, and the importance of the Church's catholicity. Gladstone awakened to the idea of civil liberty and concluded that national religion could not be imposed against colonial will, for the circumstances of colonial life differed from domestic conditions. He realized that the Church must consider itself a missionary body, and he emphasized religious liberty and the integrity of the Church.[19] If the state cannot formally and exclusively support the Church of England, he argued on March 25, 1851, it must treat all religious groups equally, and "allow the Church greater freedom to pursue its task." It must enable "the Church to develop her own 'intrinsic means' and it was to this that he looked in the future."[20] Society's regeneration could not occur through political means, which can only safeguard the ability of religious institutions to perform their tasks.

The transformation of Anglicanism resulted from the merger of diverse ideals into a comprehensive vision of the Church. Gladstone suggested an initial form of that vision in his realization that the dismantling of the establishment thrust the Church upon itself in ways which entailed global mission and heightened issues of Church identity. Adjustment to the age afforded the possibility of being a Catholic body unrestricted by English allegiance.

THE CHURCH AND POLITICS

Rates

Between 1832 and 1867 the role of the Church of England in the British state underwent a decisive realignment. It is tempting to interpret this process as an assault upon the Church, for numerous contemporary Church defenders viewed the age in precisely these terms. Granting the Church lost a considerable portion of its historic role, I argue not for the Church's decline but for its adjustment, an appropriate recognition of the ecclesiastical implications of social reality. In the wake of the Reform Bill of 1832 calls for further changes in the way government functioned appeared. In response, Whigs intended to modify government without wholesale sacrifices, to alleviate Dissent's grievances without abandoning the establishment. Thus, during the period between the Reform Bills of 1832 and 1867, the Whigs moved toward further reform incrementally, a posture which was not a ploy but the result of personal conviction.

Irish Church matters became a prominent feature of reform as the Whigs intended concessions in the Church of Ireland without threatening the Act of Union. On February 12, 1833 Althorp introduced the government's Irish Church Temporalities Bill in the Commons, a proposal to reduce the Church of Ireland's twenty-two sees to ten and its two archbishoprics to one. It also intended to reduce benefices and deaneries where there had been little pastoral activity and to cut the revenues of Armagh and Derry, the wealthiest sees. The money saved would be used to create an Ecclesiastical Commission to review the Church of England's workings. Although this bill elicited fierce Conservative opposition, it proved to be the opening salvo in a Whig program of Church reform, certain measures of which moderates like Peel endorsed. The Irish Church Bill passed with minor amendments on July 30, 1833.[21]

Meanwhile, on May 11, 1833, the United Committee, representing moderate Dissenting consensus, identified six grievances from which non-Anglicans sought relief. One item, the liability of Dissenting chapels to the poor rate, was alleviated in July. The remaining five, which became the focus of Dissenting political activity, were: marriage according to Anglican rites, the lack of civil registration of births and deaths, the inability of Dissenters to receive burial by their own rites in parish churchyards, religious tests at Oxford and Cambridge and the need for a university at London which would not require such tests, and church rates, all of which were resolved eventually through a distended process. In 1836 a Marriage Act removed the stipulation that Dissenters should have an Anglican ceremony; in 1856 subsequent legislation ended the requirement that a Dissenting marriage be reported to a Poor Law Guardian. In 1857 the Burial Acts Amendment enabled unconsecrated ground to be used by Dissenters, and the session of 1836 granted London University a charter and allowed civil registration. Removal of University Tests waited until 1871.[22]

Church rates proved less tractable than other Dissenting demands, and education became a crucial issue. These foci measure the process by which the Church of England's role in the nation was reformed. Church rates were an historic tax levied on all occupants of property in a parish, except the destitute and holders of Crown property. Income maintained the fabric of the parish Church and supplied its appurtenances, such as bread and wine and prayer books. In modern circumstances, Machin observes, the rate "symbolized the whole question of maintaining a Church establishment and its privileges." While loyalists believed the rate was a justifiable obligation, Dissenters viewed it as an affront which had been an early target of their activism. Church building efforts had prompted some refusals of rates in 1818 and 1819, and also encouraged establishment concessions, notably an act in 1818 which allowed for opposition to a levy.[23]

In the wake of the Reform Bill church rates became a major target of Dissent's political program. Early alleviation of the rate problem failed when Althorp's rate reform proposal failed in 1834, stiffening Dissenting resolve to seek disestablishment and the triumph of the voluntary principle. For a generation the issue resisted resolution but remained prominent in the evolution of Liberal politics. Church rates became the best measure of the contest between Dissent and the establishment, and of the revisions made in the way the religious establishment functioned. In turn, the progress of Lord John Russell's position on the church rates issue became the barometer of this issue's development up to 1868.

Committed to the principle of establishment, Russell intended to reform what he believed were its abuses. At first he believed that reform without alteration of the substance of establishment was possible. He maintained that a Dissenter whose rate obligation was alleviated had no basis for further attack on the system unless he or she was to contend for disestablishment and the triumph of the voluntary principle. Russell and his colleagues held that a distinction could be made between rates paid for the provision of church services, from which Dissenters should be exempt, and rates paid for the mainten-ance of the church fabric, which ensured the continuation of a religious establishment. On this point the Whig indebtedness to Coleridge and Arnold was apparent. While government should avoid becoming ensnared in sectarian loyalty, it has a responsibility to reform the established Church in order to enhance its efficiency, measured by its responsiveness to public opinion.[24] For a time, however, public opinion was sufficiently confused that no resolution of the church rate issue was possible.

Conservative defense of the established Church initially intended simply to preserve the historic form and function of establishment. The conservative side included an unlikely coalition of Evangelicals, older High Churchmen of the Hackney sort, and Tractarians. Dissenters were dismayed by the variety of parties arrayed against them, for this proliferation meant that remaking the establishment would be a complicated matter. Quite the opposite resulted as Church parties absorbed the spirit of voluntaryism. Peel was the political barometer of this shift, and Tractarians the theological one. Resistant to assaults upon establishment, Anglicans, especially Anglo-Catholics, concluded by the 1850s that "relinquishing the church's right to church rates from ratepayers of all denominations might be an acceptable sacrifice in return for greater spiritual independence of the apostolic church."[25] The 1850s became a "time of advance for opposition to church-rates." Machin points to the marshaling of Dissenters after a decade of indecision to advocate the Church's disestablishment.[26] Their sentiment was not as surprising as the conviction among prominent Anglicans that rates should be alleviated. In 1852 Blomfield suggested to Lord Derby that those not considering themselves members of the Church should be allowed to register that status. They would forfeit the right of participation in church matters, such as voting or standing for vestry election, but they would be exempted from the rate.[27]

Blomfield's plan attracted influential supporters such as Samuel Wilberforce, one of William Wilberforce's sons who was Bishop of Oxford, and Gladstone, who expressed a belief that exempting Dissenters from Church matters was desirable and could be effected in this way. Wilberforce tried to convince Henry Phillpotts, Bishop of Exeter and an influential voice, that "limiting universal church rate obligations could pay dividends in maintaining the spiritual integrity of the church."[28] He might have added that Evangelicals and Anglo-Catholics alike were troubled by the alliance of Whigs and the Broad Church tradition. Church rates smacked of Whig Erastianism,

Anglo-Catholicism's *bête noire*, and opposition to Church rates became a means of opposing Whig interference in the Church.

The great shift of political and religious forces which was underway produced a new form of Church defense which Gladstone exemplified. The Liberal posture which was emerging was to free the Church from civil encumbrances in order to protect its integrity. If Gladstone's conversion was the most dramatic of the age, Russell's change on the rate issue was almost as impressive. Russell had opposed the bill of William Clay, an Anglican voluntarist and Liberal MP, who proposed in 1853 that rates be abolished and that new revenues could be gained from pew rents and better use of Church lands. Russell hated the idea of Church exclusivity, i.e., of an established Church with sectarian features, and fought for an inclusive, Broad established Church. He had combated Gladstone's compromise rate proposal in 1854 and George Grey's efforts for a compromise in 1856. In 1859, however, Russell announced his support for the abolition of Church rates, and leading Whigs quickly joined him.[29] They had been persuaded by the failure of compromise measures and by information which proved that more parish income came from voluntary gifts than from the rates.

Nevertheless the abolition of Church rates stalled because of the strength of Conservative opposition. The frustration of Liberal hopes was due to a Church defense movement which included impressive clergy such as Christopher Wordsworth. However, the prime movers of the Church defense movement were influential laity such as Henry Hoare who viewed rates as a bulwark of the established Church. Another prominent lay voice was Benjamin Disraeli, soon to be Prime Minister and later to be more flexible on the rates issue. In the context of 1859 and 1860, Disraeli's adamant support of Church rates was calculated to vilify Liberals and to enhance his public standing.[30] Disraeli momentarily rallied nostalgia for a traditional religious establishment, but could not preserve Church rates.

When resolution of the Church rate question occurred, Gladstone was its chief architect. In office as a Liberal in the parliamentary session of 1866, Gladstone pushed his conclusion that a solution to the rates question was the key to the Church's future security. He pushed earlier proposals that ratepaying would be voluntary, and only ratepayers would have a voice in church management, a bill built on one presented by J. A. Hardcastle, a Liberal Anglican MP, on March 7, 1866. Passage of the bill stalled when the government was defeated and resigned on another matter. The progress of Gladstone and Hardcastle in this session, however, suggested that some kind of compromise was now necessary. Disraeli, who entered the Conservative cabinet, granted that Church defense as it had existed to date was finished politically.[31] In the end Gladstone's bill for abolition of the compulsory ratepaying passed on July 24, 1868, and most Anglicans and Dissenters were pleased. There was no suggestion that the Church of England was disestablished. However, there was a general sense that the Church was cast upon its own resources and needed to justify being established. Resolution of the rates issue revealed the extent of Dissent's political power, to be sure. Equally important, resolution demonstrated that Anglicans possessed great ability to adjust the Church without relinquishing its historic ideals. The fulcrum was the Anglican conviction that in modern circumstances the Church required a modern way of functioning.

Education

The controversy over Church rates illustrated the nature and extent of the Liberal, Dissenting challenge to the Church of England. The effect of this challenge was to dislodge the Church from its traditional place in the nation, compelling it to generate revenue from voluntary contributions rather than from legal assessments. Voluntaryists generally grew more radical than the Whig Liberal mainstream, which seemed to prefer partial solutions to comprehensive ones. Not content with the abolition of Church rates, militant voluntaryists formed the British Anti-State Church Association in 1844 which in 1853 became the Liberation Society. This pressure group adopted the goal of disestablishment and pursued it well into the next century in the hope of an egalitarian, pluralistic society.[32]

Few Anglicans accepted the ideal of disestablishment of the Church of England. However, liberal Anglicans generally adopted the voluntaryist position, because they viewed state maintenance as an encumbrance upon the Church and Tractarians believed the Erastian Church was a handicapped one. A broad segment of Anglican opinion concluded that ending the Church of England's reliance upon state support freed the Church for mission. Articulate clergy and laity considered the new idea of an establishment grounded not upon formal affiliation with the state but upon the effectiveness of its role in national life. An Anglican voluntaryism of a sort emerged by an informal consensus and encouraged new clerical styles and new kinds of lay initiative which, in turn, inspired Church expansion. This transition from political response to ecclesiastical initiative was evident in the controversy over education.

The education issue arose in the first session of the reformed Parliament in 1833. Radical J. A. Roebuck introduced a bill to create a national system of education. Radicals hoped for government intervention in the new, industrial towns, and, in time, a compulsory, nondenominational education system. The Whig plan, on the other hand, was a typically cautious form of state intervention, epitomized by Lord Althorp's proposal to grant £20,000 in aid of private subscriptions to erect schools for the education of poor children, a typical Whig understanding of public responsibility to augment private agency.[33] At the time, government's education grant went to two national societies in proportion to the voluntary contributions they received. The British and Foreign Schools Society, founded in 1814 and backed by Dissenters and liberal Anglicans, "provided a general and undenominational religious education, in keeping with the religious pluralism which had developed in society." In contrast, leaders of the Hackney Phalanx, notably Joshua Watson, inspired the National Society for the Education of the Children of the Poor in the Principles of the Established Church, in 1811. This society intended to promote loyalty to the established Church and to combat seditious ideas.[34] The Central Society of Education, formed in 1836, reflected the radical ideas of Roebuck and Cobden, but had little impact at first.

The government grant of 1833 satisfied none of the societies, and Liberals began to agitate for further reform. They posed a limited form of government intervention and an end to favoritism toward the established Church. Brougham encouraged an increased government grant, reform of endowed charities, and the creation of public libraries and of a normal school. One significant modification of this Liberal agenda came in 1838 when the government introduced a plan to inspect all schools receiving state aid. Inspection was becoming a prominent aspect of the "Victorian revolution in government," and its early application to education was a natural outgrowth of Liberalism's advance.[35] Education clauses in the Factory Act of 1833 and in the Poor Law Amendment Act of 1834 also broadened the scope of education as a policy question. Nevertheless, the school societies remained the focus of education and of controversy. The middle third of the century was a time of intense religious and political bickering, intensified by the Whig aims of preserving the religious establishment and of placating Dissent. These goals satisfied few persons and provoked assertive gestures by the various factions. The National Society, for instance, bolstered by support from Gladstone and the Tractarians in 1839, declared that education should be religious in nature, and that curricula should be expanded and teaching improved in the Society's schools. The National Society intended to improve rural education and teacher training, and to begin schools for middle-class children.[36]

The substance of these proposals is not as significant as the motivation of advancing the Church's scope, which bespoke a new attitude to the Church and its role in society. This was no Whig innovation, but a militant Conservatism which adopted the form of a voluntary association, such as Clapham and Hackney itself, and built upon the example of the Sunday School societies, especially Dissenting ones. This new Conservatism defended the establishment by stepping outside it, soliciting voluntary contributions and escalating religious competition in a pluralistic environment. Aggressively the National Society wed itself to the concept that the established Church could not rely upon its legal status. Instead it must persuade and educate in an effective manner to warrant being established.

Gladstone was one of a group of young Tories who took this position. Early in 1835 he became Under-Secretary for the colonies. In that position he opposed nonsectarian education plans for the recently emancipated West Indian slaves. He believed that educating former slaves was the Church's prerogative. Furthermore, Gladstone conveyed his belief to Blomfield and lamented what he viewed as the National Society's complacency. Gladstone and G. F. Mathison, an officer of the Mint, convoked a group of sympathetic young men, mostly laity, who planned to expand the National Society aggressively.[37] Defense of the establishment was adapted to the form of Liberal politics, and the initiative to a significant extent was seized by laity, using *de facto* leaders, operating by consensus rather than fiat to create new means of inspiring loyalty to the establishment. The National Society's program implicitly acknowledged the necessity of further reform in the establishment and confirmed that religious and educational issues were central.

The Conservative program inspired a significant series of domestic and foreign mission programs which responded to the political uncertainty surrounding the establishment, yet soon took on distinctive colorations. Conservative assertion of the established Church's prerogative ruffled the Whig conscience, which prized Erastianism and religious liberty and resisted the notion that establishment had an exclusive right to educate the nation. Whig alarm increased in January, 1839, when Blomfield and Howley visited Russell "to assert, as Blomfield put it, 'the claims of the Church to conduct the education of the people.'" They insisted that state-aided schools should be integrated with the local parish, that the schoolmaster be a churchman, and that the Catechism be compulsory.[38] In response, in February, 1839, Russell introduced the Whig plan for a comprehensive education program. A reaction against the National Society aggression, this plan proposed an unprecedented degree of state supervision, as well as encouragement of nondenominational education. There was no hint of religious favoritism, especially for the established Church, but a belief that moderation and toleration, incarnated in state oversight, ought to prevail, and that the Church was not equipped, economically or politically, to undertake the nation's education. Russell could not adhere to his plan entirely, for the Church's Conservative defenders held sufficient political power to compel a compromise. As a result, in 1840, Russell reached accord with Howley that the Church should have some control over school inspections and retain a favored position for receipt of state grants. However, the Conservative hope of exclusivity failed, and the Church faced the specter of a secular, government-run system of education.[39]

In these circumstances Peel's government sought to expand education of the poor as part of a Factory Act and to give the established Church significant advantages in administration and religious instruction. Graham's Factory Bill of 1843, after James Graham, the Home Secretary, intended to combine education for children of different denominations with advantage given to the Church of England. Dissenters, however, were vigorously opposed and compelled Graham to withdraw the bill on June 15, 1843.[40] This proposal portended a national system of education, for the bill's course confirmed that the political nation would not allow advantages to any religious body, especially the established one. The bill's defeat created a chasm between state schemes of education and religious ones. Government turned to plans for a system of non-sectarian education and religious groups were compelled to function as explicitly denominational efforts supported by voluntary contributions. The education controversy of 1839–43 confirmed that establishment could not preserve its historic privileges. However, forced upon its own resources, the Church was not harmed. Mission programs resulted, and Anglicanism continued its transformation on a global scale.

The Ecclesiastical Commission and its legacy

In controversies over Church rates and education Anglicans adopted the platform of political reform to adjust the Church to new social circumstances. The intention was to make the Church be in fact what it claimed to be in theory, namely, the nation's religious establishment. This Anglican pragmatism inspired the appearance of the Ecclesiastical Commission, a result of Robert Peel's desire to improve the Church's efficiency. In his "Tamworth Manifesto," the speech wherein he explained his political principles, Peel emphasized Church reform.

With regard to alterations in the laws which govern our Ecclesiastical Establishment . . . it is a subject which must undergo the fullest deliberation, and into that deliberation the Government will enter, with the sincerest desire to remove every abuse that can impair the efficiency of the Establishment, to extend the sphere of its usefulness, and to strengthen and confirm its just claims upon the respect and affections of the people.

Counseled by Blomfield and Howley, Peel in 1835 appointed a commission to propose Church reform.[41]

The Commission represented an urge to rethink the nature of established institutions. It encompassed High Church efforts at Church extension and Evangelical interest in parochial reform and a higher standard of clerical duty. The Commission was part of a massive shift in government from aristocratic assumptions to rational principles of modern organization.[42] It secured the idea that the Church must adapt to its social nexus, a politically motivated basis of legitimacy. Peel was eager to "prove to the nation that his government, far from being averse to 'sensible' reform, could be relied on to make reforms, where they were really needed, with boldness and despatch." After Peel's government fell in 1835, the new, Whig administration of Lord Melbourne, in office until 1841, afforded the Commission sufficient political stability to carry out its work.[43] While the bulk of the Commission's daily work fell to Charles Knight Murray, its energetic secretary, the Commission's soul was Charles

James Blomfield, who took the lead in discussions. Blomfield's intention to adjust the Church while preserving its form was evident in the Commission's reports. The first report proposed creation of new dioceses at Manchester and Ripon, and consolidation of two pairs of existing ones: St. Asaph with Bangor, and Llandaff with Bristol. The Commission also intended to reduce the disparity of prelates' incomes, and an income range of £4,500 to £5,500 was established, excluding the archbishops and the sees of London, Durham, and Winchester.

These proposals received immediate assent and the work proceeded, resulting in three more reports in 1836 and a fifth one in 1837.[44] The second one, which concerned episcopal revenues and the functions of cathedral and collegiate churches, created a political storm. These features of the established Church had been untouched at least since the Reformation. The commissioners envisioned a reduction of "gross inequality," so that "no income should be liable to the imputation of being overgrown and enormous, nor, on the other hand, be subjected to the charge of penury, and restricted in its pecuniary resources." Canterbury's revenue should be reduced from £17,000 to £15,000 annually, London's from £12,200 to £10,000, and Durham's from £17,800 to £8,000. Bangor, on the other hand, should rise from £3,800 to £5,200. Melbourne added pointedly that secular revenues should be reduced, notably in the case of Durham. The Commissioners felt "that the temporal and secular jurisdiction hitherto vested in the Bishop of Durham, should be hereafter separated from his ecclesiastical functions."[45] For example, Durham should be relieved of the necessity of maintaining Durham Castle, which should be appropriated by the University. The commissioners intended to demarcate the Church's proper sphere.

The next portion of the second report concerned collegiate and cathedral churches in England and Wales. The Commission proposed that nonresidential canonries be suppressed, the number of residential canons reduced to four, and the funds from estates held by certain cathedrals merged into a common fund. These combined measures would create a surplus revenue of £130,000 per annum. Melbourne emphasized "the extreme disproportion of the income of many of the clergy," a situation which "had a most unfortunate effect upon the character of the clergy, and, consequently, on the Establishment to which they belonged. It exposed them to ridicule and contempt and also to temptations which they otherwise would not be exposed to." Lord John Russell emphasized provisions in the report to restrict nonresidence of clergy and holding of plural benefices. Russell also explained that the object of surplus funds "would be to dispose of this amount in such a manner as to make it beneficial to the Church." Russell suggested that the income of one thousand poor benefices be supplemented, to a minimum income of £100 p.a. Other means to apply surplus funds could include provision of new churches. In London and Lancashire there was church accommodation for no more than one-eighth of the population. Russell observed that "while the population had very much increased, the churches and church room had not increased in proportion."[46]

Response to the second report was generally positive, as Archbishop Howley commented in the Lords that Melbourne had assured him "that had it involved the dissolution of our ecclesiastical Establishment, he should instantly have thought it his duty to retire from it." Howley endorsed it because the Commission's intention was "that it should preserve the episcopal establishment of the Church in its integrity." Howley agreed that surplus funds should be applied to "populous parishes, more especially in the metropolis, and in the northern and midland counties, where the population had greatly increased, and where, from the want of sufficient spiritual assistance, the efficiency of the Church of England had been very materially diminished." On the basis of increased efficiency Howley agreed that residence should be enforced, pluralities suppressed, and the Church reformed.[47] In the Commons, however, the proposal was challenged by Robert Inglis, an ultra-Tory, a defender of the established Church in all its historic forms, and an opponent of any alteration of its fabric. He regretted hearing a report which "would be fatal to the best interests of the Church of which he was a member." He believed "no such Commission ought ever to have been appointed." Furthermore its recommendations should not be considered by the House of Commons, because "a great portion of the Members of it did not belong to the Established Religion."[48]

Subsequent reports of the Commission reiterated the major themes of earlier ones. The third report proposed restructuring episcopal sees. The fourth report put cathedral and collegiate church goals into legislative form. The fifth report was "a revised version of the bill suggested in the fourth." Movement of these bills through parliamentary labyrinths was slow. An Act restricting the holding of plural benefices and enforcing clerical residence passed in 1838 with slight opposition. An Act dealing with deans and chapters waited until 1840 and passed only after zealous opposition in the Lords. In contrast a bill embodying the third report was introduced by Russell on May 20, 1836 and proceeded smoothly. It delegated direction of future ecclesiastical changes to the Commission, assuring its centrality in the reform of the Church. The Commission's basic principle was enshrined, namely, correction of glaring abuses in the Church and its adaptation to changed social circumstances.[49]

A provisional form of self-government for the Church, the Commission performed functions which would be picked up later in the century at the revival of Convocation and became a means to distance the Church from the state. While changes in the Church still required legislative approval, the changes which were enacted emphasized its purely religious function. Avowed defenders of establishment such as Inglis were correct in sensing that the Church was being rearranged on the basis of new principles and at the expense of its traditional form. A considerable segment of Anglican opinion remained suspicious of any change at all, notably a spectrum of High Church opinion which included the Hackney Phalanx and newer attempts to inspire a sense of Anglicanism's Catholic features such as those of the Tractarians. The response of Henry Phillpotts, Bishop of Exeter, who delayed passage of the Ecclesiastical Duties and Revenues Bill in the Lords in 1840, illustrates such opposition. Phillpotts argued at length against the bill and the Commission, noting that it originated in the aftermath of the Reform Bill, when the Government began a process of general change in the country. Fearing that the Church's integrity would be sacrificed to the principle of efficiency, Phillpotts countered that to render the Church effective in instructing the people, it was necessary "to insist that every one of those institutions be preserved in its full integrity."[50] In this case Phillpotts was defeated and the Commission's plan went ahead.

That plan bore Blomfield's imprint. An ally of Hackney, he cherished the Church's traditions and undertook their modification reluctantly. "It is always unpopular to meddle with existing institutions in the way of reform and improvement, even where vested rights are respected." However, the failure of many members of cathedral chapters to perform residential duties and, even more, "the stronger ground of necessity" required extensive measures of reform.

That "necessity is too notorious to be denied. It is admitted by all parties, that there exists in this country at the present moment an appalling amount of spiritual destitution, and all parties are equally ready to admit the absolute necessity of making some provision for remedying that fearful evil."[51] Blomfield feared that if the "principle of perfect integrity" of the Church was maintained, little would be done to "furnish spiritual food" to the destitute. Instead Blomfield asserted the "principle of re-distribution" as "one which must be acted upon from time to time, or the Church, as an endowed Church, will cease to exist." Blomfield perceived repeated instances in history where the Church's worldly aspect had been redistributed in order to enhance the Church's ability to be faithful to its mission. The Church should not fear the loss of form, for its integrity lay elsewhere. It should fear "being found unfaithful to our trust, in leaving so many of our fellow Christians under the pressure of evils which it was in our power to alleviate." It should fear "the total absence of religious principle and moral restraint" among all the social classes. Thus, reform secured the Church's integrity.[52]

In its subsequent work the Commission committed the Church to a gradual reordering. For instance, realignment of diocesan boundaries occurred throughout the century as the diocese of Ripon was created in 1836, followed by Manchester in 1847, Truro and St. Albans in 1877, Liverpool in 1880, and Newcastle in 1882.[53] These changes illustrate the restructuring of the Church of England, a process born of necessity to conform the Church to the nation in a time of social change which inspired a new sense of mission. For example, the building of new churches was already underway. The Church Building Act of 1818, inspired by the Hackney Phalanx, provided £1,000,000 in government funds for new churches and established the Church Building Commissioners to manage the fund. Whereas 55 new churches were built between 1801 and 1811, 276 appeared between 1821 and 1831. Voluntary contributions assisted church-building and became the only source of such funds after 1831. The Church began to direct its own mission.[54]

Blomfield was the single most influential source of this change. He stressed that while the Church must be united to the state, it is "a distinct and independent society, for the express purpose of keeping [the faith] alive, and in full efficacy, as the instrument of enlightening and purifying the world." The Church must be "an instrument to preserve the Gospel in the world, and to diffuse the knowledge of its truths, and to promote the practice of its precepts."[55] He believed that the Church exists for mission, and, by 1846, Blomfield noted that his efforts had shown success. Over £179,000 had been raised for additional churches in London, and another £60,000 specified for Bethnal Green, where 70,000 people had two Anglican churches and three clergy. Already sixty-three new churches had been built or were under construction. Now 205,000 people could be accommodated in church at any one time out of a population of 1,380,000. However, the metropolitan population continued to increase. Blomfield insisted that the Church could not wait for legislative aid, but must proceed by its own efforts, especially in education. Blomfield had concluded that education best awakened people to religion. Through the religious training of children, parents could be influenced, and the entire nation permeated with the Gospel. Blomfield believed that making the Church available to more people was the essence of its mission, and education was the readiest means of mission.[56]

By 1851, however, the Church's inability to keep up with population growth was apparent. Horace Mann, a barrister, directed an extensive religious census. Mann's data reflected church or chapel attendance on March 30, 1851. Mann learned that an inadequate number of places for worship existed, especially in urban, industrial areas, where there was an indifference to religion. "The masses . . . of our large and growing towns . . . form a world apart, a nation by themselves." Mann cited an absence of "local interest" among residents of poorer neighborhoods. Urban areas thwarted any sense of community, of being organically related to society. The Church of England had raised some new churches in middle-class areas by local initiative and by assistance of funds from central organizations, but in poor areas initiative was lacking. The result was a large overall increase in new church buildings, but a continuing lack of such facilities for the poor. Only the Bishop of London had provided new churches without waiting for local initiative. Without other "missionary enterprises similar to this, the mighty task of even mitigating spiritual destitution in our towns and cities hardly can be overcome."[57] "Local interest" proved insufficient.

In the Charge marking his third diocesan visitation in 1880, James Fraser, second Bishop of Manchester, reviewed the thirty-three-year history of the diocese. In 1848 there had been 280 parishes for 1,500,000 people. In 1880 there were 473 parishes and 750 clergy for 2,000,000 people. Fraser's predecessor created 110 new parishes in twenty-two years. In his eleventh year Fraser could point to 80 new parishes. Nevertheless there were still too few church seats for the populace and disheartening apathy, especially among the working classes. Fraser perceived few avowed unbelievers. He was convinced that the Church required innovative forms and greater exertion from clergy and laity alike.[58] Simply providing new buildings clearly was not enough. Mission, Fraser suggested, required another standard; nevertheless, the Church's identity was rooted in its mission.

DOMESTIC MISSION

Adjustment of ecclesiastical function encouraged new means of making the Church accessible to the middle and lower social classes. The Church's particular concern was poor, working-class persons, and its work among them stressed education and evangelism. The result was that ecclesiastical reform became not only a source of mission but also a means of ensuring the Church's integrity. Concern for the form of the Church's mission became intertwined with questions of ecclesiastical identity. The Church began to consider itself a body whose nature was mission. A concern for authenticity in the Church's mission efforts in the nineteenth century determined the forms of its ministrations.

The Ecclesiastical Commission's recommendations reflected a perception in a large segment of the Church that it was out of touch with the nation. While the Commission changed the Church's framework, in other segments of the Church a variety of new initiatives appeared. Already diffuse in its notion of ecclesiastical authority, the Church of England became suffused with multiple voluntary associations on the model of Clapham and Hackney which supported particular visions of ecclesiastical mission or identity. Though mediating between such groups would eventually become a challenge to the Church's conception of governance, an uncoordinated assortment of private initiatives enhanced the Church's claim to be the nation's establishment.

Middle-class education

An important illustration concerns the Church's relationship to middle-class England. Historians of Victorian England commonly depict the era as a time when middle-class values triumphed. This cluster of moral norms included an emphasis upon the family, a belief in the virtues of thrift and self-help, and a sense of divinely mandated national destiny. Victorian England combined the ideals of Evangelicalism and Liberalism into a middle-class ethic of service. Shopkeepers, clerks, skilled artisans, and managers saw themselves as society's backbone and fostered a belief that, through education, individuals and societies can improve.[59]

The Victorian Church became wed to middle-class values and, more than any other individual, Nathaniel Woodard advanced the Church of England's educational work among the middle classes. Woodard was an unlikely source for such an initiative because of his eccentric personality and extreme emphasis upon an Anglo-Catholic sacramentalism and the Church's distinctiveness from the state. Nevertheless he believed that education was a primary component of mission, and that a lack of adequate educational facilities for the middle classes portended a failure of the Church to extend itself to those growing social strata.[60] By 1846 Woodard, then serving in the diocese of Chichester, was raising money for a small school in his home. He opened St. Nicholas' College early in 1847 and, though the school survived as an entity only until 1853, it afforded a model for education which eventually permeated England. Woodard intended to offer a complete education at a charge which made it available to middle-class children. He combined religious and moral supervision and envisioned the schools as avenues into the Church of England. By 1855 he was proposing that schools be linked into diocesan societies dedicated to mission among the middle classes. The success of Woodard's work reflected both his ability to establish a workable model, and his sense that a network of schools would enhance their impact upon the nation.[61]

Woodard proved to be a skilled fund-raiser at public gatherings which he organized to promote the school. To his meetings Woodard attracted peers, local dignitaries, bishops, and occasional royalty. The philanthropic gathering became a kind of Victorian theater, and Woodard was a skilled impresario. His Anglo-Catholicism also stamped his approach to education. He understood his schools as religious communities and fretted over the secular influences which contested with the school in the life of each child. Though he clung to the idea of the Church as a theoretical establishment, he believed the Church's aims required distance from the state. Woodard's goal of preparing the middle classes for a Christian citizenship required schools free from state control.[62] His schools suggested the ready affinity which developed between Church teachings and such middle-class values as personal devotion, morality, and family life. The result was to solidify the Church's rootage in middle-class England.

Working class mission

The Evangelical inheritance

The Church's ministry among poor and working people was another matter. Since the last quarter of the eighteenth century there had been a variety of attempts to extend Church work among poor people. Robert Raikes' Sunday school, founded in Gloucester in 1780, became a transatlantic form of religious education for children. A decade later Hannah More, friend of William Wilberforce and member of the Clapham Sect, devoted considerable energy to the religious education of poor children. From the 1790s until well into the nineteenth century, More organized schools in the Mendip Hills area of Somerset. She also wrote numerous pamphlets for children, notably the Cheap Repository Tracts, which first appeared in 1795, and reveal the Evangelical approach to work with the poor. Though More condemned the idleness, unbelief, gaming, intemperance, and debauchery which she saw as characteristic of lower-class life, she blamed industrialism and the city for multiplying these woes. Instead she encouraged honesty, piety, respect, restraint, industry, and sobriety. More idealized rural life and condemned urban environments. She also stressed the sacredness of family life and called for renewal of domestic loyalties. In her tracts there were repeated illustrations of good wives, faithful husbands, and obedient, respectful children.[63] Similarly More encouraged renewed ties of dependence within the existing social spectrum.

Like Evangelical opinion generally, More's emphasis upon reinvigoration of existing social institutions envisioned the integration of religion into all aspects of daily life. Schools and tracts were agencies of mission, ways to saturate society with the Gospel message. Evangelicals were disturbed at the religious apathy of substantial segments of society. William Wilberforce reserved his ire for the social elite, whom he believed bore a special religious responsibility. More turned to the poor, the victims of profound social and economic upheaval. Her interest was not in remedying their circumstances but in saving their souls. She also intended to eliminate the gap between rich and poor symbolized by the popular culture of lower-class life. Instead she proposed a universal, Christian culture which would reinforce the duties of all classes and draw them into an organic sense of affinity, a vision born of the emerging upper-class sense of the social role model.[64]

Evangelical work among the poor proposed a new social ethic and implicitly criticized the upper classes for patterns of irresponsibility. This was a daring position for the early nineteenth century, when most clergy and laity of the Church of England would have endorsed the views of J. B. Sumner, Bishop of Chester. Sumner categorically rejected equality as a social ideal. "Wherever equality is found to exist . . . mankind are in the lowest and most savage state." Sumner acknowledged that English society at present revealed "each individual neglectful of the general good, and struggling merely for the advancement of his own; flourishing by the discomfiture of competitors, and elevated by the depression of his brethren. But the other side of the picture shows individual advantage terminating in public benefits, and the desire of aggrandizement which is stimulated by ambition or domestic partialities, contributing towards the welfare of the community at large." It is clear, Sumner continued, that the "state of civilization which admits and consists of a gradation of ranks and of unequal conditions, is precisely the situation which affords to man the best opportunities of performing the purposes of his being."[65]

Sumner cautiously approved of schools where poor children could learn the Bible and be rescued from ignorance. He looked to local charity as the surest way to alleviate acute distress and urged that poor people be taught to save what little money they received. "The poor man requires to be taught prudence, by seeing its advantage clearly before him." The "clergyman of the parish as the natural and legal superintendent of the establishment," working with poor children to ingrain prudence, obedience, and industry, could convey this lesson. He should also teach the poor to postpone marriage until a mature age, thus checking population growth and rendering parents more fit for their duties. These "improvements," Sumner concluded, encouraged poor people to be content with their station.[66] Such admonitions, of course, were ineffective and revealed the inadequacy of the Church's comprehension of lower-class life. Hannah More's work, on the other hand, represented the beginning of an effort to increase the Church's work among a segment of society which felt little affinity with the established Church.

James Kay's *The Moral and Physical Condition of the Working Classes*, published in 1832, noted the "absence of religious feeling, the neglect of all religious ordinances," and the "moral degradation of the community." In 1836, *The Quarterly Review*, covering Kay's and other works on the subject, lamented the prevalence of "an evil which, if not speedily checked, threatens to corrupt the whole social system . . . and bring into jeopardy . . . the safety of the empire." The evil sprang from a system of degradation, an environment in which human bonds were torn away and people were doomed to vice. The "diabolical system" overwhelmed "the laws of our moral being" and reversed "the order of nature and the precepts of revelation."[67] An important change had begun in the attitudes of Church leaders toward poverty and industrial society. Already Evangelicals such as Wilberforce had rebuked the upper classes for moral laxity and, as an Anglican criticism of industrial society developed, Evangelicals were in the forefront. Their influence within the Church pushed it toward a new sense of social mission.

Lord Shaftesbury

A notable figure in the Evangelical challenge to industrial society was Anthony Ashley Cooper, seventh Earl of Shaftesbury, a leading advocate in Parliament of measures to regulate the hours of daily work, especially the work of children. Ashley believed that human beings must prepare the world for Christ's return, a belief he carried into his leadership of diverse voluntary associations to expand the Church of England's ministry. He was a founder and president of the Church Pastoral Aid Society, organized in 1836 to raise funds for clergy in needy parishes and to offer lay assistance with parish visitations. However, Ashley's primary commitment was to parliamentary action on behalf of the poor. Ashley became the second Wilberforce, working within legislative channels to combat social evil.

On July 20, 1838, Ashley addressed the House of Commons on the subject of children working in factories. His thundering jeremiad warned of the social consequences of this labor practice. Ashley charged that if the Commons "continued idly indifferent, and obstinately shut their eyes to this great and growing evil, if they were careless to the growth of an immense population, plunged in ignorance and vice, which neither feared God nor regarded man, then . . . they must be prepared for the very worst result, that could befall a nation." Here was the Evangelical view of history, perfected by opponents of slavery, now applied to industrialism. Unless Britain repented through measures of reform, she must expect national punishment.[68]

In subsequent consideration of child labor, Ashley rose to greater rhetorical heights. On August 4, 1840, he insisted, "I have sufficiently proved that there prevails a system of slavery under the sanction of law." The employment of children retards moral and professional education. It trains them only to be criminals and paupers. The "whole course of our manufacturing system tends to these results." Instead, "my object is to appeal to, and excite the public opinion; where we cannot legislate, we can exhort, and laws may fail, where example will succeed. I must appeal to the bishops and ministers of the Church of England, nay, more, to the ministers of every denomination, to urge on the hearts of their hearers, the mischief and the danger of these covetous and cruel practices."[69] In Evangelical fashion, Ashley appealed to extra-parliamentary influence to remake the public order, indentifying the political nation with coalitions of people engaged in moral response to social problems. Ashley reflected in the parliamentary arena the Evangelical effort to bring the Gospel to a large number of people who seemed beyond its reach.

Much in Ashley's attitude was paternalistic, as was the case in Evangelical social attitudes generally. A Tory, Ashley felt that society should be hierarchical and stable, distinguished by clearly defined classes linked to one another through bonds of mutual respect. It was the duty of the higher classes to exhibit moral governance and charity to the poor, who were dependent upon their betters. Tory paternalists, including Robert Southey, Thomas Carlyle, and Benjamin Disraeli, believed in a society of mutual obligations whose values were rooted in biblical imagery, and a rural, agrarian society. Paternalism prized a nation whose people understood they belonged to a whole and accepted their social lot in order to preserve this social union.[70]

To Evangelicals such as Ashley, paternalism had an altered meaning, an ideal of organic society which did not simply look backward to the rural ideal of England's fabled past, but anticipated the society to come, with Christ's return. Reform was the means to act in accord with God's will in preparing individuals and the nation to face their creator. While Evangelicals prized the rural past, they used pastoral imagery to suggest a future of harmony under the Lordship of Christ. Ashley believed that extra-parliamentary organizations were essential to this national preparation. During the 1840s Ashley became a vice-president of the Church Missionary Society, helped to establish ragged schools for destitute children, and became a member of the committee of the Scripture Readers' Association. Founded in 1844, by a coalition of Anglican and Nonconformist Evangelicals, this society organized lay persons to read the Bible to illiterate, poor people. Evangelicals disregarded denominational identity and clerical leadership in addressing working-class ignorance of religion. Following a model used by Thomas Chalmers in Glasgow, London Evangelicals formed the District Visiting Society in 1828 and used lay persons while generally ignoring clergy and the local parish. Often the visitors were women, giving rise to women's groups dedicated to relief, education, and conversion of the poor.

In response to the needs of the poor and the initiative made by visitors, the London City Mission appeared in 1835. The LCM was a pan-Evangelical effort which attracted Whig Anglican Evangelicals such as Thomas Fowell Buxton, youngest member of the Clapham Sect and the parliamentary leader of the abolition of slavery in 1833. It distributed Scripture, organized relief, and began instruction designed to forestall vice among the poor. Despite the movement's broad initiative, it appealed only to the Whig and Evangelical sectors of the Church, because of its blurring of denominational lines. Charles James Blomfield was not impressed with an organization which ignored ecclesiastical identity, but he became supportive of the concept as Anglican Evangelicals expressed interest in uniquely Anglican forms of mission. In 1843 Blomfield rebuked Robert Hanbury, a wealthy brewer, for supporting the LCM. In reply Hanbury offered to fund an Anglican effort if Blomfield would endorse it. In 1844 Blomfield and Bishop C. R. Sumner of Winchester became chief patrons of the Scripture Readers' Association, of which Ashley was an officer. The Association emphasized lay work among the poor and lay direction of its affairs. However, SRA agents were forbidden to preach or to conduct meetings; they merely went from door to door in order to read selections from Scripture. As the clergy role was protected, the lay role was expanded.[71]

The SRA's work in London was one instance of the trend toward urban mission by Anglican Evangelicals. Birmingham was another locale where Evangelical initiative encouraged the Church's life. In 1825 the Birmingham Clerical Society appeared with the endorsement of Bishop Henry Ryder of Lichfield. There Evangelical archdeacons William Spooner and George Hodson inspired new forms of urban work and Thomas Moseley, rector of the city's central parish, organized visiting teams and divided his parish into four separate ones. He promoted new forms of charity, the distribution of tracts, and the building of schools. Anglican influence over poor children in Birmingham resulted more from a comprehensive education program as local Church leaders pressured industrialists to create factory schools and to give the Church prominence in local politics. Clergy and laity hoped to influence municipal policies concerning education and poor relief.[72] A successor, John Cale Miller, extended Moseley's initiatives when he established an association for working people and, in 1854, offered a prize for the best essay on the subject of "cooperation of the working classes and the other classes of society for the elevation of the former." Miller won workers for the Church by teaching an organic sense of social union and extending Church-sponsored schools.[73]

Urban clergy had little interest in conveying the practical skills required by industrial society. The Church emphasized elementary education for children and an introduction to the sciences and liberal arts for adults. These curricula imparted a kind of socialization which featured Christian precepts and an organic sense of social bond among all classes. Church schools encouraged the working classes to believe that they could advance socially to middle-class values and upheld nostalgia for a simpler, agrarian England. While Church work among the poor expanded impressively, it remained alien to industrial society.

W. F. Hook

Walter Farquhar Hook was the best-known urban parish priest of the mid-century. Hook was a High Churchman who embodied the Evangelical interest in the city and who applied traditional Church values to the new urban society. His ministry was spent at urban parishes in Birmingham and Coventry, followed by Leeds, where he served from 1837 to 1859, then as Dean of Chichester, where he died in 1875. Throughout his career Hook believed that the rural parish should be the urban parish's model, because rural life exemplified the personal relationship between the laity and their spiritual shepherd which should be the Church's ideal. When he found at Leeds that he had charge over fourteen churches covering the municipality, Hook set out to make changes.

Initially Hook encountered intense opposition to his program. His

vestry refused expenditures for surplices and prayer books, and for the
additional wine necessary for weekly celebration of Holy Communion. He discovered that vestry members left their coats and hats on
the altar or sat upon it at vestry meetings. Hook pushed through a
higher Church rate to cover additional expenditures. An energetic
teacher, he stressed that his principles of Church life could be tested by
Scripture. A tireless pastor, Hook became an energetic reformer and a
public figure. Church attendance improved dramatically, especially
among young adults and children, and baptisms, marriages, and
funerals were performed with new solemnity. Teaching the Scriptures
and the meaning of the Church's offices became priorities, and Hook
trained lay teachers to lead these classes.[74]

Hook believed that the Church had become too much a part of its
social locus, leading to laxity in educating its people. He argued that
being "a true and faithful member of the Church requires no little
moral courage." To contend for "a true Church, a pure Church, a
holy Church – this is different to those who court the praise of men or
fear the censure of the world." He identified the Eucharist as the
essence of the Church's distinctiveness and the center of its social
mission. When he found that the Eucharist had been celebrated
casually in Leeds, he began reforms, such as the installation of a
piscina so that consecrated wine could be disposed reverently. Hook
commented that increased care in the liturgy caused people to
"enquire whether the Eucharist is not something more than a bare
commemoration." In the Eucharist the believer finds the Holy
Spirit, who will "inspire us with holy, consolatory, rapturous
thoughts." This consolation "is such as worldly men, or the ordinary
run of those who are called religious, cannot conceive." Reception of
the Eucharist could not be undertaken lightly but required purity of
heart, achieved by devout preparation. To receive the Eucharist "is
indeed an act of much austerity" by which "we shall more and more
wean ourselves from the world, and devote ourselves to works of
charity and religion."[75] His quixotic mixture of Evangelical and
High Church piety became the basis of Hook's sense of urban
mission.

A sense of mission pervaded all that Hook did. In late 1843 he
planned the division of his unwieldy parish into fourteen independent
ones in order to make the Church and the sacraments accessible to the
poor. "I am most anxious thus to secure for my poorer brethren the
privileges of a free and unrestricted participation in the sacraments

and ordinances of our holy church; in making each church a parish church I have in view the conferring upon them a *right* to a seat or kneeling therein." Hook's use of the term "right" is significant, given the importance of the concept in liberal thought. He hoped to integrate the poor into the Church, for he believed that "unless the Church of England can be made in the manufacturing districts the church of the poor, which she certainly is not now, her days are numbered." He proposed to accomplish this through teaching in schools and churches the nature of the Church of England's distinctiveness as a liturgical community. The integrity of establishment derived from its faithfulness in mission.[76]

Christian Socialism

Hook sensed that the working classes were part of a new, urban environment, and he attempted to bring the Church to that setting through higher standards of clerical performance, education, lay voluntarism, and an ideal of the Church as an alternative society. While Hook's work succeeded, the Christian Socialists, a cluster of clerical and lay intellectuals and activists, articulated a more visionary understanding of the Church's mission. They viewed the Church's role as leadership in a process of social transformation. A founding figure was John Malcolm Ludlow, an Englishman of French upbringing who had been schooled in early French socialist thought, especially Fourier. Though he experienced a sense of conversion in 1840, he rejected what he believed was doctrinal narrowness in Evangelicalism and identified social issues as the locus of faith. In 1841 Ludlow was impressed when he heard working-class spokesmen John Bright and Richard Cobden detail the horrors of life for urban, poor people. This became a second awakening for his Christian faith, and alarm at the privations of workers guided his life's endeavors.

Compelled to organize more effective ways to dispense charity, Ludlow wondered if aspiring barristers would be good workers with the poor, and, in 1846, sought advice from the Chaplain to Lincoln's Inn, F. D. Maurice. Ludlow initially perceived Maurice as an impractical intellectual, and, impatient for solutions to the plight of the poor, he by-passed Maurice and formed a visiting society to attend poor people residing near the Inns of Court. The program had modest success, but Ludlow was dissatisfied. He was a practitioner whose search for a social vision brought him back to Maurice.[77] Although Ludlow later in life became disenchanted with Maurice, for more than a decade Ludlow idolized him and deferred to him as a superior. Maurice supplied much of the intellectual sense of what the movement might be, while Ludlow pushed the movement far past the point where Maurice felt comfortable. Maurice envisioned education for the working classes; Ludlow hoped to create a system of trade unions.

The French Revolution of 1848 excited in Ludlow a sense of possibility. If this event had been "taken in hand by earnest Christian men, able to understand and grapple with social questions, it might have regenerated France and Europe." Social issues begged for practical witness to Christianity, and Chartism, a movement of labor protest, alerted Ludlow to the silence of Christian faith in the midst of upheaval. Awed by Maurice's intellect, Ludlow turned to him, and the two men gathered a group of sympathetic colleagues, including cleric and author Charles Kingsley, and writer Thomas Hughes.[78] Out of this merger of sentiment, a newspaper, *Politics for the People*, appeared for three months in 1848, marking the birth of Christian Socialism. In a prospectus for *Politics*, the authors characterized modern life as separation of people and social classes from mutual sympathy. Moreover, "Politics have been separated from Christianity," a gap the authors intended to bridge. They acknowledged "that a Living and Righteous God is ruling in human society not less than in the natural world . . . The world is governed by God; this is the rich man's warning; this is the poor man's comfort; this is the real hope in the consideration of all questions . . . this is the pledge that Liberty, Fraternity, Unity, under some conditions or other, are intended for every people under heaven."[79]

The authors asserted that the French social ideal, "Liberty, Fraternity, Unity," lacked a center which these authors claimed they had found. "We pretend to think that an Everlasting Father has revealed Himself to men in an elder Brother, one with him and with us, who died for all." On this principle men "must learn to act and feel together as men." Differences of class and of political philosophy could diminish in Christ, where people could discover their inherent bond as children of God, and build a just society. Socialism, "the science of making men partners," was the heart of Christianity, and Christianity was the essence of socialism.[80] Inspired by this ideal, Maurice began a series of discussions with working men in March, 1849. "I never recollect," Ludlow recorded, "any meetings so interesting as were these. They were . . . fortnightly conferences between a clergyman of the Church of England and working men, the first of the kind that had ever been held."[81] In this early instance of a new conception of mission, Maurice tried to learn from the poor, to legitimize their experiences, and to position the Church to alleviate their misery. The meetings contributed to his conviction that every form of human culture possessed inherent evidence of God's presence. God's universal sovereignty became one of Maurice's basic convictions.

Maurice supplied the theoretical side of Christian Socialism, an effort to restate Christian principles in terms meaningful to contemporary social experience. Influenced by Ludlow, Maurice asserted that God's universal Kingdom is earthly and practical, as well as heavenly and spiritual. The Church's task in proclaiming the Kingdom was to better humanity, creating a new sense of social fellowship, a union of society across class lines. Christian Socialism updated the old ideal of an organic society with the Church as its core and hoped to bring the urban masses to Anglicanism. Although the movement itself faded, its goals permeated important segments of the Church and informed Anglican ideals of the Church and mission.[82]

Christian Socialism itself continued as a series of practical endeavors. Maurice nurtured his dream of a newspaper or pamphlets to convince working people that true Christianity was not the preserve of the wealthy, but the visible form of God's eternal Kingdom. Ludlow, Kingsley, and Hughes attempted sanitation reform and the formation of workingmen's associations. The Working Tailors' Association, begun in February, 1850, became the model for other groups, notably among weavers. Ludlow also suggested groups to improve the condition of women, an interest which attracted Shaftesbury's support. Though aloof from these efforts, Maurice captured the movement's flavor in his tract *Christian Socialism*. "Christianity is the only foundation of Socialism, and a true Socialism is the necessary result of a sound Christianity. The watchword of the Socialist is co-operation; the watchword of the anti-socialist is competition."[83] Maurice and his colleagues nurtured a critique of capitalism which Ludlow took into practical experiments such as prototype trade unions which failed for lack of funds and a central, coordinating body.

The movement's most notable creation was education for working-class adults. Early in its history Christian Socialism had established classes for adults which envisioned uplifting workers in morality and in political consciousness. The interest in education culminated in 1854 in the Working Men's College in London. The College became a model for similar institutions throughout Britain which offered lectures in such subjects as law, economics, history, and mathematics. These courses presented Maurice's belief that the Church was by nature the nation's educator, because education could not be distinguished as secular and sacred. Society could be regenerated through the discovery of its inherent harmony. This Christian Socialist ideal, as well as a Maurician belief in the integrity of every culture and in the role of the Church in the redemption of culture, became a constituent of the Anglican approach to mission.

FOREIGN MISSION

New forms of domestic mission were accompanied by initiatives in foreign mission. Already Evangelical humanitarianism spawned African and Indian ventures in which the Hackney Phalanx insisted upon High Church forms, so that Anglican mission became a fusion of party interests. The Church of England's program of foreign mission relied heavily upon initiatives from outside official Church structures as *ad hoc* groups created new forms of Church work. Anglicans nurtured an image of their Church as a people energized for mission, an emphasis which means that the Church must expand by public initiative and its missionary strategy entails creation of a sense of peoplehood, of an organic sense of community. This Anglican approach fastened upon the episcopate as the guarantee of the Church's authenticity as a missionary body.

Thomas Fowell Buxton

Foreign initiatives could be traced directly to the Evangelical, humanitarian tradition which had secured legislation to end British slavery in 1833. Humanitarians turned their attention to Britain's international expansion out of concern for its influence upon distant cultures and peoples. Because two sons of Clapham occupied influential positions in the foreign-policy apparatus during the early 1830s, Evangelical opinions had to be taken seriously. Charles Grant the younger (Lord Glenelg) became Secretary of State, and James Stephen the younger was Permanent Under-Secretary at the Colonial Office. Thomas Fowell Buxton remained an important

Member of Parliament and became the driving force behind the formation of the Aborigines' Protection Society in 1837. These humanitarians envisioned Britain as a global power committed to civilizing and evangelizing the peoples of the world.

Evangelical interest in foreign affairs clashed with the increasing influence of avowed imperialists such as Edward Gibbon Wakefield. This powerful lobby pursued unrestricted colonization in the hope of aggressive British expansion. Conflict between these factions intensified over New Zealand policy in the 1830s and 1840s when Wakefield and his supporters pursued massive British intervention, while Buxton and other Evangelicals wanted gradual expansion through Christian mission and the exercise of a civilizing influence. In 1838 Buxton drafted a Bill of Aboriginal Rights, arguing that just as British subjects had rights, so had people subjected to British influence. In Clapham fashion, Buxton insisted that Britain held a divinely appointed destiny to redeem the world's peoples.[84]

The zenith of Evangelical influence over foreign initiatives came in reference to Africa. In 1837 Buxton formulated a new kind of Africa policy, the idea of teaching the continent a legitimate form of commerce and exerting a civilizing influence. Buxton pondered a way to begin Africa's social redemption through British influence, and he was able to win acceptance in principle in 1839 for an African plan with key support from Lord John Russell, the new Secretary of State.[85] The plan called for an expedition supported by the government to sail up the Niger river to reach agreement with tribes in the vicinity on an end to the slave trade and the inauguration of ethical commerce, including a model farm to show how tribal society might improve. On June 1, 1840, Buxton's Africa Civilization Society sponsored a mass meeting to arouse public enthusiasm for the project. Surrounded by the Prince Consort, peers, and nine bishops, Buxton and other speakers harangued a crowd of over 5,000, including a medical student named David Livingstone. Vintage Evangelicalism, the message was that Africa awaited Britain's civilizing gesture. It seemed to be the moment of triumph for a humanitarian colonial policy.[86]

This meeting left a lasting image of Evangelicalism and empire advancing in tandem. Charles Dickens ridiculed Evangelical interest in Africa and mocked the Niger expedition, though his cynicism inadvertently offered proof of the political power Evangelicals commanded.[87] The Niger expedition was a bipartisan effort which

Whigs and Tories alike felt compelled to endorse. Over a year after the great rally, a flotilla sailed and, on August 8, 1841, assembled off the mouth of the Niger. Five days later it entered the river's mouth, and two weeks later, enacted the first treaty with a nearby tribe.[88] The expedition concluded several other treaties and selected a site for settlement. However, by mid-September the majority of the ships' crews were ill with fever and, eventually, of 145 white men among the ships, 130 became ill and 40 died. Of several young African men brought along from Sierra Leone as interpreters, none fell seriously ill. One, Samuel Ajayi Crowther, later figured prominently in a Church mission in the Niger delta.

Buxton's highly publicized endeavor left little tangible legacy, serving only to introduce British interest in the region. For Evangelicals it was a crushing defeat. The African Civilization Society soon crumbled, and government never again embraced so explicit an alliance with a humanitarian lobby, much less a religious one. Evangelical influence over colonial matters came to be exerted through groups such as the Church Missionary Society and personal contact with political figures, rather than through government endorsement of a religious agenda. The Church's relation to colonial policy occurred more in the mission field than in parliamentary corridors. In yet another way the Church had been distanced from government.

A zeal for mission

Despite the embarrassment of the Niger expedition, interest in mission intensified. A new, public mood blended romanticism, a sense of religious duty, and an eagerness to participate in remaking global affairs. The mood extended beyond an interest in evangelizing and civilizing distant cultures to public enthusiasm for building empire, and perhaps making one's fortune in an undiscovered realm. Nevertheless, for the Church of England, this encouraged a new zeal for mission. A notable expression was Anthony Grant's *The Past and Prospective Extension of the Gospel by Missions to the Heathen*, delivered as the prestigious Bampton Lectures at Oxford in 1843. Grant, a Fellow of New College, Oxford, and Vicar of Romford, gave an insightful expression of the Church of England's new zeal for mission. Assessing present possibilities for mission, Grant referred to "the insufficiency and faultiness of the recent modes of conducting missionary enterprises." Without direct references, Grant stated that the Church of England's recent missionary work was "identified with a certain cast of religious opinion and character, which caused offence to sober-minded Christians, while the work itself was discredited by others, because it was disconnected from the authority and direction of the Church." Something more than rival missionary societies and public forms of action was needed.[89]

Grant stressed the recent "wonderful expansion of the Empire of Great Britain, whereby, through her colonies, she is brought into contact with almost the entire heathen world." For Grant this meant that "it is no longer a question whether the heathen shall be left to themselves. Our colonies are already planted in the midst of them; they are our fellow-subjects; we *must*, as a nation, exercise an untold influence upon them." This influence should be a civilizing, humanitarian one, which could best be accomplished not by manifold mission societies, but by the Church itself. "Therefore must the Church extend herself with the extension of our empire." The Church must carry "her divine system into foreign settlements, [to] secure the Christianity and the true social development of these future nations."[90]

Grant believed the Church must educate other cultures in its principles in such a way that a civilizing influence would result. Mission's goal is the transplantation of the Church, which requires respectful familiarity with other cultures. It would be easy to condemn pagan religions if one did not remember that "in these traditional revelations the germ of the Gospel may be said to exist, as it did when they were first communicated to man." The Church must build upon primitive traditions as preparation for the Gospel and thus must treat other peoples humanely as children of God.[91] This idea was not original, for the Hackney Phalanx had insisted that the consecration of a bishop for India assured the integrity of the Church's mission. However, several aspects of Grant's argument represented new understandings of the necessity of the episcopate in Anglican mission. He argued that the Church's mission should be expansive beyond the bounds of empire. Grant hoped the Church would correct the failings of empire, bringing civilization in a Christian form. Grant believed the mission of the Church's role was to inspire nation-building, uplifting a culture and modernizing its traditions, themes which contemporaries of Grant expanded into the basis of modern Anglican mission. For instance, Oxford movement figure E. B. Pusey, in two sermons in 1838, argued that mission was the work neither of individuals nor of societies but of the Church. Missionaries must be accountable to bishops, who represent the succession of the Church's mission, which is to gather all nations into God's Kingdom. England's responsibility is to plant Catholic Christianity around the world.[92]

In speeches and sermons Samuel Wilberforce emphasized the themes of mission and civilization. He combined his father's zeal for humanitarian mission with an emphasis on the Church which allied him to Blomfield. He not only intended to elevate the dignity and efficiency of the Church's ministry, but grasped that the modern Church must gather its integrity from within itself and not from its connection to the political establishment. From a conviction that the Church must be distinct from society, Wilberforce derived a profound view of mission which linked foreign and domestic strategy. In an SPG sermon in 1852, Bishop Wilberforce insisted that the highest duty of a Christian people is to shape the life of an infant nation. Britain's participation in the slave trade gave her a responsibility to exhibit a civilizing influence in her global expansion, uplifting a national character to become part of the universal Christian society.[93] Britain's greatness lay in her tradition of Catholic Christianity, which should spread across the globe as a means to realize the divine intention for history.

The Church's American experience struck Wilberforce as a portent of its global challenge and possibility. In America the Church had developed features which went beyond its English heritage. In other words, in the mission field the Church, "not being subject to the same restraints" as the Church at home, realized its distinctiveness and integrity. Wilberforce believed that only in mission could the Church truly become Catholic, a vision which completed the adjustment of establishment into a sense of the Church as God's Kingdom.[94] He believed mission went beyond planting the Church and conveying civilization out of a sense of national duty; rather, the Church realized its destiny as it expanded in mission. Mission afforded the Church the chance to clarify its universality and its particularity, as Wilberforce interpreted the American example, where the historic establishment had been overcome by modern conditions. While American pluralism challenged ecclesiastical identity, it was an opportunity for mission. In Africa, Asia, and India the Church could realize its genuine identity.[95] This conviction prompted his interest in the office of missionary bishop.

Charles James Blomfield was a kindred spirit who shared

Wilberforce's emphasis upon mission. Blomfield was never more eloquent on the subject of foreign mission than on Whitsunday, 1852, when he preached in Lambeth Palace Chapel at the consecration of Owen Emeric Vidal as first Bishop of Sierra Leone. Hammering away at the words of Acts 17: 24, 26, 27, "God . . . hath made of one blood all nations of men," Blomfield found that the words reveal that "all mankind are members of one great family, springing from a common root" and "that all are religious beings, objects of God's moral government, capable of acquiring a knowledge of his will; and accountable to him for that knowledge, according to the measure of it which they possess." The various races "are but deflexions from the primitive type of perfect humanity . . . all proceeded originally from a single pair." Beneath the variety there exists "an essential identity of intellectual constitution." In all manifestations of human nature "there is the capacity for improvement," for "where reason exists, there exists a soul . . . to be saved." This is true of all peoples. "The boundaries of the kingdom of grace are not marked out by seas, or mountains, or zones, nor by lines of more or less perfect physical development of the human frame."[96]

Blomfield believed that Sierra Leone could be the entry point into Africa for the Church. That toe-hold symbolized Britain's rejection of unethical commerce and turn to a divine responsibility. The Church must be transplanted to that land by a bishop who would "offer spiritual freedom to the remoter tribes of the African continent" through "the embassy" of a "native ministry." For the time being European missionaries must conduct the work. "The African race must for the present be regarded as children; stunted . . . in their intellectual growth by a long period of harsh . . . treatment; and they must be educated with great tenderness and care." As Blomfield summarized it, the task was "to lay the foundations of an African native episcopate" and to transplant "the polity and . . . the ritual of our Reformed Church."[97] Thus, Blomfield imagined that mission would transform the Church into something it had not previously been. In addition to translating the Scriptures and the Prayer Book into "native languages," Bishop Vidal must engage in "the necessary task of adapting the ritual of our Church to the use of native Christian churches, founded beyond the limits of our colonies amongst independent tribes." Ritual would facilitate the encounter between tribal tradition and faithfulness to the Word of God. In this process, the superintendence of a bishop was needed, for the episcopate guaranteed continuity as the Church adapted.[98] He failed, however, to elaborate norms of adaptation, i.e., ways to distinguish appropriate from inappropriate modification of the Church as it engaged in mission.

The episcopate

The Colonial Bishoprics Fund

The Church of England's missionary work entailed expansion of the episcopate. The first colonial bishop was Charles Inglis of Nova Scotia, who was consecrated in 1785. Inglis was chosen because the episcopate represented an important form of colonial oversight after the American Revolution and embodied High Church commitment to the Church's authenticity. Prior to 1841 ten sees were created outside Britain and the United States, to align the episcopate with colonial administration: Nova Scotia, Quebec, Newfoundland, Toronto, Calcutta, Bombay, Madras, Barbados, Jamaica, and Australia. For example, in 1826, the Church of England in New South Wales became part of the Diocese of Calcutta with an archdeacon appointed for immediate supervision. When William Grant Broughton became archdeacon in 1829, he intensified a movement toward colonial self-government. After several years of receiving entreaties for a resident bishop, the Colonial Office acted favorably in 1836, creating the Diocese of Australia and naming Broughton as the first bishop.[99]

The consecrations of colonial bishops at first served as a means to tighten administrative control rather than to expand the Church's mission. However, a new sense of the Church's mission appeared in April, 1840, when Blomfield published a public appeal for a Fund for Endowing Additional Bishoprics in the Colonies. He believed that the time had come when "a great effort is required on the part of the Church of England, to import the full benefits of her apostolical government and discipline . . . The duty incumbent upon the government of a Christian country, of making provision for the spiritual wants of its colonies . . . was felt at far too late a period by the rulers of this Protestant country, and has at no time been completely and effectually carried out." It is not enough to send out missionaries; "we must plant the Church . . . in all its integrity."[100] Each colony must have its chief pastor, a need which Blomfield proposed to meet neither from the colonies nor from the home government. Instead financial support for the colonial episcopate must be found "in the voluntary liberality of Churchmen, creating a fund which might be administered . . . through the Archbishops and Bishops of the English Church." In time the colonists might augment support for the episcopate. Thus Blomfield made the extension of the Church's central office dependent upon the new political style of a voluntary association with public appeals for endowment, a recommendation which began a new expansion of the Church.[101]

On April 27, 1841, a public meeting was held to organize the Colonial Bishoprics Fund for the Church of England. Addressing an impressive collection of bishops, peers, and political leaders, Archbishop of Canterbury William Howley asserted in his address that "a Church without a Bishop can hardly deserve the name of Episcopal. Whatever may be the worth of the clergymen by whom it is served, whatever their numbers, it is a body without a head." Furthermore, the presence of a bishop has a great influence "on the moral and religious feeling of the population." He cited the West Indies, where the episcopate had excited a general religious improvement. Provision of its ministry is the Church's duty, Blomfield added, and the Church must "proceed on her own principles of Apostolical order and discipline;" that is, the Church "is to act . . . upon those principles which constitute her a Church." Above all the Church's mission relied upon its apostolic order. Calling for a bishop for New Zealand, Blomfield observed that to date the Church's mission had been conducted by societies loyal to the Church. But "there has not been that perfect unity of operation between them." Blomfield countered that "I have always been of opinion that the great missionary body ought to be the Church herself."[102]

An impressive list of public subscriptions resulted from the new Fund. In addition to various Church societies, leading clerics gave generously and the royal family added their contributions. Private gifts were an important feature of the Fund's growth, and Angela Burdett-Coutts, a noted Victorian philanthropist, established bishoprics at Cape Town and Adelaide in 1847, and in 1857 endowed British Columbia. During the same period she built five new churches in London, illustrating the Church's turn toward reliance upon the public.[103] Her involvement also indicates the beginning of a distinctive role for women in the Church's mission. Thus, through the Colonial Bishoprics Fund the overseas episcopate grew dramatically.

In May, 1841, only a month after the Fund's organization, Blomfield, on its behalf, offered the new see of New Zealand to George Augustus Selwyn, who became a leading colonial bishop. Thus the Fund not only multiplied the Church's leadership, but located able leaders who left an impressive example of leadership and implanted the Church indelibly in colonial areas.

The missionary bishops

Formation of the Colonial Bishoprics Fund demonstrated that a new level of interest in mission had come to focus upon the episcopate but required reliance upon private funding. The Church of England came to this realization gradually, because the state continued to be a prop for ecclesiastical identity and mission. In the United States, where social circumstances had uprooted historic forms of religious establishment, the Episcopal Church had already confronted the challenge of mission bereft of state assistance. Meeting in Philadelphia late in August, 1835, the Episcopal Church's House of Deputies in its General Convention received a committee report on the idea of missionary bishops, who would be consecrated for the purpose of beginning Church work in new areas. Since 1808 the manner of affording episcopal oversight to new states and territories in the expanding nation had been a subject of regular discussion in Church conventions. Bishops in constituted jurisdictions occasionally visited adjacent areas which lacked a bishop. However, this was an irregular function which taxed episcopal resources, human and financial. By 1835 the growth of the nation had become rapid, encompassing large territories where the Episcopal Church was not represented. Furthermore a "missionary spirit . . . has been awakened in the Church, and its missionary department puts it in the power of the Convention now to send the requisite number of bishops to those settlements." The committee added that the Church should begin to send bishops abroad, to nations where the Anglican Church had never done missionary work. A resolution proposing these measures concluded the committee report.[104]

With the proviso that missionary bishops would be elected by the General Convention until such time as a duly organized diocese could function, the measure passed in both the House of Deputies and the House of Bishops. The Bishops proceeded to select Jackson Kemper for consecration as a bishop to exercise jurisdiction in Missouri and Indiana. On September 25, 1835, Kemper was consecrated in Norwalk, Connecticut. The preacher on that occasion was George

Washington Doane, Bishop of New Jersey. Doane sensed the significance of the moment. The office of missionary bishop "is a new office in this Church . . . What we are now to do will go on record, as a precedent."[105] As "every minister of Jesus is a *Missionary*," Doane explained, "so are the Bishops, as His chief ministers, *eminently* Missionaries – *sent out* by Christ Himself to preach the Gospel – *sent* to preach it in a wider field." As the Church sends missionaries, so it must send bishops, "going *before* to organize the Church, not waiting till the Church has partially been organized." According to Doane the revival of this apostolic office was required by the times, as diverse regions of the world were within the compass of Western influence. Meanwhile the Protestant churches faltered for want of principles of union, and the Church of England "now needs her utmost succours for her own defence against the impious combination that attempts her overthrow." He failed to see that liberal assumptions undergirded the new ideal of mission.[106]

"If we believe," Doane insisted, "that our principles as Protestant Episcopalians are most in accordance with the divine will, and therefore most for the promotion of human happiness, it is our duty to demonstrate it in action." Next to the Gospel itself, God entrusted to the Episcopal Church "the maintenance, in integrity and purity, of the order of His holy apostolic Church." Doane believed that "as the truth of the blessed and glorious Gospel is attested . . . so the identity of the one, holy, apostolic Church is and will ever be established." In other words, the mission of the Church inherently led to the enhancement of its identity and the spread of its order. Or, as Doane summarized it, "how can we encourage . . . the extension or even the existence of the Church without a Bishop?"[107] The Episcopal Church regards the whole world as its field. "To every soul of man, in every part of it, the Gospel is to be preached. Everywhere, the Gospel is to be preached *by*, *through*, and *in* the Church." The Church's ministry depends upon bishops as successors of the apostles. With rhetorical flourish Doane challenged Kemper as missionary bishop to preach the Gospel, and he responded admirably. For eleven years he traveled tirelessly, establishing the Church in Illinois, Indiana, Kansas, Iowa, Missouri, Minnesota, and Wisconsin. He also made an extensive trip through Louisiana, Mississippi, Alabama, Georgia, and Florida in 1838. He personally created much of the Church's work in the midwestern United States.[108]

The episcopate became the focus of the Church's expansion. In

Tennessee and the deep South, James Otey became a commanding figure from 1834 to 1863. Similarly Leonidas K. Polk directed
the Church's growth in Arkansas and Louisiana. Polk had been a
member of the committee that recommended the consecration of a
missionary bishop. In foreign missions William J. Boone became
the founder of Anglican work in China in 1842, and in 1844 was
consecrated bishop. In 1859 Channing Moore Williams initiated
Anglican work in Japan, and in 1866 he was consecrated bishop.
Episcopalians in the United States had found a model for other
Anglicans in understanding the episcopate as the center of mission
and the Church as a missionary body. In England, Samuel
Wilberforce read Doane's sermon and became enamored of the
concepts of the missionary bishop and of the missionary Church.
Wilberforce's response began with energetic support for the Colonial Bishoprics Fund. He also attempted to secure parliamentary
approval for the concept of missionary bishops and for the
Church's responsibility in colonial areas. In 1853 bills to those
ends failed in the Commons, where Dissent's influence checked
any settlement of advantage for the established Church. The
adjustment of the Church's mission could not rely upon legislative
initiative.[109]

Late in 1856 David Livingstone returned to England from
missionary travels through central Africa. Livingstone, who had
worked on behalf of the London Missionary Society, seemed to speak
for all of Britain as he began a series of public lectures. Livingstone had
become interested in Africa after learning of Buxton's Niger
expedition, and his work reflected Buxton's ideal that Christianity,
commerce, and civilization must advance together. These priorities
linked several themes which intertwined in Livingstone's lectures. For
instance, Livingstone devoted much in his public presentations to
depicting African tribal culture as primitive. He also emphasized the
potential for missionary work and praised the peoples he met. He
found innate religious ideas, fertile land, and a propensity for trade.
"Those two pioneers of civilization – Christianity and commerce –
should ever be inseparable." "What we greatly need," Livingstone
concluded, "is more missionaries to sow the seed of spiritual truth . . . I
believe England is alive to her duty of civilizing and Christianizing
the heathen." England may not have been as alert before Livingstone
as she was after his lectures. His message electrified students,
especially at Oxford and Cambridge, where mission societies formed

in the wake of his presentations. A new era in public missionary zeal had begun.[110]

As Owen Chadwick observes, Livingstone "singly caused a revolution in the attitude of the British public towards the interior of Africa." One result of his appeal was the Central African Mission, formed by Oxford and Cambridge Universities, which were joined later by Durham and Dublin. The Mission recommended that its initial effect be directed by a bishop. Late in 1859, on November 2, the Mission resolved that Charles Frederick Mackenzie, Fellow of Gonville and Caius, Cambridge, and Archdeacon of Pietermaritzburg, Natal, be invited to head its first effort.[111] The Mission's organizers affirmed that their purpose was "the establishment of one or more stations in Southern Central Africa, which may serve as centers of Christianity and civilization, for the promotion of the spread of true religion, agriculture, and lawful commerce, and the ultimate extirpation of the slave trade." Mackenzie seemed an ideal man to embody this purpose. He had impressed Robert Gray, Bishop of Cape Town, who had contemplated using Mackenzie for one of the bishoprics he hoped would be added in South Africa. However, Gray wondered about the wisdom of the idea of missionary bishops, as did Henry Venn, Secretary of the Church Missionary Society. Each believed in the necessity of the episcopate for the Church; but, each felt that the Church must precede the episcopate. Gray, out of respect for one of his archdeacons, was willing to endorse the idea.[112]

On a wave of public sentiment the new mission proceeded. It followed a course suggested by Livingstone up the Zambezi river to Lake Nyasa, where a missionary settlement of 157 people was in place by late 1861. Sadly, illness took a severe toll, and in January, 1862, Mackenzie himself died. Mackenzie's death, however, did not impede the advance of mission, for successors established the Church in Central Africa. The office of missionary bishop proved to have limited application; but the symbolism of the episcopate in mission had immense significance. By a consensus which evolved until it pervaded the Church, Anglicans embraced domestic and foreign mission. Mission grew out of the Church's need to adapt to new constitutional circumstances. The Church seized the moment and experimented with new forms. Anglicans have characteristically sought to ensure the Church's integrity. In mission Anglicans discovered a new emphasis upon the episcopate. Mission became the primary way to ensure that the Church's identity was intact.

CHAPTER FOUR

The struggle to define the Church and its belief

ANGLO-CATHOLICISM

By 1833 two powerful movements were ascendant in the Church of England. Liberalism proposed the Church's adaptation to social and intellectual change, while Evangelicals believed that the age demanded new forms of mission, for which extensive changes in Church life could be justified. Together Liberals and Evangelicals suggested a new role for the Church of England as a virtual religious establishment, a basis for the spiritual development of a modern nation. Other Anglicans protested against the inroads of modernity into the Church's life. Invoking the High Toryism of the eighteenth century or the earlier Non-Jurors, such opposition hoped to preserve historic conceptions of the Church and its alliance with the state. However, political and social change rendered this Anglican self-understanding untenable. The Church came under a reformed Parliament which subjugated ecclesiastical traditions to considerations of political expediency. In 1833 ecclesiastical reform included changes in the Church of Ireland.

The Irish branch of the Church of England was legally established by virtue of English political control. Nevertheless less than 10 percent of the Irish population were actual members of the established Church. English political reformers seized upon this fact and proposed to reduce the Irish Church's bishoprics and to review its finances. Though these seemed natural adjuncts to political reform, the idea that government could alter the framework of the Church affronted some English clergy. Edward Burton, Regius Professor of Divinity at Oxford, insisted that the Irish Church was not bound by parliamentary decisions, a claim reminiscent of the Non-Jurors. The rallying cry for a new movement came on July 14, 1833, when John Keble preached the annual Assize Sermon at Oxford. "National

Apostasy," John Henry Newman later recalled, was "the start of the religious movement of 1833."[1]

This movement, which became known as Tractarianism, bears singular importance for the emergence of modern Anglican identity, as I suggested in chapter 1, and will discuss now. Although the Tractarians and their descendants, the Anglo-Catholic party, have sustained a legacy of protest against Anglican accommodation to the modern world, the movement's emphasis has been a positive one. This tradition forged a viable modern identity for the Church which has greatly influenced the course of Anglican life and mission. The modern sense of being Anglican, I argue, is a direct result of the Tractarian legacy. In this chapter I show how the movement evolved from protest to program and moved toward the center of Anglican life.

The Tractarians

Keble's sermon argued that a sense of national danger resulted from the willingness of government to take political measures which were indifferent to religious sentiment. In England, under "the guise of charity and toleration we are come almost to this pass . . . that the practice is becoming more common of trusting men unreservedly in the most delicate and important matters, without one serious inquiry, whether they do not hold principles which make it impossible for them to be loyal to their Creator, Redeemer, and Sanctifier." Keble criticized society's "fashionable liberality," which was much like the "temper which led the Jews voluntarily to set about degrading themselves to a level with the idolatrous Gentiles." That temper Keble labeled "Apostasy."[2] He cited a disregard for morality and revealed religion which permeated the nation and warned that God's punishment might befall Britain as it had Israel. Meanwhile, if "the apostolical Church should be forsaken, degraded . . . and despoiled by the state and people of England," Keble began, the Church should be guided by the example of Samuel – "but I will teach you the good and the right way."[3] This meant that the Church found its integrity not in close relation to the state, or to the culture or people of England, but in apostolic precedent.

The good and right way
Keble inspired like-minded friends to create a program of Church defense. Beginning at Oxford in the 1820s, Keble and his associates

considered the Church of England's outward forms were visible manifestations of what Christ bequeathed to the apostles. In 1833, a time of crisis, that apostolic character had to be recovered or risk being lost. The leading figures of the Oxford movement shared an association with Oriel College, where Edward Hawkins served as mentor to John Henry Newman, the dominant figure of the first phase of the movement. Newman became an Oriel Fellow in 1822, when Keble already held a fellowship. Richard Hurrell Froude was an undergraduate at the College and Edward Bouverie Pusey became a Fellow in 1823. Pusey later spent two years studying modern theology in Germany before returning to Oxford as Professor of Hebrew and Canon of Christ Church. Pusey found a theological sparring partner in Hugh James Rose of Trinity College, Cambridge, soon a friend to the movement's other figures.

Newman's progress in faith paralleled the advance of these men toward a shared vision of the Church. As an adolescent Newman had resolved to cultivate the religious life and, at Oriel, he learned the importance of religious tradition. Correct doctrine, verified by Scripture, is contained in the Church's formularies, such as the creeds, and the episcopate guarantees the validity of the Church's ministry. Newman read in Butler's *Analogy* of the reality of the visible Church, "the oracle of truth and a pattern of sanctity, of the duties of external religion, and of the historical character of Revelation."[4] He saw that material phenomena embody an underlying reality, an analogy which would later inspire an incarnational theology that would undergird modern Anglican thought. Newman began to consider the Church as a visible entity, grounded in Scripture and primitive tradition, existing independently of the state. He aligned himself with Keble, as well as Froude and Robert Isaac Wilberforce, who had reached similar conclusions. Their friendship, Newman recalled, had become by 1827 "the first elements of that movement afterwards called Tractarian."[5] They shared with Keble a sense that religious faith combined a habit of mind and an object of truth and believed that religious certitude was a modern religious problem. For Keble and Newman the search for certainty required that Christianity be visible, historically and morally credible, as well as the invisible form of a pervasive reality. The visible faith became authentic because it was grounded in ancient precedent, and linked sacramentally to the spiritual realm.

When Newman discovered Christian antiquity in 1828, he studied

Ignatius and Justin and the formulation of the Nicene creed, and was attracted to the school of theology at Alexandria. Combined with his reading of Church of England divines, this interest led him to the conclusion that "Antiquity was the true exponent of the doctrines of Christianity and the basis of the Church of England," and that "the works of Bishop Bull . . . were my chief introduction to this principle."[6] Newman opposed Liberalism and reforms in the Church. Blomfield, he felt, had "engaged in diluting the high orthodoxy of the Church by the introduction of members of the Evangelical body into places of influence and trust." Evangelicals "played into the hands of the Liberals" in compromising the Church's principles. With this state of affairs, Newman contrasted "that fresh vigorous Power of which I was reading in the first centuries."[7] He resolved to defend the Church Catholic and Apostolic.

At that moment, Keble preached his Assize sermon. In the wake of Keble's sermon, Hugh Rose encouraged a sense of group identity and Froude and Newman resolved to awaken the Church of England to its apostolicity through a series of tracts. When their colleagues joined them in writing tracts, the circle became known as the Tractarians. The first tract, "Thoughts on the Ministerial Commission," written by Newman, appeared on September 9, 1833. Others, often written by Newman, appeared regularly. The tracts were published to encourage "the practical revival of doctrines, which, although held by the great divines of our Church, at present have become obsolete with the majority of her members, and are withdrawn from public view even by the more learned and orthodox few who still adhere to them." The Church must substitute its apostolic integrity for secular forms of authority, the tracts repeatedly emphasized.[8] Thus, in Tract 1, Newman challenged the clergy to consider the source of their authority should "Government and Country so far forget their God as to cast off the Church, to deprive it of its temporal honours and substance." He pointed to the Church's apostolic deposit, a theme extended in Tract 2, "The Catholic Church." The idea of One, Catholic, and Apostolic Church is a reality, and "it is our duty to do our part in our generation towards its continuance."[9]

Tract 4 proceeded to ask "Why should we talk so much of an *Establishment*, and so little of an Apostolical Succession?" The Church's task is "to keep fast hold of the Church Apostolical, whereof we are actual members." Tract 7 also argued that the Church's form reflected neither a truth grounded in expediency, nor an accident of historical circumstance. Episcopacy embodies the superior form of Church governance because it perpetuates apostolic Christianity, which undergirds the visible Church and validates such ordinances as the sacraments. "A Visible Church must exist" as a specific society "so that to believe in Christ is not a mere opinion or a secret conviction, but a social or even a political principle."[10] The tracts' authors deepened their new convictions as they extended their research. Keble's biography of Thomas Wilson, the Hanoverian Bishop of Sodor and Man, revealed the Tractarians' pastoral ideal, for Wilson embodied a concern for the poor and for Church discipline which combatted spiritual laxity among clergy and laity. The reform the Church required, Keble implied, had not been achieved by the Reformation. Protestantism overlooked the apostolic nature of the Church, its discipline, clerical probity, and the sacraments. Wilson pursued his ideal not with the hope of gaining political advantage, but because of his devotion to the Church.[11]

In 1838 a posthumous collection of Hurrell Froude's writings was published as the *Remains*, an important defense of the Tractarian program. Froude cited the "recent changes which have taken place in our political constitution," which effaced in "our Civil Legislature, that character which . . . qualified it to be at the same time our Ecclesiastical Legislature, and thus to cancel the conditions on which it has been allowed to interfere in matters spiritual." The Church must secure itself through a revival of Church discipline, for a national Church had no purpose if "a national church means a Church without discipline."[12] Froude was particularly concerned with the power of the Church to set moral standards and its ability to impose spiritual conditions on its members. Froude believed discipline had decayed because the clergy prized their social status above their calling to shun evil. The Church was more interested in a pervasive religion than in a faithful, apostolic one. Though the ancient Church observed a discipline which imposed penance on notorious sinners, the modern Church ignored its charge to do likewise. The English Church needed to realize that being a Church member and being a citizen were not one and the same thing.[13]

Newman's course

Tractarianism's significance lay in its search for Anglican integrity and its protest that the Church's identity was not dependent upon its social locus. This idea gained transatlantic attention, for, in 1841, Bishop Charles McIlvaine of Ohio published a stinging criticism of "Oxford Divinity." McIlvaine identified the Church of England's decline as the betrayal of the Church's Reformation heritage. McIlvaine traced the sources of erosion to the Non-Jurors and Bishop Bull, the forefathers of the Oxford divines. He perceived the Church's abandonment of the doctrine of justification by faith, the classic Reformation doctrine. Oxford's disregard for this doctrine was "a systematic abandonment of the vital and distinguishing principle of the Protestant faith and a systematic adoption of that very root and heart of Romanism."[14] Opponents of the Oxford movement charged that it had abandoned historic Anglican belief for the doctrines of Rome, a challenge that required the Tractarians to clarify their sense of the Church of England as catholic, a child neither of Rome nor of the state, but a distinctive, apostolic Christianity. Newman undertook this task in *The Via Media of the Anglican Church, Volume I: Lectures on the Prophetical Office of the Church*. Published in 1837, the work revised Hooker's definition of Anglicanism over against Puritanism and Roman Catholicism, and encouraged a new way of defining Anglicanism.[15]

Like Coleridge, Newman discerned an "idea" of the Church, i.e., an essence which represented its authenticity as an apostolic Christianity. Anglicanism was an obscured apostolic form, an unrealized possibility for engrafting the Gospel into social life. Newman carefully developed this insight in a series of works, an achievement which made him the first truly modern Anglican theologian and established a starting point for subsequent Anglican apologetics. In his *Arians of the Fourth Century* Newman had argued that the patristic Church possessed an episcopal tradition which produced the creeds and existed alongside a prophetical tradition, embodied in the Councils and Scripture. He envisioned the Church as a community of divine origin for teaching the faith and living the Christian life. In the *Prophetical Office* Newman maintained that the Book of Common Prayer revealed a broad, religious system, centered on the Prayer Book, which allowed the Christian a life balanced between private judgment, the prophetical interpretation of Scripture in a Protestant sense, and the Church's authority in the Catholic sense. Anglicanism, as a religious system, offered the believer a *via media* between private judgment and an infallible, rather than "indefectible," as for most Anglicans, teaching authority.

Reiterating the claim of the seventeenth-century Caroline divines for the Church's apostolic authority, Newman depicted Anglicanism as a way of using authorities, a way of relating the individual to the community, and a way of prayer and discipline, in continuity with ancient precedent. The Church's prior attempts at self-understanding confirmed in Newman the idea of Anglicanism as *praxis* built upon the Prayer Book and the Church's forms. Thus he sparked a revolution in Anglican identity, for he felt that the Church of England required a "positive Church theory erected on a definite basis" in order "to withstand the Liberalism of the day." Newman conceived of an unrealized Anglicanism, grounded in antiquity, opposed to the Roman claim of catholicity. He envisioned "that the whole of Christendom should be united in one visible body," whose basis would be "not in its being a polity, but in its being a family, a race, coming down by apostolical descent from its first founders and bishops." Prior to F. D. Maurice, Newman held the view that the Church was a universal family. He set the stage for Anglican ecumenical endeavor and coined a theological category through references to "unity." This he traced to the *via media*, a model for unity at the core of Anglican identity, "a sort of remodelled and adapted Antiquity."[16]

Eventually this conviction began to crumble in Newman's mind. His studies of the ancient Monophysite heresy convinced him that the Church of the *via media* stood now where heretics once had been. In 1839 Newman discovered that the Roman party in the ancient Church had clarified historic doctrines and not fallen under civil power. Once assured that early Christianity had been monolithic and static, he realized its dynamism. Shifts in doctrine could be legitimate adaptations of the faith to changed circumstances. Newman's trust in the *via media* as a viable basis for ecclesiastical identity was eroded, and his attraction to Rome increased as he found Roman sympathies in such Anglican divines as Hooker, Taylor, and Bull, and said so in Tract 90, which appeared in February, 1841. Reviewing Anglicanism's Thirty-nine Articles, Newman argued that these were consistent with Roman Catholic doctrine, and perceived a doctrine of justification in Tridentine decrees. Having opened the door to Rome, he cautiously stepped through it, but his Church rebuked him in a heated controversy, argued largely by innuendo. Newman was troubled by criticism of Tract 90 and by the Jerusalem bishopric controversy in 1841, when the English Church and the Prussian Church cooperated in the creation of an episcopal see at Jerusalem.

Tractarians viewed this as an act of state and a dilution of Anglican identity through accepting Lutheran orders.

He verified the suspicion that Anglicanism had abandoned apostolicity in his *Essay on the Development of Christian Doctrine*. Newman's theory of development led him to the conclusion in 1845 that the true modern representative of apostolic Christianity was Rome. It remained possible to demonstrate continuity between some branch of modern Christianity and its apostolic forerunner; but, it proved inaccurate to say that this branch always adapts itself variously, as Protestantism claimed, or that a line of pure, unchanged Christianity could be traced from apostolic experience, as Anglican divines wanted to do. Christianity embodies an unrealized idea possessing a plethora of conceivable aspects, no one of which could exhaust the possibilities of its essence. Furthermore an idea acquires life when its expression arrests minds, and becomes a public principle. In the public realm it "becomes an active principle . . . leading . . . to an ever-new contemplation of itself, to an application of it in various directions." Eventually "some definite teaching emerges"; over time, "one view will be modified or expanded," until a new conception of the original idea appears.[17]

This process Newman called "development," meaning "the germination and maturation of some truth or apparent truth on a large mental field." A legitimate development retains forms of continuity while "cutting across, and thereby destroying or modifying and incorporating within itself existing modes of thinking and operating." Development represents the living out of an idea within human communities, though periodically the idea must reassert itself, otherwise development might take false forms. The heart of his study of development comprised seven criteria for genuine doctrinal development. For instance, the Church preserves certain aspects of its character while being able to assimilate a number of the features of its environment. By its sacramental quality the Church recognizes truth in pagan guise, and adapts truth to the form of the Church. Thus "the rulers of the Church from early times were prepared, should the occasion arise, to adopt, or imitate, or sanction the existing rites and customs of the populace, as well as the philosophy of the educated classes."[18] Anglicanism failed the test of authentic development because inherently it relied too much upon its cultural environment in search of a center of ecclesiastical identity; and so, in 1845, he turned to Rome. From Newman, Anglican theologians have learned to pay attention to the Church's place in a culture and to see Anglicanism as an unfulfilled, modern, apostolic Christianity.

Newman left Canterbury for Rome because he concluded that secular interference had tarnished the Church of England's apostolic character. Other Tractarians such as Henry Manning, and Robert Isaac Wilberforce and Henry Wilberforce, were persuaded by the Gorham case that Rome was where Anglicanism claimed to be. When G. C. Gorham angered his bishop, Henry Phillpotts, by attacks on Tractarianism, which he admired, Phillpotts examined Gorham's doctrinal beliefs and concluded, in March, 1848, that Gorham did not accept the doctrine of regeneration in the sacrament of Baptism. Gorham doubted that the sacrament unfailingly conveyed spiritual regeneration to an infant's soul, for, as an Evangelical, he argued that a conscious experience must confirm the sacrament's validity. Phillpotts rebutted such assertions and refused to institute Gorham to a new living.

Gorham instituted legal proceedings to compel the bishop to grant him the new cure. Whether secular authority had the right to decide doctrinal matters and to challenge a bishop's conduct became the issues. Such questions heightened Tractarian fear that Anglican apostolicity had been corrupted by secular authority. Evangelical Anglicans like Gorham disregarded the sacraments and valued the Church as a national establishment.[19] However, the High Church view seemed upheld when in August, 1849 the Court of Arches declared that Gorham held a doctrine which the Church of England opposed. Although concerned that the courts were adjudicating doctrinal disputes, Tractarians felt reassured. But the case continued on appeal to the Judicial Committee of the Privy Council, which, on March 9, 1850, declared that Gorham had not contradicted the Church's doctrine.[20]

Response to this result was tumultuous. After Phillpotts excommunicated anyone who dared to institute Gorham, he broke down the locked doors of his new parish and assumed its charge. Gladstone feared that the Church of England was lost, and Keble and Pusey denounced the court. Some leading Tractarians left for Rome, concluding that the Church of England had abandoned its divine basis. In Australia a fierce controversy erupted over the Church's relation to the state as Tractarian sympathies augmented powerful anti-Erastian feeling. In the United States, the question of the validity of the Church's sacraments prompted a few secessions to Rome, notably Bishop Levi Silliman Ives of North Carolina. Most Tractarians remained within the Church, however, giving rise to the Anglo-Catholic party, which stressed the role of ritual in fostering a sense of the Church as a distinctive, religious community.[21] The Tractarian legacy became an important component of the modern Anglican style, which I call Liberal Catholicism.

Toward an Anglican Catholicism

Maurice

The articulation of a genuinely Catholic Anglicanism was begun by F. D. Maurice, who, though not a Tractarian, stressed Anglicanism's apostolic roots. Maurice understood that Newman sought a center of ecclesiastical identity in continuity with ancient Christianity, and he agreed that Christianity possessed a fundamental idea against which the validity of development could be tested. "Most heartily then do I agree with Mr. Newman, that we need an authority the same in kind with that which the first ages had."[22] Although Newman had set the terms for Anglican self-definition, for Maurice, the "testimony of the Bible" revealed the necessary center as an invisible, divine, governing power, pervading the physical and human worlds. The "conscience of man witnesses to this living Being," to "something within him which is above nature, which has to do with a direct personal Being." There could be no visible, ecclesial system set up "in the place of conscience," for this invisible power is the legitimate center toward which Scripture and the Church direct human perceptions. "This, I think, is the principle of the Bible . . . that the unseen God is actually ruling over men . . . that just so far as they know this, and live and act in the faith of it, they are doing their right work in the world."[23]

Maurice contended that the "right work" entailed "helping to expound the laws and principles of the Divine Government," and "helping to bring man into that service which is freedom." Not doing this meant idolatry, though even idolatry could contribute to the triumph of divine governance. Idolatrous principles would dissolve, and "that dissolution is itself but the instrument of bringing out with greater clearness the real eternal principles of this order." Such a "statement may seem to Mr. Newman, and to a great many others, a vague repetition of what they have heard before."[24] But, Maurice reiterated, the Bible and the Church establish the presence of a living

God among humanity. He believed that creation was reuniting with its creator in an irreversible process which the Church makes visible through education. He found in Hebrews the principle of a living God and evidence of a gradual transition from an old dispensation to a new one, "each step in the manifestation of its being a step in [human] spiritual education." The shift from the old revelation to the new occurred with the Incarnation, which became Maurice's "essential idea of Christianity." That is, the creation contains a "Divine, Personal Centre" which is revealing its governance. Human beings mistake an outward center for the "living, eternal, invisible Centre" to which Scripture points. But the "Divine, Personal Centre" occupies the heart of the Church, what Maurice also calls "a distinct consciousness of this invisible fellowship."[25]

This "Centre" reveals the unity of the creation with its creator, and becomes the basis of the Church. For Maurice, development entailed neither the realization of an ecclesiastical ideal nor the embodiment of an essential Christianity in an institution, but was a social process leading to recovery of the inherent unity of the creation. "A development of this kind has, I believe, been going on in the Church from the earliest age in reference to the study of Scripture, under the authority not of any mortal, but of Him who has promised that He will watch over it, and that all things shall work together for its good."[26] Suggested by Newman, unity indicated the recovery of a primordial wholeness by societies, individuals, and the Church, an ideal which Maurice established as a mark of Anglican identity.

For Maurice, God's unfolding governance required a social paradigm of unity, a society, in which a "practical process of assimilation" of persons to the ideal proceeded. Through the Church, that which is eternal is being separated "from the accidents of human opinion which had clung to it."[27] The Church risks identifying its doctrines and offices as literal embodiments of the divine because they are grounded in Scripture, though here Maurice presumed a coherence in Scripture which later was severely questioned. His theology attracted widespread approval because his explanation of Christianity's essence and of the Church's development possessed a compelling dynamism and an appealing reliance upon Scripture. But his theory begged Newman's question; Maurice argued for an Anglicanism which was vaguely apostolic, manifesting an unclear essence of Christian experience in uncertain ways. Thus, Maurice helped to suggest a modern Anglican identity, but could not clarify the nature of its essence.

Pusey

Edward Bouverie Pusey articulated an Anglican Catholicism which offered a corrective to Maurice because he suggested that as the divine manifested itself, so the Church could realize itself by retrieving its apostolic character. Anglicanism's advance led to a mystical unity of God and the world through the indwelling of Christ in the Church. Two decades after Maurice replied to Newman's theory of development, Pusey's *Eirenicon* took the form of an extended letter answering charges leveled against Anglicanism by Manning, then a cardinal. Pusey insisted that the Church of England served as "a real and chief bulwark" against infidelity, because "the Church, by putting into the mouths of all her members the ancient Creeds and Prayers which embody the faith, is, yet more, a continual unchanging teacher of the truth which Christ revealed and delivered to her at the first."[28] In other words, Pusey posed a different standard for the authenticity of the Church than either Newman or Maurice, who debated a scheme of development by which the authentic Church maintained continuity with apostolic precedent. Newman saw this progression as visible; Maurice as essentially spiritual but becoming manifest in society.

Like Newman and Maurice, Pusey defined apostolic Christianity as the source of the Church's episcopal order and sacraments. He sensed a realization of the Church's unity with itself and with God which suggested Maurice's scheme of development. However, he felt that the Church's unity required faithfulness to the apostolic model, to the form of the Church which expressed its inner essence, for form offered "a necessary preservation of the Church as a whole, from error." Scripture and tradition do not conflict, for the Church must "preserve those Sacred Writings committed to her trust."[29] The Church can neither violate Scripture, nor abandon tradition, nor do more than elaborate that which was already established. For Pusey, the Church of England affirmed the indissoluble unity of Christ's Body, the Church. It claims a spiritual oneness wrought by God the Holy Spirit, and it aspires to "an organic union with one another through union with Him." This union corresponds with the union of the persons of the Trinity, "an actual mystical oneness" through Christ. "The mystery of Christ, then, was made a sort of beginning and way whereby we too might partake of the Holy Spirit, and of oneness with God."[30] God endows all people with a sense of this unity and inspires a search for organic union, of which the Church becomes the predecessor, and the means. The sacraments represent the hope of unity becoming visible and actual.

Pusey made explicit several features of what was becoming the Anglo-Catholic ideal of the Church. His concept of development offered a potent image for the unity of Christendom, especially of Anglicans with Roman Catholics and the Orthodox churches. This hope became an important source of authority in his idea of the Church. The Church exists not to realize itself through the progressive education of humanity, but to realize an ecclesial unity which is proleptic of the coming of God's Kingdom. For Pusey this meant that the Church must be faithful to its apostolic inheritance, not, as for Maurice, that it must cooperate with programs of social development. Pusey envisioned a Church distinguished by its sacraments, which transmit God's grace and draw the believer into the Body of Christ. Against the Protestant view of Baptism, for instance, which emphasized the invisible experience of God's grace, Pusey believed that "our justification is imputed to us, not through the feelings, but *through* baptism." Because the early Church did not finish defining the gifts imparted by Baptism, Pusey argued, the modern Church must extend apostolic initiative. "The view, then, held here of baptism, following the ancient church and our own, is, that we be engrafted into Christ, and thereby receive a principle of life, afterwards to be developed and enlarged by the fuller influxes of his grace."[31] Baptism engrafted the believer to Christ and his Church.

Pusey stressed the sacrament's reliance upon a typological view of Scripture. For him, the Bible presents the reality that "everything in this world can be a type or symbol of heavenly realities." "The natural world is an image of the spiritual," the two being linked by analogy. As nature imitates and reveals truth, so biblical revelation occurs through types and symbols, and Pusey insisted on the objective character of the symbol and its grounding in reality. The sacraments become archetypes of God's communication, which occurs now as it has in previous ages.[32] Preservation of sacramental form ensures perpetuation of its invisible truth. For Pusey *lex orandi* was *lex credendi*, the content of which was a mystical, contemplative spirituality. Pusey stressed the mystery of the divine presence in human life. The Incarnation represented God's grace, which becomes present in the Eucharist, and the reception of grace required participation in the divine nature through the sacraments. Thus, on the Eucharist, Pusey believed "there is a true, real, actual, though Spiritual . . . Communication of the Body and Blood of Christ to the believer through the Holy Elements" and "a true, real, spiritual Presence of Christ at the Holy Supper." This was not a carnal presence as Rome insisted, but a spiritual reality superseding yet directing the material realm.[33] Though his references to the Body and Blood of Christ identified Pusey with Rome in popular estimation, he was truly Anglican. Pusey wrote that the Eucharist, "as conveyed by type or prophecy, by the very elements chosen, or by the words of our Lord, is the support and enlargement of life and that in Him." More than the "refreshing of our souls by the invigorating of our moral nature, giving us more fixedness of purpose," the Eucharist is union with Christ.

The gathering of all creation into the creator, prefigured in the Incarnation, continues through the Eucharist. The mystery of divine love defeats sin and promotes mutual indwelling – Christ in humanity and humanity in Christ.[34] Furthermore, I emphasize that his insistence that the Church must observe a life different from that of its social environment represented a major development in Anglicanism. The Church's life entailed a recovery of its apostolic deposit which had become obscured. The restoration of the obscured Church, including the recovery of Anglicanism's apostolicity and the achievement of ecumenical unity, anchored Pusey's theology and became hallmarks of modern Anglicanism. Pusey believed the Church's apostolic character had slept since the Glorious Revolution of 1688, when the deposition of James II secured the triumph of democratic principles. The ascendancy of popular sovereignty revealed that the populace was no longer subject to "power without us, further that we have ourselves delegated the authority, and may resume it, when we will; in short, we are to govern ourselves, not be under the government of another."[35]

Pusey posed the Church as an alternative to the spirit of modernity and democracy, a stance which countered the Liberal approach to the Church, and established the Anglo-Catholic party's opposition to modern culture. Ironically enough, Anglo-Catholics would later be among the foremost supporters of Church synods, which represented the Church's self-rule, an attempted reversion to the model of apostolic Church Councils. Pusey contrasted the authority of apostolic Christianity with what he believed to be the modern understanding of authority. In a sermon on the Gorham case, he explained that Anglicanism maintained the authority of early Christianity which secured the Church's identity, for Anglicanism must resist being an individualistic Church grounded in popular fashion. The English Church possesses a "deposit," rooted in Scripture, which serves as the Church's indefectible guide. This "deposit" encompasses "the body of the Christian Faith, committed to the Church." This "sacred deposit" must be "faithfully guarded, not to be tampered with, not to be lessened, not to be adulterated . . . not to be mingled with anything foreign from itself."[36]

The body of the faith serves as an external rule, to ensure the continuity of the present Church with the ancient one. The Church's validity lies in preserving its deposit, rather than adjusting itself to each age. The faith inherited by the Church is "one, complete, uniform whole, capable neither of being increased nor lessened."[37] The Church of England must preserve its validity as Catholic, an insistence which gave the nascent Anglo-Catholic party a sense of mission. Pusey sought a living relationship to an ideal view of early Christianity, an emphasis upon antiquity which bespoke a modern Anglican paradigm for the Church. For Pusey, apostolic Christianity secured the Church against the intrusions of secular or political currents, which threatened its faith. Later figures such as R. W. Church, Dean of St. Paul's, pushed this theology of the Church toward the Anglican mainstream. Anglo-Catholicism existed as a diverse movement of pastors such as Church, spiritual writers, and theologians. The movement valued preservation of apostolic form in the Church's offices and liturgies. The reanimation of ancient liturgies, hymns, and vestments, in the context of a sacramental theology and of episcopal order, became tangible evidence of faithfulness to apostolicity for Pusey. The party which followed his direction offered a principle of apostolicity which became the center upon which Anglicanism focused as it became global and catholic.

Neale and the Cambridge Camden Society
An emphasis upon proper form as the hallmark of Anglican Catholicism became the contribution of John Mason Neale, who awakened interest in Eastern Christianity, church architecture, and religious orders, and promoted use of ancient vestments and forgotten hymns. Through Neale, Anglicans found their identity in the modern application of ancient usages throughout the Church. Neale believed that the Church's faith was one with the heirs of Christ, an expression

of the divine, organic unity itself. He shared Pusey's belief in Anglicanism's obscured apostolicity and, at the time of the Gorham crisis, expressed hope that the "English Church . . . is not compromised by the decision of the Judicial Committee." Instead the present time offers the Church an opportunity to uncover its traditions and to distinguish itself from the state.[38] Neale believed his life-time was a period when "men's minds were more disposed now than they once were to acknowledge religion a subject deserving of their best attention." For instance, he envisioned a recovery of auricular confession and he taught the literal efficacy of a priest's absolution.[39]

Such convictions had been forgotten; but the sacramental nature of the Prayer Book of 1662 was being uncovered, although "the Archbishop of Canterbury and his Evangelical allies" opposed such ideas. "His Grace appeals to Public Opinion – that is, he appeals to the World against the Church."[40] Neale emphasized the Church's liturgical possibilities as guards against the intrusion of social and cultural influences. The Church could also be an alternative to the world through religious orders, and Neale helped to found the Society of St. Margaret, one of the first of the new forms of religious life which appeared among Anglicans in the nineteenth century.[41] Neale hoped a fresh sense of the religious life would pervade the Church, and to that end he formed the Cambridge Camden Society, an energetic effort to remake forms of church architecture and decor. "If it be true," an early Society treatise insisted, "that the appearance of a Church tends to inspire those who attend it, with solemn and devotional, or with irreverent and indifferent feelings, and if there has been a palpable neglect no less in the internal than external appearance of not a few of our Churches, surely upon this ground alone the Society may proclaim themselves the advocates of a restoration to that primitive elegance combining simplicity."[42]

The reference to feelings suggests that a modern, romantic sensibility played an important role in the Society's suggestions for restoration of the Church's apostolic nature. It attacked such practices as pew rental as a means of subsidizing the Church and presented ideas for church refurbishment through easily understood pamphlets on medieval English liturgies and church construction. Although the Society reduced its scope in 1842, fearing that it was becoming another ecclesiastical party, it became a catalyst for liturgical change.[43] The Catholic party within the Anglican Church proposed a new Anglican sensibility, fusing apostolic Church forms with Church identity. That concept of apostolicity received critical scrutiny as new forms of scholarship challenged the foundations of the Church's belief.

THE CONTOURS OF A NEW WORLD

The iconoclasts

In the mid nineteenth century F. D. Maurice and E. B. Pusey suggested ways by which the Church could reinvigorate traditional understandings of Christian belief. Though they agreed that Scripture was literally true and that early Christianity possessed a divinely inspired character, their work set the stage for bitter controversy among Anglicans over the basis of Christian belief and the nature of the Church's response to a new intellectual environment. Ironically the theological radicalism of the nineteenth century helped to shape the orthodoxy of the twentieth. Such radicalism began in England with the appearance of Deism, a rigorous rationalism which blossomed in the eighteenth century, scrutinized biblical narrative, and encouraged doubts about the veracity of miracle stories. In the nineteenth century a systematic scepticism emerged with D. F. Strauss' *Life of Jesus*, which appeared in Germany in 1835, then was translated into English by the novelist George Eliot. Strauss used the concept of myth to explain that Scripture included layers of human experience that were not apparent, and to challenge the truth of miracles. Eliot also translated Ludwig Feuerbach's *The Essence of Christianity* in 1853, a work which challenged the historical character of Christianity and argued that religion was merely a psychological phenomenon. As a result of this work, Eliot joined a circle of skeptics seeking a faith without myth.[44]

The appearance of skepticism represented the triumph of a form of religious authority rooted in personal experience without implicit trust of traditional institutions. Victorian England nurtured a variety of skeptics, including Charles Hennell, Eliot's consort George Henry Lewes, Arthur Hugh Clough, and John Stuart Mill. Early in the century, skepticism remained the preserve of limited groups; but, skeptics such as Thomas Huxley and Charles Bradlaugh became public figures when large segments of society shared their doubts about the scientific truth of the Bible and felt drawn toward a humanized Christianity. A disparate group, skeptics shared the conviction that revealed religion was inimical to the modern spirit.

During the eighteenth century, religion and science were generally considered to be mutually supportive. Nature seemed to reveal the imprint of divine authorship, while the prevailing theological temper confirmed that religious belief resonated with a reasonable, ordered universe. In the nineteenth century the accommodation between religion and science unraveled. The first hints of antagonism came in 1832, when Charles Lyell's *Principles of Geology* argued convincingly that geological events resulted from natural forces. He implied that similar conclusions could be made about biology, though he was reluctant to conclude that human beings descended from primitive life-forms. *Vestiges of the Natural History of Creation*, written anonymously in 1844 by Robert Chambers, a Scottish journalist, undercut any alliance between science and religion. Chambers concluded that the creation of life by divine intervention was an impossibility and insisted that God established and sustained natural laws, rather than contravened them. Preparing the way for Darwin, he perceived that nature moved forward in an evolutionary process.[45]

The works of Lyell and Chambers provided evidence of an antagonism between science and religion. Liberal Anglicans felt the effects of this disruption acutely because liberals, such as Baden Powell, an Anglican cleric and Oxford professor, believed a harmony existed between science and faith, and perceived the Church's task as accommodation to the mind of the age. Schooled in Noetic ideas, Powell in the 1820s was convinced that scientific research "when conducted in accordance with a correct methodology, was bound to provide much support to the cause of revealed religion. The evidence it afforded of design and purpose in creation reinforced the credibility of the existence of a creator."[46] However, Powell, witnessing social change, "was convinced that scientific procedure . . . was becoming a central feature of contemporary culture." Political dissent was symptomatic of social groups which were oriented to a new, scientific world. "The modern mind was a scientific mind. Modern man considered that the standards and procedures so successfully employed by the scientific investigator were the most powerful intellectual tools humanity had forged."[47] Baden Powell did not doubt the value of modern science, nor did he doubt that science and religion would uncover their basic unity. Scientific discovery would strip away the antiquated, mythic husk of Christian religion to reveal its timeless kernel, an essence of biblical religion which became the object of the liberal search.

The hunt for the Christian essence had powerful defenders such as Renn Dickson Hampden, whose Bampton lectures in 1832 argued that the truth of Scripture must be distinguished from the form of dogma. Hampden became a despised symbol of liberalism to Tractarians and Evangelicals, who believed that his criteria for scriptural truth discarded essential beliefs. Though in 1846 Hampden was a controversial appointment as Bishop of Hereford, ironically he later opposed the conclusions of biblical critics as injurious to the faith. Hampden surpassed Maurice in disregarding the importance of the visible Church, for he believed that an invisible Christian spirit must be seen beneath the Church's forms. Yet Maurice attracted vigorous opposition, notably from H. L. Mansel, Dean of St. Paul's, whose Bampton lectures in 1858 argued brilliantly that human knowledge and experience of God is suggestive of normative forms of the religious life. Since Christianity was not a natural religion, but a revealed one, religion's truth lay in its doctrines.[48] Conservatives endowed external form with a necessity which was denied by liberals.

By 1860 a series of shocks redirected the Church of England's theological discussion. Charles Darwin's *The Origin of Species*, which appeared in 1859, built upon the work of Lyell and Chambers in arguing that nature operated according to observable forces in a discernible pattern. Darwin added that no external force operated upon nature, whose development was a struggle for survival in which chance provided some species with characteristics which permitted endurance. Since human life was the produce of blind chance in a struggle for survival, there was no divine design and no progression to a heavenly kingdom. Darwin acquired an evangelist in Thomas Huxley who, in 1860, debated with Bishop Samuel Wilberforce at Oxford. Wilberforce attempted to ridicule Huxley, but his effort was discredited, for Huxley relied upon patient exposition.[49] Public approbation for Huxley swept Britain, and Darwinians such as Herbert Spencer applied the tenets of evolution to human social experience. Spencer concluded that Darwin's image of the struggle for survival could explain disparities between cultures and nations. As the British Empire approached its zenith, this was a persuasive way to account for power without having to apologize for it.

Darwin and his intellectual offspring could be disregarded by Church leaders as cynical opponents of the faith. Less summarily dismissed, however, a cluster of clergy and theologians proposed a reinterpretation of the Christian faith in terms of critical approaches to the Bible and Christian history. Using the ideas of German scholarship and responding to the age of Darwin, a group of Anglicans in 1860 published a set of articles seeking revised views of the Church and its faith. *Essays and Reviews* was organized by Henry Bristow Wilson, a vicar and Bampton lecturer, whose own contribution, "*Séances historiques de Genève*: The National Church," has received little attention from scholars. Wilson argued a national Church should be doctrinally broad or "multitudinist," in order to be truly apostolic. He believed that both Christian doctrine and Scripture contained layers of truth. In the Bible lay an obscured, spiritual meaning retrievable only by careful dissection, a distinction between form and content which became basic for Wilson and the other essayists.[50]

Wilson's tone throughout proved biting. "It is generally the custom of those who wish to ignore the necessity for grappling with modern questions concerning Biblical interpretation, the construction of the Christian creed, the position and prospects of the Christian Church, to represent the disposition to entertain them as a disease contracted by means of German innoculation." He ridiculed opponents of the modern spirit, and challenged the Anglican image of apostolic Christianity. "Neither in doctrine nor in morals did the primitive Christian communities at all approach to the ideal which has been formed of them." He depicted Christianity as a religion of the heart which has retained moral and doctrinal flaws.[51] Thus Wilson challenged the assumption that early Christianity existed in monolithic form, an issue which would command attention a generation later.

Wilson's colleagues in *Essays and Reviews* focused their attention upon problems in biblical interpretation as well as recent English theology. Frederick Temple, a future Archbishop of Canterbury, wrote "The Education of the World," in which he presented world history as a progression of stages from childhood to adulthood. As the world absorbed new scientific knowledge, and reached adulthood, so the Bible must be read from a fresh perspective. Rowland Williams' "Bunsen's Biblical Researches" reviewed German scholarship and cast biblical revelation as progressive, encoding human experience in myth. For Williams the Church provided the context in which the Bible came alive. Baden Powell attacked the truth of miracles in "On the Study of the Evidences of Christianity," and C. W. Goodwin asserted that the Bible's creation stories were not scientific truth in "On the Mosaic Cosmogony." Mark Pattison's "Tendencies of Religious Thought in England 1688–1750" revised impressions that the age of reason was spiritually indolent. The essay was an effective, critical history, for Pattison insisted that the age of reason must be seen in its historical context, not judged in terms of religious or political parties. Theological truth demanded impartial method lest the Church succumb to dogma.[52]

The concluding essay offered the best summary of the volume's intention and the most inflamatory contribution. Benjamin Jowett was Regius Professor of Greek at Oxford when he wrote "On the Interpretation of Scripture." Skilled in biblical languages and in German philosophical and religious thought, Jowett in previous work had challenged inherited ideas about original sin and atonement, insisting that religions are historical phenomena, encased in cultural forms. Religious life expresses the life of a people, a phenomenon which, as Maurice suggested, pointed beyond itself to a supernatural reality.[53] In *Essays and Reviews* Jowett applied this conviction to study of the Bible. Its interpretation requires "a moral and religious interest which is not needed in the study of a Greek poet or philosopher." However, in the "externals of interpretation . . . that is to say, the meaning of words, the connexion of sentences, the settlement of the text, the evidence of facts, the same rules apply to the Old and New Testaments as to other books."[54] Jowett elevated the distinction between the husk and the kernel to a new plane by arguing that study of the Bible as literature would clarify its truth. A critical history of the interpretation of Scripture "would take us back to the beginning; it would present in one view the causes which have darkened the meaning of words in the course of ages; it would clear away the remains of dogmas, systems, controversies, which are encrusted upon them." Assessment of the nature of the Bible's inspiration would reveal the text's original meaning, which, in turn, would uncover a progressive revelation which finds its fulfillment within human history.[55]

It was to be expected that *Essays and Reviews* would provoke public outcry. Seven clergy had apparently undercut the Church's faith. Much criticism of the volume seized upon the thought that the search for a biblical essence was itself the product of an age and would damage the Church's identity. In a volume of responses, Samuel Wilberforce insisted that the spirit of *Essays and Reviews* was "a spirit of lawless rejection of all authority, from a daring claim for the unassisted human intellect to be able to discover, measure, and explain all things." Wilberforce sensed a modern, self-serving inclination to jettison prior example and a search for truth only within the self, according to personal inclination. This spirit disrupts the Church's "firm hold of primitive truth." Its apostolic ministry, creeds, and sacraments diverge from "the new rationalistic unbelief."[56] Advancing what became an habitual, conservative argument, Wilberforce charged that the modern spirit acknowledged only its own authority.

Wilberforce's seven co-authors replied systematically to their counterparts. Against Frederick Temple, E. M. Goulburn countered that the world's education could not be progressive, moral improvement, because the Fall could be overcome only by God's grace. Corrupted humanity could not trust its own instinct in interpreting God's Word. Thus liberal optimism about human nature and a conservative pessimism stood in clear relief. Hugh Rose, in response to Rowland Williams, maintained that the Hebrew Scriptures were predictions of Christ's coming. C. A. Heurtley of Christ Church, Oxford, opposed Baden Powell in arguing that Christianity's truth must be attested by miracles recorded in Scripture. It "seems inconceivable, how, without miracles . . . it could sufficiently have commended itself to men's belief." Upon the appeal to miracles, "both our Lord's and those of the Apostles, the Church of Christ was built up in the beginning."[57] These essayists envisaged dire consequences for the Church's biblical and apostolic foundations from the influence of modern criticism.

The response to *Essays and Reviews* proved as heated as it was inconclusive. Convocation of the Church of England condemned the book. Two of its authors, Wilson and Williams, were indicted for heresy by the Court of Arches, but exonerated by the Judicial Committee of the Privy Council. Although Anglican controversies frequently appeared inconclusive, *Essays and Reviews* signaled that a variety of changes in the Church and its belief were underway. Controversy over critical biblical study encouraged the reliance upon such synodical forms of Church governance as Convocation and the Lambeth Conferences. In order to resolve internal tensions, the Church required a deliberative forum, modeled upon the ancient Councils. In modern circumstances even Church defense demanded innovative forms.

Another impetus to move toward synodical government resulted

from the case of Bishop John William Colenso, whose name came to
be associated with scandal. Since 1853 Colenso had been Bishop of
Natal, South Africa, under the jurisdiction of Robert Gray, first
Bishop of Cape Town. When he was a student at Cambridge,
Colenso's views were shaped by reading Coleridge and Arnold, and
meeting Maurice, whose sense of God's presence throughout culture
formed the basis of Colenso's theology of mission. As the new bishop
traversed Natal, acquainting himself with Zulu life in 1854, he
concluded that the world is not divided between Christian and
heathen, enlightened and barbarian. Christians should meet non-
Christians "half way, as it were, upon the ground of our common
humanity, and with the recollection that that humanity is now
blessed and redeemed in Christ."[58] Colenso advocated cultural
adaptation and a humanitarian posture on the part of the mission
Church.

Missionary experience moved Colenso to examine Scripture from
a critical perspective. In 1861 he published a commentary on
Romans, and in 1862 the first part of a massive study on the
Pentateuch appeared. The content of these works, on the heels of
Darwin and *Essays and Reviews*, with a missionary bishop as author,
triggered a major crisis in Anglican life as modern forms of biblical
interpretation penetrated the Church's ministry and teaching
authority. Colenso even questioned the idea that the sinner and the
non-Christian, especially those removed from Christian culture,
would be condemned to eternal damnation. He rejected the
traditional view of Christ's atonement, that Christ's death was a
punishment or penalty for human sins. Colenso also insisted that
persons who had never heard of Jesus Christ could be righteous. He
believed that Baptism and the Eucharist did not guarantee that one
was acceptable to God but pointed to God's presence among all
peoples.[59]

Like other advocates of revisionist views of the Bible, Colenso was
propelled by a modern, historical sense. He read Scripture as a human
document, robed in the garb of a particular culture, pointing beyond
itself to the God of all creation. In a non-Western culture, Colenso's
theological revisionism translated into a tolerant humanism. For
instance, while he disliked polygamy, which he commonly encountered, he refused to condemn polygamous families, a position which
the Lambeth Conference subsequently adopted. "The price of
conversion to Christianity should never be the dissolution of the

family and perhaps the destitution of wives and children."[60] Outspoken, Colenso saw his role as that of exponent of a compassionate honesty, caring for people and shaking his Church free of dogmatism. That style left an important example for the Church's development in southern Africa, but engendered controversy in Britain. Colenso intended his study of the Pentateuch to be a public statement on biblical interpretation. In 1870, eight years after the first part of the work appeared, he produced a one-volume set of conclusions. That book acknowledged that he had become notorious, condemned by Church synods including the first Lambeth Conference, but it explained his positions without apology. Although Colenso denied that Moses wrote the Pentateuch and challenged the literal truth of the creation and the flood, his opinions were not extreme. His message galled because a bishop dared to question historic belief.

Colenso insisted that a "wide-spread distrust does exist among the intelligent Laity in England, as to the soundness of the traditional view of Scripture Inspiration," and, as a bishop, he proposed to repair the Church's one foundation.[61] He persisted, eventually with a sense of isolation and martyrdom, because he believed that "multitudes have already broken loose from the restraints of that traditional religious teaching, which they know to be contradicted by some of the most familiar results of modern Science, now made the common heritage of every educated English child."[62] Thus Colenso believed that the mission field was not only Africa, but the modern world. This doggedness has characterized a tiny succession of iconoclastic Anglicans, whose willingness to speak critically has driven them to a lonely role. Anglicanism has rarely welcomed such persons; but the Church has inevitably incorporated their witness.

The mediators

In 1858 A. C. Tait, Bishop of London and later Archbishop of Canterbury, expressed the anxiety many Church leaders felt. "It is not to be denied that there is, in this age, a great danger of what we may call intellectualism . . . Students in our Universities, wearied of the dogmatism which ruled unchecked there some years ago, are very apt now to regard every maxim of theology or philosophy as an open question."[63] Tait was appalled by the findings of *Essays and Reviews* and Colenso. Nevertheless he bespoke a moderation which sustained most Anglicans, for he granted that there were difficult intellectual questions "which cannot in this age be avoided by men of inquiring minds. But I have no fear of such questions if they are approached in a reverential, truth-loving, prayerful spirit. There are exceptions of minds peculiarly formed; but, as a general rule, I have no fear of a man becoming sceptical, if he has not a secret love of the independence of scepticism."[64] Tait worried that the Church might splinter because of "self-sufficient" individuals whose work eroded the Church's foundations and required moderating influences. The adjustment of the Church's belief called for mediators who suggested how Anglicans could absorb new ideas.

One of the foremost mediators became Benjamin Jowett, whose idiosyncrasies made him a difficult person to categorize, but whose admirers viewed him as a prophet. Jowett understood the depth of spiritual and intellectual dislocation which resulted from new knowledge and the abandonment of old, dogmatic forms of thought. There could be no turning back, for "if we insist on retaining all that we have received from antiquity, we must insensibly impair the divine image in the soul."[65] Direct, unmediated knowledge of God was available if the past could be stripped away. Jowett believed truth had an underlying unity, which would eclipse the opposition between religion and science. Fellow essayist Frederick Temple insisted that God governs the world by fixed laws, assuring permanence amid change. Nature's uniformity reveals God's moral law and demonstrates the presence of God in each human heart. The present afforded an opportunity to recover essential truth. "Truths of all sorts have existed from the beginning of time which are either hidden from us or of which we are only just beginning to be conscious."[66]

Christ represents the "rock which neither the winds of opinion nor the waves of human life and action can overturn." When dogmas turn stale, the human heart can find assurance in seeking the life Christ exemplified. Jowett taught that belief demands "the inward evidence we have ourselves obtained of the truth of the Gospel ... Custom, and habit, and knowledge, and convention are poor staffs for a man to lean upon ..." Instead human beings are capable of inwardly grasping a spiritual essence, "the high and permanent element of religion."[67] "To this simple life Christ invites us; to return to the beginning of Christianity ... He speaks to use across the ages still, telling us to come back to the first principles of religion. And of this simple religion we have the assurance in ourselves, and the better we become the more assured we are of it." However, Jowett did not say Christ was necessary for this "spirit of life – the spirit of peace and love." There was no sense of any biblical basis, or for that matter of any verifiable principle or particular social expression of this life, other than vague references to moral improvement. Jowett's opposition to religious systems left only an aesthetic, religious sense, a timeless essence the Church should embody.[68]

That outlook endured in like-minded colleagues such as Arthur Penrhyn Stanley, Dean of Westminster and biographer of Thomas Arnold, whom Jowett eulogized on October 16, 1881. "It has been said both of him and of others," Jowett observed, "that a liberal clergyman has no true place in the Church of England, that he subscribes what he does not believe, that he repeats words in a sense which they do not mean." Stanley believed in toleration, not permissiveness, a religion of truth united to morality. Seeking those essential Christian ideas which would "bind the present with the past," "he would have liked to see the Church and the Universities freed from restriction, but still rooted in the past."[69] Though Stanley criticized points in *Essays and Reviews* and Colenso, the movement to censure them alarmed him. Authors who revised the Church's faith ought to be tolerated or the Church would lose the respect of intelligent laity. Stanley believed the Church should take a pastoral, middle ground, between criticism and dogmatism. He valued a Church which accepted diversity, inviting Pusey and Jowett with equal relish to preach at Westminster. When Pusey hesitated, Stanley replied that "nothing you say at all shakes my conviction that we have a common Christianity."[70] He could accept the shifts of the age without fear that the ground of belief was shaken.

Stanley demarcated his middle ground by a set of unassailable Christian principles. He stated that beneath "the sentiments and usages which have accumulated round the forms of Christianity, it is believed that there is a class of principles – a Religion as it were behind the religion – which, however dimly expressed, has given them whatever vitality they possess." Such principles eluded earlier generations of Christians, but the timeless character of their essences "give to these ancient institutions a use in times and circumstances most different from those in which they originated." The discovery of the universality of Christian faith endowed the Church's forms with unanticipated truth. Baptism expressed a universal principle of cleansing, which revealed God's grace, and the Eucharist conveyed a sense of spiritual feeding. Stanley used Maurice's sense of God's presence in human culture to argue that the Church's historic forms embody the human experience of God. He believed the Church's traditions gained importance when modern experience revealed their underlying meaning.[71]

If Stanley suggested a pastoral way to modernize the Church, T. H. Green offered it a modern intellectual basis. As Jowett commented in his eulogy on April 16, Green "gathered around him a band of disciples" attracted to his "Christian and philosophical life." Jowett was too modest to add that he had introduced Green to Hegel and to German biblical scholarship. Green drew upon German Idealism to challenge the idea that God and the world were opposites, for he believed that God represents that unity of traditional beliefs with a modern metaphysic which the human spirit is becoming.[72] Though Green's argumentation was dense, he inspired the idea that God's presence to humanity exemplified the divine nature. Thus he suggested a new view of the Incarnation, the pivotal doctrine of modern Anglican belief.

Jowett's most fervent disciple proved to be W. H. Fremantle, Dean of Ripon, who extended his sense of modern Christianity's basis. Fremantle believed that Christianity should not be identified with a tradition of "religious ordinances." The Church system "seems to need a closer connection with the social progress at which all Christian bodies are in some way aiming."[73] He envisioned an ecumenical Christianity as the means for the faith to perform its proper social role. Resistant to dogma and tradition, Fremantle believed the Oxford movement "encouraged the corporate and social idea of life, and so far was a help to the object aimed at in these lectures; but it was a hindrance to that object in that it restricted the social idea to the fellowship of those bound together by ordinances." He endorsed the impact of modern scholarship upon traditional Church identity. "The idea of a church system of any kind having been imposed by authority appears to be giving way before historical investigation." However, there is "some danger that men may . . . think that the whole apparatus of religious ordinances is valueless for moral and social purposes." Since religion was identified with the visible Church, the danger was that many people would imagine "that we must turn away from religion if we would insure moral and social progress." Fremantle stressed that though "all ordinances are essentially secondary and mutable," nevertheless "ordinances have still a perfectly valid ground, and that they may be made to serve powerfully the ends of social righteousness."[74]

Because human experience occurs in social contexts, Fremantle noted that religious life requires corporate forms. Experience "shows that . . . both faith and righteousness are in a large measure dependent for their support upon worship and sacraments . . . which may be adapted to the needs of our time, and especially to that social progress on which the mind of all the more advanced sections of the Christian Church is set."[75] The "body of faithful men banded together for the establishment of Christ's righteousness in the world," the Church's "natural religion" requires its own ordinances in order to anticipate the Kingdom of God. It must "work out its sovereign position by blending with human life, and with the general development of the whole system of nature which God has made."[76] Absorbing Green's sense of history moving through stages toward a culmination, Fremantle believed that the Church must encourage progress in particular people and nations. Mediators such as Fremantle have suggested patterns of Anglican adaptation through the absorption of social experience and envision the Church as the source of progress. Suspicious of inherited authority, they insist upon the primacy of human experience over dogma and anticipate important shifts in Anglican life.

THE EMERGENCE OF LIBERAL CATHOLICISM

A new way for the Church

By 1871 the Church of England's parties had experienced a variety of change. Evangelicalism retained its emphasis upon mission, but suffered under the weight of biblical criticism. The Broad Church group encouraged adaptation to the modern world but lacked a coherent program for doing so, although they advanced a new combination of liberalism and sacramentalism. Profound change altered the High Church party as the Hackney concern to preserve a Church that was established and apostolic was eclipsed by the Oxford movement's contrast between apostolicity and establishment. As some Tractarians crossed over the border to Rome, the movement impressed a concern for ritual upon Anglicanism. In its own way each party contributed to a consensus about the nature of Anglican identity which emerged between 1871 and 1914. Not conclusive, this consensus nevertheless afforded the Church a means to adjust to modern experience.

The emergence of a Liberal Catholic sense of Anglican identity represented a major feature of the transformation of Anglicanism. Liberal Catholicism, a marriage of Broad and High Church concerns, became the means of adapting ecclesiastical tradition to modern life. Accepting critical biblical scholarship, Liberal Catholics believed that Scripture revealed an historical progress of the creation toward final unity. They interpreted the Bible as a cosmic paradigm which encouraged optimism about human nature and history. Liberals believed the Church must absorb social trends in order to realize its nature and purpose and that its ability to absorb challenges verified Christianity's truth. This conviction was shared by liberals of all Christian varieties, as well as by modernizing forms of other world religions. Anglican liberals also possessed the conviction that modern experience enhanced the authority of apostolic precedent. Anglican liberalism proved instinctively to be a Catholic liberalism, and believed its task entailed revitalization of an apostolic model for Church life. This model relied upon the ministry of bishops, priests, and deacons, the centrality of Baptism and the Eucharist as sacraments, and the historic creeds. Believing apostolic Christianity could stimulate social progress, Liberal Catholicism affirmed that the modern world offered apostolic Christianity the context in which to become truly Catholic, the basis for ecumenical union among Christians, and a means for conquering the strains of modern life. The Church could inspire social progress in the non-Western world, and unite people across racial and cultural barriers. Liberals proclaimed the unity of history and envisioned the world and the Church becoming one under the Gospel. Modern life would discover a timeless Church as its destiny.

Liberal Catholicism became the predominant form of Anglicanism without being consistent within itself about the nature of the Church. Nevertheless, Liberal Catholicism became the dominant form of modern Anglicanism, and a major purpose of this book is to illustrate its role in the Church's transformation. The Liberal Catholic platform emerged as a synthesis of Tractarian tenets with higher criticism in 1871, when F. J. A. Hort, a Cambridge divinity professor, delivered the Hulsean lectures, published a generation later as *The Way the Truth the Life*. Hort suggested the emphasis of the Liberal

Catholic position began with human experience; the "human search precedes Divine revelation." Jesus appealed to human experience by using the disciples' questions, and his answers suggested a way of faith beneath the literal meaning of his words, a way which revealed "a future and progressive satisfaction." The human questions expressed doubts about where Jesus was going and what his disciples would do when he was gone. In response Jesus depicted a way of life which could be known "only so far as the way of God is known."[77]

Hort described the Way as a life of discipleship which entails a "necessary expansion of the individual Way into the universal Way." Both individually and corporately, Christian belief as a Way encounters "seasons of crisis" which test the Way's truth. In the modern world, where "it becomes manifest that a Christian world is ceasing to exist," Christ's followers naturally feel as if "He were once more leaving them to themselves." For Hort this meant that Christianity's "temporal and external characteristics" were no longer familiar. The reconsideration of Christian faith, which the modern world demanded, was an opportunity for the Church "to go forward in the Spirit." Tradition and custom from the past inspire the growth of a life of service to the Way.[78] Hort believed that Christian faith is bound to the world in ways that are no longer plain, but are revealed progressively. John's Gospel presents Christianity as an "underlying universal truth which was intended to be known." At pivotal moments in human history that Way becomes newly apparent, as the Incarnation was revealed within the fullness of time. The modern world "must ultimately reinvigorate theology by throwing into stronger relief its character as simply truth" and "give promise to aid powerfully in bringing to light the unity of all truth in Him."[79] The achievement of unity in God's creation requires that universal truth take specific form. The ancient Church appropriated the Gospel in terms of ordinary life, creating a sphere within which the whole of life was claimed progressively for God. This intention gave the apostolic Church a normative character which Anglicanism must maintain in modern life.

In a preface to Hort's work, in 1893, Bishop Brooke Foss Westcott of Durham cited the Incarnation as Hort's central theme, and unity as the Incarnation's fulfillment. From 1853 to 1881 he and Hort collaborated on a revised edition of the Greek New Testament. Like Hort, Westcott respected Maurice's theology and concluded that modern life compelled reconsideration of the Church's belief, especially the Incarnation. "The temper of the age leads us to trace out as far as we can the beginnings of things. In this way we feel the grandeur of our heritage." The basic truth was that "man is born religious. He is by his very nature impelled to seek some interpretation of his being and his conduct by reference to an unseen power. He strives to establish a harmony between himself, the world, and God."[80] The Church's discovery of its essence epitomizes the modern search for truth and suggests a personal and social paradigm.

Like many religious liberals, Westcott adopted a progressive view of Scripture's revelation and of Church history. He observed that "the Church welcomes the experience of the past not as exhaustive or finally authoritative, but as educative." "Nothing is added to *the faith which was once for all delivered unto the saints* (Jude 3). That was fixed during the Apostolic age and enshrined in the New Testament. But the Faith itself is brought to bear upon fresh problems and through them is itself illuminated." Or, as he expressed it shortly thereafter, "each age in order to apprehend rightly the new lessons which are brought to it, must guard its inheritance though it may see it transfigured." The Church advances, but it does not start afresh in each age. The early Church fixed norms of Church life, notably creeds and Scripture, which arose "by common usage, that is, by the Christian consciousness." The consciousness is timeless, though its expression changes.[81] Thus, Westcott wondered, "is Catholicity determined by reference to the past alone? Can we call an opinion or a practice 'Catholic' when it is opposed to the deliberate convictions of multitudes of believers, not less fertile than we are in Christian works?" The English Church, because it "unites in itself the old and the new, is best able to meet the grave problems which are thus raised."[82] The English Church is disinclined to seek its completeness in a theological system alone, but "looks to finding truth through life rather than through logic, for truth is not of the intellect only." The Church finds truth's basis in "the historic elements of our Creed" which are "of life; and unto life; and through life."[83]

The two parties which divided the English Church – Evangelicalism and Tractarianism – proved insufficient means to a comprehensive truth. The Church must learn from the new science, historical criticism of the Bible, and socialism. Science afforded a new view of nature's unity, while higher criticism showed that the Bible's message comes "from living men like ourselves among whom God is shown to be working: it enables us to feel that He is working . . . now among us."

Socialism teaches that Christ's redemption occurs in and through the world and suggests the overall message of the Church.[84] Christ's Incarnation "connects us with all Nature; and it reaches also to all life. This thought of fellowship with the Father in Christ, which places us in a living connexion with all that is, gives a new dignity and meaning to all that we think and say and do." A vision of fellowship "with the Father in Christ is, I believe, our message." "It is not the observance of legal ordinances but fellowship with the Father in Christ which brings life." "We must then set forth afresh this sovereign truth of fellowship with the Father in Christ if we are to offer a Gospel which uses and satisfies the aspirations of our age."[85]

Westcott was vague about the exact nature of this fellowship, but insistent upon its importance. He stressed that the Church's use of the forms of each age to become what it claimed to be, namely, the center of life, inspired a new concept of fellowship. Thus "through the Incarnation we have the fellowship of sons with Him of Whom lawgiver and prophet and psalmist spoke. This fellowship under the limitations of earth is the preparation for fuller fellowship in heaven."[86] The Church offered a unity of faith and life which overcame modern estrangement. Although he advanced the idea that the Church is an apostolic ideal with an unrealized destiny, unlike Newman, Westcott concluded that this destiny did not lead the Church away from the world, but into it, offering society the fellowship for which it hungered.

Westcott expressed the key points of Liberal Catholicism in a manner which permits clear summary. He emphasized that the Church must adapt to the forces of the modern world without necessarily sanctioning them. Modernity benefited the Church by compelling a recovery of apostolic faith, grounded in the Incarnation. The process of redrafting the Church's apostolic nature would inspire a new sense of fellowship within the Church and throughout society, based upon an ideal of unity. Clarification of these points demanded new understandings of the nature of faith, of the person of Jesus, and of the nature of the Church. These pursuits represented the pillars of Liberal Catholicism and the major themes of modern Anglicanism.

The meaning of faith

In 1889 the pivotal statement of Liberal Catholicism appeared in *Lux Mundi*, a volume of essays written by clergy who had sought a coherent theological position at Oxford between 1875 and 1885. The volume's editor was Charles Gore, then Principal of Pusey House, Oxford, and later Bishop of Birmingham and of Oxford. The central Liberal Catholic figure, the emblem of its balance of tradition and modernity, Gore called the book an attempt "to put the Catholic faith into its right relation to modern intellectual and moral problems." Gore believed "that if the true meaning of the faith is to be made sufficiently conspicuous it needs disencumbering, reinterpreting, explaining."[87] The authors of the essays wrote as "servants of the Catholic Creed and Church with the conviction that the epoch in which we live is one of profound transformation, certain therefore to involve great changes in the outlying departments of theology, and to necessitate some general restatement of its claim and meaning." Gore distinguished between innovation in theology and legitimate development. "The real development of theology is rather the process in which the Church, standing firm in her old truths, enters into the apprehension of the new social and intellectual movements of each age" and shows "her power of witnessing under changed conditions to the catholic capacity of her faith and life."[88]

The coterie sought a new basis of Christian belief which would be consistent with Catholic experience. In Bible study, Westcott insisted that an historical critical approach to the Bible could uncover a sense of growth and development, "a moral progress wrought out under the discipline of experience." The Bible reveals patterns of God's counsel to human beings amid the vicissitudes of their experience. It posits the evolution of a higher life as a human experience of increasing closeness to God. Scripture reconciles diverse persons into a unity, creating a human fellowship which expands gradually throughout the narrative, joining the visible world with an invisible order.[89]

Modern study brings the Bible into close connection with life. "When we have realised with vital distinctness how God spoke in and through the past, we shall be prepared to recognise and to interpret His message for us to-day." The Bible must be "read in the light of our own time, by the help of the same Spirit through which it was written," in which case, "we shall find that view of the working of God and of the destiny of man which will be our inspiration and our support."[90] Thus, Westcott and other Liberal Catholics stressed the authority of modern experience in understanding Catholic Christianity's truth. Modernity and catholicity were essentially one, a unity. This meant that beneath the apparent disharmony of historic faith and modern life lay a bedrock of unified truth, which the historic Catholic faith of Anglicanism embodied. Liberal Catholicism's task was to reveal and to disseminate that unity. Study of the Bible entailed upheaval, but resulted in a realization of God's presence in creation.

Personal experience was Liberal Catholicism's standard for interpreting the Bible. Here the imprint of T. H. Green was perceptible, especially upon Henry Scott Holland, author of the first essay, "Faith," in *Lux Mundi*. Holland anticipated the "personalism" which would become influential in modern theology. That is, Holland located faith's ground in personal experience rather than in objective forms or doctrines. This was a decisively modern turn, first suggested by German theologian F. D. E. Schleiermacher, who called religion a feeling of absolute dependence. Holland similarly depicted faith as religion's basic instinct in the person, preceding conscious expression. An "elemental energy of the soul," faith is "an inner and vital relation of the soul to its source" which is "most certainly elsewhere." "Faith is the sense in us that we are Another's creature, Another's making." Further, it is "an instinct of relationship based on an inner actual fact."[91]

Faith encourages a discovery of one's sonship, and the growth of faith is a "gradual increase of this personal contact, this spiritual intimacy between Father and son."[92] The self uncovers its capacity to move closer to God, and finds its quest verified in external forms of faith. This point required elaboration, for Liberal Catholics, prizing modern experience and the believer's selfhood, required expressions of faith conformable to the Church's tradition. They found a link between faith and its expression in the Incarnation where human and divine met.

The appearance of Liberal Catholicism transcended the Church of England. In the United States, William Porcher DuBose understood faith as a dynamic, historical process, rooted in Scripture and the Catholic form of the Church. A Southerner caught up in the American Civil War, DuBose later became a professor at the University of the South, Sewanee, Tennessee. From 1871 until his death in 1918 he created an indelible, Liberal Catholic influence upon that institution and the Episcopal Church. For him this position derived from a study of biblical criticism and from a realization of the personal dynamic of faith. DuBose concluded that faith entailed more than conversion and adherence to doctrine. He sought a vision of the Church which accounted for the tragedy and fragmentation of modern life.[93] The central problem of modern theology concerned the coherence of the human and the divine. In 1878 DuBose decided that the divine could be known only through the human in a process of realization whose possibility existed in each person. DuBose believed that each person possesses an unrealized true self, a divine sonship. Analogously the churches could uncover their essential unity with one another. Thus the Incarnation was a paradigmatic event, which set in motion a process by which creation was discovering its underlying unity. The Church must herald the realization of this destiny.[94]

DuBose grounded his theology in New Testament study, in a style he called "epexegesis," in which he isolated essential features of New Testament doctrine. He postulated that the Bible revealed the development of human realization of the unity of creation. This process drew human beings into relationship with God and actualized the possibility of fulfillment expressed in Christ's Incarnation. Human nature errs in seeking itself apart from dependence upon God. Through faith, "the highest and most distinctive function and activity of the spirit of man," a "marvelous assimilative and transforming power," unites human beings to Christ's life, for "Christ is not another instead of myself, but is only my true, divine, selfhood and self."[95] Harmonizing human personality with truth, faith in Jesus Christ means "unity with the entire working of all things as they are in the world," which fosters a cooperative sense of working for the divine purpose. Unity is the correspondence between reality and personhood, a "personal acting" in the world in harmony with its creator. For DuBose, the Christian way represented life in the "mind of the spirit" grounded in the revelation of God through Christ. The human spirit and its divine counterpart become one, advancing the creation toward its unity with God.[96]

DuBose's reference to life in the Spirit was echoed by Charles Gore's essay in *Lux Mundi*. "The Holy Spirit and Inspiration" stressed that Christianity entails a particular "appeal to experience" which "is essential to Christianity, because Christianity professes to be not a mere record of the past, but a present life, and there is no life where there is no experience." The experience of the Spirit encourages individuals to seek mutual reliance as it reforms the Church's faith. The Spirit unites the mind of Scripture and the apostolic Church with the mind of the present age. Faith, Gore insisted, is a belief inspired by the Spirit, which speaks now as it has done since the time of Christ.[97] Gore, DuBose, Holland, and Westcott shared a Liberal Catholic conviction that a dynamic, personal realization is the heart of modern faith. This perception entailed particular conceptions of the person and work of Jesus Christ.

The person and work of Jesus Christ

The Incarnation

A belief that in Jesus God took human form pervaded *Lux Mundi*. E. S. Talbot's essay "Preparation in History for Christ" set the Incarnation in the context of historical development. Talbot believed that "our own time is one which is specially fitted to appreciate and handle this aspect of the Christian truth." Modern historical method forms "a habit of mind" which recognizes the "relation of the Truth to the world into which it came." Critical study identifies the process in nature and society which, in turn, enables the Christian to "behold the facts and method of God's Redemptive Work." The divine ordering of life prepared the world for the Incarnation and inaugurated hope for the ultimate unity of the creation with its creator. Talbot perceived a process of historical development toward the Incarnation through the Old Testament and the ancient world.[98]

J. R. Illingworth maintained the Incarnation was compatible with the scientific theory of evolution. He emphasized that all creation moves inexorably toward higher forms of life. The Incarnation "introduced a new species into the world, – a Divine man transcending past humanity, as humanity transcended the rest of the animal creation, and communcating His vital energy by a spiritual process to subsequent generations of men." The Incarnation not only "opened heaven for it was the revelation of the Word; but it also re-consecrated earth, for the Word was made Flesh and dwelt among us." This moral event began a gradual overcoming of evil in the material order, a sense of human possibility for regenerate life. The Incarnation restored humanity's divine nature, and with it the hope that heaven and earth ultimately would be reunited.[99] Similarly R. C. Moberly called the Incarnation basic to the Church's belief; however, he did not defend dogma on *a priori* grounds but traced a development of doctrine leading to forms which modern study endorsed. Moberly depicted historical experience as a process which clarified the truth of dogma, unveiling the Incarnation, for instance, as a progressive indwelling of the divine among the human.[100]

Lux Mundi justified the human emphasis in religious life by reference to the humanity of Jesus. This theme pervaded Charles Gore's *The Incarnation*, which appeared in 1891. Upholding the idea of a process which prepared the creation for Jesus' coming, Gore stressed that Jesus was a human embodiment of the divine. This truth of the Incarnation was embedded in the Bible and entrusted to the Church's corporate development. A common faith appeared from the first, and to this the Church must hold fast.[101] Thus the Church balances continuity and progress. As it passed from simple faith to a credal one, "a corporate consciousness" took shape, like "the genius of a nation or a society finding expression." The decree of the Council of Chalcedon represented a *via media*, "which means not the way of compromise, but the way of combination and impartiality." Christ's humanity and divinity were balanced, as were the Church's eternal and historical natures. What is variable and changing embodies the eternal and absolute, so the Incarnation becomes the Church's paradigm, conforming its nature to history.[102]

The subjection of the divine to the human represented Gore's more provocative emphasis. Accounting for Jesus' humanity, Gore asserted that the divine expresses its intentions in accordance with nature, necessitating a self-limited God. In order for God to become human, "it was necessary that He should be without the exercise of such divine prerogatives as would have made human experience or progress impossible." Citing Philippians 2:5, Gore said that Paul taught a doctrine of *kenosis*. Jesus emptied himself of equality with God in order to become fully human, a means of dignifying God's creation.[103] Gore retained his balanced approach to the human and divine as he remarked that Anglicanism is an apostolic system which leads its members through a process of education that grounds personal growth in eternal truth. The Incarnation is the model for each believer's life because it inspires "personal conviction and enlightenment." In turn the Church exists as a visible society of early Christian origin which upholds the individuality of each believer's development. To grow in personal faith is to recapitulate the experience of apostolic witness, and to make one's own the truths enshrined in creeds and sacraments. For each believer the Incarnation becomes the means by which life dwells in Christ and Christ in life.[104]

An emphasis upon the centrality of the Incarnation was the Anglican genius and the essential idea of Liberal Catholicism. By incorporating a process compatible with scientific and critical methods, Gore described the Incarnation as creation's pervasive reality. He envisioned humanity's fulfillment as an incorporation of what was already bequeathed, not a synthesis of new truth or a wholesale abandonment of past experience. Future and past would meet, he suggested, revealing the importance attached to the idea of unity for the Liberal Catholic notion of the Incarnation. B. F. Westcott applied the conviction that the Incarnation reveals human nature's possibility to social life. In light of the idea of the Incarnation human beings could learn to make the Gospel the rule of life. Westcott insisted that human aspirations became intelligible only in light of the relation between God and creation. In Christ human nature is restored and directed toward its proper end. In light of the Incarnation a new basis for fellowship becomes actual. In the Epistle to the Hebrews Westcott sensed that Christ leads his Church toward completion. The Fall is overcome, and the common life begins its gradual perfection.[105]

The atonement

Liberal Catholics also contributed an innovative approach to the traditional idea of the atonement. R. C. Moberly, Regius Professor of Pastoral Theology at Oxford, published *Atonement and Personality* in 1901, a work which has been overlooked generally. Moberly sought to recover the "inferential structures" of the apostolic idea of atonement, the implications of the doctrine apart from its forms.[106] This historical recovery of essential religious truth would draw theology into the marrow of modern experience. Moberly explained the atonement in terms of the completion of personality. Individuality meant the "self-identification of the Christian with the Spirit of Christ ... which is the key to the explication of atonement ...." Moberly intended personal deliverance from sin to be a real change from what has been into what might be. Sin's defeat can occur only when a person realizes an innate identification with Christ's spirit. In genuine penitence, forgiveness is provisional "unless and until it is consummated in the holiness of the penitent, and in the perfect embrace, by love because it is love, of the holy penitent because of the holiness that is in him."[107]

Each believer faces the challenge of making personal the Incarnation, and thus of living as a changed, forgiven person. Atonement is not an external transaction requiring no personal initiative. Christ's self-sacrifice awakens the divine spirit in each person, a gift of grace which the believer must make actual and so grasp the unity of human personality with all creation. As Jesus identified with people, so his followers gain a "sympathetic self-identity with others." The Spirit of Christ allows human personality to realize itself and to unite with others. This is "a real transformation of the conditions and possibilities of Humanity" which requires external references such as sacraments and the Bible.[108] Though criticized for construing the atonement in subjective terms, Moberly intended to bridge the gap between its objective and subjective aspects. In his view a contemporary work by Congregationalist R. W. Dale failed to link Christ's death to the Holy Spirit and the life of the Church. Dale erred in defining the atonement's objective side as Christ's suffering in place of humanity.[109] Moberly explained that the atonement awakened human possibility and engaged the Church as mediator of God's Kingdom.

Liberal Catholics were convinced that the Church of England possessed an unrealized identity, congruent with tradition as well as with modern experience. Catholicism was "identifiable as a historical tradition within which Scripture has been interpreted in terms of a continuing experience under varying circumstances." They located that tradition within ancient creeds and Councils, the writings of patristic figures, and the liturgical practices of early Christian communities.[110] Historical investigation of early Christian experience became a prominent feature of Liberal Catholic endeavor, marking increasing precision in the search for what modern Anglicanism should be. An early instance of such work was *The Idea of Atonement in Christian Theology*, the Bampton lectures for 1915, given by Hastings Rashdall, Dean of Carlisle.

Rashdall served notice of his intention in 1898, when his *Doctrine and Development* appeared. Holding that liberal theology had an objective basis, he stressed that doctrine must develop. "All theology arises, he believes, from the attempt to set the facts of moral and religious consciousness in due relation to science and history." In *The Idea of Atonement* he reiterated this point. Praising Adolf von Harnack's work on the history of dogma, he argued that historical inquiry allows the Church to rethink its belief. Rashdall felt that traditional concepts "will be found to be far more patient of a reasonable and a modern interpretation than is often supposed." The question of how one knows one is saved leads one through the tradition back to Jesus himself.[111]

Jesus proclaimed a messianic kingdom using language which was "the accidental historical dress in which the ethical and religious ideas of Jesus would appear to have clothed themselves." In subsequent ages those same ideas appeared in different garb, all of which

Rashdall wanted to strip away. He believed the essential view of atonement "was that men were to be judged according to their works, including in the conception of works the state of the heart and intentions as scrutinized by an all-seeing God." To Rashdall this meant that Christ suffered in order to convey love and forgiveness and to lead humanity to a new way of life. "The atonement is the very central doctrine of Christianity in so far as it proclaims, and brings home to the heart of man, the supreme Christian truth that God is love, and that love is the most precious thing in human life."[112]

This conclusion afforded Rashdall a criterion by which he assessed the history of Christian writings on atonement. Rashdall explained that the idea was expressed in various ways because experience must take objective form. However, the "actual, objective fact of forgiveness" became lost in the construction of dogma. Paul diminished the impact of his experience by emphasis upon Christ's sacrifice as propitiation. In the Epistle to the Hebrews symbolic language obscured the fact of forgiveness, just as John's Gospel increased the gulf between the Church and the world. Augustine, the ultimate villain to Rashdall, denied human freedom and imposed a juridical meaning.[113]

Rashdall cited Irenaeus for the idea of an important parallel between the Fall through Adam and the redemption through the second Adam. He developed this analogy into a theory "of a peculiar fitness in the method of redemption actually adopted by God," a recapitulation of all things in Christ. Christ, as the embodiment of ideal humanity, makes it possible for humanity to recover its goodness and unity. Atonement was not "retrospective forgiveness" for Adam's sin, but the offer to all people of a realization of full humanity, because of the restoration of their unity with God. Rashdall transferred the Liberal Catholic idea of the Church's destiny to the person, as the center of God's creation. He praised Origen and the Greek Fathers for a progressive view of atonement and found in Anselm and Abelard a similar idea that Christ came to complete humanity.[114] The modern mind comprehends only a person-centered revelation.

The quest for a Catholic Church

Liberal Catholicism achieved a consensus about the nature of historical process and the meaning of Incarnation and atonement which adapted the Church's belief to modern experience. However, this consensus failed to resolve a basic tension in modern Anglicanism, for Liberal Catholics stressed the Church's historic ministry, creeds, and sacraments without agreeing about the literal truth of the Church's outward forms. Did Christ himself commission Catholic order? Or, were visible forms accidental expression of inner, timeless truths, and thus capable of being modified? This tension became endemic to modern Anglicanism, and Charles Gore illustrates one early response to the issue. In four lectures published as *The Mission of the Church* in 1892, Gore explained the Catholic principle of apostolic succession in ministry. He emphasized that Christ gives his grace through "a visible body, a visible Church." That body possesses outward ceremonies, such as Baptism and the Eucharist, "intended for the conveyance of spiritual gifts." Because the Church transmits these gifts to present life, it is a Catholic society, whose validity is ensured by a "succession of persons . . . bearing the apostolic commission for ministry." The center of the Church's life is "a perpetual stewardship of the grace and truth which came by Jesus Christ" which also "acts as the link of continuity, binding the churches of all ages and of all nations into visible unity with the Apostolic college."[115]

Gore believed a visible, historic ministry, with creeds and sacraments, were "parts of the organism of the Spirit." They afforded a context for the Bible which distinguished the Anglican from the Roman Church. Since the Reformation, Anglicans have "repudiated neither the ancient structure of Catholicism, nor the newer and freer movement." Upon ancient foundation, England's Church "opened her arms to the new learning, the new appeal to Scripture, the freedom of historical criticism and the duty of private judgment." Anglicanism "stands in such a unique condition of promise at the present moment," embodying both the imperfection and the promise of all Christendom.[116] The Church expresses its faith through a ministry rooted in divine commission, one of Gore's most important books, *The Church and the Ministry*, first argued in 1888. In the preface to the fourth edition in 1900, Gore construed his book as a critique of F. J. A. Hort's *The Christian Ecclesia*. Here the rift in Liberal Catholicism appeared as Hort argued that discipleship, not apostleship, was the primary function assigned to Christ's followers. Christians must possess "the inward characteristics of the Christian Ecclesia,' especially servanthood and ministry. Function takes priority over visible form, if the Church becomes the people of God.[117]

Hort stated that the Church's apostolic ministry was "founded on direct personal discipleship" without "in the New Testament any clear definition of the Apostolic office." Apostolic Christianity was distinguished by its teaching and by its fellowship, not by its uniform offices. Its authority was "moral rather than formal."[118] Founded not by Christ himself, but by the apostles and prophets who were determined to continue Christ's teaching, the Church was a community of disciples. Its offices "were the creation of successive experiences and changes of circumstance." The Church's outward forms must continue to adapt in order to keep Christ's message vivid.[119] Although Hort believed that apostolic Christianity was normative for the Church's identity, Gore was troubled that he invalidated the visible society which Christ instituted and undercut the significance of apostolic succession as the Church's basis. Both Hippolytus and Clement of Rome upheld the episcopacy as the local authority in a regularized ministry. An early Christian course of development resulted in the appearance of a ministry that finalized a portion of the Christian character, as Scripture and the creeds were final. The Church is not a fluid association in which believers are free "to organize themselves on any model which seems from time to time to promise the best results."[120]

The Church "is naturally of a piece with the Incarnation", which "has a finality which belongs to its very essence." Although Christ's religion faces further development, "it is a religion which in its principles and essence is final – which contains in itself all the forces which the future will need." No ministry is valid which is not thus derived. No ministry is valid "which is assumed, which a man takes upon himself, or which is merely delegated to him from below." It must be in continuity with the Christian tradition, "a transmitted trust." Apostolic succession is a principle of harmony between Christ and his Church. External, visible faithfulness secures the ministry of redemption and hastens the realization of unity.[121]

Gore's *Lux Mundi* colleague R. C. Moberly concurred with this view of Anglican catholicity. Though the Church has developed continuously, Christ delivered to it a truth which apostolic succession enshrines. The three-fold ministry was "the form which a certain divine and essential principle had already taken from the earliest moment at which it could be recognized as having any definite form at all." Outward form is not dispensable, because form incarnates principle. Furthermore ministry is received through divine commission, by the Church's transmission. To disregard outward form is to threaten the Church's validity.[122]

Moberly scolded J. B. Lightfoot for insufficient emphasis on the

Church's form and continuity. Lightfoot followed Hort in diluting the idea that Christ inspired a Church of particular form. He held that episcopacy was a late development which appeared haphazardly in the second century in response to changing social conditions. Bishops at first were presbyters in supervisory roles, and their functions remained similar in kind. Episcopacy appeared because of "the pressing needs of the Church," especially the need for order. Ignatius of Antioch, Irenaeus, and Cyprian secondarily linked the office to apostolic tradition, shifting its rationales from practical consider- ations to a matter of principle. Still later episcopacy acquired a sacramental function. Throughout, however, the ministry gained its validity from the Church's life, not vice versa.[123]

Convinced that the Church's tradition encourages adaptation to modern life, Liberal Catholicism has never agreed within itself about the nature of adaptation. As their writings suggest, Liberal Catholics never resolved the meaning of a Catholic ministry. Gore offered the most centrist Liberal Catholic theology, but he attracted opposition both from liberal and conservative Anglicans. As a liberal, Hastings Rashdall questioned Gore's idea of *kenosis* in Christ's Incarnation, while the conservative H. P. Liddon was horrified that *Lux Mundi* condoned liberal views of the Bible. American Anglo-Catholic Francis J. Hall argued that *kenosis* was an unscriptural abandonment of Catholic faith.[124] Though Liberal Catholicism became accepted generally, its meaning lacked conclusive definition.

Liberal Catholicism blended modern inquiry with the agenda of John Henry Newman and E. B. Pusey, who affirmed apostolic succession and the authority of ancient creeds and liturgies. New- man's idea that the Church was an unfulfilled reality realizing its essence through historical experience became the basis of Liberal Catholicism and a principal theme of modern Anglican thought. Tractarians intended their theory as a defense of the Church against modern innovations; ironically they inspired a modern means of identifying the Church's essence. Liberals even cited evolution as an historical dynamic resulting in eventual harmony between science and religion and unity among Christians.

The juxtaposition of traditional form and modern thought reflected Liberal Catholicism's characteristic division over the nature of the Church's outward forms. Could liturgy and ministry originally have been cultural adaptations rather than divine institutions, and could they be readily modified as an aspect of cultural adaptation?

Modern Anglicans have disagreed about the possibility of adapting the Church, while agreeing that it is an apostolic society seeking its completion in the unity of the human and the divine. This conviction afforded Anglicanism a modern basis for the Church's ministry and a tension in its identity.

CHAPTER FIVE

The Church and empire

"We seem, as it were, to have conquered and peopled half the world in a fit of absence of mind," John Seeley wrote in 1883. Seeley sensed that loss of a large portion of North America and the enhancement of India's importance constituted a decisive new phase of empire. He understood that empire involved the expansion of one people to encompass others in patterns of trade and cultural influence. Seeley wondered whether colonial experience could acquire a unified character and mistakenly dismissed the influence of nationalism in most of Britain's possessions. Despite his awareness of the new phase of empire, he misread its direction.[1] The idea that empire was imperialist appeared in 1902, in John Hobson's *Imperialism*, which linked empire with exploitation of colonial areas, an idea which became fundamental.[2] In this view the Church of England served as an extension of imperialism.

Nevertheless Britain expanded randomly without a clear goal. Australia started life as a penal colony and Sierra Leone as an humanitarian project. Widening trade found important centers in Nigeria and Hong Kong. In the second half of the nineteenth century Britain consolidated control over India and became a major player in the Scramble for Africa. By the early twentieth century a coherent imperial identity had appeared, but this was never complete and soon began to fracture. R. E. Robinson and J. A. Gallagher have shown that some of empire's most important features were informal, including cultural and economic influence loosely related to actual rule. Development of "Free-Trade" imperialism was a continuous process through the nineteenth century, "a constant interaction between the expanding metropolis and a host of less developed societies." Though Britain was not feverishly acquisitive, empire became the basis of British power and the guise in which the Anglican Church spread to the non-Western world. The Church readily adopted the role of religious establishment to the empire, seeing itself as the vanguard of historical progress. Yet within this pattern of adaptation to the form of empire, influential segments of Anglican life sought an indigenous Church, freed of the constraints imposed by the imperial mind.[3]

The British Empire was a nexus of effective control of subordinate societies by a metropole, or central power. Empire included outright rule, as well as effective influence, and entailed policies of shared rule, by which colonial subjects absorbed some of the burden of their own affairs. Calls for local autonomy emerged in Canada, Australia, and New Zealand, signaling the rise of colonial nationalism. Similarly deliberate British disengagement, or devolution of authority, became a characteristic policy goal as colonies replicated British patterns of representative government. The image of British rule was an ephemeral one, for the pressing policy question was how power was to be transferred. Missionaries often prolonged control over the indigenous Church, for they doubted its readiness for autonomy.[4] Yet I shall demonstrate that the Church moved toward an ideal of autonomous branches, directing their own affairs, much as the branches of empire developed local legislatures and later became a commonwealth of nations. Anglicanism became a confederation of churches, paralleling the rise of the British commonwealth.

Though the Empire lacked a coherent character, patterns of imperial experience can be detected. Similarly, while the Anglican presence within the Empire was diverse, the Church understood its role to be that of a public religion, instilling a national identity under God's aegis into non-Western cultures. Missionaries envisioned the creation of an indigenous Church as the basis for social betterment. Though the Church thought of itself as encapsulating the Christian essence of English culture, colonial circumstances distanced it from imperial control and encouraged it to become self-governing with indigenous influences. Four examples illustrate the role of the Church in empire. In each case I mean to show how the Church participated in the various phases of empire in a consistent pattern which stressed ecclesiastical identity without sacrificing it to mere political motives. Nigeria represents the commercial growth which accompanied empire, and India portrays the Church's relation to the rise of imperial forms of administration. Japan fell outside imperial rule, but rapidly modernized under British and American influence. Japanese experience illustrates cultural forms of imperialism. Uganda exemplifies the last burst of imperial expansion, which began late in the nineteenth century. Throughout their imperial experience, Anglicans attempted to function as a local religious establishment, rooting the Church more in local culture than in empire.

Nigeria – commerce and Christianity

The expedition organized by Thomas Buxton in 1841 to the Niger secured the linkage of the Church's mission to Britain's expansion. This union had its roots in the antislavery movement, in which Buxton and members of the Clapham Sect had been prominent figures. They concluded that eradication of slavery at its sources entailed the substitution of "legitimate commerce," which the Niger effort hoped to foster. Although that expedition failed, the idea of "legitimate commerce" remained influential for a generation. Trade became the focus of British expansion in Nigeria and the basis for cultural influence as well as Christian mission. The Church encouraged a civilizing process for which commercial and industrial skills were important. Until secular political goals appeared in the late nineteenth century, this entente between Christianity and commerce remained influential in Nigerian affairs.[5] As British foreign trade grew eight-fold between 1840 and 1870, traders joined humanitarians in the belief that moral forms of commerce would be financially successful. They pressured the British government to challenge the international slave trade at its sources. In 1840, the schooner HMS *Wanderer* attacked a slave base off Nigeria. The Aberdeen Act of 1845 empowered the Royal Navy to intercept slave ships wherever they were found.[6]

Nigeria was a revealing instance of the missionary role as empire expanded. In 1842 Church Missionary Society worker Henry Townsend arrived at Badagry in Yorubaland to establish a missionary base. Townsend "saw his work in Africa in political terms, and possessed the ability to carry it out." By March, 1845, the CMS had begun regular worship services and missionaries were studying the Yoruba language to translate the Bible and the Prayer Book. They planted vegetable gardens and built a corn mill. There were few converts, however, and Badagry remained a slave and rum trading post.[7] In 1846 chiefs in the vicinity of nearby Abeokuta agreed to admit missionaries to their territory. Townsend and the CMS moved their base from Badagry and made Abeokuta into a model site for early Anglican work in Nigeria. By 1849 there were usually 500 persons attending church services, with 80 communicants and 200 candidates for Baptism. By 1861 there were 1,500 converts and 800 communicants. Sunday schools bulged with children, and elementary education programs were popular. Meanwhile the CMS emphasized industrial education in carpentry, brickmaking, and cotton cultivation. Prince Albert donated a corn mill, and missionaries interested Thomas Hutton & Co., a trading firm, in establishing a factory. Trade created a context for mission and facilitated Britain's expansion in the region.[8]

Although missionaries often criticized the morality of traders, missionary work relied heavily upon a symbiotic relationship with the merchants. CMS Yoruba work found itself dependent upon contributions from prosperous merchants. Until regular mail-boat service began in 1853, missionaries reached the Nigerian field as passengers on merchant vessels. It was often the case that trading companies waived or reduced the cost of passage. Periodically the companies donated supplies to the mission or ensured missionaries safe transit. In 1846, when Thomas Hutton visited his company factory at Badagry, he toured mission schools and contributed generously to mission funds.[9] In return missionaries taught the traders to comprehend indigenous cultures. The missionary community afforded a social center for the merchant crews and local peoples received instruction in literacy and Western ideals of honesty, thrift, and morality, as well as agricultural and industrial skills.[10] Eager to end slavery, missionaries encouraged palm-oil trade and cultivation of cotton. Missionary work provided the rationale for expanding Britain's economic web.

Cooperation between missionaries and merchants sometimes became formal. In 1856 CMS Secretary Henry Venn convinced Thomas Clegg of Manchester to provide equipment and training for the nascent cotton industry. He also promoted creation of an Industrial Institution at Abeokuta where carpentry and brickmaking would be taught. This facility's profits were turned over to the Church and the Institution played a central role in the cotton industry.[11] Pursuit of "legitimate commerce" by the Church enhanced Britain's imperial expansion. Missionaries and traders also joined forces in a political lobby. In 1849 a House of Commons committee recommended the recall of a Royal Navy squadron from West Africa, although missionaries viewed the squadron as a deterrent to the slave trade and protection for their endeavors. Venn asked Henry Townsend, who was visiting Britain, to assess the necessity for a firm British presence to safeguard the missionary intention. Townsend depicted conversion, commerce, and the extension of civilization as the most desirable British policy. When Venn organized parliamentary witnesses, including military and economic experts, Clapham's lobby seemed resurrected.[12]

Ensuing events led to Britain's intervention on the Niger coast and rapid movement toward formal rule. Late in 1849, Foreign Secretary Lord Palmerstone dispatched John Beecroft on a diplomatic mission of inquiry to Abeokuta. He concluded that Britain must intervene and recommended Lagos as a natural center of future development. To facilitate intervention Beecroft advised that Britain assist Akitoye, dethroned King of Lagos, in regaining power, in return for favorable commercial and diplomatic arrangements.[13] In return Akitoye ceded five plots to the CMS for churches, and a service was conducted at Lagos in 1852 by catechist James White, an émigré from Sierra Leone.

CMS workers became key figures in probing Nigeria's interior. The foremost was Samuel Crowther, a Sierra Leonean of Yoruba descent, who had survived Buxton's disastrous Niger expedition. Ordained priest in 1843, and in 1864, the first black Anglican bishop, Crowther participated in 1854 in a new expedition up the Niger, sponsored by the British government and Macgregor Laird, an influential shipbuilder. Crowther sensed the missionary potential of uncharted territory, and linked mission to the training of indigenous leadership and to the pursuit of commerce, especially palm-oil trade, in inland Nigeria. Crowther also called attention to large stores of ivory, to the suitability of the land for cotton cultivation, and to access to existing caravan routes. Laird appreciated what Crowther envisioned and afforded him regular transit on his Niger river steamers.[14] Crowther joined subsequent expeditions and, in 1857, opened a mission station at Igbebe and performed the first baptisms in Nigeria's north. In 1861 he established work at Akassa and in 1864 he was invited to Bonny by King Pepple. Like other CMS workers, Crowther encouraged the burgeoning trade network because, in his mind, commerce encouraged conversion. The association became personal in 1873 when his son, Josiah, became Agent General of the West Africa Company.[15]

By mid-century it was assumed in Church circles that the

introduction of Christianity should proceed in the context of a civilizing mission. Religion was a relationship of exchange and commerce offered the basis mission required.[16] That assumption proved ephemeral, for the relationship between traders and missionaries in Nigeria was an affair of opportunity, never a marriage of conviction. Missionaries focused upon Church growth, neglecting industrial education and denigrating the necessity of trade. Traders grew suspicious of missionaries and developed independent influence over government policy. By the 1880s, traders and missionaries viewed each other as irrelevant.[17]

India – education and administration

On January 4, 1858, in the Nigerian countryside, Samuel Crowther commented on news of the India mutiny. "The reputation of the unjust disparagement on the missionary work as being the cause of this barbarous mutiny in India will open the eyes of those who opposed the conversion of the Sepoys, to see what advantage it is to any community to have converted natives mingled with it, who are like salt in the midst of a mass corruption."[18] Crowther expressed the searing effect of the India Mutiny upon the imperial imagination. After the Mutiny, missionaries, like British policymakers generally, became suspicious of indigenous control and administered Church work closely. Prior to the Mutiny, English missionaries in India focused upon education as a form of influence. In 1793, Baptist missionary William Carey started a school where he taught reading and writing, arithmetic and accounting, and basic Christian concepts. "The children were expected to learn by heart simple catechisms, portions of scripture, and hymns, which were simultaneously used as exercises in reading and writing." The missionary message was that Christianity offered access to Western commerce.[19]

Revision of the East India Company Charter in 1813 created an Indian episcopate and commissioned Anglican missionary work in Company territories. Initial Anglican mission work stressed education, and, after 1816, the SPCK, SPG, and CMS expanded and taught basic literacy skills blended with biblical stories and theological concepts. Anglican missionaries hoped to demonstrate to Indians how their own culture pointed toward the moral and religious truth which English civilization embodied. By the middle of the century, however, a spirited controversy pitted Anglicizers, who advocated an education in English for the sake of transforming India's cultures, versus Vernacularists, who wanted instruction in local languages. In India and Britain from the late eighteenth century influential Orientalists such as William Jones and H. H. Wilson attempted to preserve India's traditions, although Indians like Ram Mohan Roy and the Brahmo Samaj hoped to purify Hinduism through Western education.[20]

Few missionaries believed that Christianity and the non-Christian religions could be blended. Most felt that India needed a saving faith which Western culture could provide, and joined with educators and government officials in a policy of Anglicizing India. Governor-General William Bentinck, an Evangelical, believed colonial influence should produce religious and cultural conversion, and Anglicans followed his example. Bishop Daniel Wilson challenged the basis of the caste system in his congregations in the 1830s. The policy of Anglicization was most clearly expressed in the Indian Education Minute, a policy statement drafted in 1835 by T. B. Macaulay, a son of Clapham. Macaulay advocated India's cultural transformation through raising a new, educated, Western-style middle class.[21] Until the late 1850s, English education appeared to be an effective civilizing influence. In 1853, Charles Trevelyan, a prominent defender of education in English, testified before a House of Lords committee that Britain was cultivating a cultural and commercial bond with India which would endure.[22] British policymakers encouraged the Church's influence as synonymous with a program of modernization.

British opinion presumed that indirect influence would reduce resentment of the imperial power. That assumption proved a naïve one, for in 1857 three regiments of Indian troops garrisoned at Meerut rebelled after being issued a new model Enfield rifle using cartridges greased with cow and pig fat, animals forbidden to Hindus and Muslims. The Mutiny quickly spread through northwest India, a cataclysm which represented the failure of indirect rule, and numerous English men, women, and children were massacred. Missionaries seemed to be agents of state, and were treated accordingly.[23] When peace was declared in July, 1859, British shock hardened into a determination that she would forcefully continue her presence in India. Government policy shifted from education and paternalistic authority to an exclusion of Indians from leadership positions and direct British rule, although notable differences appeared.[24] Conservatives, under Disraeli, introduced ceremony to their country's rule in order to create a sense of deference among the Indian population. Disraeli proclaimed Queen Victoria Empress of India and retitled the Governor-General Viceroy.[25]

In 1880, on the other hand, the Liberal viceroyalty of Lord Ripon in India began. He attempted municipal reform, created low-level Indian civil servants, and ensured opportunities for technical training of Indian people. Liberals believed that education and administrative reform would unify the Indian and British cultures; instead, they encouraged nationalism, symbolized by the organization of the Indian National Congress in 1885. The Church of England's work during this period varied little from the colonial government's emphasis upon administration. In 1867, Bishop of Calcutta Robert Milman conducted an extensive tour of the country during which he visited government schools and colleges in order to examine students in metaphysics. The Church legitimated the westernization imposed by British rule, and this role of willing partner became a hallmark of Anglican activity in India. Milman also toured an opium factory at Patna. Britain organized opium production for Indian and Chinese consumption, and Milman approved of the industrial skills this effort entailed.

Milman reviewed government facilities at Agra for famine relief and, at an orphanage, he "went over the various workshops, printing, paper-making, carpentering, smithery, &c. It seemed to me a wonderfully complete and well-conducted establishment."[26] Throughout his tour, Milman devoted more attention to secular matters than to spiritual oversight and endorsed government policies. Near Cawnpore he found a church where government "had taken over the funds which had been collected for its erection soon after suppression of the Mutiny." After the bishop "made a strong representation to the Government on the subject, an engineer was added to the overworked staff at Cawnpore, and the building of the Church was proceeded with."[27] The bishop became an adversary of government when the Church's prerogatives seemed threatened.

The expansion of India's rail network was a triumph of British administration. This work relied upon British subjects transported to India to serve as laborers, and Milman paid close attention to a mission to the railways. At Jamalpore late in 1868, Milman reached an important rail center. "Here a church had been built which the Bishop consecrated, and then held a confirmation in it. He addressed about 180 railway operatives in the Station Library . . . The increase of railways in Indian and the consequent multiplication of English artizans, with wives and children, forming a population for which increased church and school accommodation was needed, was a source of constant anxiety to the Bishop."[28] Milman was a thorough administrator concerned to expand the efficiency of the Church's ministry. Late in 1868 he wrote government officials advising them of his intention to create a council of clergy and laity to advise him in ecclesiastical matters. He also plotted procedures to ensure that only Indian persons known to missionaries would be ordained deacon or priest. Although there had been Indian clergy for decades, in post-Mutiny circumstances Milman stressed that Indian ordinands must be nominated by the CMS or SPG and recommended by a British missionary. Acceptability to fellow "native Christians" was less of a priority.[29]

After the Mutiny a period of Anglican consolidation began. Following the government's example, the Church expanded its administration. New episcopal sees were created for Lahore and Chota Nagpur, and in 1883, the nine bishops of India and Ceylon met in Calcutta. Milman's successor, Edward Ralph Johnson, served from 1876 to 1898, and consolidated the office of Metropolitan, i.e., of a presiding bishop. Assisting the effort to create an Indian middle class, Church schools grew impressively. Although one report observed that "educational work has not produced any great results in the form of individual conversions to the Christian faith," there was a sense that the Church legitimized British administration and assisted in the birth of a modern society.[30]

Japan – influence without rule

The idea of a modernizing influence became a significant theme in the Church's role in empire. Even beyond the bounds of formal empire, the Church presumed its function was to be an agent of Western influence. Japan well illustrates this kind of missionary influence. Here the Church was not simply an extension of Western commercial and administrative control; Anglican missionaries assumed that social improvement resulted from Christian belief. They intended to reproduce Western culture, believing as they did that cultural conversion provided a fertile soil in which their Church might be planted. Anglican missionaries realized that they must adopt particular ways in which a foreign society might find Christianity suited to its own idiom. In Japan, as elsewhere, missionaries offered an education which helped to transfer the West's culture to a non-Christian society. Japan exemplified the nature of Anglican missionary work in the age of empire.

Though Christianity reached Japan in the sixteenth century with the Roman Catholicism of Francis Xavier, by the early seventeenth century emergence of the Tokugawa shogunate led to repression of Christian belief and expulsion of foreigners. Until the appearance of America's Commodore Matthew Perry, Japan remained closed to foreign influence. But in 1859 Episcopalians Channing Moore Williams and John Liggins, and Presbyterian J. C. Hepburn, began Protestant work at Nagasaki. Williams became the first Anglican bishop to work in Japan after consecration in the United States in 1866. He remained nearly fifty years in Japan and left an indelibly pastoral image upon the Church. Japan tested the missionaries' patience severely. Until 1873 Williams reported few converts and could call upon few co-workers. Funds were limited, and language and cultural barriers seemed insuperable. Though Japan had admitted Westerners and did not renew persecution of individual Christians, the faith was officially discouraged. However, a modernizing sentiment in ruling circles appeared as a younger, pragmatic nobility believed Japan must learn from the Western nations or face the prospect of being overwhelmed culturally and economically by them. In 1868, in a transfer of power called the Meiji Restoration, younger Samurai interested in modernization gained power.[31]

Japanese modernizers believed they could assimilate modern technology, commerce, and even forms of dress, without succumbing to cultural domination by the West. They were willing to accept Christianity as a matter of private opinion so long as Christians exhibited social loyalty. Legal barriers against Western intrusion turned into a psychological accommodation to modernization. Thus, in 1873, official proscription of Christianity ended and a large number of Western missionaries entered the country. The Church of England's SPG sent Alexander Croft Shaw as its first worker in 1873. The CMS had begun work in 1869.

Modernization in Japan entailed a rapid reform of society as railways, a modern military, telephones, and the telegraph appeared. A new legal system emerged, and the government's bureaucracy revamped itself along Western administrative lines. In the last quarter of the nineteenth century Japan seemed to plunge into a program of total westernization, in which foreigners came to play the role of teacher. The populace looked increasingly to education as the means to turn their nation around and, after 1873, their eagerness to learn from foreigners increased dramatically. In 1874 Bishop Channing Moore Williams wrote to Episcopal authorities in New York that he had performed twenty-one baptisms and twenty-one confirmations. He established St. Paul's School for boys in Tokyo, and reported there were more applicants than he could accommodate. Girls' schools opened in Osaka and Tokyo. A boys' school in Osaka led by missionary Arthur R. Morris grew suddenly to fifty students after having struggled for several years.[32] Episcopalians were seeing the new Japanese hunger for modern knowledge and taught young Japanese that the Church could offer access to the cultural power of the West.

Japanese modernizers hoped that Western forms would enhance the national spirit. Mori Arinori, who later became Minister of Education, advocated westernization and expressed a sympathy for Christianity. For the decade of the 1880s, there was passionate public interest in Christianity, and missionaries dared to dream of Japan as a Christian society. On June 30, 1880, Channing Williams wrote "that the seed so diligently sown in past years is beginning to bear fruit." He added, however, that the Church must "counteract the infidel influences which are poisoning the minds of the youth of Japan."[33] Williams observed that fascination with Western learning often led students to Mill, Huxley, and Spencer, not to the Bible. But Episcopal missionaries believed that conveying the Gospel entailed teaching cultural values as well as building the Church. In 1887, British and American Anglicans agreed on a constitution for the Japanese Church, or Nippon Sei Ko Kai, after they had formulated a Japanese Prayer Book. In the 1880s Japanese clergy were groomed and Deacons Kanai Nobori and Tai Masakazu were ordained in 1883. The first priest, Isaac Yokoyama, had been ordained in the United States in 1877 but proved a disappointment, and served the Church only briefly. His successors turned out to be able, and the Church ordained large numbers of Japanese men, while keeping control of the Church firmly in missionary hands.

Although its schools were popular, the Church struggled to grow as an institution. On September 8, 1883, for example, Channing Williams observed that "our Church has not a single Mission which can be called a successful one." On the other hand "there is a widespread & growing conviction among the higher classes that Japan needs a religion and that Christianity is the only religion which can meet the deep needs of the Country."[34] Popular response to Church schools suggested that Japanese people endorsed Williams' conviction. Anglican workers believed that cultural influence foreshadowed waves of individual conversions, and the emergence of the Church as the core of modern Japanese culture. Though all denominations adopted a similar approach, Episcopalians had one advantage over their competitors. Diplomats such as America's Townsend Harris and Britain's Sir Harry Parkes were sympathetic to Anglican work. Such influence encouraged Anglican missionaries to become an informal establishment, and they sought contacts with the ruling class. Thus, on May 3, 1886, missionary Henry Page wrote that he was teaching in a "school for special courses in law, political economy, and English founded and patronized by a nobleman who is very liberal in his ideas, and who, tho not a believer himself, is desirous that his students should know what Christianity is." On January 17, 1888, Bishop Williams announced he was searching for a teacher at the Ladies' Institute of Osaka. "All the members of our Mission in Osaka think this is such a good opportunity for doing good among ladies of the higher classes that we should not let it slip. Some of the best people in the City have the management of the Institution." Mission work included finding the proper social niche.[35]

While Japanese society prized Western ideals, there was room for Church work. In the 1890s, however, a tide of nationalism swept Japan, and allegiance to the emperor and reverence for cultural traditions threatened missionary work. Missionaries adapted to the new mood by insisting that Christianity was a socially stabilizing force. This wave of nationalism seemed to have passed by 1900, and missionaries recovered a feeling of security. In 1904, Bishop John McKim of Tokyo wrote that "the modern civilization of Japan is essentially Occidental. She has abandoned the hegemonic principles of Oriental countries and has placed herself in line with the leading nations of the West. It is generally acknowledged that the basic ideas underlying Western civilization are Christian in character."[36] McKim proclaimed the triumph of Western cultural influence and of the success of the Church's mission. In so far as Japan has assimilated Western ideas, "just so far may she be considered a Christian empire."

But Western forms without Christian faith were incomplete, because Christian education brought lessons in loyalty, responsibility, and morality in all facets of life. The establishment of Church schools influenced a generation of Japan's future leaders. "While a large proportion of the boys and young men educated in such schools have not become Christians, they have imbibed religious and moral principles which can never be forgotten and must influence them for good all their lives."[37] The Church also stressed the importance of educating women, offering them new roles in a modern society. Although it remained small, the Church contributed significantly to the modernization of Japan.

Uganda – the Scramble for Africa

In the age of empire, Anglicans consistently sought advantages from proximity to secular power, and contributed informally to the expansion of empire. In the late nineteenth century the pace of expansion increased notably, and the administration of empire became formal for both British and American interests. In the last quarter of the century a "Scramble" for new territory engaged the great European powers. The Scramble began on January 4, 1877, when Britain annexed the Transvaal to its holdings in South Africa. The move was intended by policymakers to be the initial step in a plan of federation. It was urged by a variety of local interests in South Africa, especially an acquisitive commercial element dominated by Cecil Rhodes, and humanitarians such as Bishop John Colenso of Natal, who argued that British rule would ensure a just social policy for indigenous peoples.[38] Imperial expansion included tensions between local leaders and distant politicians.

Uganda illustrates how the Anglican Church abetted expansion. Anglican missionaries were among the earliest explorers of eastern Africa. In 1844 Johan Krapf of the Church Missionary Society landed at Mombasa, on the coast of Africa bordering the Indian Ocean, and made initial forays into Africa's interior. After the British explorer Speke reached the kingdom of Buganda in 1862, and Henry Stanley followed in 1875, CMS missionaries arrived in 1877. They discovered a kingdom under powerful rule with considerable Islamic influence, and they met opposition from the Roman Catholic White Fathers.[39] Nonetheless conversions to Christianity increased dramatically and the Church of England dispatched Bishop James Hannington to serve as missionary Bishop of Central Africa. In 1885 Hannington and his small party were killed on orders from King Mwanga, who feared a threat to his power. Undeterred, the Imperial British East African (IBEA) Company sent a party under Captain (later Lord) Frederick Lugard to explore the commercial possibilities of the area. In east Africa the Scramble had begun.

Lugard's arrival in 1890 coincided with a decisive turn in Uganda's circumstances in favor of British interests. In that year indigenous Christians defeated a Muslim army and acquired political dominance. Despite tensions between Anglicans and Roman Catholics, initial steps toward accommodation of both groups began. Anglicans received a great impetus as British power proved dominant in the area by 1892. While Uganda remained apparently tribal, the basis of its life slowly became colonial. The Church's work received a further boost when Bishop Alfred R. Tucker arrived in 1890. Tucker believed that "Christianity can never be evolved out of civilization. Civilization, in its best sense, follows in the wake of Christianity." While Tucker cooperated in the work of empire, and expected advantages for the Church, he believed the Church possessed an integrity apart from imperial association.[40] Tucker dispelled any impression that he viewed himself as an adjunct to empire; rather he understood his goal as the creation of a Christian community. Tucker began educational programs which featured the New Testament and the Book of Common Prayer, and he planned the emergence of an indigenous Church. "Again I say our hope for Africa (under God) must be in the African himself."[41]

Lugard, Britain's chief representative in Uganda, on the other hand, realized he had to accommodate Roman Catholics. He pressured Tucker to acknowledge Catholic grievances while assuring him that the IBEA Company would not encroach on Church goals. Tucker and Anglican missionaries rejected the idea that Church expansion should reflect Company priorities, but they assailed Lugard and the IBEA for inadequate assistance to Church work.[42] Upholding the Church's distinctive mission, Tucker observed that as "a general rule, it may be laid down that Missionaries should hold aloof from interfering in the politics of the country in which their lot is cast." But, he added, "there are conceivable circumstances where such interference becomes not only a duty but an absolute necessity."[43] Anglicans in Uganda took this position when they successfully petitioned Lugard to be exempted from taxation, and insisted that they were Britain's primary representatives in Uganda, because they served longer terms than IBEA agents. CMS workers felt they should have veto power over Company matters. When the Company hesitated, missionaries requested a government takeover of British affairs.[44] In 1892 Lugard expressed concern about missionary pressure for the expansion of British influence.

In 1892, Lord Rosebery, Foreign Secretary in Gladstone's government, appointed Sir Gerald Portal as Commissioner to investigate Ugandan affairs, a move which reflected Cabinet uncertainty over a continuing British presence there. The IBEA Co. had indicated it would quit Uganda, and leading cabinet figures, including the Prime Minister, were content to let the matter rest. Rosebery, however, linked Uganda to British influence in Egypt, and warned that evacuation would lead to massacres of Christian converts and create public outrage in Britain.[45] Rosebery's warnings swayed cabinet sentiment and coincided with missionary intentions, though he considered the situation in terms of what strategic advantage might be gained for British interests. The turn to Gerald Portal and a commission of inquiry was designed to muster evidence commending absorption of Uganda into empire. But Portal did not seem to share his superior's ambitions. Bishop Tucker interpreted Portal's work as a precursor of evacuation from Uganda. On September 21, 1892 Tucker warned Portal that "if this intimation implies that Her Majesty's Government disclaims all responsibility for the safety of the English Missionaries in Uganda . . . then such disclaimer, in my opinion, does not relieve Her Majesty's Government of such responsibility."[46]

Tucker insisted that "the home Government, I maintain, has no right to compromise the Missionaries. And this, I submit, Her Majesty's Government has done with respect to Uganda." He was alarmed when Portal considered enhancing Catholic territories, but partition of the country along religious lines advanced colonial administration and benefited Anglicans. Tucker functioned as the main intermediary between Portal and tribal leaders. A treaty, signed in 1893, signaled Uganda's emergence as a colony with Anglicanism as the established Church. The rise of British sovereignty over Uganda did not erase tensions between Church and state. Tucker fretted that necessities of state would conflict with his hopes for

Church expansion. Reliance upon empire would interfere with the achievement of indigenous forms of Anglicanism.

THE CHURCH AND THE MAINTENANCE OF EMPIRE

The imperial mentality

Praising the creation of West African "Native Independent Bishoprics," the *Sierra Leone Weekly News* for March 8, 1913 emphasized that "one great hindrance in the spread of Christianity since it came to Europe has been the imperialistic idea imported into it." The Roman Church adopted the outlook of "imperial Rome," and Protestants "are now trying to reserve the monopoly of superintending and governing to members only of their own race, as if the grace of God and the operations of the Spirit were confined to race or colour." The editorial praised Anglicans for envisioning a Church that would be self-supporting because the Church "must be an alien and exotic institution" until its leadership "ceased to be foreigners" and comprised instead "members of our own race."[47] However, there were few signs that missionaries had transferred authority to an indigenous branch. Intent on furthering the Church's development, Anglicans assumed the mentality and the form of imperialism. In Singapore, where Anglican work started in 1826, no Church work among the Malay Chinese people took place until 1884, despite their dominance in the population. Diocesan leadership remained in English hands, and cathedral programs were geared to the English population. Work among the Asian population began in earnest only in 1910, and then attracted only a few, Anglicized Asian people.[48]

"None of us feels that we know much about the native character," Bishop Charles Brent reported from the Philippines early in 1903. "I am both impatient and sad because I am unable to speak the tongue of the people." Brent commended American residents who tackled language study, and called for missionary work among the Filipino people. Upon his arrival in Manila in 1902, he found only one Holy Communion service in Spanish "attended by a few Filipinos, but beyond this no attempt has been made in Manila to provide services for the natives."[49] When Mercer G. Johnston, rector of the cathedral parish in Manila, reported his activities for 1906, he listed 200 families as members, 24 baptisms, 13 confirmations, 30 marriages, and 7 burials. He had attended 200 meetings, including work for the

YMCA and for an antigambling crusade. But little of this activity had touched the indigenous people, and his congregation suffered a notable loss of members "when the troops stationed in Manila were moved to Fort McKinley."[50] Burma offers equally striking testimony to the imperial outlook adopted by the Church. At the Annual Meeting of the Rangoon Diocesan Association in 1906, A. R. Birks, a judge, distinguished between "the work among the Europeans and the work among the natives. There are some 11 Government Chaplains and 5 Additional Clergy Chaplains, drawing salaries in part from the Government, who deal with the first branch of the work." Birks added that "33 missionaries, half of whom are natives," worked with the Burmese population. He professed no knowledge of that work, but noted "a great improvement in the tone of English Society in Rangoon since I last came to Burma."[51]

English residents often viewed Burma with patronizing amusement and treated their time in that society as something of a lark. One lay person traveling to an Anglican missions conference expressed delight at being carried for three miles in chairs fastened to bamboo poles by Burmese: "We were a happy party trudging along over paddy fields, along bullock tracks, up and down . . . We stopped at a stream after we had crossed it on a wooden bridge. While the rest of the party ate sweets provided by Miss Knight, we ate chocolates." Meals at the conference were "picnicky . . . in fact, now that it is all over, I can comfort myself by calling the whole thing a picnic." Church work often resembled a social event as much as a missionary responsibility.[52] The colonial Church created separate European and Burmese congregations under English control with little initial thought to a self-governing, indigenous Church. Even where extensive work among indigenous people occurred, Anglican missionaries attempted to remake local cultures along Western lines rather than incorporate them into Church life. At Kuching, Sarawak, in eastern Malaysia, mission school graduates in the city "sometimes became Westernized and alienated from their communities by their command of English and consequent deficiency in their own languages." In the age of empire, the Church sometimes debilitated cultures.[53]

Behind this sense of separation between cultures lay the assumption that indigenous peoples required guidance because of their limited capacity for self-betterment, a clue to the role of racist ideas in imperial experience. By the late nineteenth century earlier, benevolent British tendencies in the expansion of empire had shifted toward a justification of domination based upon notions of innate Anglo-Saxon superiority. Anglican missionaries, however, believed their responsibility was to improve people less fortunate than themselves. Retaining a sense of benevolence, missionaries looked paternalistically upon peoples under their influence, and presumed control of the Church would remain in English hands.[54] This benevolent sense of superiority permeates Anglican missionary literature. In 1906, Eleanor Knight, sister of Bishop Arthur Knight of Rangoon, accompanied her brother on a tour of mission stations. Miss Knight gushed that "as my attendant I have *Becky*, the prettiest little Burmese maid you can imagine! . . . She is a Christian and speaks English, and she is so dainty . . . she is a pleasure to look at, and I feel more like petting and waiting on *her* than letting her wait on *me*."[55] Other English people boasted that "our native converts have stood firm" and that "the life of these Christian natives was in most cases satisfactory." Such common expressions approved of converts as childlike and uncorrupted by modern vices.[56]

A few African missionaries expressed explicitly racist views. John Widdicombe, Canon of Bloemfontein, South Africa, wrote in 1895 that "all natives are fond of dancing, most of them passionately so. Almost any pretext will suffice for a feast – which, of course, usually ends with a dance. Sometimes, when there is a great 'beer-drinking' going on at a heathen village, the dance which accompanies it terminates in an orgy. The dancers of both sexes become thoroughly intoxicated, and then ensues a scene of bestial revelry." Often missionaries noted the prevalence of superstition. Bishop Edward Steere, third missionary Bishop of Central Africa, told an Oxford audience in 1874 that "just as the outward life of an African is full of fear and uncertainty, so his inward life is all fear and uncertainty too . . . A man gropes his way through his life, peopling the darkness round him with fearful shapes, and on the continual look-out for some omen."[57]

The imperial age fostered an assurance of Anglo-Saxon superiority. In 1857 Bishop John Henry Hopkins of Vermont endorsed racial separatism when he called America a Christian nation in which religious toleration should be limited. Only Jews, as people of the Covenant, should be acknowledged. Others, including Muslims, Mormons, Hindus, and Roman Catholics, should not be permitted to enjoy religious equality.[58] By 1889, Bishop Maurice Baldwin of Huron, Canada, insisted in a Jubilee Sermon for the Diocese of Toronto that "we ought to be devoutly grateful to God, that we sprang from that great Anglo-Saxon nation, which has been so especially raised up and commissioned by Him to propagate His glory, and advance the kingdom of his Son."[59] God had endowed England with a unique mission and vast mission fields, and English expansion had succeeding in diffusing the truth embodied in Jesus on a global scale. The imperial Church prized its ability to cooperate with policymakers in a *de facto* establishment. Eulogizing the life of wealthy Philadelphian Anthony J. Drexel, Bishop Henry Codman Potter of New York, on January 20, 1894, praised the entrepreneur's role as a calling and wealth as a force for good. Drexel exemplified a "moral nobleness in business – a kind of financial statesmanship touched with the finest sensibility, and lifted to the most exalted conception of great responsibilities and opportunities."[60] In 1897, Bishop William Lawrence of Massachusetts lectured on "The Mission of the Church to the Privileged Classes" and noted that "there are in the Church men of the largest leadership in social, commercial, educational and all lines of life, men of the deepest piety and loyalty to the Church, and of the widest influence." When he organized a Pension Fund for Episcopal clergy, Lawrence sought guidance from financier J. Pierpont Morgan, an active layman. The Church's privileged ties to corporate America offered a resource for its mission.[61]

Toward a public religion

Nevertheless Anglicans were not content to identify the Church as an extension of the Empire, because they saw themselves as a public religion, encouraging a Christian sense of national identity in each culture with which they interacted. Anglicans believed that this identity included a sense of participation in the advance of God's Kingdom within history, the realization that God's redemption occurred within history as national life modernized. Ugandan Samwiri Rubaraza Karugire has written that to missionaries, empire did not connote economic and strategic advantage as it did to policymakers. In the Philippines, for instance, Episcopal missionaries feared that the expansion of civilization would corrupt indigenous peoples. The Church's task was "to invigorate their spiritual and moral character," to preserve something of their purity, yet to prepare them for life in the modern world. Of all missionaries in the Philippines, only Episcopalians believed that such preparation was their highest priority.[62]

The superiority Anglican missionaries felt toward their charges revealed a sense of responsibility to improve non-Western peoples. Future Bishop of the Melanesian Islands, John Coleridge Patteson wrote from Auckland in 1855 of his early impressions of the Maoris. "I like the natives in this school very much. The regular wild untamed fellow is not so pleasant at first. It only wants a little practice to overcome one's English feelings about dress, civilisation, etc." Similarly Chauncy Maples, later Bishop of Likoma, central Africa, noted from Zanzibar in 1876 that "I am not able to get over my astonishment at the general forwardness and proficiency of our boys, as well as at their general behaviour and moral character. It seems to me so perfectly natural somehow to be working amongst them that I do not and cannot see any difference between them and English boys." Although missionaries generally believed that empire possessed providential importance, they understood that it included debilitating effects. Imperial influence must encourage proper cultural advance, not merely overturn ancient societies. The missionaries viewed indigenous peoples as misguided, not irretrievably corrupted, and censured improper moral examples given by Westerners. In this vein, Archdeacon Cory of Burma cautioned in 1909 that missionary work "among the natives" should not "belittle in your minds the value of the work among the Europeans or Eurasians." He emphasized that the colonial Church must inculcate morality among the Europeans.[63]

At the Convocation of the Missionary District of Cuba in 1919, Bishop Hiram Richard Hulse gave a clear summary of the Church's role in a world he characterized as both disturbed and hopeful. "We face a new world . . . we can never go back to the old order of things." "The world is facing new and revolutionary schemes, the Church likewise confronts strange proposals springing up out of the spiritual unrest of the times. What should be our attitude towards all these evidences of social breakup and spiritual ferment? It must be sympathetic, we must look forward and not backward."[64] Hulse depicted Anglican mission as divinely appointed. "The world needs as never before the leadership of the Church, if it is to go forward and not slip back, if it is to come up out of the muck of competition and warfare onto the solid ground of free co-operation between the nations it must pay heed to the teachings of the Christ. The Church was established that it might bring those teachings to bear on the problems of the world." That charge suggested a stance for Church life. "We who come from the neighbor land to the North do not come altogether as foreigners, we are one with the rest of you in the household of Faith. But as the Church becomes at home among the nations it must do it from within as it uses those who are native to the soil."[65]

In the age of empire the Anglican understanding of mission developed into the creation of a modern nation suffused with a sense of Christian identity. Often missionaries stressed their cultural role at the expense of teaching indigenous people the distinctiveness of the Church's beliefs and practices. The imperial mentality dictated a civilizing influence rooted in a perception of God's activity among nations and cultures. But a countervailing opinion emerged that the participation of missionaries in God's direction of history must emphasize the distinctiveness of the Church's identity. The intention to create a modern nation required an indigenous Church rather than perpetual missionary control.[66] The idea of a public religion can be seen in India, where education became a prominent feature of the Church's mission. The Church Missionary Society created new schools after the Mutiny with special interest in boarding-schools for boys. Residential schools created an all-encompassing Christian environment where students might learn a new way of life. Education produced "social and municipal reform," attention to orphans, the sick, widows, and the destitute, the Cawnpore mission reported in 1909. While conversions were few, the Church in India encouraged a philanthropy and inculcated in future leaders a sense of public commitment.[67]

In Basoga, Uganda, between 1891 and 1918, education created a professional class of catechists and schoolmasters. The Church Missionary Society developed training for teachers and a program for ordinands among the indigenous people. The CMS goal was the creation of a "self-governing, self-supporting, and self-extending Church," which would shape the development of Basoga society. In western Uganda, the CMS founded the first dispensary in Toro in 1899. By 1904 there was a hospital with major nursing and surgical facilities at Kabarole. The CMS offered to train the mothers of young children in infant care and hygiene, an illustration of its interest in new attitudes toward public health.[68] Although English missionaries had difficulty relinquishing their direct control, they grasped the need for an indigenous professional class and for shared responsibilities. The result was social development, from building construction and methods of farming, to hygiene and disease prevention, and new notions of social hierarchy, morality, and personal improvement. The Ugandan Church substituted a national consciousness for tribal identities.[69]

In this effort CMS workers sought influence with tribal leaders. As representatives of the Church of the imperial power, Anglican missionaries believed their work deserved attention from the leadership of the host society. Furthermore the missionaries viewed the conversion of acknowledged leaders as the most effective means to convert the entire society. However, they received powerful Muslim opposition and faced Roman Catholic pressure, and so made few converts at first. Resistance from Muslim chiefs was an especial concern to government officials and missionaries, since Islam had profound political influence. But by 1900 Britain's Ugandan administration persuaded recalcitrant chiefs that missionary work enjoyed government sanction, with the result that the unconverted began to cooperate with missionary programs.[70]

Anglican reliance upon colonial resources suggested to a host society that the Church was in the forefront of social development. In the early history of Zimbabwe, the Church conducted a "Railway Mission." Clergy rode trains to inland areas as track construction advanced. In Burma, Bishops Knight and Fyfe traveled by steamer donated by the Lieutenant-Governor.[71] Such reliance upon the technological sophistication of the Empire was representative of an intention to create a public religion, and bring about a national religious consciousness. In Burma, Bishop Arthur Knight stated the goal of mission to Karen tribal people was to teach them that "in the Unity of the One Body are harmonized and co-ordinated the special and characteristic gifts of God to the different races, so as to promote the edification of the whole." In Cuba, Bishop Hulse said that the Church "recognises the national feeling, it enobles and sanctifies the Spirit of Patriotism, and has a place in its economy for each nation."[72]

The concept of a national Church became a primary reference point as missionary strategy developed. In *The World as the Subject of Redemption*, in 1885, W. H. Fremantle asserted that the Church is more than a private society where worship is the focus. "In contrast to this limited view of its functions, the Church will be here presented as the Social State in which the Spirit of Christ reigns; as embracing the general life and society of men, and identifying itself with these as much as possible; as having for its object to imbue all human relations with the spirit of Christ's self-renouncing love, and thus to change the

world into the kingdom of God." That transformation required the
Church to reveal the inherent "unity of the various spheres of moral
and intellectual life." The Church must consider itself as the
"important redeeming part" of the entire nation.[73]

Fremantle believed that although sin flawed human nature, the
recovery of harmony was possible. He emphasized the responsibility
the Church had to extend a vision of unity in social relations. Human
history "may also be traced out as a progress towards unity and the
organization of moral relations." The coalescence of a universal
Church, a "supreme Christian federation," would foreshadow the
arrival of God's Kingdom on earth.[74] Fremantle advanced the idea of
unity beyond Maurice's thought by linking it both to the nation and
to the nature of the Church. The idea of the national Church became
an influential Anglican theme in which unity appeared as the pivotal
concept. In the United States, William Reed Huntington published
in 1870 *The Church Idea: An Essay Towards Unity*, and followed this
with *A National Church* in 1898.[75] Huntington viewed the Church as
harbinger of God's Kingdom, a social institution, "visibly, as well as
spiritually one," revealing the unity of the creation. This sense of the
Church's mission led him to articulate four marks of its identity which
inspired the Chicago–Lambeth Quadrilateral.[76]

Other Anglican figures arose in support of unity. In Canada, in the
1880s, William J. Ashley of Toronto and Herbert Symonds of
Peterborough gained influence. In the United States, President
Eliphalet N. Potter of Hobart College depicted unity as the goal of
Church and national life in a sermon to the graduating class of Lehigh
University in 1889. Because education revealed the unity of truth
amid life's variety, the Church assumed the role of national educator,
for Church and nation are "harmonious parts of one system." True
Catholicity, through education, "paves the way for the best national
and Christian unity."[77]

This image of unity, and the concept of a national Church,
provided the rationale for Anglican mission. Non-Western peoples
were regarded as children of God in less developed form. The Church
advanced social development both by identifying with imperial
intentions and by adapting to indigenous culture.[78] In Britain and
North America, however, concern arose that a national Church must
safeguard marks of its uniqueness. Bishop Henry Codman Potter of
New York advocated the construction of vast cathedrals for the
Episcopal Church because he believed that "religion has never

survived anywhere without the due recognition and conservation of the instinct of worship." Religion best performs its social function by witnessing to its essential nature. Thus "the cathedral is a long-neglected witness which we may sorely need." A neo-gothic revival in church architecture, encouraged by the work of Ralph Cram, spawned the construction of massive cathedrals in New York City and Washington, D.C., and influenced the design of numerous other church structures.[79]

The concept of unity masked a tension that is perpetual in Christian history between evangelizing a culture by embracing it, and protecting the Church's distinctiveness from that culture. That tension burst upon Anglicans in the early twentieth century in the Kikuyu controversy. Anglican missionaries in east Africa endorsed ecumenical conferences which proposed joint forms of worship and structures of ministry. The possibility of a union Church jolted Anglo-Catholics who feared the surrender of apostolic ministry and sacraments; the same possibility, however, pleased Anglicans who prized ecumenical scope in a public religion. Though federation in east Africa later failed, in 1913, Anglican Bishop J. J. Willis of Uganda insisted that the necessity of a public influence encouraged ecumenical forms of the Church. "We are dealing with a nation in a formative stage," Willis commented. "Christianity is touching and moulding the inmost life of the people."[80]

While pagan superstition and Islamic resistance hindered the development of Ugandan Christianity, Willis expressed greater fear of the effects of modernization. Construction of a railway had produced "pathetic" consequences, for "the whole fabric of this country, social and political, has been upheaved," "a complete reversal of the whole national life within so short a time." Willis concluded that the spread of modernity brought social declension. "We must not assume that the establishment of Christianity will, of itself, necessarily regenerate a country."[81] Christian missionaries searched for the most effective form of an east African Church. When the Kikuyu conversations produced in 1913 a "Scheme of Federation" for a united Church, Bishops Willis and W. G. Peel of Mombasa participated. They based the move toward a federated Church on the Lambeth Quadrilateral, which was intended to "safeguard essentials" as well as to "facilitate Reunion."[82]

Missions constituted a crucial aspect of the recovery of unity. "The Mission field might be expected to witness the earliest attempts to translate into action the spirit and the intention of the Lambeth Quadrilateral." Mission churches "tend more closely to approximate to primitive conditions." Moreover "the actual conditions of the Mission field make some measure of 'effective and visible co-operation' a practical and 'imperative necessity.'" New forms of cooperation raised Anglican hope of movement toward that unity of Christians which foreshadowed the establishment of God's Kingdom. Peel and Willis emphasized that Kikuyu satisfied three of the four Quadrilateral points. Only episcopacy was in doubt, but the office might become the basis of a federated Church.[83]

Mission has produced Anglican debates about the nature of ecclesiastical identity. Kikuyu's proposal elicited opposition from Bishop Frank Weston of Zanzibar, east Africa, an influential Anglo-Catholic, who felt the demands of mission did not justify compromise of the Church's deposit. Weston viewed Kikuyu and the theological modernism expressed in *Foundations*, a recent volume by Oxford theologians, as gestures which threatened the Church. Such senti-ments allowed "any priest to deny the Trustworthiness of the Bible, the Authority of the Church, and the Infallibility of Christ." Weston lamented that Anglicanism allowed heretics to remain in the Church, and that Kikuyu undercut the basis of the Church's validity. These were twin signs of the same crisis.[84] Less alarmed, Randall Davidson, Archbishop of Canterbury, sought a middle ground within the duty of "upbuilding the Church of Christ among all nations and kindreds and peoples and tongues." The Church must incorporate "the characteristics of the people of that land" and avoid "divisions and nomenclatures which trace their origin and meaning to some distant chapter in our own local life." But Kikuyu must be approached with due respect for Anglican form and with sanction from the wider Anglican fellowship. Davidson showed how for modern Anglicans an issue in one sector of the Church created a dilemma which required a general means of arbitration.[85]

Few persons shared Davidson's modern approach. Charles Gore declared "that the zealous love of principles characterizes every period of real spiritual progress and power in the Church." Further, "no human organization, and especially no religious organization, can maintain itself unless it understands and lets other people understand what principles it stands for." The Church of England "has stood for what can, I think, be best described as a liberal or scriptural catholicism; that is, it maintained the Catholic creeds, conciliar decisions, sacraments, and apostolic ministry." It appealed to the Bible as the "safeguard of liberty against the constant tendency to exaggerate ecclesiastical authority and to accumulate dogma."[86] But the Anglican affinity with both Catholics and Protestants must not imperil the Church's identity. Gore valued a "common perception" of Church principles, which must be recovered, or the Church faced dissolution. Genuine comprehensiveness meant "a body which can tolerate much difference of opinion and practice among its members because it is at the basis bound strongly together by principles held in common."[87] Kikuyu's proposals were "specimens of a very wide-spread tendency" to reject the Church's historical basis, and to disregard "the obligation of all Christians to submit to the authority . . . of the one body." The Church's cohesion lay in " a continuous ministry," representing "the authority of the whole body," which branches of the Church must respect, or risk the Church's validity. At present, the Anglican "conditions of validity" were imperiled.[88]

Gore called the Lambeth Quadrilateral "a bare minimum," and only then if Baptism were presumed to include Confirmation. Yet these four points suggested that Anglicans should not federate with an ecumenical, national entity, but should "deliver our special message and maintain our type of Christian life, as much in Asia and Africa as in America and Europe. The days may be beginning when African and Asiatic Christians will be numerous and strong enough to manage their own affairs." Therefore they must maintain the "principles of the undivided Church and (we believe) of the Bible."[89] Revealing a new idea, Gore argued that mission entailed heightened expressions of the Church's uniqueness. This position later became central to the Anglican theology of mission.

Gore's broadside elicited responses from liberals such as H. M. Gwatkin, Dixie Professor at Cambridge, who argued that "the future Churches of Africa, India, or China will develop new types of Christian thought, so that nothing but harm can come of attempts to fix them in our present Western models." Regarding the historic episcopate, the "alleged necessity of a mechanical succession does not do well with our Lord's warnings against tradition," and "non-episcopal Churches show no very notable moral inferiority to others." J. F. Bethune-Baker, Lady Margaret Professor at Cambridge, one of the Church's most avowed liberals, claimed Gore had confused belief and forms of belief. Unity required distinguishing what was essential in Christianity from what was reliant upon particular forms.[90] Unrepentant, Gore in 1915 declared there to be a crisis in Church and state which stemmed from confusion about the Church's vocation. He reiterated that the Church's missionary strategy entailed extending its Catholic nature, which involved no surrender of the "special national capacities in religion."[91]

In 1920 Gore's Essex Hall lecture, published with an introduction by R. H. Tawney, depicted Christianity as membership in a visible society demarcated by apostolic ministry and sacraments. Acceptance of the Church into the Roman Empire, and the amalgamation of Protestantism with the nation-state, compromised the idea of the Church, though in the modern world, its essence could be recovered. For Gore, social experience shaped character, and the Church as a society must remain distinct, or confuse its mission with secular aims. As Tawney commented, the conception of an established Church of England "as a society co-extensive with the nation, preaching a colourless and inoffensive Christianity to congregations who were churchmen because they were first citizens, was abhorrent to him." Gore preferred "principles to expediency," "authority" to acquiescence in the "whole social system of the country." He "desired the Church's disestablishment . . . as a measure indispensible to its spiritual health."[92] He was both a critic of empire and a defender of Catholic Christianity.

The Church's experience in empire in the end provides evidence of its concern for integrity, not of its capitulation to colonial circumstances. The Church developed distinctive structures as it encountered disestablishment and pluralism. The concept of unity, the appearance of synods, and the tension which resulted from Kikuyu revealed the need for a global structure capable of embracing the Church's diversity and adjudicating its tensions. The Lambeth Conference addressed these requirements.

THE MEANS OF DISTINCTIVE IDENTITY

Church synods

In their search for a public religion, Anglicans created ecclesiastical forms of self-governance which diverged from empire. Church growth paralleled the rise of colonial government and fostered Anglican reliance upon colonial structures; however, religious pluralism in colonial settings confronted Anglicans with disestablishment. Colonial circumstances forced the Church to develop self-governance and resulted in tensions between Church and society. For instance, should colonial bishops receive their office by virtue of Letters Patent issued by the Crown, or through the colonial Church's structure and procedures? How could the Church resolve the tension between effective forms of mission and the preservation of an essential identity? It was also apparent that events in one branch of the Church often required a general means of amelioration. The colonial context encouraged the Church to develop a transnational forum.

The idea of synodical government appeared when the Church in the United States organized national and diocesan synods in which Church governance was shared by bishops, clergy, and male laity. The colonial Church grasped the synod as a form which embraced all strata of the Church and adjusted its governance to the realities of disestablishment and religious pluralism. The earliest movement toward a colonial Church synod occurred in New Zealand, where Bishop G. A. Selwyn zealously promoted a conciliar process for Church governance. Selwyn realized in 1844 that the synod of clergy he called for infringed royal initiative, which was the only legal means of calling a synod. But he reasoned that the colonial Church could not exist as the Church of England did. In New Zealand he could discover "what the actual system of the Church of England can do, when disencumbered of its earthly load of seats in Parliament, Erastian compromises, corruption of patronage, confusion of orders, synodless bishops, and an unorganized clergy."[93]

Selwyn called another synod for 1847 and in the interim drafted a constitution for the New Zealand Church which organized it on the basis of voluntary consensus rather than affiliation with the Crown and a monarchical episcopate. Selwyn's approach coincided with the sentiments of influential laity who drafted an appeal to Selwyn in 1850. This document noted that the New Zealand Church's duty was "aiding in the foundation of a great nation, and in the moulding of its institutions." Additionally there were "many native inhabitants of these islands who have not yet embraced the doctrines of Christianity." Although the "European members of the Church of England" were "bound together by a common faith, and have common duties to perform," they lacked "the usual ties of long and familiar acquaintance" and a "system of local organization which might tend to draw us together as members of the same Church." The New Zealand

Church required "the speedy establishment of some system of Church-government amongst us, which by assigning to each order in the Church its appropriate duties, might call forth the energies of all, and thus enable the whole body of the Church most efficiently to perform its functions."[94]

This was a clear statement of an important aspect of modern Anglican experience. The encounter with unprecedented social circumstances stimulated a sense of mission and a need for new forms of governance; yet, the Church's drift away from imperial moorings created uncertainty regarding the nature of its mission. Such dynamics appeared first in New Zealand, where Church leaders believed that the American "plan of Church-government" would afford "security for the ultimate establishment of that system" because it would conform to popular wishes in their own country. In other words, the Church was compelled to organize itself according to public sentiment, which favored disestablishment. In the 1850s the New Zealand parliament ceased to pay the stipends of colonial chaplains and questioned paying the bishop from public funds. The presence of non-Anglican Christians created an effective political lobby in the 1850s. Church property in 1858 was transferred from government control to newly chosen Church trustees.[95]

Selwyn endorsed this change in the Church's situation and responded with a plan of endowment whereby clergy received half of their salary from the local parish and half from a general Church fund. He also encouraged public meetings in 1852 and 1853 to consider a Constitution for the Church in New Zealand. Selwyn believed it was beneficial that the Church had been forced to find its own funding, because it encouraged the Church toward mission. He rejoiced in 1857 when a Church Conference created a triennial General Synod consisting of the bishops and of elected delegates with control over matters of patronage, property, and finance. The Synod also received power of discipline over clergy and Church officials.[96] Addressing the first Synod in 1859, Selwyn noted that it had become necessary in 1847 for lay people to be represented. Though legal recognition was slow in coming, a recent change of opinion legitimated autonomous Church governance. Selwyn had a powerful ally in Gladstone, then at the Colonial Office, who supported the movement toward colonial self-rule. He observed that in New Zealand, unlike Canada and Australia, the Church had avoided the colonial legislature because alliance with government had become an encumbrance. The Church organized itself on the basis of "mutual and voluntary compact."[97]

The influence of pluralism was overtaking the Australian and Canadian churches as well. Those churches also faced the practical necessity of self-governance through synodical structures. In Australia, the first bishop, William Grant Broughton, realized the anomalous position of the Letters Patent in the creation of his see. Those Letters presumed the English religious establishment, but in the colony there existed no system of parishes and patronage; indeed, pluralism prevented the rise of the English kind of religious establishment. Broughton's own Letters Patent were redrafted in 1847 to designate him as Metropolitan of Australasia, the senior bishop of that church. Such designation was a response to a series of challenges to his authority by Australian clergy and by the colonial courts. In 1844 the Lieutenant-Governor informed Broughton that he lacked the power to discipline two clergy whose licenses he had suspended. Such power was vested in the Crown, which alone could oversee colonial clergy. Court proceedings in Australia proved inconclusive in resolving the nature of a colonial bishop's authority. During the 1840s the Australian episcopate appeared anomalous, a dilemma which encouraged bishops to seek distance from colonial authority by creating ecclesiastical procedures.[98]

The rise of ecclesiastical governance was also encouraged by the emphasis on lay participation by the newly appointed bishops of Melbourne, Adelaide, and Newcastle, who arrived in 1847. Charles Perry, of Melbourne, wrote to Broughton in 1850 that the Church "will never gain a hold of the affections of the people, unless there be something of the popular element introduced into its constitution." Perry hoped that lay participation would resolve uncertainty about episcopal authority. He proposed a diocesan organization which involved laity, and he encouraged bills in the colonial legislature which would legitimate Church discipline. Those bills were withdrawn after vigorous opposition to what was perceived to be the taint of Erastianism. Repudiated in the public arena, the Church devised its own process of self-definition.[99] Broughton realized that, despite the advantages it enjoyed over other religious bodies, the Church in Australia was compelled to exist as a voluntary religious entity. He believed that adjustment to this situation entailed bringing laity into direct control over Church affairs. He further concluded that measures of ecclesiastical adaptation should be discussed by the region's bishops. Accordingly, in October, 1850, he organized a conference of Australian bishops which included Selwyn. Broughton decided that conventions of laity and synods of bishops and clergy represented the proper forum for responding to the Church's challenges.[100]

Perry feared that English law prohibited such synods, but Broughton replied that prohibition implied the Church possessed privileges of establishment. Short of Adelaide found English precedent for their meeting in the idea of a visitation by the Metropolitan, and Broughton pushed the concept of a synodical meeting of bishops. Unlike Selwyn, he dismissed the American precedent as ineffectual and urged the adoption of ancient, conciliar models. Perry wanted bishops and clergy united in all the functions of the Church, and Selwyn insisted upon the proper role of the laity. The compromise which emerged outlined bishops and clergy seated in synods and laity meeting in a concurrent convention. The session represented an important breakthrough to a synodical model of Church governance which became a precedent.[101] Broughton hoped to follow up the meeting of 1850 with a general meeting of Sydney diocesan clergy in April, 1852 and argued that, outside England, such a meeting did not require royal assent because the Act of Supremacy was not applicable in the colonial world. He encouraged clergy to call meetings to receive their parishioners' views, and he persisted in the hope of a concurrent forum for laity. A number of laity attended the session in 1852, though it was actually intended solely for the clergy. Broughton hinted that a provincial synod should be called, and convinced Bishop Tyrrell of Newcastle to assemble his clergy. Nevertheless Broughton was unable to carry through his aims and the mantle of reform passed to his successor, Frederic Barker.

In January, 1858 Barker asked several lawyers to draft a Constitution for the diocese which would incorporate the synodical idea. In November he called his clergy and representative Sydney laity to a meeting where the idea of synods was discussed and urged that the Church's missionary responsibilities required it to have a structure for managing its property and for administering discipline. The Church could not rely upon the government, but must act autonomously. Synods would permit the Church to safeguard that autonomy and to assume its mission.[102] Ironically enough, Barker hoped that the colonial legislature might approve creation of a synodical structure for the Australian Church. The measure proposing that structure was carried in the Legislature Council on March 14, 1861, but fourteen of the fifteen Council members were Anglicans and thus favorably disposed. The full Assembly was less receptive to the proposal, with Roman Catholic members complaining that the Anglican Church was seeking dominance by a legislative subterfuge. Efforts to dilute the bill centered on limitations to the bishop's power in a synod, a measure Barker accepted in his eagerness to ensure the bill was passed. But Tyrrell's diocese of Newcastle generally opposed diminution of episcopal authority and, with Anglicans lacking unity among themselves, the bill was withdrawn. The legislative attempt at a synodical constitution for New South Wales failed.[103]

Synodical government would not arise out of secular legislation. The movement toward involving the laity in Church governance was driven forward by assertive bishops who wished the Church to have an ecclesiastical identity which functioned like, but was disentangled from, secular authority. Barker and Tyrrell accordingly moved without legislative sanction. By 1866 the dioceses in New South Wales had collaborated on ecclesiastical constitutions and included provision for a provincial synod.

Synods became the primary means of distancing the Church from formal connection to political authority and of enhancing the particularity of the Church's identity and mission. Though the rise of synods was prominent in the south Pacific, a comparable trend was underway in Canada. In 1850 Peter Boyle De Blanquière, a member of the Canadian Legislative Council, unveiled a plan for a Church Legislature based upon the American model. The Act would have established procedures for the appointment of bishops, for provincial conventions, and for ecclesiastical discipline. In 1851 Bishop Strachan of Toronto met with his clergy and laity and incorporated Boyle's plan in a proposal that the Queen permit creation of a diocesan synod. On June 7, 1851, Strachan wrote the Archbishop of Canterbury that English Church precedent did not apply in missionary jurisdictions, leaving Church administration ill defined. A synod would unite bishop, clergy, and laity in mission and provide competent management of Church business.[104]

Strachan's action had wider ramifications. In September, 1851, the five Canadian bishops resolved their dioceses should adopt synodical governance. Synods would include a house of bishops and one of presbyters and laity. Bishop G. J. Mountain of Quebec emerged as a major proponent of synods, and dioceses rapidly organized synods, with Toronto forming in 1853, Nova Scotia in 1856, and Montreal and Quebec in 1859. In 1857 the Canadian legislature approved of synods and created the office of Metropolitan and formed a provincial synod of all Canadian dioceses.[105] Francis Fulford, Bishop of Montreal, was another advocate of synods. In 1852, when he addressed students at New York's General Theological Seminary, Fulford noted that it had "interested me most deeply to inquire into the particulars of your ecclesiastical constitution and discipline; for circumstanced as we are in the Colonial Branch of the English Church, we are in many respects looking to our Brethren in the United States as the model after which we may ourselves hope to be organized."[106] As Metropolitan, Fulford advocated a provincial synod despite the sentiment of Toronto lawyers who argued that it had no binding authority over any diocese. Fulford gained legal opinion to bolster his authority as Metropolitan to call a synod and to show that a provincial meeting was authorized by "the mere concurrence of all the Dioceses in Canada," expressed by the fact that diocesan synods had taken place. Clergy and laity of Erastian opinion who opposed a provincial synod protested in vain.[107]

In 1858, G. J. Mountain revealed the thinking of those who promoted a Canadian synodical structure and of those who opposed it. Mountain commented that the "synodical movement originated here, as in other parts of the empire, with the Bishops. The government of the Church is committed to their hands: they, voluntarily . . . came forward to divest themselves of an exclusive authority, and under such just reservations only as are connected with the essential maintenance of the principle of Episcopacy, to share their authority with their brethren of other orders in the body ecclesiastical." Synods were not creations of the Colonial Legislature, but of the Church itself. There were parties, he added, "who should desire to prevent our engaging in a course of proceeding" which was right. An Erastian party in Mountain's diocese prized the Church of England's affiliation with the state and sought that status for the Canadian Church.[108]

Mountain replied that his diocesan synod had respected the principles of the Church of England, making the worship of the Holy Communion the synod's central act. The meeting granted equal status to bishop, clergy, and laity, in a spirit of prayer and mission. In Canada there was no national establishment to guide Church affairs and thus no ready means of participation without the creation of a specific forum. Anglican synods were not like those of Baptists or Presbyterians because they were safeguarded by the principle of episcopacy. At the initiative of her bishops, the Church intended to "carry on our affairs and frame our regulations in conjunction with the Laity, *making their consent necessary* to every provision or regulation with which the Synod will have to deal."[109] Even contrary opinion gained a hearing in a synod.

By 1860 diocesan synods had appeared widely in colonial Anglican experience, the concept of provincial synods was gaining approval, and several colonial bishops had conferred with one another in England. These trends received considerable impetus from events in South Africa. Robert Gray became the first South African bishop when he assumed the see of Cape Town in 1848. Gray inherited seventeen clergy, most of whom were paid by government, and 10,000 Anglicans, most of whom were English. The South African Church at first was little more than a colonial chaplaincy.[110] Gray began meeting with tribal leaders to plan Church work among non-English people. He applied for SPG funds and planned a system of schools. Gray exemplified the Tractarian impact upon the Church's mission, and illustrated how mission brought issues of Church identity to the fore. Perceiving a laxity in Church life which he ascribed to Erastianism, he began regional meetings with his clergy and, in 1849, raised the possibility of applying to the government for a Church constitution. Though fourteen of the fifteen clergy present opposed him, Gray insisted that the colonial government should not "in any way legislate for the internal affairs of our Church. Considering that our future Government is sure to be adverse to the Church, this is a most important question."[111]

With disestablishment looming, Gray began an energetic program of fundraising and building construction. The Church "must, if it would take deep root in this land, depend mainly on its own exertions. It is by its own efforts that the Church in every age has extended itself." The Church's structure could no longer rely upon state support. "Meantime, in our present circumstances, we must be dependent upon the voluntary offerings of our people." Mission was a task undertaken by the entire Church and, in 1851, Gray proposed to a clergy synod that he consult in England for the best methods of "inviting the co-operation of the Laity in the regulation of the affairs of our Church."[112] Gray was elevated to the rank of Metropolitan and received episcopal assistance in the persons of John Armstrong as

Bishop of Grahamstown and John William Colenso as Bishop of Natal. The three bishops were suspect to Erastian clergy and laity as ritualists who emphasized the monarchical episcopate and the need for autonomous Church organization. Gray even envisioned a general synod of the Church in South Africa. "It was necessary at first, in an infant missionary Church like ours, that the whole burden and responsibility of what was done should rest upon the Bishop . . . But we have arrived at that period of our history when such a state of things ought not to continue. It is not in accordance with the principles of our branch of the Church, or of the Primitive and Apostolic Church that the Bishop should, by his sole authority, settle all questions which may arise, and conduct the affairs of the Church through all their details."[113] The Church should be run by bishops, clergy, and laity in a joint forum, and the first synod met in 1856.

Gray's plan for a synod ran into opposition from laity and clergy who believed the Crown summoned Church assemblies. One priest, William Long of Mowbray, refused to attend the Church's synods, and in 1861 ignored Church court proceedings against him and was suspended. Losing an appeal to the colony's Supreme Court, Long appealed to the Judicial Committee of the Privy Council in England. As a cleric of the established Church in a colonial setting, Long argued that he should be able to go through English legal channels. Gray countered that developments in England supported his case against Long. A powerful movement for revival of the Convocations of the Church of England had begun. Suspended since 1717, Convocation remained theoretically in effect in each English province, Canterbury and York, and met perfunctorily at the beginning of each Parliament. The lack of a functioning Convocation meant the Church of England lacked its own legislative assembly.

Reforms undertaken by the Ecclesiastical Commission in the 1830s and the surge of Tractarian sentiment contributed to a movement for the revival of Convocation in the Church of England. The effort entailed not merely a restoration of the institution but a change in its nature toward a deliberative body, a sign of the Church's ability to govern itself, and, by 1850, it was supported by such bishops as Blomfield and Wilberforce. Convocation at first seemed more a means of Church defense than a democratic innovation. Henry Hoare, a lay organizer of the movement for Convocation, cited the Church's colonial experience. He was aware that Australasian bishops had met in 1850 to plan Church synods. Neither Hoare nor Wilberforce could achieve parliamentary sanction, but regular meetings of Convocation took on enhanced importance, and an increasing amount of Church business began to flow through this neglected channel.[114]

I believe Convocation's example was instructive for Britain's colonial Church. When Bishop Gray of South Africa argued that he possessed the authority to call Church synods, he claimed that the South African Church was not identical to the Church of England. Despite its heritage and its colonial setting, the Church in South Africa must be free of outside influence, especially from English secular courts, and South African synods must settle the Church's affairs. But, in 1863, the Judicial Committee of the Privy Council reversed the South African decision and challenged synodical action against Long. That decision foreshadowed the furore over Colenso.[115]

Colenso had challenged Moses' authorship of the Pentateuch and questioned the veracity of biblical miracles. He also advocated the Church's absorption of African tribal customs and the Baptism of polygamists. He taught that the sacraments were little more than vague signs, with Baptism conveying no radical change, and the Eucharist serving simply as an aid to personal devotion. Adapting Maurice to the mission field, Colenso's belief that the Church should be the spiritual heart of a nation became the basis of a mission to the Zulus. Gray, however, and most South African clergy, held Tractarian views. They feared the Church's absorption into culture, whether colonial or tribal, and defended the efficacy of the sacraments and the truth of Scripture. On May 18, 1863, the Dean of Cape Town and the Archdeacons of Grahamstown and George brought charges of heresy against Colenso.[116] The proceedings which followed constituted a watershed for the colonial Church and for Anglican treatment of controversial personalities. Colenso emerged as the first of a succession of figures who have challenged the Church's authority and extended Anglican thinking beyond traditional categories. Although his name became synonymous with unrepentant heresy, his case stimulated constructive discussion about Anglican identity. More than any other individual, Colenso served notice of the Church's need for a global forum.

The South African trial of Colenso culminated in his conviction late in 1863, and deposition from office. The Church court concluded that his beliefs varied from the standard which was expected of Anglicans.

Failing to secure his argument that the Church court lacked jurisdiction except by his consent, Colenso, in June, 1864, appealed to the Crown, and his petition was referred to the Judicial Committee of the Privy Council.[117] Gray objected to this appeal by resorting to both legal and ecclesiastical principles. He cited his Letters Patent, which bequeathed him authority as Metropolitan. Appeals beyond Cape Town should proceed only to the Archibishop of Canterbury, not to secular jurisdictions. On the other hand, since the Judicial Committee had ruled in the Long case that colonial bishops were not to be equated with bishops of the established Church, Gray claimed to be separate from English authority. Such a protest proved in vain, for the Judicial Committee found for Colenso on March 20, 1865. He proceeded to win continuance of his salary from the Colonial Bishoprics Fund and gained a judgment allowing him access to Church property in Natal. Yet intricate questions of Anglican identity remained. What was the relationship between a colonial Church and the Church of England? Must the Church resort to secular authority to resolve its disputes? To what extent could the Church determine the limits of belief, and discipline violations of those limits?

The Colenso stalemate taxed the Church's ability to resolve anomaly and to live with quixotic personalities. After Colenso took possession of the cathedral at Natal and attempted to function as bishop, Gray excommunicated him in January, 1860. Desiring a new bishop, Gray consulted England, where the matter was debated in Convocation in May and June, 1866. Samuel Wilberforce believed that the situation required a formal statement of the South African Church's beliefs, the selection of a new bishop by South African clergy and laity, and the consecration of the man by the Archbishop of Canterbury. Although W. K. Macrorie accepted the see of Natal in 1869, Colenso continued to function, focusing upon work with the Zulus and leading regular worship at the cathedral.[118]

In light of this circumstance, Gray concluded that colonial churches should be represented in England, and in 1866 he designated an emissary. The colonial churches did not feel bound to the English establishment, but hoped for a means of accord with it. This became the formal position of the South African Church when, in 1876, it declared that although it stood in continuity with the Church of England, the Church was bound only by its own tribunals.

The Colenso matter led Robert Gray to claim a profound degree of independence for the colonial Church in South Africa.

The meaning of the Lambeth Conference

The appearance of synods represented an Anglican adaptation to colonial circumstances. The bishops who charted this course believed that synods enhanced the distinctiveness of the Church's mission and identity. Gray was convinced that the colonial Church should shed identification with the state. The Colenso affair drew attention to both the Church's lack of a central authority and the global scope of its ministry. Calls for an international Anglican forum had begun in 1851, when John Henry Hopkins, the American Presiding Bishop, received an invitation from the Archbishop of Canterbury to celebrate foundation of the SPG in 1701. Hopkins replied that there should be a meeting "in the good old fashion of Synodical action. How natural and reasonable would it seem to be if . . . there should be a Council of all the Bishops in communion with your Grace!"[119] Bishop William Whittingham of Maryland echoed this suggestion in 1852, and, in 1854, Fulford of Montreal, preaching at the consecration of Potter of New York, hoped that a global meeting might unify the Church. Impetus toward a global structure increased with the growth of provincial synods and the revival of Convocation. The need for self-direction further increased in 1864, when the Crown ceased to issue Letters Patent as the basis of a colonial bishop's authority and a sense of uncertainty appeared among colonial bishops. Bishop John Travers Lewis of Ontario proposed a global forum in 1864, and in 1865 all of the Canadian bishops publicly joined him. In December, 1866, a sermon by Fulford at Christ Church, Oxford excited great interest in a "Pan-Anglican synod." The initiation of this important concept was at hand.[120]

The concept of a meeting of Anglican bishops required English assent and, after personal persuasion by Lewis of Ontario, C. T. Longley, Archbishop of Canterbury, agreed to consult bishops within and beyond England. Given Longley's cautious conduct in office, little might have been expected of him. However, in February, 1867, he invited the 151 Anglican bishops to Lambeth Palace on September 24 for four days of meetings. He cited both the request made by the Canadian bishops for such a gathering and the concurrence of

Convocation. He added that a recent meeting of English, Irish, and colonial bishops endorsed the proposal, and that this meeting would address "many practical questions," the resolution of which "would tend to the advancement of the Kingdom of our Lord and Master Jesus Christ, and to the maintenance of greater union in our Missionary work, and to encreased intercommunion among ourselves." The meeting would not "make declarations, or lay down definitions on points of doctrine." But "united worship and common counsels" would promote Church unity. Seventy-six bishops accepted Longley's invitation.[121]

A moderate anti-Erastian, with a high regard for episcopacy and a sympathy with synodical developments, Longley recognized that the revival of Convocation and the revision of English canon signified the need for a full consultation among Anglicans.[122] The appearance of *Essays and Reviews*, together with Colenso's writings, suggested that the Church lacked a proper means of defining its beliefs. When, in February, 1867, colonial bishops met at Lambeth with English bishops, Longley, responding to Samuel Wilberforce's entreaty, drafted the invitation to the first Lambeth Conference. He explained that colonial bishops desired the meeting in order to clarify their relation to the Church of England. When he solicited subjects for discussion, major interest centered on the clarification of doctrinal standards, and of the relationships between branches of the Church, as well as the role of laity in the Church and of the Church's response to social questions. Accordingly, the Conference's agenda, drawn up by Longley, devoted the first day to relations between Anglicans, the second to colonial churches, and the third to missionary cooperation with resolutions on each topic compiled by Gray and Wilberforce. In his opening address, Longley reminded participants that their actions were collegial rather than binding. The mere fact of meeting, however, conveyed a hope of unity in faith and mission.[123]

Unity seemed a vain hope, because Evangelical and Broad Church bishops were hostile to the Conference, while High Church and Tractarian bishops viewed Lambeth as a vindication of their principles. Gray lobbied hard for discussion of the Colenso affair and moderate bishops such as Tait of London and Thirlwall of St. David's wanted no judgment which would reflect negatively on the Church's relation to the state. Colonial bishops hoped that a Pan-Anglican synod would result from the discussions. Lambeth Conference, and Church synods generally, revealed a series of conflicts among parties and personalities, and energetic political maneuvering to create power blocs which might sway the proceedings. Democratic process proved a laborious way to clarify the Church's mission, and obstacles to consensus appeared in the discussion of a general preamble to the session which characterized the Anglican Church's beliefs. The original draft defined Anglicanism as the "faith of the primitive and undivided Church," based upon Scripture, the first four general Councils, and the English Reformation, and announced the assembled prelates' sorrow at the divisions of Christendom. This affirmation did not survive in its original form as proposals to amend it cited various theological agendas. Evangelicals cared little for ancient Councils; Tractarians desired greater emphasis on the creeds. Thus it was difficult to perceive that Lambeth would serve as a means for clarification of the Church's identity.[124]

Lambeth's major achievements in 1867 concerned synodical structure. Selwyn, Fulford, and Gray directed the session toward this pivotal subject, and moderates and colonial bishops prevailed. Cotterill of Grahamstown stressed that the relations between the Church of England and its offspring required clarification. As Gray added, the union of Anglicans represented a communion of churches, a "self-constituted, spiritual subjection, by their consent to yield obedience to the decision of some higher synod."[125] The final form of the Conference's main resolutions reflected this sentiment. The bishops concurred that "wherever the Church is not established by law, it is . . . essential to order and good government that the Diocese should be organised by a Synod." This statement upheld the diocese as Anglicanism's fundamental unit, but advised that the diocese required assent from a provincial synod. The resolution recommended a synodical form with bishop, clergy, and laity sitting together and voting concurrently under the Bishop's presidency. Each Provincial Synod retained the authority to define its particular form and procedures.[126]

Lambeth also urged the creation of a "voluntary spiritual Tribunal" consisting of representatives from each Anglican province to resolve disagreement among Anglican branches and "to secure unity in matters of Faith and uniformity in matters of Discipline." Fulford and Cotterill, who authored the resolution advocating this structure, recognized that such a tribunal might transgress "the liberties of the Colonial Churches" or collide with "the Courts established by law, either here or in Her Majesty's foreign possessions.''[127] Longley guided the assembly's handling of the Colenso matter toward consensus which bridged the sentiment of Anglo-Catholic bishops such as Fulford, Selwyn, and Cotterill, who rallied around Gray, and Evangelical and Broad Church bishops who held out for latitude in doctrinal standards. The resolution noted that the "Anglican Communion is deeply injured by the present condition of the church in Natal," and appointed a committee to propose a solution. Thirty-five bishops voted confidence in Gray and in the South African Church's stance against Colenso.[128]

The first Lambeth Conference concluded with affirmation of the council format and the ideals of Church unity and ecumenical reunion. Those themes became important reference points for later Lambeths and for Anglicans generally. Lambeth secured its authority by guiding a process of discussion out of party channels, upholding Anglican principles, and suggesting resolution of intractable conflicts. However, despite approval in principle, in Canada and the United States, much work remained to explain to Anglicans the further necessity of such a meeting; fortunately, Selwyn and Tait addressed these needs. Selwyn, in 1868, relinquished the see of New Zealand for the English see of Lichfield. He thus was able to bridge the colonial and English churches, and became the foremost international bishop. In 1871, Selwyn preached before the Episcopal Church's General Convention in Baltimore. He examined the nature of intercommunion among Anglicans in light of controversy over ritualism and declared that "every branch of the church hath authority to ordain and change ceremonies and rites of the church ordained only by man's authority . . . It is the duty of all loving members of the Church of England to submit their own private opinion, in matters indifferent, to the judgment of their brethren; for truth of doctrine and fervency of devotion are best promoted when Christian men are seen to be of one heart and soul."

There should be "no servile uniformity" in the Church, "if there be but a recognized authority, which all are willing to obey. The whole of our church is interested in obtaining this happy combination of elastic freedom with efficient control." Here lay the essence of the modern Anglican ideal.[129] Its realization entailed visible unity embodied in an international synod of bishops, clergy, and laity, as recommended by the American Church. Selwyn added that the Archbishop of Canterbury should be considered Patriarch of the Anglican Communion, and that the convening of a second meeting of bishops seemed advisable. In 1873 Selwyn addressed Convocation and noted that Anglicanism had become a confederation whose unity, which relied not upon the state but upon voluntary compact among the Church's branches, now demanded a council of bishops and the patriarchate of Canterbury.[130] He hesitated to promote the American idea of a global synod, and the proposal to appoint an Anglican patriarch proved controversial. By general assent, a sure sign of Anglican authority, the idea of a second council of bishops proceeded.

Tait, by now Archbishop of Canterbury, agreed that a global legislative body and a patriarch would offend important Church parties and threaten the Communion's unity. On the other hand he held out hope for a voluntary tribunal of appeal and recognized the acceptance of a regular meeting of bishops. Writing to the American bishops in June, 1875 about discussion of a second Lambeth Conference, Tait cautioned that such a meeting could not achieve an "authoritative explanation of doctrine." "Each Church is naturally guided in the interpretation of its formularies by its recognised authorities," a note struck by Selwyn three years earlier.[131] Similarly, no branch of the Church could interfere with the matters of any other. "Each is considered qualified to regulate its own separate affairs, while all are united in the maintenance of the one faith." The propriety of a meeting of bishops revolved around the presence of issues "relating to the brotherly intercourse of the various branches of the Anglican Communion," on which its chief pastors might shed light. Before Convocation, Tait explained that the Church of England desired to encourage among its branches conversation so that "we may be able by friendly intercourse to strengthen each other's hands." The issues which emerged included relations among Anglicans, doctrinal questions, and the idea of a tribunal to resolve intra-Anglican conflict.[132]

In July, 1878 Tait welcomed a hundred bishops to Lambeth. His opening speech praised both the Church of England's tradition as an established Church and the varieties of governance exhibited by its offspring. Establishment of the Church meant that "the Civil Power is a delegation from Him, and that the laity, who are entitled and admitted in every well-ordered community to a voice in matters ecclesiastical, are fairly and well represented according to our Constitution by the influence of the Civil Power." The established Church's proximity to civil authority encouraged the progress of its mission; however, in other circumstances the Church found new forms of governance and avenues of influence. Anglicanism's diversity intensified the search for "essential union" through clarity about "those verities by which Christians live."[133]

In 1878, Lambeth first engaged the question of a board of arbitration. Barker of Australia felt keenly the need for this structure, but no Lambeth consensus appeared. American bishops refused to discuss the matter. In its final report on the matter, Lambeth simply urged each province to determine the circumstances under which it would refer a question for wider discussion, evidence, as Selwyn stated in 1871, that Anglicans aspired to a unity which respected their diversity, and, as Tait held, to a union with civil society which protected the Church's distinctiveness. The Church required an apostolic method which would balance its unity and diversity, and it settled upon regular meetings of the Anglican bishops at Lambeth as the proper forum. Such meetings honored the Church's diocesan and provincial levels of authority, but addressed common concerns and clarified common beliefs. In 1878 ritualism concerned the bishops, and in 1888, temperance, socialism, and polygamy received attention. Relations between Anglicans has been a perennial theme, and the Committee on Mutual Relations in 1888 reminded their colleagues that the Conference lacked authority to impose standards upon the Church. It was even permissible for the provinces to revise the Prayer Book, though consultation would be advisable on such a matter.[134] In 1888 Lambeth also accepted a statement of Anglican principles which the American priest W. R. Huntington had advocated as a basis for ecumenical discussions, and which was adopted by the American General Convention of 1886 at Chicago. Their resolution defined the Scriptures of the Old and New Testaments, the Apostles' and Nicene creeds, the sacraments of Baptism, and the Lord's Supper, and the historic episcopate as the four foundations of Anglicanism. The bishops viewed these principles as a basis for Anglican identity as well as for ecumenical reunion, although some doubted that the ministries of other Christian bodies could be accepted.[135]

With a consensus about these principles, and the need for regular Lambeth Conferences, Anglicans were able to coordinate the Church's mission. In 1897 and 1908, for instance, Anglican bishops addressed the question of "Native Churches" and industrial conditions. In 1897 sentiment against an Anglican patriarch proved determinative, but hints of interest in a consultative body surfaced.

Anglicans have used Lambeth to ponder other forms of cooperation among themselves. In 1908, the first Pan-Anglican synod involved bishops, clergy, and laity in a massive discussion of Church life. Thus, the Lambeth Conference embodied the synodical principle without itself being a synod and evinced the Church's desire to be a public religion without recourse to civil society's structures. It represented the Church's longing to function as a spiritual kingdom, and it confirmed the Church's unity amid diversity, and recognized its heritage without positing the necessity of allegiance to England. The age of empire produced a series of paradoxes which became inherent in a Church torn between what it had been and what it aspired to become.

CHAPTER SIX

Anglicanism confronts cultural diversity

THE SOCIALIST IMPERATIVE

The convergence of Anglicans and radicals

The adjustment of Anglicanism to the form of empire raised the issue of the Church's distinctiveness from culture. The tension between adaptation and preservation of its essence pointed to a modern dilemma. Beginning with the Tractarians, a movement to loosen the Church from its English, imperial moorings advanced. The question of the Church's relation to culture became pivotal as new forms of Anglicanism posed alternative expressions of religious life. These popular sentiments suggested that the modern Church embodied an apostolic order, distinct from the political establishment, grounded in local religious community. Indeed I argue that a profound feature of modern life has been the appearance of popular opinion as a basis for political and religious authority. In diverse forms, grassroots religious movements have challenged institutional prerogative. For Anglicans the onset of modernity awakened a fascination with local culture and encouraged a sacramental sense of community as the Church's identity. Inherent in this turn to local culture was a critique of modern life which distanced the Church from association with empire.[1]

In his analysis of late nineteenth-century American religion Martin Marty identified the search for a lost wholeness as pervasive. Modernity produced the "schisms and divisions" of urban, industrial life which alienated all social classes from redemptive community. A variety of figures viewed the crisis as a cry for recovery of a lost, premodern wholeness. In England and in America Anglicans played central roles in the emergence of this social gospel. Political scientist Richard Ely of the University of Wisconsin observed in 1889 that the social crisis was characterized by "an international, world-wide stirring of the masses," that a movement of "profound social reconstruction" emerged to remake "the foundations of the social order." Ely believed the churches must direct this impulse to the recovery of a religious sense of social wholeness.[2]

The quest for wholeness raised the issue of the Church's integrity as articulate Anglicans criticized the Church for its compliance in the social establishment. The idea of disengaging the Church gained momentum as a result of a new brand of politics. From 1870 in Britain, socialist political organizations encouraged the Church toward an apostolic ideal of religious community. This view awakened the pervasive tension in the Anglican response to modernity, between the defense of social order and the search for true religious community. That tension emerged in the late nineteenth century when Whig-Liberalism encountered severe challenges from the political left. This new radicalism developed as a fusion of Nonconformity and working-class concerns with skepticism and free-thought. It drew the Liberals toward the initiation of further reform measures and, in 1868, Gladstone was returned to office with a large majority supporting his pledge to disestablish the Church of Ireland and to seek Irish Home Rule. Temporarily these issues offered the Liberal Party unity and influence it would never again achieve.

Gladstone believed that the Church's integrity necessitated its independence from the state, and he encouraged self-determination for distinctive cultures, endorsing colonial self-government and the mission Church's right to direct its own life. Consistent with these convictions was his support for the disestablishment of a Church which attracted only 10 percent of the Irish population. Gladstone located public authority in popular opinion. The Church which took account of social realities need not fear the loss of social privilege. In 1869, accordingly, the Church of Ireland was disestablished, the first fissure in Britain's alliance of Church and state. Because this achievement had clear implications for England and Wales, articulate defenders of traditional Church privilege emerged. The Church Defence Institution, originally organized in 1859, revamped itself and gained adherents in 1871. Embodying the Whig-Liberal principle of accommodation to social reality, the Church Reform Union, formed in 1870, and later – in 1895 – the Church Reform League urged a greater degree of self-government to preserve the essence of religious establishment. During the 1870s and 1880s a furious debate over disestablishing the Church of England proceeded without resolution.

The issue remained a sensitive one so long as religious issues remained at the forefront of political debate.[3]

The Church of England attempted to secure its role as the religious establishment through reforms of its life and extensions of its mission. Defenders of the Church pointed proudly to the dramatic signs of new life that were visible in the Church. However, an influential Congregationalist wrote in 1877 that an "institution so ancient, so venerable, and having so many claims to public respect as the Church of England, ought to be able to stand on its own merits, or it is tolerably certain that it will not long be able to stand at all." Evidence of new life in the Church, and increased toleration for Nonconformity, did not justify continuation of the religious establishment. On the contrary, new life demonstrated the Church's readiness to endure the loss of its privileged position as the religious establishment. Thus the author concluded, "we are all opposed to the Establishment, and we are all equally ready to admire and honour whatever is good in the Church."[4]

By the 1870s, after a century of Nonconformist pressure, the Liberation Society amassed sufficient political muscle to challenge the Church's historic place in the nation. The novelty of this moment was that Anglicans began to concur that the Church's new life failed to justify continuation of formal establishment, and augured for a reconsideration of the Church's nature. A defense of Anglican identity entailed distinguishing between its social locus and its apostolic ideal of sacramental community. This point of view emerged in 1877, when Alexander H. Mackonochie argued that the "whole state of things as regards the relation of the Church to the State, and of the State to the Church, has altered entirely." The Church and the State share certain common ends; however, the Church "is a kingdom which differs from all human organisations in that it has to do only with the souls of men; it affects their spiritual interests only, but affects them with an exclusive jurisdiction, with which no one who does not belong to the Church can interfere." Furthermore, social circumstances had "so changed as to make the old relations" between Church and state untenable. Parliament no longer spoke for the Church, and the reappearance of Convocation signaled the Church's ability to govern itself had matured.[5]

Sounding like a secular critic, Mackonochie questioned the effectiveness of the religious establishment. He acknowledged that every village had included "an educated gentleman, with his wife and family, disseminating a high moral, religious, and civilising tone on all around." But "three centuries of the system's work has [*sic*] failed to raise our rural population to any great height of religion, morality, or civilisation." The Church has imprinted rural life with "little more trace of itself than the tradition found by the next comer of the gifts and amiability of the rector's wife." Recent "gigantic efforts" which extended "the Church's work both in town and country, at home and abroad," demonstrated that its success resulted little from its political privileges but greatly from voluntary endeavor, for the identity of the Church lay outside political order.[6] Establishment "could not prevent the zeal of individual clergymen," but it colored the Church's work in Britain and, in colonial areas, restricted the occurrence both of confirmation and of ordination. At home the Church often fell victim to corruption and heresy. Far from being a focus of unity, it had encouraged Dissent and confused political control with apostolic order. The anomaly of the Church's situation suggested the necessity of disestablishment as a means to recover its integrity.

Mackonochie embodied the fusion of Anglo-Catholic ideals with political radicalism. In 1865 he became one of the Anglo-Catholic priests to be prosecuted for use of excessive ceremonial in conducting public worship. He adopted what hitherto had been Roman Catholic vestments such as copes and chasubles, faced eastward in conducting a Romanized form of the Holy Communion, and urged his parishioners to practice auricular confession.[7] To much of British public opinion such practices indicated a seditious attraction to Rome which threatened the Church's role in enhancing social order. To an emerging segment of Anglican opinion, overriding criteria determined the Church's integrity. The Church must relate itself to common people through a dramatic statement of its apostolic nature, rather than its alliance with the state. At first controversial, this perspective would evolve into the central expression of Anglican self-understanding. The reconstitution of Anglicanism's Catholic heritage represents a significant feature of its transformation.

In the decade of the 1870s radical ideas moved from the periphery to the heart of British life. Radicalism offered visible evidence of its prowess in the Labour Party, which consolidated working-class experiences with new political enclaves. Socialism, the core of Labour's political thought, turned reform away from the Liberalism which had dominated its agenda. As Machin explains, "the movement's motivation was partly religious, springing from the experiences obtained by many of its members as Sunday school pupils and teachers, lay preachers, and attenders at church services and meetings."[8] This social gospel attracted support among various denominations. Born of working-class, Noncomformist experience, Labour found a home among some Anglicans. Despite the prominence of antireligious radicalism among Labour, the party offered a segment of Anglican opinion a means to regenerate society while guarding the independence of the Church. For the High Church party the attraction of reform combined with ecclesiastical distinctiveness proved irresistible. High Churchmen hoped to "popularise the notion of the universal Church catholic." Releasing the Church from the state freed it to stand upon its sacramental integrity.[9]

In the late nineteenth century High Church and Labour convictions appeared synonymous. Freeing the Church from the state was the ecclesiastical equivalent of Irish Home Rule, or colonial self-government. The Church, as Henry Parry Liddon (a High Church cleric and biographer of Pusey) noted, existed as a sacramental community to inspire social harmony through "holy fellowship." Stewart Headlam, the source of a new vision of Christian Socialism, believed that the Church must "get men to live as brethren," challenging all that impedes human development. Charles Gore put forward the apostolic community of the Church as the model for reconstructing industrial society. These suggestions represented the germination of a new kind of Anglicanism.[10] Figures such as Liddon, Headlam, and Gore could not appreciate that religious issues would lose political energy. The moment of the High Church–radical entente coincided with the shift in the political world from religious concerns to social ones. Irish Church disestablishment had been a pivotal question in 1869, but by 1921 Welsh Church disestablishment offered little that proved momentous. The idea of a High Church, reformist politics faded, though political influence alone had never been its intention.[11] The goal had been the reconstitution of Anglican identity, a search which encouraged a social critique grounded in an ideal of apostolic community. The incarnate Lord offered a model of wholeness for which industrial society hungered. The Church's integrity lay in its social mission.

Proponents of a new Anglicanism

Stewart Headlam

"I hope, then," commented Stewart Headlam in 1892, "that I have said sufficient to make it clear that, so far as Christ's works and teachings are concerned, not only is there no contradiction between the adjective 'Christian' and the noun 'Socialism,' but that, if you want to be a good Christian, you must be something very much like a good Socialist."[12] Headlam's article, published by the Fabian Society which he helped to found, illustrated the convergence between socialism and a new Anglican self-understanding. Christ's work, he argued, alleviated the social ills of this world. Jesus taught his followers that they were members of God's Kingdom, "the righteous society to be established upon earth." "Live, Christ said, all of you together, not each of you by himself; live as members of the righteous society which I have come to found upon earth."[13]

This society must "stir up a divine discontent in the hearts and minds of the people with the evils which surround them." The greatest evils were economic, for "those who work the hardest and produce the most, have the least of the good things of this world for their consumption; and those who work very little and produce nothing . . . have the most of the good things of this world for their consumption." Christian Socialism sought a day when "work will be a joy instead of the 'grind' it is at present, and to bring about the time when robbers shall be utterly abolished." Christ taught that "the rich man was in Hell simply because he allowed the contrast between rich and poor to go on as a matter of course, day after day, without taking any kind of pains to put a stop to it."[14]

Headlam's message focused on the nature of the Church. Christian Socialism relocated ecclesiastical identity away from the social establishment and toward identification with the dispossessed. For Headlam, and Christian Socialism generally, this transfer of the Church's locus enabled recovery of its apostolic integrity, embodied in sacramental forms of expression. The Church must undertake "on a large scale throughout the world those secular socialistic works which Christ did on a small scale in Palestine." It expresses this purpose in Baptism, where "every little baby born into the world [is] the equal with every other little baby." In the Holy Communion, the "very name tells you that those who partake of it are bound to live in brotherhood, in fellowship, with one another."[15] The generation of Christian Socialists which included Maurice, Ludlow, and Kingsley emphasized an innate human sense of God, an ideal of the Kingdom of God, the importance of the sacraments as marks of the Church's distinctiveness, and a concern to relate the Church to the emerging working classes. The Maurician program encouraged workers to better themselves, rather than refocus the Church or articulate a critique of economic life. Nevertheless Headlam, who graduated from Cambridge in 1868, had attended lectures on moral philosophy given by the aging Maurice and credited his example with a call to ordination.[16]

Headlam applied the Gospel to working people's lives when, from 1870 to 1873, he served as a curate at St. John's, Drury Lane, London. He visited tirelessly within the parish and eagerly conveyed the Maurician message that God sought the salvation of all. Headlam also met Thomas Wodehouse, an eccentric cleric who had written *The Grammar of Socialism*, which linked Christianity and socialism in catechetical form; and Henry George, whose *Progress and Poverty* traced social ills to rapacious landlords, whose control of land and labor afforded unnaturally high profits, which George's Single Tax proposed to turn to public benefit. Wodehouse and George convinced Headlam of the necessity for the Church to be an alternative to modernity. At Bethnal Green, where he had gone as curate in 1873, Headlam invited controversy by creating the Church and Stage Guild in 1879. He defended popular theater and ministered to the actors and dancers who provided working-class entertainment. The association scandalized ecclesiastical sensibilities and cost Headlam his curacy.[17]

Without regret Headlam never returned to a strictly parochial ministry. In 1877, at Bethnal Green, he founded the Guild of St. Matthew, which embodied what Headlam had concluded the Church's role in society should be. Coterminous with human life, the Church, as Ludlow had suggested, must change social conditions, preaching Jesus as "the founder of the great socialistic society for the promotion of righteousness, the preacher of a revolution, the denouncer of kings." Christ's rule over human hearts must sweep across social circumstances, an amalgamation dramatized by the Church's sacraments, especially the Eucharist. Therefore, it "becomes impossible for a priest, who knows what the Lord's Supper means, not to take a part to the best of his power in every work of political or social emancipation."[18] Embodying this conviction that socialism and sacramentalism should be juxtaposed, the Guild was intended to be a model for what the entire Church should become.

By the 1880s various ideals of authentic community had appeared in English social philosophy, and the Guild of St. Matthew was the first body to manifest a new ideal for the Church. The Guild made a decisive break with the reform tradition in its advocacy of George's Single Tax as the basis for a general redistribution of wealth, of giving common people a direct voice in their own government, and abolishing "false standards of worth and dignity." Images of human community and economic morality combined to produce the first Christian Socialist political platform.[19] From the mid 1880s to the mid 1890s this message had an admirable impact. Guild membership grew steadily from 100 (with 35 clergy included) in 1884 to 364 (99 of whom were clergy) by 1895. Headlam chose Frederick Verinder as administrator, and Verinder founded active branches. The Oxford chapter contacted sympathetic American Episcopalians, and the Bristol chapter helped to popularize George's tax as a Christian response to the age. Verinder became known in socialist circles and legitimated the connection between reform and Anglicanism. His credibility afforded the Guild an influence disproportionate to its membership.[20]

The Guild received attention not only for its political activities but also for its sacramental emphasis. Guild publications regularly promoted "frequent and reverent worship in the Holy Communion." Guild leaders stressed that the Communion should not be celebrated "for the select few," and the service should be "surrounded with all dignity and beauty of ritual and symbolism." This reflected Headlam's conviction that "Baptism conferred a franchise, that the Church is a real society, and that each person admitted to that society has rights and duties to perform." Elevation of "the Mass to its true position as the one, common, necessary service" freed the Church from the political shackles of its past to become the society its founder intended. Exalting Christ's Lordship, the Mass instilled in the Church a sense of "brotherhood, solidarity, cooperation."[21] This linkage of the sacraments with socialism proved to be a fertile association for Anglicanism. It offered a form of mission through its identification with poor people in industrial society or with the indigenous people of the non-Western world. As Maurice had envisioned, a heightened sense of the sacraments dramatized an Anglican image of God's Kingdom and of God's call for social justice. The rites of the Church became the fabric of religious community and formed a bond between people and the divine.

Headlam elaborated this connection no further. He appeared ill at ease with organizations and succeeded only as a provocateur. In the late 1870s he joined three radical clergy – George Sarson, Thomas Hancock, and John Elliotson Symes – in heckling speeches delivered by atheists and distributing socialist leaflets to astonished Church meetings. Headlam outdid all his contemporaries in terms of iconoclasm. He scorned Anglo-Catholics but adopted a sacramental theology. He emphasized his priesthood but derided clerical garb. He praised the Church's ideals but lampooned its leadership. With no sense of contradiction Headlam ridiculed religious skeptics and yet defended atheist Charles Bradlaugh's right to a seat in the House of Commons. But Headlam overstepped the mark in 1895 when he offered bail for Oscar Wilde, the noted writer who – as a homosexual – had been jailed on a morals charge. In Victorian society this act lost Headlam and the Guild a good deal of sympathy.[22] Nevertheless Headlam and the Guild encouraged the emergence of a distinctively socialist philosophy. Headlam became a leading figure in the Fabian Society, although he criticized the Society's drift toward Marxism. Headlam's Fabian role was an idiosyncratic one, since his feisty independence left him ill at ease with conformity to any ideology.[23] His sacramental Christianity isolated him among cultured despisers of religion. He achieved a linkage of socialism to Christianity, believing that the Church should accommodate all forms of social experience. He felt there "was no distinction between the sacred and the secular because all work for humanity was God's work, and all human experience conveyed divine truth." The sacraments emphasized the Church as a human community which challenges the state by offering a model of what it should be.[24]

The Christian Social Union
Socialist ideas moved into the mainstream thought of the Church when Charles Gore, Henry Scott Holland, and J. R. Illingworth created the Christian Social Union at Oxford. The Oxford branch of the Guild soon defected to the Union, a trend which broadened through the 1890s and which brought Headlam's ideas deeper into the Church of England. The founders of the CSU were the authors of *Lux Mundi* and the progenitors of a Liberal Catholic theology which absorbed socialist ideas and extended the conviction that the Church was a sacramental community which required distance from the social hierarchy. The Union's founders claimed "for the Christian Law the ultimate authority to rule social practice," and application of "the moral truths and principles of Christianity to the social and

economic difficulties of the present time." They intended to "present Christ in practical life as . . . the enemy of wrong and selfishness." Some Union members, such as F. Lewis Donaldson, an activist cleric, had in mind a more radical role for the group. Donaldson, who led marches for fair wages and decent working conditions, inspired a narrow strand of Anglican activists.[25] Between 1889 and 1913, sixteen of fifty-three appointments to the episcopate came to Union members. They brought into office a socialist emphasis upon Anglicanism's apostolic origins and reshaped the Church's leadership to accord with these ideals. "Only Church people sharing the same Sacramental system could awaken their fellows to the real social meaning of their baptism, their confirmation and their Holy Communion."[26]

The key theological plank of the Union's founders was the Incarnation, which became the pivotal category in late Victorian thought. It succeeded an Evangelical approach to social policy which had encouraged free-trade capitalism. Evangelical ideology carried the imprint of the atonement, i.e., that events in the social order benefited or harmed a society in response to its moral character. The newer ideology stressed the oppression of basically decent individuals by dysfunctional social circumstances. Social reform entailed not moral retribution but the recalculation of social order to free persons so that they might realize their inherent goodness.[27] Christian Socialism, the progenitor of this shift of social motifs, began with Maurice's perception that modern life had sundered the inherent continuity between humanity and nature. Incarnation implied the recovery of social wholeness by awakening a reverence for nature and a hunger for community so that human beings could cooperate with God and one another to build an organic society. The means of awakening lay in organizing the Church as the model of what creation should be.[28]

Charles Gore suggested the Liberal Catholic view of the Incarnation, and several of his colleagues in the Union popularized it as a theological theme and applied it to social questions. B. F. Westcott's incarnational theology gave Christian Socialism respectability. He depicted God's revelation as progressive, socialist, and revealed by the Church's sacraments. Westcott strove to bring the Church into sympathy with the workers' plight, just as Christ cared for persons in need. His reputation was enhanced when he helped to settle the Durham coalminers' strike in 1892.[29] A biblical theologian, Westcott dictated that spiritual truth must be found in social and material terms through the proper ordering of relationships, for which the Church presents an ideal of community. "We must then set forth afresh this sovereign truth of fellowship with the Father in Christ if we are to offer a Gospel which uses and satisfies the aspirations of our age." Through the Incarnation "we have the fellowship of sons with Him," and a model of social relations based upon equality and fellowship.[30]

The image of fellowship grounded in the Incarnation became Westcott's theme. He argued that working conditions should be organized to promote human dignity and mutuality. Thus he praised trade unions as creating among workers "a new spirit of confidence, self-respect, and of generous independence." A Christian Socialist who followed in the footsteps of Maurice and Headlam, Westcott aligned himself with workers for motives which differed significantly from their political and economic agendas. Instead Christian Socialism viewed social conditions as the embodiments of spiritual malaise, to be met with compassion grounded in an incarnational theology. This was as much an act of ecclesiastical reorganization as it was of social reform.[31]

The goal of a new Christian social emphasis brought to light a further theological category of pivotal importance in modern Anglican thought. Unity took on a mystical aspect as Anglican reformers justified their sense of the Church's social role. Acknowledging the disharmony of modernity, the Church represents the ultimate unity of God's creation and offers hope for a recovery of the unity between the divine and the human. Westcott made the connection between the Incarnation and the plight of the individual in modern life, which he took to be a search for personal fulfillment and for social fellowship. In Christ's Body "the most perfect development of the individual is combined with the social completeness of the whole."[32] Westcott's emphasis upon fellowship helped to popularize Christian Socialism.

Two other Christian Socialist thinkers applied the concept of the Incarnation more substantively to social questions. Henry Scott Holland wrote in the preface to Wilfrid Richmond's *Economic Morals* in 1890 that "it was the Incarnation . . . with which [Christian Socialists] desired to see the laws of political economy brought into contact." Holland, Canon of St. Paul's Cathedral and a contributor to *Lux Mundi*, meant thereby that the Incarnation united economic and political conditions with the reality underlying them. An advocate of government intervention to redress social ills, Holland persuaded the Christian Social Union to endorse the ideal of a Christian state. Not an affirmation of the historic religious establishment, this ideal presented the Church as the incarnation of an eternal fellowship. The Church must inspire the state to act against the woes of industrial society in favor of cooperation with God and one another. Holland's message centered upon awakening the Church to see its true nature and social task, so that it could galvanize the modern state.[33] Because of his belief that the Church must be a catalyst for social reform, Holland favored the Church's disestablishment as a means of equipping it spiritually for its social role. Holland emphasized "the primal idea of the spiritual Church, in its integrity and its purity, that we may see clearly wherein its true glory consists." The Church's social role "reveals the workings of an inner spirit." In modern society Anglicans must reach "beneath all the shell and husk" of the Church to recognize "the substance of that spiritual act by which we inhere in Christ our King." Churchmanship must reflect "the innermost motions of our being as it exercises its faith."[34]

In Holland's writings one sees a profound nostalgia for a lost world. He feared that modernity had fragmented the ties which should unite people to creation and to one another. Instead the Church gave people the hope of recovering a personal centeredness grounded in the Incarnation. Holland contrasted the city – "possessed and filled from end to end with its busy throngs, thick as ants that bustle and hurry in and through and about the living heap which is their home" – with the village, where "the peasant and the old Earth understand one another." In the country "man is co-operating with a vast system of Nature which he cannot bring under his control, or force into definite grooves. He must make his venture, and then leave it to slow, silent, unseen, incalculable processes to work out for him." Nature offered a vision of wholeness. Furthermore "it is, we know, in the labour of the country that He sees the form and fashion of this kingdom which He has come to found." The Church attunes humanity to the kingdom which germinates steadily amid the frenzy of modern life.[35]

In Holland's view, the Church recognized that a human desire for wholeness exists in misdirected form. The revival of a Catholic sense enabled the Church "to face this new social aspiration." A Catholic sensibility recognized the social struggle as the individual's fight for dignity. The Church must quicken personal conscience, awakening a consciousness of its responsibilities to society. The "true message and gift of the Church" concerns "the value of the individual life." "The idea of the Church raises the personal existence to a higher power and so evokes in it a fuller ethical temper."[36] Thus the Church served as a model of social possibility and a "house of healing." Christian Socialist thought emphasized that the correct relationship between self and society came about through the agency of "conscience." Holland's friend Wilfrid Richmond cited conscience as "the organ in the individual personality of the impulse towards collective life in the region of action." Less needed in premodern circumstances, this faculty gained authority in modern life.[37]

Richmond gave special attention to economic conditions which, he argued, had been regulated by custom and mutual obligation. In the medieval world (like Holland, his touchstone of comparison) a sense of "connectedness" pervaded society. In modern economic life that relation to one another and to nature – depicted by the "official influence of morality and religion" – and any sense of the divine will as regulating social relations had vanished. In "the showing forth of social truths, and in the working out of their practice," the church substitutes conscience, rather than law, as the best, modern expression of the divine will, the power "to see and say what is good with authority."[38] Conscience translates into a feeling of obligation in human relationships, including economic forms of exchange. "It is a revelation from within; it rises up at the first touch of common life." Conscience inspires life's governance, which springs from this basic instinct. "Deep down in the human heart itself lie the instincts that grow to be the principles of life. They are part of the lines of the original foundation. They are hidden in the structure of the seed that is to grow into a mighty tree. They cannot be imposed from without unless they can be evoked from within."[39]

This assertion offered a clear insight into the cherished assumptions of Christian Socialism. Its recovery of a sense of wholeness rested upon the reintegration of persons and societies through an awakening of the self. Furthermore, Christian Socialism envisioned an inherent level of religious authority within each person which, when correctly expressed, would reveal the unity of social relationships and the harmony of Christian faith with human experience. An innate bond existed between persons and with God of which conscience offered evidence. Conscience could be trusted as "the voice and the power of God. It is through these you see that He rules this economic world." It also "leads me to depend on others . . . I am not, I do not exist as, I cannot live as, a mere unit. I am part and parcel with this man over against me."[40] Of such mutuality, modeled in the Church, a just society could arise, valuing cooperation rather than competition.

The Union's leaders moved Liberal Catholic notions of social life toward the Church's center in Britain and beyond. An American branch of the CSU appeared, with Richard Ely as one of its key spokesmen. For Ely, the Church represented God's heavenly Kingdom, demarcated from the world by love of humanity and responsible use of material goods. "This I regard as the grand distinctive feature of Christianity, the exaltation of humanity." Christianity, Ely continued, emphasizes "a sort of oneness with people," a kind of an empathy. As Charles Kingsley understood, in industrial society the lot of individuals improves as social arrangements are reformed. The Church's religious culture suggests new social possibilities and inspires state intervention to realize them. This position became the basis for radical forms of Christian Socialism.[41]

The proliferation of the Anglican Left

In the summer of 1908, the Pan-Anglican Congress brought to London the variety of movements and cultures the Church had encompassed. Designed as a consultation on mission, the Congress offered a clear view of the Church's continuing transformation from an agency of the British state to global communion. The Congress and the Lambeth Conference of 1908, discussed socialism's meaning for Christianity with Charles Gore offering a clear sense of the relation between the two. Gore insisted that "there is nothing in the socialistic idea of the constitution of society which is antagonistic to Christianity, and that its main idea is closely allied to the Christian idea." "For Christianity is to work in all stages of social organization . . . inspiring men with the consciousness and power of divine sonship and human brotherhood." Furthermore the Gospel indicts the "present social organization" and "the official Church" with a prophetic wrath because they allow poverty and degradation. The legitimate Church upholds an ideal of "social obligation and fellowship" upon which to model reform.[42]

Gore's message was widely accepted by 1908, as new forms of Christian Socialism appeared. In 1892 Gore founded a religious order, the Community of the Resurrection, which marked the spread of religious socialism into a new religious community and gave birth to the Church Socialist League in 1906. From the beginning Christian Socialism attracted a radical fringe. The Guild of St. Matthew, for example, included W. E. Moll and H. C. Shuttleworth, two outspoken clerics. But religious radicalism was not secured in Anglican life until it acquired a model for community. The Community of the Resurrection and the League exhibited aspects of the emerging Christian Socialist character.[43]

The Community of the Resurrection nurtured ideas for Anglican reform and for social witness. Gore soon passed leadership to W. H. Frere, who led liturgical renewal and became a revered theologian of the spiritual life. Frere inspired within the tiny band a sense of community bound to a regimen of worship and work. Here the ideals propagated by the Christian Social Union found a sacramental example. The Community carried these principles into the mission field, especially South Africa, where it sustained a number of schools among indigenous people. The Community believed education and sacramental piety created the conditions for justice, and attracted talented men who popularized its convictions.[44] Paul Bull believed that the Church functions as a sacramental brotherhood which works for a society where cooperation prevails over competition. John Neville Figgis, a theologian and a literary scholar, believed the Church should recover a sense of true human society from the snares of modernity. Because of such men, the Community exercised a profound influence upon the Church.

In 1906 Paul Bull and W. H. Frere directed a conference of sixty Anglican clergy out of which the Church Socialist League appeared. Politically radical, the League emphasized the link between socialism and the sacraments in the Church. Conrad Noel, the League's key figure, intended its scope to be theologically and politically broad, and its program to be not theological publicity but social action. It hoped to attract wide support, but, as another leader, Percy Widdrington, stressed, the tenets of sacramental socialism precluded broad consensus.[45] Nevertheless the connection between sacramentalism and socialism proved fecund. Percy Dearmer, a friend of Gore and Noel, also sympathized with social activism on behalf of workers. Dearmer also became a key figure in liturgical renewal and in a new, pastoral sense of the sacramental life. Noel drifted toward a more radical style when, in 1918, he founded the Catholic Crusade. In a similar spirit Widdrington took those who remained with the League into the new League of the Kingdom of God.[46] The fragmentation of the CSL should not obscure the influence of these smaller groups upon the Church. Their ideal of religious life and a critique of industrial society left an enduring imprint upon Anglicanism.

That configuration of socialism and sacramentalism was to be found in America. James O. S. Huntington, founder of the Order of the Holy Cross, united the ideals of religious life, sacramental emphasis, and a socialist critique of capitalist society. Son of Frederick Dan Huntington, Unitarian convert to the Episcopal Church, noted preacher, and Bishop of Central New York, the younger Huntington became a priest in 1880 and began work among poor people in Syracuse, New York. Maurice's theology inspired the commitments to which he dedicated himself and encouraged his sense that the human family hungered for Christ's redemptive love. Huntington concluded that the Church could recover its true nature through the witness of the religious life.[47] An advocate of George's Single Tax and of labor organization, Huntington founded the Church Association for the Advancement of the Interests of Labor (CAIL). Its organization emerged as a result of the work of William Dwight Porter Bliss, who pushed the group toward mediation in labor conflict. Bliss, steeped in Maurice's theology, brought social concerns to the attention of the Church's mainstream. Although his vision was a revolutionary one, his means were gradualist and practical. He founded a mission church, the Church of the Carpenter, in 1890 in Boston, which he hoped would express what the entire Church, and the society, should be.[48]

Although the Church of the Carpenter declined, Bliss remained convinced that Christian Socialism expressed an earthly image of God's Kingdom, where "there shall be the highest individuality for every member realized in the most highly developed social organism."[49] That ideal persisted in the work of Vida Dutton Scudder, who, in 1917, called "the social awakening of the churches" the "great fact" of modern life. Official Church groups had adopted "advanced positions . . . concerning social justice." "Concrete and stinging must be the application of Christian ideals made by the Church to modern civilization and modern Christian lives."[50]

The progress of the Episcopal Church illustrated this trend. Although the Church was popularly considered to be the church of the wealthy, the Church's General Convention in 1916 created a Social Service Commission upon which diocesan groups were modeled. In 1913 and 1916 the General Convention affirmed that "the Church stands for the ideal of social justice and that it demands the achievement of a social order in which the social cause of poverty ... shall be eliminated." The Church now called every communicant to a social ministry in "warm sympathy with the class struggle," for "the struggle for freedom is righteous and religious, whether it be found in striking miner or in outraged nation, and Christian hearts must recognize in it the motions of the Lord and Giver of Life."[51] The Church "knows that the world is wrong" and views humanity as capable of rising to "disinterested social action." Even more, the Church "must not only call to action, she must show the way to it." The Church teaches individuals a new attitude toward the world which entails the hope of a new form of common life. "The day is to the common life, the common effort. What we are not able to do as individuals, we may do all together, or through group-action." "Social action becomes the swift correlative of spiritual," and, for Scudder, the Church's common life stimulated a new ideal for society.[52]

Scudder interwove the various threads of Christian Socialism into a seamless garment. She prized the individual conscience, and absorbed Maurice's sacramental representation of the Kingdom of God. Fabian ideals merged with the Tractarian theology she had encountered when she studied at Oxford in the early 1880s. She felt the alienation of being a woman, and an American who had lived outside the country. But Christian Socialism taught her that human beings "can only be satisfied by a vision of the whole." In its modern struggles the Church is freed from privilege, and through socialism it recovers its true nature as the community of Christ's followers.[53]

THE CHURCH AS AN ALTERNATIVE CULTURE

The need for distinctiveness

"There is a heaven and an earth in every man; first in his nature, then in his experience," Phillips Brooks postulated, "and it is on the cordial working together of these two parts of his life that the healthiness and completeness of any man's existence depends." Representing truth and righteousness, one dimension "springs out of the earth," and the other "must look down from heaven." Life languishes until these two worlds "work in harmony with one another, to make the perfect man."[54] Compassion for the poor reveals life's unity in Christ, who appears through "the common motive or purpose out of which an infinite diversity of many actions may proceed." "He who insists on looking through the material to the spiritual" finds personal harmony.[55]

Brooks articulated the Liberal Catholic principles spreading throughout the Church. Rector of Trinity Church, Boston, though his last months were spent as Bishop of Massachusetts, Brooks gained fame as a preacher whose ministry exemplified an important aspect of modern Anglican life. The parish became the point where the Church's distinctiveness and its social concern merged. As social changes eroded any facile identification of the Church with its environment, many Anglicans looked to the parish in the hope of creating a distinctively religious ethos. Thus, Frederick Dan Huntington noted that "the social constitution of man, and the revelation in Christ, are the two correlated, complemented forces, which bear forward the progress of the world."[56] He believed the Church must implant "the great truths of Christianity" in "the actual forms" of society. For "it is through men's social relations and affections, that Christ, the Head of the race, proposes to construct his spiritual empire, his church."[57] This sense of human cooperation with divine intention evoked a sense of the parish as the meeting point of heaven and earth.

In April, 1876, the great American financier John Jacob Astor proposed to the vestry of Trinity Church, New York, that he donate a new reredos both as a memorial to his father, William B. Astor, and as an offering to the glory of God.[58] The conjuncture of material and spiritual captured the Anglican outlook of the period. The parish demarcated a religious sphere, conversant with, but separate from, the corridors of power. Under Morgan Dix, Rector from 1862 to 1908, Trinity became a model of parish reform. Pew rental had been an American means of fundraising which elevated a financial elite in many parishes. By the late 1880s Dix had ended pew rental at Trinity and its affiliated chapels. As a result, "William Waldorf Astor, a vestryman, was seen standing at the rear of the Church and sharing his hymnal with a colored man who stood beside him."[59] Dix expanded the schools sponsored by the parish and initiated extensive new forms of mission. Trinity supported the work of Bishop William Hobart Hare among Dakota territory Indians in the 1870s. Phillips Brooks' parish financed an astonishing variety of charities, schools, mission agencies, and relief projects, signs of a determination to engage the world's concerns as the Church rather than as the embodiment of social order.

The new assertiveness apparent in many parishes resulted from drastically changed circumstances. During the nineteenth century the old English model of the parish as the embodiment of local life broke apart. English reforms of clerical nonresidence, building programs, and the rise of Sunday schools could not alter the basic social realities. While English parish life faced adjustment to an industrial order, outside England the parish system was impossible to replicate, and alternative parish forms resulted.[60] Parish life benefited from the nineteenth-century religious revival. In the United States, Episcopal churches often benefited from the evangelical Protestant consensus. In 1858, when religious awakening swept the eastern United States, Low Church Episcopalians "welcomed the awakening with more abandon" than many other Protestant clergy, and the Episcopal Church gained numerous converts, Frederick Dan Huntington being one of the most prominent. These converts enhanced the Church's sense of being a religious community.[61]

The church architecture of the period revealed the search that went on for ways to demarcate the religious life. In the seventeenth and eighteenth centuries a neoclassical style in England and America linked church design to the general style of public buildings. But in the nineteenth century a Gothic revival, advanced by the Cambridge Camden Society, appeared. Architect Richard Upjohn encouraged the American revival, and Bishop John Henry Hopkins popularized it.[62] Gothic forms idealized the Middle Ages as a religious environment and encouraged the Episcopal form of worship to veer toward heightened ceremonial. At the beginning of the nineteenth century Episcopalians followed an informal, Protestant expression of the Book of Common Prayer. Many churches used only a small table, not an elaborate altar, and Communion would not be celebrated weekly or even monthly. There was no procession of clergy and choir before or after worship. Choirs never wore vestments, and gathered in a church gallery from which they sang. Clergy entered the church with an equal lack of ceremony, sometimes chatting with parishioners as they did so. There were no acolytes, no processional crosses, and no altar candles. Vestments consisted of a surplice, worn without stole, and an academic gown worn for preaching. Communion was celebrated from the north end of the altar so that the minister would not be turned away from the congregation in the Roman fashion.[63] Baptisms were often performed in homes, and Confirmation was administered irregularly.

The style of Anglican worship was changing profoundly though not uniformly. Evangelicals emphasized preaching, while the Broad Church and Anglo-Catholic parties responded to Tractarian priorities. In general, however, heightened formality accompanied an emphasis upon teaching the intention of the Church's rites. Baptism acquired new importance as the rite of entrance into the Church, and preparation of parents and godparents intensified. Emphasis on the bishop's sacramental role raised the importance of Confirmation. New stress on the duties of the clergy in conducting worship paralleled emphasis upon clerical professionalism.[64] For clergy of the eighteenth-century Church of England there was little sense of being distinct from local gentry, as they assumed a variety of public duties, such as magistrate or public health officer. Clergy hunted and fished, farmed and raced horses, rented land to poor tenants and socialized with the squirearchy. Though many clergy frowned on excessive social indulgence, a genial sense of blending with society prevailed.[65]

"The congruity of the clergyman's role with traditional society made it particularly vulnerable to the changes which industrialization and urbanization brought to society." Furthermore the Evangelical and Tractarian movements encouraged higher standards of clergy performance. Evangelicals insisted upon the spiritual nature of the ministry and encouraged weekly celebrations of the Holy Communion and regular parish visitation. Tractarians saw "the need for the Church to establish its autonomy and to underline its distinctive nature and values," an emphasis upon teaching and pastoral duties. These parties pressured the clergy to relinquish their civic functions for religious tasks. Ironically this was the religious equivalent of the professionalization which affected medicine and law, teaching and engineering. Standards for entry into the trade tightened, and societies appeared to guard norms of performance.[66] For clergy the tasks of preaching and worship leadership gained significance. Mission and social relief required that clergy assume administrative chores to ensure adequate institutional performance, and counseling became an important duty as clergy became spiritual guides amid the crises of modern, secular life.

A bishop such as Samuel Wilberforce enhanced the office's stature, for he was less inclined to dwell on his perquisites than to fret over his duties. He spent large amounts of time visiting parishes, directing clergy, or leading retreats for ordinands. Wilberforce impressed upon his clergy the importance of their piety and care for their parishes. His candidates for ordination faced grueling examinations and extensive scrutiny of their backgrounds. He encouraged the formation of theological schools because he considered attendance at Oxford or Cambridge to be insufficient preparation for ordination, which required a separate environment.[67] A similar attention to clerical training and performance appeared in the United States. Episcopalians founded a number of theological seminaries, two of the earliest being the General Seminary in New York City and the Virginia Seminary in Alexandria. In his lectures at Virginia, Bishop William Meade depicted the ministry as being set apart from the world in order to serve it. He prized "personal holiness," rather than learning or zeal, which entailed willingness to follow the examples of great figures such as "the pious Cotton Mather," and being "experimentally acquainted" with divine wisdom and human frailty. Preaching was stressed as the compelling means of presenting God's truth.[68]

Experiments in religious community

The search for models

The attempt to demarcate the Church from the society manifested new forms of religious community. William Augustus Muhlenberg, an American, exemplified this sense of community in various parish reforms. Muhlenberg pioneered in vesting choirs, having a procession, and bringing parish music to the fore. Author of the Muhlenberg Memorial, an early ecumenical statement, Muhlenberg had, in 1827, founded a boys' school at Flushing, New York and later – in Manhattan – initiated a mission to prostitutes and a hospital. These innovations derived from an incarnational theology. "The coming of our Lord in the flesh creates a new relation in the human family. In Him men are bound together by an original tie, arising out of their union with Him." Thus the Church must be a society "whose bond of unity is in Christ, whose relationships of person to person are most commonly represented in the New Testament as those of brotherhood."[69] Muhlenberg was one of the first Anglicans, alongside Pusey and Neale, to sense the need for new communal forms to express this incarnational faith. As a result, Anne Ayres became the first sister of the Holy Communion in 1845, a religious order Muhlenberg began for hospital work. He retained personal direction over the sisters' hospital duties and organized communal living and regular occasions of prayer. Muhlenberg, who later envisioned a rural community, "St. Johnland," on Long Island, pioneered the communal impulse, linking the religious life to forms of charity, and encouraging women to play an important role. However, his communities lacked a coherent organization and a clear sense of the role of worship.

James Lloyd Breck envisioned expansion of the Church in Minnesota by means of mission communities to attract Indian converts. While a student at New York's General Seminary, Breck worshiped at Muhlenberg's Church of the Holy Communion, where he absorbed the ideal of religious community as the basis of mission, and that model persisted. When George Worthington became Bishop of Nebraska in 1885, he created "associate missions." Worthington brought together a group of recent General Seminary graduates into a residential community, intending them to become a model for Church life and a source of clergy for mission churches. The associate mission in Omaha from 1891 to 1902 developed an elaborate pattern of daily work, prayer, and study. The mission role of the community diminished as its own spiritual life grew rigorous and the group finally disbanded.[70] New forms of community included efforts to blend spirituality and social reform. In Britain, Toynbee Hall (a settlement house) reflected the ideals of Thomas Arnold and T. H. Green in its pursuit of a harmonious, class-free society. Toynbee Hall blended Christian Socialist and Fabian ideals in its effort to make sense of East London realities. Canon Samuel Barnett, the founder, could be heartless to the poor, but inspiring in his holiness. The result was an oasis of middle-class spirituality removed from the desperation around it.[71]

Tractarian influence inspired Bishop Levi Silliman Ives of North Carolina to create Valle Crucis in 1844, a mission center, seminary, and monastery. When the Bishop became a Roman Catholic, the community declined. However, its observances of private confession, reserved sacrament, and prayers to the Virgin and the saints found other outlets. Several new sisterhoods followed Muhlenberg's Sisterhood of the Holy Communion. In 1865 Harriet Starr Cannon led the creation of the Community of St. Mary. The Sisterhood of St. Margaret (1873), the Community of St. John Baptist (1881), and the Sisterhood of the Holy Nativity (1882) followed. Men's orders included the Community of the Resurrection and the Order of the

Holy Cross. The Cowley Fathers, or the Society of St. John the Evangelist, became an important, transatlantic order. In 1866 an American priest, Charles Grafton, joined two English clergy, Richard Meux Benson and Simeon Wilberforce O'Neill, in the religious life, adopting a simple habit and daily recitation of the choir office. Their mission of spiritual leadership found a center at Boston's Church of the Advent, where Grafton had been confirmed. Benson understood the basis of religious community as a search for corporate participation in the divine. "The authenticity of the Christian revelation . . . lies in its vision of a God whose personality is inherently social."[72] The Church's mission is distinguished by its search for the realization of human nature.

The accommodation of separateness

Women The Church's effort to become an ideal community stumbled on the limits of social equality. As Anglicans expanded their work among women, American Indians, and blacks, problems ensued because evangelism entailed white, male control of those who were incorporated. The Church accommodated by creating separate enclaves, not by transcending social barriers for the sake of religious community. By the late nineteenth century, for instance, the roles available to women in the Church expanded beyond traditionally limited ones. Under the influence of the missionary, Tractarian, and social Gospel movements the place of women in the Anglican communion changed. In addition to the growth of religious orders for women, the Episcopal Church hired women workers. The Church's Freedmen's Commission, which worked among the former slaves after the Civil War, needed teachers. With little training, often raising funds themselves to support the work, women went south and persevered in austere circumstances. The Church's work among black people grew impressively and a number of black clergy were groomed. Black parishes, schools, and colleges (such as St. Paul's College in Lawrenceville, Virginia and St. Augustine's College in Raleigh, North Carolina) evolved from women's initiatives.[73] Women teachers and child-care workers appeared in the foreign mission field from about 1870 and surmounted hardships to make notable contributions. Nellie G. Eddy, one of the first Episcopal women in Japan, noted that "a woman missionary should be more or less a prodigy in all things." Missions offered women the opportunity to assume leadership roles in ecclesiastical life.

By the early twentieth century the typical Episcopal parish

included more women staff members than men. Women served as organists, schoolteachers, secretaries, and outreach workers. The General Convention of 1889 created the order of deaconesses to serve as teachers and social workers affiliated with a parish rather than with a religious order, thus imparting the example of the sisterhood into parish life. The idea of distinctively women's ministry further developed with the King's Daughters, Young Married Women's Society, and, especially, the Women's Auxiliary. In the Church of England, the Mothers' Union, founded in 1887, enhanced a sense of women's fellowship and of religious vocation.[74] Women achieved a high level of organization at the national level in 1871 as the Women's Auxiliary to the Episcopal Church's Board of Missions appeared. Mary Abbot Emery, followed by her sister Julia Chester Emery, successively served as the national secretary from 1872 to 1916. They envisioned an organization to coordinate Episcopal women's work, planned a network of parish and diocesan groups, and publicized the variety of duties undertaken by women in the mission field.[75]

In the Church of England more women than men regularly attended church services. A committee appointed by the Archibishop of Canterbury in 1919 found that women pioneered much of the expansion of the Church's ministries through voluntary work. Nevertheless the Church of England rejected the expansion of women's work as a violation of biblically codified subordination. From all quarters of the Church's male leadership, even many Christian Socialist ones, came endorsements for the subordination of women.[76] Yet English women moved toward new responsibilities, as effective leadership emerged in the persons of Maude Royden and Louise Creighton. An advocate of women's suffrage, Royden became a lay preacher and an "advocate of speaking out on sex." Louise Creighton, wife of Bishop Mandell Creighton, worked within Church channels to expand women's opportunities. She addressed the Pan-Anglican Congress as well as missionary meetings, and served on various Church committees. Each woman, in her own way, reflected the movement to grant women equality in the Church, which was gaining momentum.[77] As the Church assumed its own governance, many women argued, they should receive increased leadership roles. In 1898, a petition signed by 1,100 Church women demanded the Canterbury Convocation permit the election of women to parish councils. The all-male Convocation defeated the measure, banning women from parish councils officially until 1914, although the ban was ignored in some localities.[78]

Church women campaigned for parliamentary suffrage through

the Church League for Women's Suffrage. They received support from clergy, notably William Temple; however, women failed to assume pastoral or liturgical duties. Opponents of women speaking in church or ministering in any fashion sensed a trend which might lead to the ordination of women. A report in 1919 to the Canterbury Convocation agreed that the ordination of women would violate Catholic custom, but urged that limited speaking and praying roles be expanded to include special worship services for children and women. Thus, the Church sought ways to accommodate women.[79]

American Indians The Church also attempted to absorb American Indians to its framework without modifying any of its cultural presumptions. Since the colonial era only occasional Anglican work among Indians in North America had occurred. Episcopalians maintained only one Indian mission until 1852, when work began in northern Minnesota and, in 1859, Henry Whipple became the first Bishop of Minnesota. During Whipple's tenure of forty-two years a new awareness about Indian life emerged.[80] Following Whipple and the episcopate of William Hobart Hare in the Dakotas from 1873 to 1901, the Church's mission to American Indians grew in the Midwest. Whipple ordained Enmegahbowh, an Ottawa Indian who was converted by Breck and ordained deacon by Jackson Kemper, in 1867 as the first Indian priest and sent Samuel Hinman to begin a ministry among the Santee Sioux, who had attacked white settlers in 1862. Hinman was notorious among whites as an apologist for the Indians. Yet, on one visit, Whipple confirmed a hundred Santee whom Hinman converted.

The Church gained the reputation of being an advocate for Indians. Whipple brought to the Church's House of Bishops an awareness of the destructive effects of white expansion. The Church's response included establishing the missionary jurisdiction of Niobrara in 1872 and, in the same year, creating a Standing Committee for Indians' Affairs, whose first chair, William Welsh, represented a wealthy Philadelphia family which would later establish the Indian Rights Association. Whipple single-handedly awakened Episcopal consciences to a new form of advocacy.[81] The Church also benefited in 1872 when President Ulysses S. Grant announced a "peace plan," placing particular denominations in charge of mission work among certain tribes. The plan gave Episcopalians jurisdiction in the Dakota territory with some duties among the Shoshone-Bannock in Wyoming and the Ponca in Nebraska. Between 1871 and 1882 the Church sent eighty new Indian missionaries, and ordained twenty Indian deacons and two priests. Bishop William Hobart Hare, an advocate of Indian rights, opposed General George Custer's expedition in 1874 in search of gold as white encroachment on Indian soil. Hare founded schools which produced future Indian leaders and groomed young Indian men for ordination.[82]

The Church took root among American Indians because of its advocacy of their rights and because the Church's Prayer Book struck a chord with Indian ceremonial, especially its strictures about the observance of feast days and its rites of passage. The Church encouraged respect for Indian community as white settlers assaulted it and translated the Bible and the Prayer Book into Indian tongues. The Church's image as an advocate of Indian rights seemed confirmed in the early twentieth century by the work of Hudson Stuck, the great Alaskan missionary. Stuck gained national attention through books and articles defending Alaska's Indian cultures. It is possible to describe the Church's Indian ministry as a defense of their cultural prerogatives.[83] Nevertheless cultural barriers restricted the Church's adaptation to Indian life. Even Bishop Whipple assumed that "for an Indian to be a Christian he must cut his hair, wear shoes, get behind a plow and wholly subscribe to the white man's tenets regarding private property." Indian converts must renounce what the Church viewed as "pagan spirituality," those features of traditional religion deemed offensive to Christian belief. Hare, for example, denounced the Ghost Dance, a messianic movement incorporating Christian eschatology and promising the departure of whites from Indian land.

As early as 1870 the Church in the Niobrara Convocation, the earliest Dakota jurisdiction, passed resolutions which condemned the Indian custom of regarding the daughter as belonging to her mother even after marriage. Instead the Church presented the husband's authority as absolute according to biblical tenets. More to the point, the Convocation resolved that "it is evidently impossible for the Indian Tribes to live any longer as Indians," and, "if they can be saved, it must be by learning the ways and religion of the whites."[84] The leadership of the Church remained white, and the Church's message promoted cultural upheaval as much as religious change. Not until 1971 would an Indian bishop be consecrated – Harold S.

Jones as suffragan of South Dakota. The American Church found a way to incorporate Indians while preserving white prerogatives. Among unfamiliar cultures, the Church tended to reinforce Western values and to create separate cultural enclaves.

American blacks The experience of the American Civil War awakened the Church's ministry among black people. In 1862 the bishops of the Church in the Confederacy acknowledged a sense of duty because many of the Church's members were slave-owners. In 1860 a Virginia diocesan committee reported the need for "instruction of the colored population" and affirmed that the Church's worship was "admirably adapted to such persons." One Southern bishop, Leonidas Polk of Louisiana, owned four hundred slaves and undertook extensive evangelism among them.[85] In the old South, the Church abetted the slave system, an arrangement which appeared doomed after the Civil War. The General Convention of 1865 created the Freedmen's Commission and initiated extensive work among the former slaves. A new era dawned in one Southern church as black people became communicants alongside white. "They were not required to wait, but came to the altar with whites, kneeling side by side with our best citizens." In Virginia, in 1890, Bishop Francis Whittle stated that "our colored brethren" "ought to have some voice in the legislation which affects them, and some means by which the influence of their laity may be felt among them."[86]

Leading voices in the Church expressed fears for the state of black life. "Every intelligent person, be he white or colored, must see how very degraded a large portion of our colored brethren is becoming, especially since they have gotten to flock so to themselves in our cities and towns, and have put themselves out of contact with the refining influences of the better class of white people," a white layman reported at Virginia's Council in 1901. In 1911, one Church magazine reported that "city Negroes" faced racial hatred and economic exploitation. Many Episcopalians realized that changing social circumstance brought new forms of degradation.[87]

The Church fostered limited forms of black self-government. In 1879, the *Spirit of Missions*, the Church's monthly magazine, reported that the ministers of a black congregation in Brunswick County, Virginia, had joined the Church. One convert, James S. Russell, became one of the Church's pioneering black clergy. In Georgia, in

1903, a white archdeacon explained this effort to absorb black congregations and ordain black clergy. The Church "puts colored clergymen in charge of parishes and missions and gives them a close white supervision. As organization and as individuals, their relations are the same to their Bishop and their Archdeacon as that of their white neighbors." Thus "every provision is made to give the colored people all the information and education possessed by the whites . . . and they receive it through the only channels they will permanently recognize, the better informed members of their own race."[88] Alert Church leaders realized black Episcopalians should control their own ministries. In June, 1910, one observer wrote that the "Church experiences . . . both the strength and the weakness of the Anglo-Saxon ideal of responsibility for self-government and of the catholic or democratic ideal." "There is a widespread feeling among the Negroes that the Church offers them no opportunity for the exercise of responsibility in self-government." The Church's convocations "offer some opportunity for initiative and leadership," while white control of the Church remained intact. Thus "the system in general keeps the Negro religious life . . . in intimate relation with the religious life of the white people."[89]

The white sensibility appeared clearly in 1902 when Bishop C. K. Nelson of Georgia praised an ecumenical congress of young black people which met in Atlanta. "Neither socialism, anarchy nor race antagonism received encouragement. Following the teachings enunciated at this congress, every man's life, property and honor are safe. Social intrusion is impossible, and a race of law abiding, self-respecting, industrious, happy and successful citizens would be evolved by the application of the superior forces of morality, thrift, judgment and perseverance."[90] In other words, the Church encouraged black emulation for white priorities, while barring blacks from assuming all the privileges of Church life. In South Carolina in 1875 the diocesan convention denied seats to delegates from a black parish, because, as one white priest declared, "convention possesses the right of excluding from this body all such delegates . . . as it shall hereafter regard likely to interrupt the peace of the Church." In the 1880s when white laity tried to prevent the admission of black clergy, most white clergy balked, and two black priests were seated, causing laity from twenty parishes to boycott diocesan proceedings. A commentator denied that the "object and effect of the seating of a colored presbyter in Convention is and will be social equality," for the real issue, he felt, was clergy privilege.[91] Though the Church resisted the implications of its mission, cultural diversity forced reconsideration of the nature of modern Anglican identity.

Ritualism

The emergence of a party

The Anglo-Catholic movement was inspired by Pusey, who sensed that industrial society needed Catholic worship to instil in it a redemptive sense of community through a dramatic sense of the divine. A conviction which proved momentous for Anglican identity, this insight became the basis of Puseyite parishes created by loyal disciples across England from the 1850s on. From the start Anglo-Catholicism, or Puseyism, identified a theological and liturgical subculture whose development is a modern Anglican saga. St. Saviour's in Leeds (founded by Pusey himself in 1839) exemplified the development of this network of parishes. Initially encouraged by W. F. Hook, St. Saviour's intended to combine urban ministry with sound Church principles. Tension grew in the parish in 1845 when its clergy began observance of monastic hours, starting with Prime at 7 a.m. and ending with Compline at 10 p.m. In 1846 an assistant who declared that departed saints pray for the living received suspension from the bishop in reply. In 1848 the choir began to wear robes and the Sunday Eucharist became adorned with altar frontals, chalice veils, and colored stoles. Hymnody grew in popularity and processional lights and acolytes appeared. Ominous rumors of Romish conspiracies spread beyond the parish as a few parishioners crossed over to Rome. In reality modestly Anglo-Catholic, the parish seemed a center of sedition.[92]

Anglo-Catholicism grew as urban ministry melded with liturgical expression. "Slum priests" such as A. H. Mackonochie, Charles Lowder, and George Rundle Prynne created a Catholic image of community in their parishes during the 1850s. In 1855 Lowder led the formation of the Society of the Holy Cross, an order which influenced Benson, Grafton, and Liddon among others. Lowder wanted to introduce the model of St. Vincent de Paul from seventeenth-century France and proposed to inspire clerical spirituality, defend the Church's faith, and carry on its mission. Lowder idealized the Church as a community, and established a monastic regimen with Mackonochie in 1857. Ministry to the surrounding area entailed correct practices if the parish was to be genuinely Christian.[93] The idea of an Anglican expression of Catholicism led to ritualism in the late 1850s as slum priests risked confrontation with Church authorities for the sake of maintaining what they regarded as a correct order. It took a decision by the Judicial Committee of the Privy Council and an admonition by Bishop Tait of London to keep Robert Liddell from using a stone altar cross or a cross attached to the reredos. Liddell also complied with orders to remove candles from his altar. In 1858, when Tait ordered Edward Stuart to cease usage of lit altar candles "except when they may reasonably be considered necessary or convenient for purpose of light," Stuart declined, arguing that liturgical candles had been used during the reign of Edward VI and were therefore legitimated by history.[94]

For the sake of Church identity, ritualists cited the authority of conscience and urged the Church hierarchy to endorse their views. Tait expressed sympathy with their position in 1868 when he addressed the Canterbury Convocation. "I desire that my own conscience shall be respected, and I desire also that the consciences of others shall be respected, and whether in matters of doctrine, or in allowable matters of practice, I think that within due limits in the National Church we ought, as completely as we possibly can, to act upon that principle."[95] Tait took a middle ground which doubted that ritualism was a conspiracy to demolish the Church. However, public fear abounded and, in 1859, at St. George's Church in east London, riots broke out as Lowder and his colleagues advanced the parish's ritual. Such disorder seemed tame in comparison to the furor that broke upon the Church.

Tait (who in 1869 became Archbishop of Canterbury) worried over the ritualist tendency to ignore a bishop's counsel and defended the religious establishment. He thus joined with Evangelicals in endorsing a Bill for the Regulation of Public Worship in 1874. The bill established English diocesan tribunals to work in concert with the local bishop to investigate complaints of irregular ritual and included appointment of a lay judge to rule in matters of questionable ritual. The right of appeal to the Archbishop could be invoked, and this clause won approval for the bill in ecclesiastical circles. Tait had been disturbed by reports that some clergy muttered prayers to the Virgin Mary and the Twelve Apostles at the celebration of Communion, a Roman practice. He upheld episcopal authority as the basis of

Anglican collegiality and affirmed the bill as an extension of Anglican principles.[96]

Despite considerable revision of the bill, it proved difficult to specify where inappropriate ritual began. In many quarters, an obvious discomfort appeared over this parliamentary intrusion into worship. Gladstone violently attacked the bill as an assault on the Church's diversity. Anti-Roman, Erastian figures finally prevailed, although some of them felt the bill did not go far enough.[97] The Act proved momentous in several respects. Disraeli's Conservative government seriously underestimated the political strength of the ritualists. Passage of the measure drove ritualists and their political sympathizers away from Conservatives and Liberals, who now seemed tepid, toward the Labour and socialist coteries. Public condemnation cemented ritualism's affinity for the political left and confirmed its sense that the true Church must be critical of inherited political authority. Headlam's connection of socialism with ritualism gained adherents after passage of the ritual bill.[98]

The Act to regulate public worship cited criteria for normative Anglican worship in the rubrics of the Prayer Book and the authority of bishops and archdeacons. It added procedural means to adjudicate allegations of excessive ritual, though the meanings of violations remained vague. Nevertheless, in an environment where fears of Rome and of disestablishment fueled desperate measures, the Act did elicit instances of prosecution. Soon proceedings began against C. J. Risdale of Folkestone for using wafers at Communion, wearing Catholic vestments, facing eastward to celebrate Communion, and adorning the church with candles and a crucifix. The Privy Council ruled that these practices were unacceptable in the English Church, with only surplice, scarf, and hood as Anglican vesture. The decision evoked expressions of support for Risdale, but he lost heart and threw himself on the mercy of Archbishop Tait.[99]

The Rev. Arthur Tooth proved intransigent. Failing to appear for court proceedings against him, Tooth received a citation for contempt of court and was jailed for twenty-eight days. The incident resulted in a public relations coup for the ritualists and a headache for Tait. Tooth argued that court action failed to express the Church's mind and Tait remonstrated that Tooth opened himself to prosecution because he failed to grant his bishop's authority. Tooth's lawyers, appointed by the Anglo-Catholic English Church Union, proved that action against him had been illegal for being conducted south of the

Thames, outside the appropriate jurisidictions. By late 1877 Tooth seemed to have been vindicated.[100] Other ritualists were imprisoned for contempt of court, notably Sidney F. Green in 1881. However, the Victorian *cause célèbre* concerned Bishop Edward King of Lincoln. King entered the episcopate in 1885 convinced "that he could do nothing better than hand on the teaching of the Tractarians." He viewed the Church as a spiritual organism, believed in Christ's real presence in the Eucharist, and taught that priesthood entailed sanctity and sacrifice. King offered a rallying point for ritualist hopes and a target for antiritualist aggression.[101]

King's trial came about as a result of his manner of celebrating the Eucharist at one of his parishes in 1887. The trial began early in 1890 under the personal jurisdiction of Archbishop Edward Benson, who sympathized with a man generally viewed as pastoral and gentle. King stuck to his guns, intent on vindicating the Catholic nature of Anglicanism, and his position triumphed in the court of public opinion. Benson condemned the mixture of wine and water in the chalice during the Eucharist and the sign of the cross at absolution and blessing, but condoned the eastward position and ritual ablutions, allowing standards of permissible ritual to change.[102] Ritualists defended Catholic order on the basis of the authority of conscience and the technique of appealing to popular sentiment. Intent on retrieving the practices of the past, Anglo-Catholicism was a modern construct.

The Fond du Lac Circus

A similar situation developed within the Episcopal Church as ritualism gained a following. The chief American ritualist, James DeKoven, upheld the sacraments as efficacious links between the earthly kingdom and God's eternal verities. He argued that American society yearned for apostolic Christianity grounded in "care for sick, and poor, and desolate, and wounded, and dying." DeKoven believed the true national Church should be demarcated from society by the sacrament of the altar.[103] In America a network of clergy and parishes developed as DeKoven's theology gained adherents. In major cities one or two Anglo-Catholic parishes formed, while in the upper Midwest the movement engulfed entire dioceses. American ritualists found common ground in ceremonial, which they viewed as Anglicanism's safeguard. Their hopes leaped when John Henry Hopkins, Presiding Bishop and one-time anti-Tractarian, endorsed ritual in his *The Law of Ritualism* in 1866.[104] As was the case in

England, ritualism generated feverish efforts to root it out by the Church's General Convention. DeKoven, a deputy to the Convention, defended a eucharistic theology of Christ's real presence, which was the key issue in the American debate. In 1874, the same year as England's Public Worship Act, the issue dominated the Convention's agenda. Lay deputies, irritated at what they saw as High Church aggression, passed a canon which condemned any actions at the altar that implied adoration of the bread and wine. As a result, one Philadelphia priest was admonished for excessive ritual, but ritualism persisted.[105]

Anglo-Catholicism intended to redefine the worship of the Episcopal Church. The consecration of Reginald Heber Weller as Bishop Coadjutor of Fond du Lac in 1900 pointed to the confidence of the movement. Weller was consecrated by ten bishops, among whom were one Polish Catholic and one Russian Orthodox, wearing elaborate copes and miters. Dubbed the "Fond du Lac Circus" by the press, the event resulted from the influence of Weller's predecessor, Charles Grafton, one of the great American ritualists. Several bishops were forced to defend their participation, and the Reformed Episcopal Church, a tiny schismatic group led by Bishop George David Cummins, broke with the Church in 1873 because Roman ritual seemed ascendant. Cummins accurately sensed that a large segment of the Church was elaborating its liturgy, symbolizing a new ideal of the Church as a community. Ritual could accommodate cultural diversity, a task which foreign mission made acute. There the Church met with further intimations of modernity.[106]

THE RESPONSE TO NON-WESTERN CULTURE

Transplanting the Church

Henry Venn

The influence of ritualism in the Church was evidence of a tension within Anglicanism between an assertion of the Church's distinctiveness from society and a desire to retain an historic social base. Although the Church absorbed diverse cultures in the mission field, a few Anglicans showed how the Church could retain its identity while adapting itself to non-Western culture. At first the goal of foreign mission seemed simply to work for the salvation of "the heathen," but the creation of Church structures gave rise to bewildering cultural issues. Should the Church retain Western form or find an indigenous mode? When Henry Venn became Secretary of the Church Missionary Society in 1841, he recognized that the nature of the Church as a religious community raised pressing questions about its traditions and its Western control. The integrity of the mission Church had to be reconciled with its missionary enterprise, and Venn offered an important ideal. Venn's grandfather was one of the leading spiritual writers of the eighteenth-century Evangelical awakening, and his father had been parish priest at Clapham. By 1841 a new concern for the Church appeared among Evangelicals, and Henry Venn carried this awareness into the design of mission. He never personally traveled to the mission field; but, in response to the reports crossing his London desk, Venn devised the goal of the self-supporting Church.

Self-support "The ultimate object of a Mission," Venn wrote, must be "the settlement of a Native Church under Native Pastors upon a self-supporting system," which "depends upon the training up and location of Native Pastors." Converts "should be habituated to the idea that the support of a Native Ministry must eventually fall upon themselves." Mission advances when the "Native Church" grooms its own pastors to work with European missionaries. Venn intended this cooperation to foreshadow a transition from a European toward an indigenous Church.[107] The essence of Christian mission lay in sharing an experience of the Spirit, Venn observed. He found that Acts said little concerning ecclesiastical order, and he concluded that time and place could modify the Church's form.[108] However, he also demonstrated a characteristically English tendency in his respect for the religious establishment and in his concern to maintain continuity with Western forms of worship and Church order. Venn believed that the missionary goal of transferring the Church blended indigenous forms with Western experience.

The Church's adaptation to indigenous culture required oversight. Missionaries must explore the social framework for common points with Christian beliefs and take redemptive roles in social struggles. However, they were expected to resist some local practices, such as polygamy, which seemed unambiguously idolatrous. Venn implied that mission involved a process of sifting between what could be accepted or should be rejected from a particular culture. Finally, Venn believed, the indigenous Church should aspire to being a "national institution," molding the life of a particular people into a modern, Christian nation.[109] Venn recognized that European control could not be perpetuated and pondered the means of disengagement. He fretted that missionaries might become immersed in administrative duties rather than living as a transitional figure until the new Church could sustain itself.

Samuel Crowther In 1860 in Sierra Leone, the CMS's initial outpost, local clergy formed the "Native Pastorate Organization," a transitional entity which resulted in the parish structure of a Sierra Leone Church. Further progress was hampered because the CMS retained control of four parishes until 1877 and English bishops supervised the Church until the mid twentieth century. In fact, no Sierra Leonean became bishop until T. S. Johnson became assistant bishop in 1937. Venn did not believe that a bishop guaranteed the mission's spiritual integrity, but he viewed the office as the historic basis of the Church. Venn pointed to the creation of an indigenous episcopate as a crucial step toward self-support. In connection with this advance, however, the tension between diversity and order in Anglican mission heightened. When Samuel Adjai Crowther was consecrated the first black Anglican bishop at Canterbury Cathedral on June 29, 1864, it was a moment of triumph laden with future difficulty. Venn respected Crowther as a man who remained above the petty power struggles which sometimes surfaced among missionaries. Unlike Henry Townsend, Crowther rejected ambitious scheming, and possessed "great tact, remarkable knowledge of human psychology and a consequent ability to feel for others, understand them and, if necessary, manage them." Venn viewed Crowther as the Niger Mission's key figure and believed his elevation vindicated the theory of self-support.[110]

Townsend, however, considered direction of the Niger Mission to be his prerogative. He had established an impressive tenure and shown organizational ability; however, his ambition detracted from his other qualities and he frustrated Venn by opposing the idea of self-support. In 1858 Townsend confronted Venn in a letter with the claim that "the purely native Church is an idea, I think, not soon to be realized . . . The change of religion in a country is a revolution of the most extensive kind and the commanding minds that introduce these changes must and do become leaders."[111] Bolstered by feelings of racial and cultural superiority, this attitude was redolent of the fear that a missionary Church shorn of missionary direction would cease to be recognizable as the Church. English missionaries disagreed with one another over the extent to which the Church could transfer control to indigenous forces. Venn took an optimistic line which has had enduring influence yet has repeatedly been constrained by a cautious concern for order.

As Crowther's episcopate began, Townsend's suspicions grew. Crowther's relationship with English missionaries proved to be problematic. Church expansion preoccupied him and he worked to build the Church, adopting Venn's goal of a national Church with a vaguely English heritage and indigenous forms which would encourage modernization. During the 1860s and 1870s the Church grew unspectacularly but steadily, despite little increase in CMS support. Crowther proved resourceful in creating educational facilities along Western lines. He believed that the Church should blend indigenous and modern forms into a model for cultural development, and witnessed the acceptance of his vision.[112]

To English missionaries this attitude appeared syncretistic. Combined with Crowther's casual administration, the Church appeared imperiled. Such fear increased in the 1870s when a new generation of English missionaries arrived in the Niger region. They were both evangelical and racist, attuned to the Church's form and more jealous of European control than their predecessors. Meanwhile, Townsend proposed to divide Crowther's jurisdiction by the consecration of another African bishop, James Johnson. Ever modest, Crowther endorsed the plan and in 1877 Johnson superintended the CMS Yoruba mission and, in 1900, became Assistant Bishop of the Niger Delta.[113]

Johnson shared Crowther's emphasis upon education as the means of modernization. Militantly he advocated adjustment of the Church to local conditions. He cited liturgy as the means of Church adaptation to local culture. He despaired that Christianity cut people off from their cultural origins and he urged that Anglicanism allow cultural flexibility. The tide turned against him, however, as he and Crowther faced missionary suspicion. Africans, such as Crowther's son Josiah, lost responsible positions in the West Africa Company as imperialism stiffened. Similarly CMS workers urged an investigation of the Crowther episcopate and dogged the aging bishop's moves. Sadly Crowther's consecration may have been the moment of his greatest glory.[114]

Roland Allen

In the late Victorian era, the imperial mentality of domination challenged Venn's dream of an indigenous Church. Yet the idea gained ground because it won the loyalty of articulate figures whose beliefs went beyond racial and cultural norms toward a transcendent sense of the Church. Roland Allen went further than Venn in pursuit of indigenous forms of a universal faith. Having returned from China after missionary service from 1895 to 1903, Allen became a great theorist who stressed that mission should not perpetuate particular forms of authority but should convey a quality of the divine Spirit from whose benefits none was excluded. Allen believed that the mission Church should evolve from individual experience of the Spirit toward a corporate expression of it. In China he concluded that the Church could come into being if the first converts were "so fully equipped with all spiritual authority that they could multiply themselves without any *necessary* reference to us." Local congregations of indigenous Christians should receive "full power and authority," and missionaries must acknowledge that "foreigners can never successfully direct the propagation of any faith throughout a whole country." Allen emphasized that a national Church structure could not appear without "the substructure of the local church." Self-support meant not autonomous organization, but truly local church forms. "If the faith does not become naturalized and expand among the people by its own vital power, it exercises an alarming and hateful influence, and men fear and shun it as something alien."[115]

Missionary work for Allen had the intention of creating communities of believers who were inspired by the Spirit, just as the apostles had been. "This administration of the Spirit is the key of the apostolic work," he wrote. By nature the Spirit thus is "world-wide, all embracing." It "is not bound by material local and temporal chains." "Obedience to the commands of the Gospel is a spiritual act." Though the Gospel appears in the form of Law, beneath outward form lies its spiritual essence. Law becomes valid when it is "an expression of the mind of the Spirit." Indeed the "essential characteristic of the Gospel," Allen claimed, "is that it is an administration of the Spirit."[116]

In Allen's view, the nature of Christianity as an implanting of the Spirit firmly established its essential characteristics. Christ did not impart a new doctrine or found a new institution. Christ "imparted His own Spirit, He implanted His own Divine Life in the souls of His people." For Allen a spirit could not be compared with "a system of directions." "Christ imparts the Spirit from which the command emanates . . . Christ gives an internal power which grows stronger and stronger and works out our salvation in Him."[117] Christianity therefore was a principle of life looking for practical realization. Missionary work should emulate Christ's Incarnation, where God's essence assumed human form.

The expression of Christ's revelation entailed "the growth and progress of the Church." It encountered a tension between spirit and form, the universal and the particular. For Allen, the Incarnation was a light which guided the Church through the dangerous waters of this tension to a safe haven. An incarnational missionary approach meant, finally, that the universal assumed the form of the particular. The Church could not bind itself up with the particularities of Western culture but realized "that a world-wide communion does not involve the destruction of local characteristics, that a world-wide communion is a communion, a unity, Catholic, apostolic, not a loose federation of mutually suspicious societies. This sense of the corporate unity has come to us late, and we have scarcely begun to see what it is; but we see that it is the manifestation of Christ."[118] Allen feared that missionaries easily equated the Gospel with Western institutional form and noted that missionaries had become overseers of budgets and programs, distancing themselves from the people they were charged to serve, and accumulating an authority which they were reluctant to relinquish. Missionaries often lost sight of the provisional, spiritual nature of their work. Through a recovery of the incarnational basis of the Gospel, the Church could reconstitute what apostolic Christianity had been, namely, a confederation of indigenous Christian communities constituting a universal faith.

The mission Church as religious community

Allen's idea of the Church as a community based on the ideal of apostolic Christianity developed through the influence of Oxford and Cambridge Universities, which founded missionary communities in India in the late nineteenth century. The Mission to Calcutta established a house where missionaries maintained a daily regimen of worship in the manner of an Oxford college chapel. Despite weekly lectures at the house designed to convert India's educated classes, many of the missionaries feared the destructive impact of the West on a culture they admired. They were committed to inspire an amalgamation of the best of both cultures, rooted in Christianity, where the English worldview would prevail.[119] This intention could also be seen in Church Missionary Society work in east Africa. In Kenya the CMS created mission stations which "formed a subculture sharing common attributes." The Kenyan station offered education and medical care which facilitated evangelism. African Christianity seemed bound up with notions of Western cultural superiority and thus nurtured aspirations toward social ascent, in addition to inculcating religious values among African people. Conversion to Jesus Christ, the missionaries stressed, entailed concrete, behavioral changes, which converts often associated with material opportunities. Often Christianity seemed to be the gateway not so much to the Kingdom of Heaven as to terrestrial sophistication.[120]

Though missionaries recognized "that African life provided a basis for morality," some features, such as polygamy, provoked their concerted opposition. There were over three dozen Kaguru practices which the CMS energetically opposed, including general ones such as "consulting a soothsayer," "wearing charms," and "practicing witchcraft," to more specific habits such as "boring lobes of ears and wearing discs in them" or "washing in urine." Anglican missionaries "encouraged an independence from tradition which eventually led to confrontation between paternalistic missionaries and converts." Reliance upon English values often proved decisive in making converts and instilling alternative social norms. In this respect conversion and colonial intention proved thoroughly symbiotic.[121]

Two factors mitigated the alignment of the Church with the colonial order. On the one hand, missionaries frequently developed profound sympathy with indigenous people, and came to see mission stations as local villages rather than as colonial outposts. Opposition to indigenous culture fastened not so much upon given cultural differences as upon religious practices and religious forms of authority clearly incompatible with Christian beliefs and forms. Even in the case of polygamy, an issue of perennial Anglican concern, missionaries set out to provide medical care for all wives and education for children. On the other hand missionaries expressed doubts about the kind of influence Western culture might have over colonialized people. They feared that converts would adopt the destructive side of Western life, not what they regarded as its spiritual substance. The yardstick by which this distinction could be measured was provided by the Church, as a religious community whose distinctiveness the mission station embodied.

The idea of the Church as a catalyst for a new kind of society characterized the missionary tactic of the Anglo-Catholic party, whose earliest representative body became the Universities' Mission to Central Africa. The UMCA rose up in response to David Livingstone's clarion call, and sponsored Mackenzie's disastrous effort as a missionary bishop. In the wake of that calamity the UMCA fell back to Zanzibar, where it intended to regroup. William G. Tozer was consecrated central Africa's second bishop (although an island off the coast served as his see), and between 1863 and 1873, he succeeded in giving the UMCA a characteristic style. His successor, Edward Steere, moved the mission further toward a Catholic expression of Livingstone's vision of a Christian civilization with an indigenous leadership. Until his death in 1882, Steere moved decisively in that direction. The great symbol of his episcopate, Christ Church (later the Cathedral of Zanzibar) proclaimed the Church as the source of a particular kind of civilization. Steere ordained local clergy and learned Swahili. At Christmastime, 1877, a service of Matins in Swahili was conducted in Christ Church, and in May, 1879, translation of the Eucharist into Swahili was completed. Steere achieved a cultural breakthrough in a remarkably short time.[122]

The great Anglo-Catholic Bishop of Zanzibar proved to be Frank Weston, prelate from 1908 until his death in 1924. Weston's conviction that the Church "is the human race as God meant it to be" placed him at the forefront of the emerging Anglican theology of mission.[123] As a student Weston expressed devotion to Catholicism and socialism after attending Gore's lectures, and he resolved to move to the mission field. Attracted to the UMCA, he left for Zanzibar in 1898 and there concluded that commerce, African or European, could not produce true civilization. Instead Weston aspired to an indigenous Church, whose forms stamped it as both local and Catholic. He resisted the Kikuyu idea of an ecumenical mission as a dilution of Catholic Christianity. Weston glimpsed an indigenous Church which possessed a sacramental character, not one grounded in a particular culture. In pursuit of his dream he mastered Swahili and created a community at Mazizini, where he decreed a strict regimen of daily work and prayer. "He had a passion for system and uniformity," and he grasped that "with a Christian Church the African was capable of developing a civilisation of his own."[124] Weston was not content with a Church that accepted African life uncritically. He condemned polygamy and criticized traditional initiatory rites for boys and girls. He upheld monogamy and Western family life as expressions of sound moral principles and rejected Islam as an assault upon African tribal organization. Believing the integrity of ecclesiastical order ensured the fulfillment of social mission, Weston formed the Community of the Sacred Passion of Jesus, which brought the Eucharist to bear upon social development.[125]

The Community of the Resurrection's South African mission followed the same approach. In July, 1902, the Community received an invitation to South Africa from Bishop Carter, who was acting as Vicar-General of the Diocese of Pretoria. Carter imagined that the introduction of a Community house to South Africa would enhance its development. In his correspondence Carter repeatedly called such a house "a centre of spiritual life." His views were formed in the context of a diocese which had been shattered by the recent Boer War, and which had cut African people off from the roots of their tribal life. He was looking for an example of social wholeness in the form of a worldly monasticism. In January, 1903, three priests of the Community arrived in Johannesburg.[126]

The small band began visitations among African villages and European settlements in an area called the Reef, where goldmining was growing rapidly. Training African catechists and clergy became a special commitment, although education generally was the priests' most visible work. Meanwhile the daily worship cycle of Eucharist, Daily Office, and times for meditation and prayer afforded their own center and social model. "To me it is very sad to see the native and white work being separated," one priest commented in December, 1904. "Of course it is quite obvious that the natives just emerging from savagery cannot be treated in the same way as whites, there must be restrictions, there must be in many ways separations. But when they have become Christians it does seem to me that the Altar is one place where they certainly can meet, but it is not so."[127] This was an expression of how the search for religious wholeness found Catholic expression and posed fundamental questions about the nature of society itself. The Community adopted the goal of an African Christianity from which English control would disengage.

The Community feared the debilitating effects of modern civilization. Johannesburg had become as industrial and commercial as any European center. "A great awakening is taking place to-day among the Bantu tribes," Father Francis Hill wrote in 1913. "And a great deal in the future of South Africa depends upon the kind of education they get. They are already imbibing a lot of bad education from the darker side of our civilization on the Rand . . . Christian education is what they need. The Christian Church has alone maintained the true ideal of education as a training of character and of the whole personality as opposed to the idea of merely imparting information."[128] A number of the Community's protégés took jobs as domestic servants and were often viewed as assertive and articulate. Missionaries offered the hope of an enhanced status which challenged social restrictions.

The Community expanded the roles of women as well as of indigenous peoples. In 1907 three women workers arrived to care for the needs of African women. They visited shanty towns adjoining industrial sites, led worship, began education, and assessed medical and social needs.[129] When training-schools for girls appeared the imprint of women missionaries became indelible. In 1913 a conference of Anglican women missionaries met at Bloemfontein. The women affirmed that missionary work intended to "develop Native character on right lines," and to initiate forms of social organization, such as the Native Church Women's Society. Women missionaries also prepared candidates for Baptism and Confirmation.[130] The forms of the Community's life promised social wholeness.

Adapting Anglicanism to other cultures

The Church's forms had to be modified to make them decipherable to non-English cultures, and the most obvious adaptation was translation of the Bible and Prayer Book. An American missionary to China, Samuel Isaac Joseph Schereschewsky, in 1860 indicated in his first report his intention of mastering China's major languages. "A missionary without a respectable knowledge of the book language of China could not reasonably expect to have any access to the educated Chinese. Besides, the Chinese literary language is the embodiment of the Chinese mind." By 1864 he not only had "contact with some of the highest authorities in China," but had joined a colleague in translating "portions of the Prayer Book into the Mandarin dialect, which I am now using every Sunday in the chapel. I am, besides, engaged in translating the Scriptures into the same Mandarin dialect."[131] Translation remained his life's work after his elevation to the episcopate in 1876. He considered ways to convey the key Christian concepts, such as which Chinese term to use for God. He preferred "Lord of Heaven," a term also used by the Roman and Orthodox churches.

In their search for ways to accommodate non-Western peoples, some Anglicans uncovered a great appreciation of non-Western peoples and a new image of religious community. The notorious Bishop Colenso of Natal upheld the Maurician ideal of human reason and conscience which made inherent knowledge of God possible. He saw in Zulu society rudiments of the culture he intended to create, namely, a replica of British civilization with the Church in a parental role. Colenso idealized the English family as the framework for a proper religious education and the role of the state as guarantor of justice.[132] Colenso believed God had elected Britain and her established Church to evangelize the world. Consistent with this belief was the close friendship he formed with Theophilus Shepstone, the Secretary for Native Affairs in Natal and whose control over black people within Natal he aided. In 1854 he accompanied Shepstone on tours through tribal areas, often serving as interpreter. Church work and political hegemony seemed to be twin expressions of a colonial responsibility. "Happily, the present moment is full of encourage-ment. The light is beginning to break at length out of the thick clouds, which have so long wrapped in gloom and misery the tribes of this part of Africa." Celebrating the appointment of Sir George Grey as Governor to the Cape Colony, Colenso anticipated the achievement of "pacification and improvement of the native races."[133]

Late in 1854, as he ordained Henry Callaway for missionary service among the Zulus, Colenso affirmed that "God's Love is not confined to a few, here and there, of His creatures, but extends, like the light and warmth of His glorious sun, to all." This sentiment sounded like another jingoistic call to mission. It served notice, however, that Colenso had begun to extend Maurice's convictions away from the presumption of Western superiority toward an exploration of Zulu culture. In 1855 Colenso published *Ten Weeks in Natal*, a travel narrative in which he considered how Christianity could be commu-nicated by one culture to another. He concluded that polygamy could be tolerated as a cultural phenomenon so long as the polygamist convert refrained from taking more wives. Colenso also envisioned the creation of a black Christian kingdom with Zulu bishops out of the string of mission stations he established. Still adhering to the Church–state alliance, Colenso began to move away from an unquestioning assumption of the superiority of English cultural forms.[134] Eventually

Colenso was to see his Church–state theory shattered because of his unpopularity in official circles and a belligerent colonial attitude toward the Zulus. During the Zulu war of the late 1870s Colenso championed Zulu claims and the integrity of Zulu culture. He believed that Zulu life should be modernized, but he abandoned his ideal of England's established Church and its role in Western domination in favor of a Church in which the Gospel would stand apart from imperial design.

Henry Callaway moved beyond Colenso's conclusions about the Church and Western culture. Callaway, a physician raised as a Quaker, converted to the Church of England in 1853 when he was thirty-six years old. The impact of Maurice's writings and his acquaintance convinced Callaway that Anglicanism alone could supply the sense of unity which might "resuscitate Protestantism." Callaway felt a universal human longing among all social classes for a shared, public form of unity; "not a notion but a reality," human relationships should be modeled on Christ's prayer "that His disciples might be one." The conviction that this message was desperately needed led Callaway to the Anglican mission field.[135] He reached Natal late in 1854 and, as he studied Zulu language and culture, he reached a conclusion Colenso shared. "It is quite clear that they have a knowledge of good and evil, although low and perverted." As an Englishman bringing the norms of Western civilization, he believed there "is not a single thing that the Kaffirs [*sic*] do not require to be taught, from the washing of their bodies to the building of their houses." As a missionary equipped by Maurice to seek an underlying, universal human nature, however, Callaway found something else, namely, Zulu notions of divinity inherently compatible with Christian sensibility.[136]

Intent on forming a new kind of society to express the underlying human unity, Callaway, in 1858, began a mission station at Spring Vale. His converts numbered over forty by then, and for their sake he built a small church, complete with a chancel and English appointments. Anglicanism, he felt, might become the appropriate expression of this basic human unity. Meanwhile Callaway pondered the extent to which his converts must separate from the unconverted among their tribe. "I have endeavoured as much as possible to prevent a feeling of class springing up between Christian and heathen. There is very soon apparent a marked difference between them . . . The time will possibly come when a separation must come."[137] Because he hoped to overcome cultural differences, Callaway dreaded such a prospect; however, he feared more the loss of the Christian expression of this culture, which he was constructing gradually. More important than a general unity was the Church's embodiment of a particular culture because in the Church that culture found its most legitimate expression. In Callaway one finds early evidence of a shift in Liberal sensibility away from the cause of bringing about unity toward upholding specific forms of cultural integrity.

Callaway's absorption in Zulu life led him to question the direction of colonial society. "There is a feeling among the colonists of Natal which would very easily pass into a disposition to enslave," he wrote in 1859. He also distanced his views from Colenso's, who, as late as 1862, continued to regard colonial intentions as benevolent. Colenso wanted the land on which Spring Vale stood surrendered to government control. Callaway resisted effectively as Colenso was hampered by the doctrinal stain which engulfed him. Meanwhile Callaway searched for ways to bridge Christian precept and Zulu practice. In opposition to Colenso he opposed polygamy because it enforced a cruel status upon women. Callaway wanted to overturn cultural forms which, he felt, threatened innate human dignity. He was adamant that within the Church, a respect for human dignity should prevail. Christianity must immerse itself in the life of a people and stimulate their expression of the divine as the basis for a just, indigenous society. The Church, for Callaway, was human nature recovering its primordial, social goodness.[138]

In Callaway these ideas (which later became prominent among Anglicans) remained only suggestions. His study of Zulu religion proved more complete, resulting in *The Religious System of the Amazulu*, published in 1871, a pioneering effort in comparative religion, which influenced Max Muller and E. B. Tyler. In a "Fragment" appended to the work Callaway illustrated how a vision of the Church in mission led him to an appreciation of Zulu life. Study of another religion should moderate Western "self-assertion" and reveal "some great principles which lie at the basis of all religions, even of our own." The study of "Natural Religion" should "enable us to see that the struggles which are going on in our time have gone on among other peoples; that there are fundamental truths which stand unaltered . . . and a final truth, to which . . . all these strugglings have really tended; that 'revealed truth' has no more escaped the corruptions of ignorance than truth which man has discovered for himself."[139]

Though Callaway became a bishop, he remained first and foremost a student of comparative religion. He rejected the notion that there could be no salvation outside the Church. He sensed the imprint God had made upon all cultures, not merely European ones. Moreover, Christianity, in its essence, represented for him a religion of humanity, a divine governance encompassing all the parameters of human experience. Callaway suggested that an original image of God lay in the "natural affections," prior to the constraints of laws, doctrines, governments, or religious systems. True reverence must focus upon the natural human being, God's finest creation. True religion inspires passion to recover this natural self, the primordial image of God. Beyond traditional Christianity there lies a deeper, universal religion, toward which Anglicanism must point. Thus Callaway foresaw the direction which Christian Socialism would take in the twentieth century when the psychological notion of the self and the image of social justice would be refined. Callaway's sense of a universal religion represented a significant and continuing Anglican theme.

Charles Freer Andrews also experienced Anglicanism as a springboard toward the realization of human unity. A student who imbibed B. F. Westcott's ideas, he became active in a Cambridge chapter of the Christian Social Union that was organized in 1892. Westcott encouraged in Andrews a human sense of community that transcended cultural boundaries and taught him that India could bring to light the true meaning of Christ in the unity of human and divine.[140] Andrews was ordained a priest in 1897 and in 1903 he joined the Cambridge Mission to India, which he served for over six years. A Christian Socialist ideal of union with God prompted him to search for a form of religious unity that would have general relevance. By 1912 he doubted that the Church could fulfil India's need for unity because the Church was inherently Western. He suspected that the Church obstructed the realization of a Christ who transcended cultural terms, and he concluded that the Christian must abandon ecclesiastical order.[141]

Andrews set out on an iconoclastic path. Hearing of a young Indian lawyer mobilizing public support for civil rights in South Africa, Andrews joined Mohandas Gandhi, and a firm friendship resulted. He concluded that God was found within each culture, the discovery of whose essence would also reveal the unity of human nature as made in God's image. Liberalism inspired a search for the essence of religion that lay beyond dogma and institutions, and Andrews epitomized the logical end of Liberalism. He moved to the periphery of the Church and returned to India, where he pursued Indian forms of religious community. Gandhi offered the form of unity to which Andrews devoted his life.[142]

The quest for a Christian community which found God throughout culture challenged Anglican reliance upon Western priorities. As the Church encountered new forms of culture, a number of Anglicans wanted the Church to remain English and American. At the other end of the spectrum, a few others were ready, like Andrews, to abandon Western forms altogether. Most Anglicans believed that the Church should accommodate cultural diversity without surrendering Western assumptions and forms of control, a balance which held for the moment. However, a suspicion was developing that Anglicans should distance themselves from Western cultural norms as Catholic sensibilities placed new emphasis upon the Church. The Anglican cultural diversity nurtured a tension between its historic order and the hope that the Church would embody a unity embracing other cultures. In the twentieth century this tension came to dominate Anglican self-understanding.

CHAPTER SEVEN

The crisis of Church and culture

THE AGE OF NEW REALITIES

"War is fatal to Liberalism," Winston Churchill declared in 1906, when he sensed that Liberalism faced severe challenges from socialism and Labour in Britain and tensions in Europe and South Africa; however, he could not foresee that world wars, economic hardship, and rapid changes would erode the Liberal assumptions which had fostered Western civilization's advance.[1] The erosion of Liberalism which began in the twentieth century was a turning point for Anglican identity. The modern Anglican achievement had become the articulation of a Liberal Catholic sense of the Church which seemed to adjust belief and worship to modern circumstances. Preserving the role of *de facto* religious establishment proved a vital feature of the Liberal Catholic program, but one which became problematic as Liberal social ideology declined.

Liberalism's loss of influence stripped Anglicans of their assurance that they could balance a prominent role in society with regard for Church order. As Liberal convictions unraveled, Anglicans began to experience a tension among themselves between the possibility of adjusting the Church to modern circumstances and the necessity of distinguishing Church order from social order. The modern Anglican transformation, I believe, entered a new, troubling phase increasingly characterized by uncertainty within the Church over its nature and relation to society. Anglicans concurred among themselves that they sought a form of Church life which did not subordinate belief to social assumptions, but upheld a critical role in society for the Church. A critical social stance, I argue, implied no particular Anglican identity, but inspired a variety of grassroots agendas in various Anglican locales. The loss of Liberal assurance, which I see as the second phase of modern Anglican experience, has proven devastating to Anglican self-confidence.

Liberalism had been a "unity of feeling," a merger of optimistic theological and social attitudes which emphasized human freedom, culture's inherent goodness, middle-class values, and Western society's inevitable growth.[2] This consensus attempted a political coalition uniting the laboring with the entrepreneurial and intellectual classes. So long as social experience reinforced its assumptions, Liberalism could encourage class and cultural self-expression as part of its sense of historical progress. The ability to encompass diverse social forms confirmed the Liberal presumption that Western ideals applied to culture generally, and the resultant imperialism shifted the nature of Liberalism from humanitarianism to social control. The Church of England's mission embodied these principles, which supplied a sense of order. The Church benefited from Western society's expansion but suffered from its liabilities.

In the late nineteenth and early twentieth centuries, however, Liberal assumptions frayed in the English political fabric. The Labour Party, which in its infancy was the ally of Liberalism, showed signs of restiveness and, as real wages fell in 1910, the trade unions began independent action. Liberalism had promoted sympathy with the downtrodden, but economic difficulties encouraged the working classes to rely upon their own means of organization. Meanwhile the issue of Home Rule for Ireland, which had been a pillar of Liberal doctrine, pushed the Tory Party into more strident expressions of invective. George Dangerfield speaks of "The Tory Rebellion" to describe the militant Conservatism which erupted around 1910.[3] Similarly an unprecedented political assertiveness by women appeared. Sparked by Emmeline Pankhurst and her daughters, a nascent political organization rejected Victorian role-expectations for women and demanded the right to vote. Liberalism's ideal of "upward mobility" gave way by the early twentieth century to a "desire for self-determination" grounded in "organizations that would express that spirit of community autonomy." Liberal society's weakness was apparent in its "fragmentation into a multiplicity of sections or classes with differing standards and notions of respectability, as well as differing living standards." Each group "operated its own social controls" and, though traditional aristocracy retained its social dominance for the time being, "the ruling class was no longer quite clear about its own identity, or certain of its grip on power."

"It was an orderly and well-defined society," writes F. M. L. Thompson, "but it was not an inherently stable one. The Victorian experience bequeathed structural problems, identity problems, and authority problems to the twentieth century."[4]

Secularism was one aspect of this malaise prior to the First World War. Throughout the Victorian age the Church of England succeeded in "making public deference to religious values – and public acknowledgment of the importance of religion – almost universal among the upper and middle classes." The Church's rites of passage and "social welfare institutions" enabled the Church to encompass important aspects of working-class life, although it must be said that the working classes did not adopt the pattern of Sunday church attendance which characterized the other strata of Britain's social order. The Church encountered working-class people at the level of "diffusive Christianity," the intersection where Church schools, rites, and local parish events built bridges between Church and people. In the late nineteenth century those links weakened as class divisions hardened. The Church of England lost its function among working-class people when government agencies offered them comprehensive forms of social relief and when popular belief was divorced from institutional life. Secularization was not simply a loss of religious belief, but was a manifestation of the decline of the Church's "drawing power."[5] Religious ideas and piety "do not exist in some 'pure' religious form – in a social vacuum." They "only exist within a complicated network of institutional and social relationships" and a "unique set of historical circumstances." For much of the nineteenth century those circumstances facilitated the Church's adaptation to modern life. As the Liberal consensus began to disintegrate, the Church's social role became problematic because its middle-class base declined in influence throughout the social spectrum.[6]

By the late nineteenth century the Church of England's role as the religious establishment had become problematic. Following disestablishment of the Church of Ireland in 1869, Liberal politicians had trained their sights on the Church in Wales. Though slowed by attention to more pressing parliamentary issues, Welsh disestablishment advanced gradually, to the dismay of conservative defenders of establishment. They sensed that disestablishment was a tide which would eventually swamp the English Church. After a Welsh Church Commission report formally recommended disestablishment in 1910, the measure steadily advanced and received final approval in September, 1914, shortly after the outbreak of war.

The First World War intensified the impact of new social forces upon the old order. "The Great War illuminated the strengths, and also the deficiencies, of the British society that had been developing for the previous half-century." It began in 1914 as "the first middle-class war in history," remarkable for the depth of patriotism which imbued the civilian population. It relied upon propaganda and it used the news media to publicize the promised military success. However, expressions of duty gave way to a weary melancholy as the war bogged men down in the trenches. Instead of military triumphs the media detailed the horrors of modern warfare. The destructiveness of such technological weapons as tanks and submarines broke the illusion of British invincibility.[7]

Images of empire abounded as British forces included thousands of troops from Canada, Australia, New Zealand, and South Africa. Evidence of imperial might, however, obscured the signs that the Empire had begun to disintegrate. The war-time Prime Minister, Lloyd George, accepted the concept of national self-determination, and talk arose of greater participation in government by subjugated peoples. At home the war necessitated massive industrialization, and the classes who labored to bring this about focused their aspirations upon the acquisition of political power. Industrial mobilization brought into focus notions of equality and civil rights which previously had been muted.[8] Such trends were scarcely visible at the start of the war in 1914, when morale in Britain soared as a result of popular belief in the righteousness of the cause. The Great War became a crusade on behalf of decency and civilization, the "Holy War of English Liberal idealism." It promised social renewal and personal fulfillment in a cause which pitted good against evil, and enlisted God's nation against the Hun's atrocities. Such confidence collapsed as industrial strikes were accompanied by news of battlefront losses.[9]

The loss of faith in Western civilization was epitomized by a fatalistic sense of social decline. "The future of the West is not a limitless tending upwards and onwards for all time towards our present ideals," Oswald Spengler wrote in a widely debated critique, "but a single phenomenon of history, strictly limited and defined as to form and duration, which covers a few centuries and can be viewed and, in essentials, calculated from available precedents." Western civilization "has ripened to its limit," and the present "represents a transitional phase which occurs with certainty under particular conditions," a sign of irreversible decline.[10] In British and American religious circles, a sense of tragedy took hold. "The confusion of the present time has for many persons but little of cheer," read an advertisement for a new hymnal in America's most prominent Protestant magazine. "To them modern life is inspired by a spirit of selfishness and hatred that can lead only to chaos." A Protestant minister insisted that "the only hope of civilization lies in the religion of Jesus." The Anglo-American outlook had changed from hope to despair, from the ideal of self-sacrifice to the need for self-preservation.[11]

Both in Britain and in America there was a desperate search for a realistic view of society and a comprehensive understanding of the self. "I am convinced that the world is looking for a fresher, truer and larger vision of the religion of Jesus Christ, and that it is justified in requiring it," wrote H. R. L. ("Dick") Sheppard, Vicar of St. Martin-in-the-Fields, London, in 1927.[12] This was a new perspective for Anglicans, who were awakening to sober, social realities. At first, support for the war was broad and deep within the Church. Later Bishop of Durham, Herbert Hensley Henson endorsed the war enthusiastically. A. F. Winnington-Ingram, Bishop of London, served as Senior Chaplain of the London Territorial Rifle Brigade. He preached sermons designed to boost enlistment, and often wore a military uniform with his clerical collar.[13] A few prominent clergy expressed misgivings about the war. J. N. Figgis of the Community of the Resurrection sensed a "death of the pot" of modern civilization. Charles Gore believed Britain must participate only reluctantly and should not indulge in unbridled nationalism. John Percival, Bishop of Hereford, believed Britain should be neutral, and called upon his parishes to pray for peace.[14] Such sentiments were overwhelmed by the Church's rush to join the war effort. Nearly one-third of the students at several theological colleges suspended their studies to enlist in the military. Archbishop Randall Davidson encouraged noncombative roles for clergy at home or at the front. The war deepened the Church's sense that society needed its pastoral role.[15]

The National Mission of Repentance and Hope, organized late in 1916, was the Church of England's first systematic response to the public loss of morale. It reflected the realization among Church leadership that the Church was not addressing the nation's spiritual needs and that popular religion could not be guided by the Church's influence. When Archbishop Davidson called for a National Mission, he chose twelve men as its leaders. One of those twelve was the young

William Temple, then Rector of St. James', Piccadilly. Son of Archbishop of Canterbury Frederick Temple, William Temple had attracted notice for his conviction that God's presence permeated creation, and that the Church bore the divine imprint. Concerned by the nation's religious needs, he hoped that the Church of England could generate a national mood of renewal. He shared Henry Scott Holland's belief that "if only the world had been Christian, it would not be at war." But the "big affairs of the world go on their way as if [the Church] were not there."[16]

A need for realism, rather than the assurance of progress, was emerging. The National Mission was an early Anglican expression of the hope for which Temple would become a prominent spokesman. It called for repentence from the moral ills of war, including strikes, war profiteering, gambling, brothels, and lack of respect for the Sabbath, which seemed to threaten national purpose. Reviving the ideals of Christian Socialism, the National Mission called for rededication to the Kingdom of God on earth. However, Hensley Henson called the Mission "a grave practical blunder," and the radical Christian Socialist Conrad Noel derided it as the "Mission of Funk and Despair."[17] Most of the people who responded were already active in the Church, a clue that the Church's ability to revive the nation had faded but that its efforts to inspire its own followers would intensify. Social crisis solidified the devotion of persons securely within the Anglican fold to resisting the malign influences of modernity.

The National Mission's sense of purpose carried over into "Life and Liberty," a group organized by Temple and Dick Sheppard to consider a new sense of mission for the Church of England. They began meeting in 1917 at Sheppard's vicarage in London and soon agreed that the Church was riddled with shortcomings. Before "the Church could hope to catch the ear of the nation, it must set its own house in order."[18] This plank in the reformist platform recalled the conviction of the 1830s that Anglicans best ministered to the world when they were properly organized among themselves. Anomalies of clerical life such as low pay, inadequate housing, low pensions, and inequities of Church patronage now included insufficient attention to the clergy's lives. These last concerns constituted evidence that war brought about a profound emphasis upon the individual's moral and spiritual development.

Life and Liberty's leadership hoped to disestablish the Church, believing that when Church reforms no longer required Parliament's approval, it would become the spiritual voice of the nation. Since the revival of the English Convocations in the nineteenth century and the appearance of synodical government throughout the Anglican communion created means of self-government, a prominent swath of the Church of England had supported its formal disestablishment. Late in the nineteenth century the Church Reform League had been the most influential network for encouraging further forms of ecclesiastical self-government. The League enlisted such important figures as Westcott and Gore to its cause. Mandell Creighton joined in calling for increased lay involvement in Church affairs. At its various local chapters the League spread grassroots support for the Church's autonomy.

After the war, enhancing the Church's self-governance seemed the means of freeing it for the task of social mission. An Enabling Bill passed Parliament in 1919, allowing formation of a representative Church Assembly to legislate on ecclesiastical matters, subject to parliamentary oversight. In this context the supporters of Life and Liberty, such as Gore, called for full disestablishment as the route to spiritual integrity. Others, notably Hensley Henson, Bishop of Durham, feared that the loss of connection to the state would hinder, not advance, the Church of England's social role. Though disestablishment was not formally achieved, a practical distancing of the Church from the state continued. Anglicans increasingly looked to sacramental and pastoral measures of ecclesiastical identity, rather than the privileges of establishment.

Meanwhile most Anglicans of the postwar years continued to aspire to being a *de facto* religious establishment, and articulate Church leaders posed the ideal of a critical role in times of crisis. Life and Liberty portended a new concern for the Church's pastoral role in society, and the needs of British troops awakened army chaplains to the importance of the Eucharist and to the necessity for instruction in forms of prayer. Soldiers facing death epitomized modernity's lonely individualism and posed the Church's sacraments as assurances that one was to be included in the Kingdom of God. Military chaplains grasped that the men to whom they ministered were frequently from working-class backgrounds and bore great suspicion of the established Church. These chaplains concluded that the Church must shed the trappings of privilege and that liturgy must be recast with a sacramental emphasis. G. A. Studdert Kennedy, John Groser, and J. M. Stanhope Walker were among the chaplains who won acclaim for battlefield ministry. Thirteen members of the Community of the Resurrection served, as well as members of the Cowley Fathers and the Society of the Sacred Mission, Kelham. They resolved that the Church must remake its liturgy in order to overcome social division.[19]

The war raised moral issues whose discussion symbolized the Church's search for critical distance from society. Citing the plight of noncombatants, Archibishop Davidson led the Church's bishops in cautioning their countrymen not to succumb to an attitude of reprisal against Germany. The employment of women in Britain's war industries generated calls for expanded roles for women within the Church, including reading portions of worship such as Scripture lessons and prayers. Anglicans felt the war had precipitated social changes which allowed for progress in the Church. There was a sense, however, that war "imposed a continuous moral and physical strain, producing numbness of the mind and fatigue of the soul." The moral strain could be seen in alcoholism, divorce, and sexual permissiveness, and opportunities for mission arose within the Church's critique of social life.[20]

Such caution also appeared at the Episcopal Church's General Convention in 1916, where the sense of crisis was palpable. "It was but a moment ago that we were basking in the thought that the human race was steadily coming to recognize the community of its interests the world over," the Pastoral Letter of the Church's bishops observed. "The fact that our Nation is not at war," the bishops noted, "affords no ground for smugness, much less for self-applause. It throws upon us the searching responsibility of exalting the true ideals of peace and incorporating them in our national life." Church leaders were concerned to a greater extent about domestic turmoil than European conflict. "America is still in danger of race antipathy flaming into hatred." War in Europe distracted Americans from their responsibilities to all races. "With the Incarnation as the corner-stone of the Faith, our common humanity contains in itself God's assurance that we have capacity for universal brotherhood." The Church is "God's executive agency for bringing in His Kingdom," which meets its responsibility by the moral precepts exemplified in Christ's life.[21] Episcopalians resolved that expanding their ministries among non-European people made them harbingers of social progress.

The same General Convention adopted the report of the Joint Commission on the Racial Episcopate which proposed the consecration of black suffragan bishops. The report insisted that the

Church must help "the Negro to the achievement of racial self-sufficiency, which is born of accomplishment, to self-mastery, which follows moral victory, and to . . . passion for social integrity." "Racial development is made through racial leaders . . . In this process the Church is fulfilling her highest and holiest purpose, when she has brought the incarnation of all virtues and all powers from on High to the race, and has created the conditions of its free development."[22] Though Anglicans retained a patronizing attitude toward non-white peoples, they embarked on what was then a progressive, moral critique of American racism.

Throughout the Anglican Church, this new sense of mission was expressed clearly by William Temple. In lectures at the General Theological Seminary in New York, Temple argued that the Church exists to instil in the nation the spirit of God's Kingdom. The Church must balance its optimism for social possibility with awareness of national life's moral failings. Temple could support the war because he believed its outcome would determine "whether in the next period the Christian or the directly anti-Christian method shall have an increase of influence." Advocacy of war in the name of Christ may have been the only way to serve God's Kingdom in a fallen world.[23] This new assumption which permeated Anglicanism was that society would make "progress precisely in that degree in which it realises more and more a relationship of love between its various members, and becomes the Kingdom which Christ came on earth to found."[24] Society advances only when the Church properly performs its tasks and assumes its correct form. Because the Church "will be chiefly concerned to seek and to save that which is lost, calling men everywhere to repent," it must be "a quite definite society, with a coherent constitution and a known basis of membership." The Church "must keep itself in some sense separate from the world," but could reconcile the world to Christ if it preserved its distinctive order.[25] How to balance proximity to society with distance from it became the Anglican dilemma. The loss of reliance upon modernity provoked a search for tangible standards of Anglican identity.

THE MEANS OF CRITICAL DISTANCE

"The Great War has brought home impressively to us that we are no longer living in modern times," wrote Leicester C. Lewis of the Western Theological Seminary, Chicago, in 1918. A period had

begun in which "it may be expected that the ultimate theological tone
... will differ quite radically from that in the recent past." This sense
of change was cited by Dickinson S. Miller of the General Seminary,
when he discussed the problem of evil. Miller noted that "the religion
of Christ arises in the conflict with evil. Men are to be redeemed from
evil. It is the formidable enemy." The reality of evil had become a
snare for liberal theology, which viewed human nature optimistically
and tended, "by way of justifying God, to explain away Evil."[26]
Because social progress could no longer be presumed, the Church
must come to grips with the reality of evil. A new theological realism
emerged, characterized by fresh efforts to distinguish the Church's
convictions from social mores.

Marriage and divorce

The Episcopal Church's General Convention in 1916 received a
report from its "Joint Commission on Legislation on Matters Relating
to Holy Matrimony" that marriage and family life were being eroded
in the United States. Reiterating the Christian belief in monogamous,
faithful unions, the Commission felt that marriage "should be made a
matter for careful instruction by the clergy much more frequently
than is now common. The teaching of true marriage is one of the best
defences against divorce and other evils which now afflict and
threaten the nation." Such instruction must emphasize the clear
distinction between "marriages which are allowed by the civil law,
representing all that can be imposed upon people of varying and of no
religious beliefs, and marriages which can be sanctioned and blessed
by the Church as conformable to God's will and the teaching of Our
Lord Jesus Christ." In that respect "the Commission feels justified in
recommending an entire refusal to solemnize with the Church's
blessing the marriage of any person who has a divorced partner still
living." The Commission was willing for Church standards regarding
marriage to reflect civil statutes prohibiting consanguinity in
marriage.[27]

There was dramatic evidence to account for this concern about
marriage. In England between 1914 and 1917 there was an average of
846 divorces annually, but that average increased to 1,407 in 1918,
then escalated dramatically to 2,610 in 1919, 2,985 in 1920, and 3,956
in 1921. In the United States an annual average of 111,340 divorces
between 1914 and 1918 rose 40 per cent to 155,070 between 1919 and

1921.[28] Alarmed at the incidence of divorce and the deterioration of domestic life, the Episcopal Church's General Convention devoted much time to this crisis. The Church's "Joint Commission on Home and the Family Life in its Relation to Religion and Morals" noted that "during the exigencies of war, the home life more or less disintegrated by the extraordinary demands upon each member." "Whatever attacks the home is a menace to the national life," they continued. At home children learn reverence to God and see themselves as members of a human family which God has created. Christ must be the head of the home, drawing many homes together in the wider family which is the Church. Christians must "fight the forces which prey upon family life," for they threaten the Church and the nation as well. Such forces included industrial conditions and the burdens shouldered by poor immigrants, the need for education in family life and especially in family religious observance, and renewed Church teaching on the purpose of marriage and on the threats of divorce and "indiscriminate marriage."[29]

In the face of social dissolution Episcopalians searched for ways to reinvigorate the social order. They developed a social critique which paid attention to society's most basic institution – the family – and they insisted upon the distinctiveness of the Church's values. In an age of moral alarm, when the Church's rigor safeguarded its mission to the world, it "must face the question whether it can continue to give indiscriminate sanction to all sorts of marriages," and "should also continually set forth the sacredness and inviolability of Christian marriage." America's fate was at stake, the Commission concluded, for "this Nation will decay and finally perish when American homes cease to revere God. Advanced culture did not save past civilizations, did not prevent Germany plunging into a gulf of infamy. Upon America's consecration to God depends her fate."[30] The General Convention also condemned the alarming usage by Americans of "narcotic drugs," especially opium, and urged the laity to moral vigor in their communities against all such threats to family security. The Church's social priority became a call to public morality.[31]

Anglicans widely shared this concern. The "Encyclical Letter" issued by the Church's Lambeth Conference in 1920 commented that "there is sad evidence at the present time of a widespread leavening of moral conditions. The increased number of illegitimate births . . . the multiplication of divorces . . . the widespread existence of venereal diseases . . . all sound a note of serious alarm and warning. It is easy in this, as in other matters," the bishops observed astutely, "to throw blame upon the war. To a large extent . . . the war probably disclosed conditions already existing, to which people generally were accustomed to shut their eyes."

Anglicans believed that moral rigor was the proper response to the situation, and the Conference suggested a tightening of the Church's standards. The "Church must take its full share of blame in having failed to give plain teaching about marriage, and, before this, about purity." Purity was a revealing word, illustrating the Church's new desire for boundaries between itself and the world. Concern for purity and a strict moral theology allowed the Church to distinguish itself from the world, though the result at times could sound harsh. On the matter of divorce, Lambeth's bishops suggested that adultery might constitute one valid circumstance for divorce. They insisted, however, that "no comparison for present hardships in particular cases can justify the lowering for all of the standard of Christ." The Church's defense of this norm "justifies the welfare of society and of the race."[32] This response to marriage and divorce signaled a change in the Church's stance. Sensing public turmoil, the Church's leadership embraced moral rigor. Christian mission required demarcation of the Church from the ways of the world, in order to preserve a form of life which the world needed. The Church was becoming the bearer of an alternative vision or order, a tactical withdrawal from society in order to assault modernity's mistaken assumptions.

The Church's Evangelical Party moved dramatically in this direction. One recent history of the Church of England's Evangelicals calls the period after the First World War "The Defensive Years." Unlike the old days of the Clapham Sect and the Earl of Shaftesbury, Evangelicals "conceived the means of grace much more in terms of the weekly bible study and prayer meeting than in the sacrament of Holy Communion and they eschewed, on the whole, anything like real social concern and involvement." Evangelicals in the late nineteenth century rejected Liberal Catholicism, with its emphasis upon a sacramental theology and a socialist politics. They turned vigorously to Scripture and to preaching, and insisted upon Anglicanism's place within the Protestant heritage. They valued the idea of the National Church as a product of the Reformation and felt no threat to its integrity from parliamentary oversight. Genuine religion, Evangelicals insisted, lay not in ceremonial but within the heart, guided by God's revealed Word.[33]

A sense of withdrawal dominated the mood of the Church's

Catholic Party. By the 1920s Anglo-Catholics could justifiably claim nearly a century of triumph. From the first rounds fired by the Oxford movement, Anglo-Catholics had sent volleys of invective against Protestant tendencies in the Church. The movement succeeded as a party and as a source of Liberal Catholicism. But most Anglo-Catholics retained the sensibility of their forebears that the world could easily corrupt the Church. After the war, that sense reappeared, and contributed to the Church's new rigor. "This Miserable and Naughty World" Francis J. Hall entitled an article he published in the *Anglican Theological Review* in October, 1920. Hall, a Catholic-style theologian teaching at the General Seminary, challenged the utilitarian, rational basis of modern science and philosophy. He doubted that human beings naturally could work together for mutual benefit and individual reward. Hall, a prominent author and a familiar voice on Church commissions, countered the modern spirit with the fact of social injustice and moral disarray. He presented the Christian life as an alternative, based upon repentance from evil, leading to the eternal order of the Kingdom of God. Human beings, he reiterated, exist to glorify God, not vice versa. Rather than personal happiness, individuals find fulfillment in Christian service. Life's goal must be an eternal, not a temporal, reward.[34]

As the collapse of Liberalism proceeded, I argue that the first phase of modern Anglican experience ended and the second phase began. Convinced of the Church's Liberal Catholic nature, Anglicans generally resolved to distance themselves from society through increasingly elaborate forms of social criticism.

The Liberal Catholic social critique

The heirs of Anglicanism's Liberal Catholic tradition were not censorious over the world's "miserable and naughty" nature. But they shared the perception of all Anglicans that the world required the Church's moral influence. Liberal Catholics also considered the Church's distinctiveness from the world to be the guarantor of its truth and, in their own way, helped form a new consensus about the Church's nature. Their goal had been to achieve what Ernst Troeltsch described as "a Church-directed civilisation" in modern theological and sacramental guise.[35] That goal remained intact as a new generation of Liberal Catholics attempted to reform industrial society. The war had occasioned "a new militancy and expectation among those who had previously been poor but acquiescent to their fate." Labour unrest was manifest throughout Britain early in 1919. Railway workers' stoppages in Glasgow led to a violent strike requiring troops to restore calm, and unrest spread to Edinburgh and Belfast. Wildcat strikes afflicted the coal industry, and there was talk of union coalition leading to a general strike. In Glasgow a red flag flew briefly before the Town Hall. A temperate response by the government remedied flagrant instances of insufficient wages; but, it was felt by those involved in the disputes that the root causes of unrest had not been addressed properly.[36]

Several adherents to the Liberal Catholic tradition began a new style of social ministry. Shortly after the war the Industrial Christian Fellowship united religious and political reformers and sponsored massive crusades at which such public speakers as G. A. Studdert Kennedy, or "Woodbine Willie," explained the causes of social woes. The Fellowship continued the tradition of the Christian Social Union, officially blending its structure with that of the Navvy Mission, which had supplied missionaries to construction sites. Four-fifths of the ICF's leadership were Church of England clergy and laity, and the tone set by the group was decidedly Christian Socialist.[37] From its inception the ICF credited F. D. Maurice's belief in society's organic nature as its basis and attracted figures such as Gore, Frere, and Donaldson. The new ingredient was the legacy of social dislocation left by the war. The Church's message needed restating, and Studdert Kennedy became an effective example because of the notice his front-line ministry had acquired and because his fervent oratory made a powerful impact. He brought the aristocratic Church of England to the general public with dramatic preaching, giving his hearers a vision of public life which grasped God's intention for humanity. The course of history, he argued, could be redirected by faithful people toward social cooperation.[38]

This message, which became the backbone of ICF doctrine, secured Studdert Kennedy's place among such Anglican social thinkers as Gore, R. H. Tawney, and William Temple. Less idealistic and sacramental than Gore, he was more interested in individuals and less inclined to think of social relationships in terms of power, as did Tawney, an economist whose book *Religion and the Rise of Capitalism* achieved renown. Influenced by the Anglican economist William Cunningham, Studdert Kennedy conceived of society in terms of fellowship and the advance of the individual into a system of cooperation. Studdert Kennedy was not optimistic about society's prospects, or even about the potential of the individual himself. He appreciated Temple's early ideas about the beneficent nature of society's evolution and of personality, but he could not neglect the malaise inflicted by war. His sense of realism drew a diverse public to the ICF's new style of Anglican ministry.[39]

"The greatest evil of our time is the secularisation of a large part of life – the sense that somehow or other it lies outside the sphere of God's purpose." When he made this observation in 1924, William Temple was becoming Anglicanism's magisterial twentieth-century figure. A member of the Labour Party since 1918, he was an activist who became Bishop of Manchester in 1920 and was on the verge of "ascendancy over the social teaching of the Church of England." Describing Temple's ideas as "unoriginal," "second-hand," and "inept," even the acerbic E. R. Norman acknowledges that Temple's views achieved "an ascendancy in the Church of his day." Temple's vision of the Church left an indelible mark upon its ministry.[40]

"The function of the Church," Temple declared in 1924, "is to bring to fulfillment what we may also discover to be the main hopes and aspirations of human progress in all the ages." He believed that history revealed a search for fellowship, that is, a union of individual wills into a corporate personality. This "fundamental principle" of human experience found its perfect manifestation in the Church, whose Catholic and Evangelical capabilities alert humanity to seek God and to view the world as the embodiment of God's purpose. The Church, therefore, fulfils itself through "its relationship to the other organised activities of mankind." The Church contains "the secret and the power of perfection" which the world needs. It recognizes common tasks with the state, such as the rule of law, and even enters into a public establishment of religion. At times, however, the Church must reproach the state and appeal beyond it for justice. Therefore, he suggested, "we need to begin – gradually perhaps, but we need to begin – to disentangle the Church in some respects from the State."[41]

At first Temple believed in a benevolent world process and trusted that society was sufficiently plastic to respond to the Church's influence. His sense, however, that the Church might distance itself from the state suggested that a new readiness for social criticism came about from his notion of personality. In exploring the Incarnation, such theologians as Gore drew attention to the fact of Christ's humanity and raised questions about the meaning of personal experience. R. C. Moberly's *Atonement and Personality* (1901) viewed Christ's sacrifice for humanity as the model for sacramental theology if not for the Christian life itself. The ground of historic christology and atonement theology shifted for Anglicans from an interest in objective dogma toward a subjective sense of relationship with an empathic deity.[42] Temple extended this incarnation emphasis in two ways. He explored the meaning of world process as an expression of the divine mind and he sought clues for the nature of this process in personal experience. For Temple both aspects were related as the objective and subjective expressions of a pervasive reality in which the self could hope for eventual unity. In an earlier phase of his work, Temple believed that personal wholeness resulted in a community of selves united in common purpose. He stressed the objective character of "moral convictions, which have grown up out of this experience of the race, as our guide." Moral conventions reflect a principle of fellowship which opens to individuals a future of common purpose.[43]

As his thinking matured, Temple retained this stress on the social context as the basis of personal development. However, he became critical of society as a worthy standard of value and stressed that true fellowship resulted from personal fulfillment with God in the Church. Temple's shift confirmed Anglican suspicion that the world's fallenness obscures history's true purpose. The Church became for Temple the repository of "the inner meaning of human history," the organ of "His Will for the accomplishment of His Purpose in the world." "Christianity is the religion of the redemption of the world, and profession of it involves membership of a society which is to show in itself the fruits of that redemption."[44] This revision of the basis of fellowship led him to believe that the modern Church required objective standards instead of liberal assumptions, visible "notes" demarcating it from the world, as "One, Holy, Catholic, and Apostolic." Temple felt that the Church's Catholic features served as objective standards.[45] These "notes" facilitated the development of Christian social principles which Temple outlined as the sacredness of personality, the duty of service, fellow-membership, and the power of sacrifice. These principles embodied his effort to reconcile the Church's proximity to the world with its distinctiveness from it.[46]

Temple increasingly distinguished the Church from the world, equating loyalty to the nation with a false allegiance. He acknowledged the necessity of government and applauded democracy as a political philosophy conducive to furthering the Christian intention for society. But he took care to enunciate the reforms he, as a Christian, believed industrial order required. On matters of personal integrity such as gambling and divorce, moreover, he declared that Christians could not allow the state to set their moral standards. "The State," he argued, "has to legislate for many who are not Christians at all and who make no use of the Christian means of grace. The Christian citizen cannot wish to impose on them, under sanction of legal penalties, a stricter law than some authorities find in the teaching given by Christ Himself to His disciples." Temple suggested that being a citizen and being a Christian no longer amounted to the same thing. For a Church which historically had been an arm of the state, this heralded a significant shift in self-understanding. Temple reoriented the Church's nature toward personality and a kind of fellowship that it should try to bring about between individuals.[47]

This represented a sea change for Anglicans, for Temple had been regarded as an energetic reformer who felt the Church must transform society. The culmination of such conviction was reached in Birmingham in April, 1924, where Temple organized the Conference on Christian Politics, Economics, and Citizenship (COPEC). The Conference marked Temple as an ecumenical leader and spokesman for social justice. He never lost those attributes, nor did he relent from belief in the necessity of the Church's social mission. However, his experience with COPEC completed his turn toward the distinctiveness of the Church which began in his search for Christian views of personality and fellowship, and his realization of the pervasiveness of evil.[48]

The Conference attracted over 1,500 delegates from various denominations throughout the British Isles, Europe, China, and Japan. This meeting advanced ecumenical thinking and enhanced the sense of a mainstream Christian phalanx standing for justice. But tensions were evident at the Conference between those who wanted to put individual conversion at the center and those who stressed the need for structural reform in society at large. There was a sense among some attendees that the Church spoke of a spiritual hope, rather than of a political one. Thus the Conference achieved more of a unified critique of industrial society than of a coherent remedy for its ills.[49] For Temple, COPEC marked the transition from an emphasis he had placed on the Church's social role toward an elevation of its distinctive features. Temple was part of an Anglican turn toward an exploration of the source of Christian faith in personality and its expression in fellowship.

The psychological reformation

The turn to the self

In describing the Reformation of the sixteenth century, Ernst Troeltsch said the Protestant "aim is simply to place the pure word of God on the candlestick, and it needs . . . only a provision for the pure preaching of the word and the administration of the sacrament."[50] The Protestant search for a pure expression of Christian belief reappeared among Anglicans after the First World War in personal and corporate forms and became a fixture within modern Anglican sensibility. In seeking ways to make the Church's ministry to the world more compelling, Anglicans not only emphasized the Church's distinctiveness from the world, but examined the nature of religious experience and its relation to the Church's worship.

This new turn in modern Anglicanism began as an interest in the nature of the self. In 1926, W. R. Inge, Dean of St. Paul's, commented that "the centre of gravity in religion has shifted from authority and tradition to experience. The evidences of religion are no longer external and miraculous; they are those which faith itself supplies." By the 1920s the impact of psychology upon religious understanding was undeniable. Psychological categories brought about a fervent search for the personal basis of religious practice as a means to uncover the essence of religious meaning. Thus one Episcopal seminary professor diagnosed the malady of Saul which I Samuel 16:14b had recounted in this way: "an evil spirit from Yahweh troubled him." Instead, Saul suffered from "functional rather than organic nervousness," suggesting "melancholia, morbid dissatisfaction and flashes of dementia." He struggled between noble impulses and ambition according to this account.[51]

Such analysis reflected the intellectual revolution created by the rise of psychology, which developed rapidly in Europe and North America from the beginning of the twentieth century. The appearance of William James' *Varieties of Religious Experience* in 1902, and his *Pragmatism* in 1907, created an international sensation. The French philosopher Henri Bergson realized, with the force of a religious revelation, that "only through a concentration on one's own consciousness could one arrive at a realization of human experience in its fullness and actuality." He called this sympathetic comprehension "intuition" and argued, in 1903, that personality – the self – constitutes an enduring reality which can be grasped when all other realities prove elusive.[52]

James and Bergson inaugurated a new approach to human inquiry, though Sigmund Freud and C. G. Jung became more acknowledged. But a proliferation of psychological approaches to human behavior appeared in the early decades of the twentieth century. Though divided in many aspects of their conclusions, the proponents of psychology were united in their search for primal layers of human reality and shared a tendency to reduce all human experience to intrapersonal forces. Psychology represented the ultimate frontier, whose conquest became urgent as social conflict intensified. It portended the loss of illusion including, Freud believed, the illusion of religion.

Within the Church, psychology attracted adherents who sought a means of recovering the essence of religion from doctrinal and social expressions. In 1906 Elwood Worcester, Rector of Emmanuel Church, Boston, opened a clinic at the church to treat such ailments as hysteria, hypochondria, alcoholism, and drug usage psychologically. Worcester, who had earned a German doctorate in psychology and philosophy, shared the caseload with his assistant, Samuel McComb, and enlisted several psychiatrists and physicians as support personnel. This Emmanuel movement became a model for parish counselling centers and for innovative pastoral care. It legitimated the marriage between religion and psychology and encouraged interest in spiritual forms of healing.[53]

In 1908, after two years of experience, Worcester and McComb explained their convictions. They sensed the dawn of a new day for the Church. The "time is come when the Church must enter more deeply into the personal lives of the people and make a freer use of the means modern science and the Gospel of Christ place at her disposal if she is to continue even to hold her own. It is evident that people to-day desire spiritual help and sustenance which they are not receiving, but which the Church as the representative of Christ is able to give them." The Church must "dispense with the tedious processes of criticism and dogma to return to the Christ of the Gospels and to accept His words in a more literal sense." This essential Christianity, the authors felt, led to modern psychology and physiology, whose views "as to the essential unity of human nature and the mutual relations of mind and body have sunk so deep into the popular conscience that the Church can no longer address men as disembodied spirits."[54] Together religion and medicine can define the "whole man" and demonstrate that "spiritual states can affect health and that physical blessings will follow spiritual exercises." A "general revolt in the name of the soul" promised to invigorate prayer, mysticism, and worship as means of healing.

Citing William James, the Emmanuel authors argued that in the subconscious mind physical experience, the psychological state, and religious cognition meet. The nonrational aspect of religion preponderates, but this renders the self subject to suggestion, the greatest source of which is religion. The world's greatest healer, Christ understood that "disease and sin are parts of a complex order – the kingdom of evil – to overcome which He felt himself sent by God." Christ posed an alternative order, instilling the Kingdom of God into the lives of individuals by means of healing. He suggested a way of life both faithful and therapeutic, which conveyed a sense of personal wholeness. Dormant within each person, wholeness could be realized through religious forms of suggestion to the subconscious. For the Church, this required a recovery of the apostolic sensibility. The early Church offered "the source of innumerable moral regenerations" which could not be found elsewhere. The modern Church must recapture this spiritual power, for it "is not bringing the whole force of the Christian religion to bear upon the lives of the people."[55]

The Emmanuel movement inspired widespread interest in healing and evoked discussion of the relationship between psychology and religious experience. In 1925 Angus Dun of the Episcopal Theological School argued that a psychological inquiry could clarify what religious "practices do for those practicing them and how they do it." It is "good to know what goes on in the people in the pews and what we might reasonably expect to go on under the circumstances." Dun cautioned against preoccupation with psychological states lest one "fall into that fallacy that what is outside does not matter; and neglect questions of truth and outer effectiveness." But he enumerated several psychological features of religious practices.[56] Religious behavior and objects center personal attention on God. They "expose men to religious suggestions" and further the human quest for unity, wholeness. "It says to him that it is only by being one, or at-one, that he can gain power or peace or happiness, and tells him that the only way to become one is to unify his life around the Love of God. The task of religion is the task of atonement, of reconciliation of man with himself, with nature, with his fellows, by reconciling him with God, who as the center and crown of reality holds the secret of life in Himself." Finally, religious practices arouse "that special form of consciousness which we may call the awareness of God."[57]

The idea of a special consciousness dramatized the search for religious certainty. In 1926, W. R. Inge observed "a revived interest in what is called mysticism." Inge had gained recognition as a student of religious psychology and, in 1899, he argued that the study of mysticism clarified the nature of religion, and of the distinctiveness of Christianity from other religions. Mysticism, defined as "the attempt to realise, in thought and feeling, the immanence of the temporal in the eternal, and of the eternal in the temporal," formed a bridge between religion and other forms of knowledge. Conveying its message by means of symbols, mysticism has produced "a revival of spirituality in the midst of formalism or unbelief." It encourages the self to be remade by the influence of transpersonal reality and so to find wholeness. Inge's work offered an early Anglican attempt to recover this form of Christian experience as a means to express the nature of religion.[58]

Inge acknowledged the dangers of subjectivism and pantheism in establishing the veracity of mystical experience. He took care to demonstrate that such individual experiences held an honored place in the Christian tradition. Faith encouraged virtue and wholeness, and thus brought the individual to the path toward salvation. Inge defended the spontaneous character of this process and proposed a view of religious authority which guarded the individual from dogma and institutional presumption. While Inge stressed that mystical perception could build up the Church, he prized individual religious experience against the encroachments of religious traditions and dogmas. His work signaled a turn toward the priority of the self in religious authority.[59]

The assertion of personal religious prerogative intensified in the work of Evelyn Underhill, the religious writer whose own search for certainty led her to Anglicanism. Her major concern was less to develop an Anglican apologetic than it was to uncover the human features of religious experience. This exploration reinforced her thesis that religion lay behind physical reality, loosely engaged with religious institutions but buried within the self's capacity for spiritual perception. For Underhill, religious institutions manifest features of that perception, always risking the substitution of form for substance. As with the self, the Church must look within its customary patterns to discern the divine imprint and, periodically, to recover it.[60]

Underhill's writings articulated a spiritual grammar for modern life. She recognized the loss of religious references and posed the spiritual life as the uncovering of a basic reality which alone could unite the self. Underhill pioneered a new emphasis upon prayer, spirituality, and worship which allowed lay persons to make sense of them. She moved spirituality from the arcane toward the mundane, making spirituality more necessary to human perseverance in the world. She gave the anxious self access to another dimension and she posed an alternative sense of the Church based upon group organization. "Right group suggestion reinforces, stimulates, does not stultify such individual action." Group consciousness endows the self with a context in which its quest is enriched, disciplined, and perfected. The Church grounds personal experience in a tradition of spiritual perception and in an environment of fellow seekers. Religious institutions must direct personal experience to its proper development in small groups which offer the proper environment for the self's religious completion.[61]

The turn toward small groups

"This past spring I began putting down some of the convictions which have grown up out of our work at Calvary Church, New York, where we have had the exciting and rewarding adventure of working out a 'new' religious movement in an old local parish." Samuel Shoemaker, Calvary's Rector, became a popular writer on the spiritual life, noted for his insistence on personal conversion through "surrender" and for his conviction that religion was simple and practical. In 1932, when he published *The Conversion of the Church*, Shoemaker announced his loyalty to the Oxford Group movement. This movement "only believes what the Church believes, is only re-emphasizing the inwardness of the Church's message, and only does what the Church does at its best. It is simply the Church at work in the lives of individuals." Every church "should be a group," for the early Church "was often called 'the Fellowship.'" Such groups could transform the "timid, ineffective, over-organized Church" into "the Church which Christ intended."[62]

The Oxford movement of the twentieth century was a far cry from the Tractarian movement of a century before. Shoemaker had absorbed the ideas of Frank Buchman, a Lutheran minister in Pennsylvania, whose ideal became popular throughout Europe and North America. Buchmanites guided the desire for salvation to the step of self-surrender to God's will in a group context followed by a life of prayer and personal witness. Buchmanite groups met in homes for mutual guidance and claimed that this genuine Christian fellowship posed the possibility of social renewal through conversion and "moral rearmament." The movement attracted scrutiny from Church leaders as its influence grew beyond its actual membership. Critics of the movement challenged its exclusivism and questioned the extent of the changes it inspired.

Herbert Hensley Henson, Bishop of Durham, characterized the movement as a symptom of a disturbed era, when "a chasm opens between the Christian Church and the Christian conscience, and men are perforce driven to seek for themselves as best they can the guidance and spiritual provision which normally they would receive from the Church, and which the Church is divinely commissioned to provide."[63] The Christian conscience has always "maintained an attitude of critical reserve towards the system, hierarchical and sacramental, of the Christian Church." Separatist movements express spiritual aspirations which the institutional Church cannot contain. Such groups therefore "bring to the Church a potential discipline of real value." On the other hand, this movement repudiates the "system of the Church," and its attempt to reproduce the apostolic age "cannot reasonably be made," because it is impossible "to restore either the mentality of the first converts, or the circumstances in which it found expression." "We are the children of our own age. We must perforce relate the Gospel to our own environment, and colour it by our own presuppositions."[64]

Henson criticized the Oxford emphasis upon group guidance as unwholesome, and other observers concurred that the movement addressed Church renewal in a simplistic fashion. This need to repudiate the Oxford Groups points to their influence among Anglicans during the 1920s and 1930s. They revealed the aspirations of an influential minority to remake the Church according to an alternative norm. It would become a series of small groups using apostolic forms of prayer and guidance. The appeal that the movement had was to be found in the implication that genuine Christianity could be distinguished from its institutional husk. The true Church would fall from its shell, and find in group experience its authentic locus.[65] Buchmanite groups were evidence of a disturbing turn in the Church as its social locus disintegrated. Anglicanism, like all forms of mainstream Protestantism, was buffeted by the emergence of subgroups offering competing visions of ecclesiastical identity and often expressing criticisms of the Church's hierarchy. As uncertainty over the center of Anglicanism intensified, grassroots movements claimed, in idiosyncratic ways, to embody the essence of religious identity.

The turn toward liturgy

The Anglican search for a definitive social identity came to focus on liturgy. "In England as in America the question is frequently asked, How has the Great War affected the religion of the people?" When W. R. Inge considered this question in 1926, he cited the "reports of chaplains who served with the forces" who noted "that only sacramental religion and what they call Catholic teaching has any attraction for the soldier."[66] Inge sensed that ritualism, which had secured an Anglican niche, now exerted a general influence. As the noted writer Wilfred Knox commented in 1923, "in its broad outlines ... the movement has won its place in the English Church. Without excluding the more old-fashioned types of Anglican piety ... it has made room for the development of other types more suited to the needs of an age which is largely dominated by a love of variety and sensation."[67] Knox realized that Catholic liturgical expression distinguished religious from secular experience.

Once suspect, ritualism's influence spread in the twentieth century. A Royal Commission on Ecclesiastical Discipline in 1904 investigated "the conduct of Divine Service in the Church of England" and considered means of eliminating anomalies. Rather than proscribing unfamiliar ritual, as many clergy hoped, the Commission declared that the Church's standards required clearly understood norms. It also concluded that "the law of public worship in the Church of England is too narrow for the religious life of the present generation." The study passed to the Convocations, where discussion began of proposed rubrics which would determine appropriate vesture and of modifications in the Church's statutes regarding worship to "secure greater elasticity."[68] The issue moved slowly through the Church's labyrinthine procedural networks and would have remained unresolved had not war and W. H. Frere intervened. Frere, a key figure in the Community of the Resurrection, had introduced the first weekly

Eucharist, or Parish Communion, as a parish priest in 1890. With Percy Dearmer he incited a liturgical revolution on behalf of Catholic ceremonial and emphasized a priestly sense of clerical office. Eventually to become Bishop of Truro, Frere moved readily between liturgical scholarship, Church committees, and the life of a religious community. He galvanized an influential, clerical coterie who shared a desire to make Anglican liturgy more Catholic. This was not simply a party mentality, but a vision of Anglican identity as such. At a time of uncertainty about the Church's social locus and liturgical standards, the Catholic vision gave Anglicans a sense of ecclesiastical identity. Agitation for the Parish Communion gained support before the First World War.[69]

By 1911 Frere had also made a case for revision of the Book of Common Prayer of 1662, the Church of England's standard text. He bluntly insisted that "it is not healthy that a Church of the twentieth century, in praying for the needs of the day, should be hampered by still using the categories of the seventeenth century, and limited, in its explicit scope at any rate, to the outlook of two and a half centuries ago." He urged that the "deadening power in unchanging use" proved most dangerous in "matters of devotion." The Church "must be rich in its varieties" and "ready to review its whole methods from time to time." Frere understood that action by Convocation and Parliament would be lengthy and patiently reiterated the need for revision. This became a curious argument in its usage of prior example to satisfy present need. Frere scorned sixteenth- and seventeenth-century forms of worship, for Anglicans then had prized establishment above other marks of the Church. Now the Church should substitute ancient precedent for more recent custom. "The reform which is needed is not altogether an innovation; it is in some respects a recurrence to the older customs of the Church." He searched for the Church's Catholic heritage, and found an emphasis upon Scripture and historic chant, as well as medieval vesture and the Eucharist.[70]

These points became the enduring characteristics of Anglican liturgical renewal, and Frere became their patient shepherd. He encouraged more usage of the Psalms in worship and an expanded lectionary to include diverse portions of the Bible. He pushed for alternative versions of Morning and Evening Prayer, and advocated frequent usage of the Litany. Citing England's medieval Sarum Missal, he endorsed the use of incense and provision of a lavabo, a basin for ceremonial washing of the priest's hands during the eucharistic liturgy. The Canon of the Eucharist should be rearranged along ancient lines and Compline should be revived as an evening service. Frere involved himself in technical, historical questions and revamped the Church's sense of worship.[71]

Frere sensed that Anglicans responded wholeheartedly to the direction of his work. "It may be well to realize how far spread this movement is," he wrote in 1912. He immersed himself in the details of Church procedure and consulted with Anglicans in South Africa, Japan, and China about new forms of the Prayer Book. His sentiments affected the Church leadership and provoked questions about worship in the National Mission and Life and Liberty respectively. He publicized the views of military chaplains and the conclusions of the Liturgical movement, which emerged among Roman Catholics in Europe after the war. Frere was not the only publicist and cited the work of E. S. Talbot and Percy Dearmer; to a greater extent than any other figure, however, it was Frere who articulated the motives and means of liturgical revision.[72]

The movement which Frere built up encouraged Parliament to consider an alternative version of the Book of Common Prayer. Despite opposition from Evangelicals, which dated back to the work of the Royal Commission in 1904, the idea of an alternative Prayer Book gained support in Church circles. The Church's bishops, as Hensley Henson later recalled, grasped that liturgical revision represented a means of enhancing the Church's sense of order and of renewing an outmoded system of worship. For Henson, however, there was a contradiction between attempting to enhance the Church's ancient discipline and adapting its forms to modern circumstances. He cited this confusion, and Evangelical resistance, as reasons why the proposal for a revised Prayer Book failed to pass through the House of Commons in December, 1927. Despite this defeat the Prayer Book was published in 1928 and used unofficially.[73] The failure to approve a new Prayer Book in England was not repeated in the United States, where a new Book won approval in 1928. That process moved smoothly because the Book was designed to adjust the Church's stated forms of worship to accepted practice rather than to a Catholic agenda. Yet such influence grew because of the appeal of Catholic forms to a new generation. "The real trend of religion among the younger generation is away from dogmatic and institutional Christianity," Inge observed, "and towards an individual and personal faith resting not on authority but on experience." Inge personally regretted the loss of Protestant forms and the growth of Catholic influence. He stood for a Protestantism which "has never yet been actually, the expression of a Christian civilization on its spiritual side."[74]

Such expression took Catholic shape as the most pragmatic way of disengaging the Church from the constraints of the state. Defeat of the proposed Book accelerated the turn toward a Catholic liturgical sensibility among Anglicans, suggesting that liturgical renewal must arise as a grassroots phenomenon, and was not a matter for hierarchical definition. While Frere worked within the Church's legislative channels, another liturgical innovator, A. G. Hebert, appealed to clergy and laity on behalf of a liturgical revolution. A member of the Society of the Sacred Mission, Kelham, Hebert emphasized not merely the Eucharist as the Sunday norm, but the role that liturgy had in sustaining the Church's mission to the world.[75] *Liturgy and Society*, Hebert's great work, articulated a liturgical vision of Anglicanism which confirmed the shift of the Church's identity away from establishment. While planning a book on worship, Hebert discovered that because Christianity exists to redeem the world, "the things done and said in church must have a direct relation to the things done and said everywhere else." Thus "the sacraments and the liturgy exist in order to give to human life its true direction in relation to God, and to bind men in fellowship with one another." Because modern Europe lost its common faith and witnessed the disintegration of its social life, the Church must "show the way, the only way, to the recovery of a common faith and a true social life." Hebert concluded that the Church's liturgy had a social contribution to make.[76]

Hebert appealed to the Church's "common faith" and tradition "embodied in concrete form in the sacraments." This was a reliance upon the authority of habitual practices shaped by historic consensus. Such authority revealed the Church to be an organic society which can unite humanity in fellowship. Hebert hoped to disengage the Church from liberalism's corruptions and to clarify the liturgical nature of the Church's social mission.[77] The ideals of social progress and theological modernism promised freedom for the individual from dogma and tyranny, but they led to war, to authoritarianism in religion and politics, and to isolation and alienation in urban, industrial society. Human beings continued "groping after God," in acute need but with few means of access to the divine. Modernity inspired false means of fulfillment.

Hebert called for recovery of the early Church's sacramental vision and understanding of the Incarnation from the corruptions of medieval influences as well as liberal theology. He took heart at the work of William James and the rise of psychology, which "gives way to a sympathetic interest in the phenomena of religious experience." This approach laid bare Christianity's true nature as a faith and as a pattern of ritual. Study of patristic Christianity revealed a community of faithful people united by their liturgy. As the Liturgical movement taught, Christianity is a fellowship dominated by the mystery of hope expressed in worship. The Church manifests God's "goodness in the Incarnation," the redemption of humanity "continuing in Christ's mystical Body." Liturgy joins individuals into this common sense, and exhibits "the aim and meaning of human life in the light of the Incarnation."[78]

There has been confusion about the Church of England's identity. "Is she the Church of the English nation, or is she really a group of denominations held together by an accidental bond of establishment? Is she authentically Catholic or is she Protestant? Does she hold a definite belief? If so, why does she not enforce conformity of belief?" Hebert's questions sparked debate about the role of liturgy, and his answers made a great impact in Anglican circles. Recovery of ancient liturgy ensured the Church's integrity. Liturgy is the center of the Church's life, and its patristic and sacramental patterns formed the surest basis for its mission. The Church must stress the Eucharist as its supreme form of worship, in which the drama of the Incarnation posed hope of redemption from the tragedy of modern life. Hebert became the foremost exponent of the Parish Communion, for he felt that the Eucharist could inspire the local church to realize the possibility of apostolic fellowship in its midst. In the Eucharist, the parish anticipates the eternal community.[79]

Hebert's sense of liturgy's social role and of the Eucharist as the Church's foundation led a young liturgical scholar named Gregory Dix to pose the notion of the Church as the people of God. He argued that "the primitive eucharistic rite" demonstrated "the strong consciousness" of early Christians that they were a people, a race, formed by God, in anticipation of the creation's redemption. This sense of peoplehood had wrongly turned to a dogmatic, sacerdotal sense of sacrament in the Middle Ages, when, in the erroneous "attempt to gain the whole world for God the Church came very near to losing her own Soul."[80] Now the Church was moving toward seeming a liturgical people of God, upholding ancient precedent in opposition to modernity's erroneous assumptions. The liturgical vision of ancient Christianity facilitated a moral critique of modern life and generated images of religious community.[81]

This influence was apparent as the Church expanded its healing ministries and the ministries of women. Adopting psychological categories and the format of small groups, Anglicans explored the possibility of physical and spiritual healing and the relationship between body and soul in the life of faith. Consideration of the Church's heritage encouraged the belief that apostolic Christianity had professed care for the total person, not merely the soul. There were ancient rites worthy of use in modern times, when the need for healing from disease and anxiety alike were acute.[82] If the Church should be a healing community, a few Anglicans reasoned, it must project images of social wholeness. Some Anglicans, such as Roland Allen, argued that the Church's notion of priesthood had become professional, isolating sacramental and teaching functions from the shared ministry of the Church. But priesthood should express the creation's unity, and a few Anglicans took this to mean that the priesthood should be open to women. In 1929, Charles Raven argued that social crisis provoked a need for wholeness. The Church could witness to social redemption by including women in its ministry because their presence would strengthen the Church's offer of healing to the world.[83]

The idea of ordaining women gained few other supporters at the time, but its appearance was evidence that Anglicans now possessed a vision of the Church as comprising liturgical fellowship. This guidepost gained importance because it clarified Anglicanism's nature and mission. A new confidence in Anglican identity seemed to appear, until further upheaval caused it to vanish like a mirage.

THE ILLUSION OF ANGLICAN CONSENSUS

A chastened liberalism

"It is probable," William Temple wrote in November, 1939, "that the outbreak of war will prove to have intensified a sense of divergence between older and younger theologians which . . . was already acute."

Temple was one of the younger group who shared an emphasis upon the reality of evil and realized that the Church must rethink "the standards of life to which a society must aim at conforming if it is to be in any sense a Christian society." The Church must "recover our apprehension of the Gospel alike in its essence and in its impact upon ourselves and the world." Temple hoped that theology would "offer to a new Christendom its Christian map of life, its Christo-centric metaphysic." That hope put into perspective the nature of the Anglican identity which emerged in the 1930s.[84] An influential Anglo-Catholic, E. L. Mascall noted that liberalism set out to "rehabilitate orthodoxy" but "would seem to have been a temporary divergence from the main stream of Anglicanism, largely due to pressure of circumstances and by no means wholly valueless, but incomplete, lacking continuity with the past, and without solid foundation." Mascall believed the biblical theology of Karl Barth would encourage study of the great Anglican divines and inspire future Anglican thought.[85]

During the 1930s there were signs of a post-liberal, Anglican theology. The suggestion that the Church was a liturgical fellowship and the sense of a new theological generation came into focus as Anglicans searched for an ecclesiastical identity. Although it was not clearly understood, a tension loomed between how to reconcile the preservation of Church order and the expansion of the Church's role in society. Most Anglicans believed that they could be a virtual religious establishment, encouraging a new Christendom, by recovering the Church's biblical and theological sources. This chastened liberalism functioned only as long as the nature of the Church's offices and of its social task were mutually agreed upon by Anglicans. What seemed to be a modern consensus proved a temporary moundbank amid modernity's shifting sands.

During the 1930s, the old liberalism could yet be seen in J. F. Bethune-Baker, who attempted to explain early Christian experience in modern, human terms. Bethune-Baker viewed history as an inexorable progress toward cosmic completion. In response, the Church must refashion its self-understanding in the assurance that ancient creeds, offices, and liturgies could withstand modern scrutiny.[86] Similarly Charles Raven believed religion "is essentially a relationship of love to God and man, and if all its activities must manifest this love, then there is no room for the primary insistence upon the credal, ceremonial and constitutional niceties which so often engross the attention of churchmen." Raven acknowledged that social dislocation had stimulated a search for Christianity's roots and for a purified Church. He scorned, however, what he believed were the externals of the Church's belief. He grasped psychology as the tool for uncovering genuine Christianity, which lay in personality and in fellowship unfettered by forms. This outline of a Church stripped of nonessentials was as vague as his image of Anglican identity was imprecise.[87]

The change in William Temple's thought signaled the path most Anglicans took toward a different view of the Church's nature. In his early work Temple believed in a benevolent cosmic process which underlay nature as well as personality. He never repudiated this belief, because he perceived within the creation a "principle of unity" through which, "by a right apprehension . . . a man can make his life part of an artistic or perfect whole." Unity demonstrated the supremacy of divine purpose and instructed human beings in their social duty. The Church reveals God's unity as the divine intention for creation and the locus of divine action within history.[88] Temple had characterized evil as false perceptions and misguided actions; but, his dread of evil deepened in the 1930s as he was influenced by his American friend Reinhold Niebuhr, the noted exponent of realism who taught at Union Theological Seminary in New York. Niebuhr convinced Temple that, as he searched for unity in creation, he must address the fact of evil head-on and offer a theological vision of justice. Niebuhr proved to be cynical about the capacity of groups and nations to act morally. He preferred to regard the individual as a moral agent, while Temple, clinging to a hope that the creation could be redeemed, prized human fellowship. Temple conceded the power of evil, but he turned toward the Church as the progenitor of a new world order.[89]

Instead of living for others, evil tempts the self to seek its own gratification and abandon moral considerations. An innate moral consciousness, however, is awakened by its apprehensions within the world and serves as the medium of revelation. The hope of redemption derives from the Incarnation, when God entered the world in human form, set a moral example, and inspired a principle of fellowship which was grounded in a sacramental sense of reality. These ideals became embedded in the Church, to which the promise of salvation has been entrusted, but which embodies the human dilemma. Although it offers the sinful self the promise of spiritual guidance, it

may bind the self to a lesser collective identity than the Kingdom of
God. In the past the Church has linked human hope to national,
political aspirations. But the Church's task is to reveal God's intention
as a "Commonwealth of Value," the "unity of all spirits of all periods
of time" with one another and God. The struggle against evil is not a
battle for the individual soul, but a universal struggle to establish
God's eternal Kingdom.[90]

Though he could no longer rely upon human rationality or the
world's intelligibility, Temple retained the ideal of unity, which he
accommodated to the reality of evil by means of a sacramental
theology. Worship expressed the Church's intention and the sacraments, especially the Eucharist, alerted believers to the drama of
history. The Eucharist illustrated the pattern by which people should
live, and anticipated the commonwealth to come. By the late 1930s,
Temple emphasized the Church's Catholic features, which allow it to
mediate between the human and the divine, the present and the
future, the factual and the eventual realities. Spirit arises within
matter, he believed, leading the material world toward its destina-
tion. This hope appears vividly through the Church's sacraments,
which offer "hope of making human both politics and economics and
of making effectual both faith and love."[91]

Thus a sober realization of evil led Temple to emphasize the
Church's distinctive offices and to distinguish between the nature of
the Church and that of the state. Temple now stressed that the
"Christian's ultimate loyalty is due, not to his earthly State, but to the
Kingdom of God, wherein all nations are provinces." Yet he
continued to grant the state a role in achieving the divine goal, which
might entail ordering its citizens to war, when conflict resulted from
opposition to clearly evil powers. But, as the Second World War
broke, Temple emphasized that Christians fought not for national
vindication but "for the opportunity to make the ordering of human
life increasingly Christian." The Christian must be a citizen both of
earth and of heaven, finding in worship the ultimate loyalty due in
times of conflict. Worship orients the Christian to the highest of all
priorities. The "distinctive and specially characteristic activity of the
Church," worship sustains the believer as a moral agent amid a fallen
world.[92]

Temple discovered a way to balance the Anglican need for Church
order with the opportunity for ministry in its social context. He
achieved this by defining the Church as a worshiping community

whose Catholic features revealed its moral voice as the harbinger of an eternal fellowship. He became cautious about the Church's ability to dictate social and political programs, but he reserved for the Church a right to intervene in humanitarian fashion. Early in 1943 he proposed to the House of Lords that Britain, through an unspecified neutral country, should encourage Germany to release all Jewish people in concentration camps to British care, in which the Church should play a leading part. As the horror of the Holocaust became apparent, Temple concluded that the Church must pursue a redemptive policy.[93]

Moral categories constituted the substance of the Church's critical distance from society, just as worship defined the hope entrusted to the Church. Although a sense of crisis had taken hold, Anglicans became confident that the Church had an understanding of events which was lacking in the political sphere. This assumption led the Church toward innovative views of social relations. In South Africa, Anglicans resisted the entrenchment of racial segregation in the 1930s in favor of a social philosophy which included black people in economic development. Not presumed to be egalitarian, this was a relegation of blacks to the role of "Junior Partner" on terms dictated by white interests, notably mining capital. Nonetheless, in that context advocacy of any role for black people beyond that of serf meant outright opposition to the incipient apartheid system. In Australia, during the 1940s, a visionary Anglican group, the Christian Social Order Movement, revived the ideas of Christian Socialism. They wanted to lead the reconstruction of Australian life after the Second World War by founding a social order dependent for its operation upon Christian precepts. Guided by a theological vision of God's Kingdom, the CSOM believed the Church must be a catalyst for an organic sense of society responding to life's needs with social cooperation. Stymied by its vague idealism, the movement failed in 1951. Nevertheless Anglicans generally distanced themselves from dominant social values in order to ensure that their moral voice was heard.[94]

The appeal of moral rigorism

Heightened attention to moral categories led some Anglican thinkers to explore the nature of moral obligation. W. R. Inge, who exemplified this approach, identified perversions of Christian life which had threatened the validity of the Church's witness. He cited "an extreme asceticism," which he equated with medieval monasticism, and "the monstrous growth of a theocratic Empire in Europe," meaning the papacy, as distortions of the Church's moral purpose. Inge also criticized the liberal tendency to reduce religious expressions to peculiarities of particular times and places. He characterized Christian ethical norms as universally true because they were reasonable and conformable to Scripture. Christian ethics originates in the life of Jesus, who embodied God's eternal will and taught his followers to die to sin and be reborn in righteousness. The Christian can be motivated to take Christ's path not by fear but by the love of truth and goodness.[95]

Inge understood that modern circumstances had affected Christianity's social role. "That our religion no longer attracts those who are shaping the thought of our time is notorious." Christians should adopt the *Zeitgeist* when its tendencies seem even slightly favorable to moral progress. But "there are ideals now popular which Christians must resist without compromise. Practical materialism, secularity, and the negation of discipline, are . . . really contrary to the laws of life as ordained by God and revealed in Christ. We are meant to live in fairly hard training," and "it would be well if Christians quite openly professed and acted upon a higher standard than that of the world around them."[96] K. E. Kirk adopted a similar moral rigorism, arguing in 1933 that marriage is an indissoluble, sacramental bond and that Jesus never countenanced remarriage after divorce. In fact divorce could occur morally only in rare instances such as adultery by one party. Thus the Church of England maintained moral standards of a higher order than that countenanced by society.[97]

Kirk (who was Bishop of Oxford) represented a moderate Anglican Catholicism which sought to take modern issues seriously. Clarifying the distinction between Church and world led Kirk to become a prominent moral authority. He appealed to the modern need for religious certainty, which he rooted in "Scripture, Christian experience, and the agreed results of free inquiry into human character." Kirk meant by this that psychology revealed the compatibility of experience with the truths contained in Scripture and Christian tradition. The modern search for good and for assurance could uphold Christian verities by correct use of reason and reliance upon Church tradition. In turn the Church best served the world by maintaining clear ethical norms. "Moral education, then, cannot dispense with the enumeration of duties or right actions."[98] Like other Anglican theologians between the world wars, Kirk decried current morality and appealed for Christians to consider themselves a people set apart from the world. Kirk attributed the superiority of Christian morality to its distinctive sources in Scripture and Christian tradition, whose nature seemed clearly established. The apparent consistency of the sacraments with Jesus' teaching verified that the Church embodied a reality which provided the certitude modern convictions lacked.

Kirk, however, sensed there was something fragile about this assumption of personal conscience's role in the moral life. He wondered if the Church of England's respect for conscience compromised its ability to be a clear moral voice or an expression of Catholic tradition. Yet he was confident that "there is no lack of general agreement as to Christian morality," and though the Church of England encourages divergences of opinion, its genius was an underlying sense of a clearly acknowledged Anglican tradition. Kirk believed that conscience's eventual grasp of truth would uphold the Church's polity and worship. The Church's truth results from its faithfulness to "the fundamental principles of moral theology" while interpreting them "with a wise discretion." The Church tolerates conscience while requiring of it loyalty to the collective wisdom of the present, which accords with the accepted traditions of the past, though he did not specify how.[99] He believed in the Church's capacity for consensus, and he was convinced that morality, discerned by personal conscience, accords with the Church's standards, which do not vary from age to age. Conscience upholds the unity of the creation which the Church is charged to reveal.

The vision of unity

The idea of unity encouraged two forms of Anglican interest in ecumenical discussions. Following the Christian Socialist tradition, many Anglicans concluded that cooperation by Christians in social mission portended creation's eventual unity. Other Anglicans, swayed by the Church's Catholic wing, sought ecumenical unity through defining the Church. They intended to preserve important features such as the historic episcopate and the sacraments of Baptism and the Eucharist. The influence of liberalism made it seem possible to balance mission and Church order. But when liberalism became problematic, Anglicans stressed that particular marks of Church life guaranteed Church identity. Anglican ecumenism began in 1853 with the publication of the Muhlenberg Memorial, a petition to the Episcopal Church's General Convention inspired by William A. Muhlenberg, which called for Christian unity through the creation of an ecclesiastical system broader than that of the Episcopal Church. The Memorialists observed that any system should be "identical with that Church in all its great principles, yet providing for as much freedom in opinion, discipline and worship, as is compatible with the essential faith and order of the Gospel."[100]

The preservation of the Church's essence permeated Lambeth's Quadrilateral, but the idea of unity initially overshadowed consideration of the Church's nature. Herbert Symonds, the Anglican President of the Canadian Society of Christian Unity, in 1899 called unity "no merely transitory wave of feeling" but "the necessary outcome, of the circumstances of our time, which cannot therefore be stayed or turned aside until it has reached its appointed goal." Christian unity was a key feature of the age, accompanying scientific and political developments. The differences among churches were inconsequential and could be overcome.[101] Hensley Henson struck a hopeful chord when he preached at Westminster Abbey early in the twentieth century. He expressed confidence that Christians could become one as in apostolic days, supplant the state, and guide the "aspirations of humanity." Taking over the role of the nation became a prominent theme in Anglican missionary work. The state posed misguided loyalty, while the Church pointed to creation's unity.[102]

The World Missionary Conference which met in Edinburgh in 1910 "focused much of the previous century's movement for uniting Christians in giving the Gospel to the world." Led by Methodist John R. Mott, it rallied ecumenical zeal and inspired the Faith and Order movement, which contributed to founding the World Council of Churches.[103] A leading figure at Edinburgh was Charles H. Brent, Bishop of the Philippines and later Bishop of Western New York. Brent believed that Christians must cooperate in practical fashion for mission without being deterred by differences in doctrine, polity, or worship. Nevertheless, sounding a note which would characterize future Anglican ecumenical endeavor, Brent called for consideration of Church order. There could be no mission without attention to the causes of division among Christians. With William T. Manning, later Bishop of New York, Brent organized an Episcopal Commission on

Faith and Order. In 1912, a deputation led by Charles P. Anderson, Bishop of Chicago, went to persuade the Church of England of the wisdom of ecumenical discussions.[104]

Anderson and Manning called for ecumenical talks as means to bolster the Christian social mission but cautioned that ecumenism did not entail the surrender of Church identity into a vague, undenominational structure.[105] With discussion of the Lambeth Quadrilateral in the 1890s, Anglicans began to prize features of their Church structure as rallying points for Church unity. Charles Briggs migrated from the Presbyterian to the Episcopal Church at the end of the nineteenth century as his emphasis on the episcopate increased. A noted scholar of the New Testament and early Christian history at Union Theological Seminary in New York, Briggs confirmed Anglican suspicion that ecumenical unity required delineation of Church structure.[106] The Church's Anglo-Catholic wing particularly stressed that unity was inseparable from the holiness of the Church derived from its sacraments and ministry. The Kikuyu controversy in Africa awakened fear that unity might compromise the Church's apostolic deposit which Anglo-Catholics guarded.[107]

Nevertheless, after the First World War, the hope of Church unity as a prelude to history's decisive advance encouraged Anglicans to take a leading role in the ecumenical movement. Ecumenism in the 1920s and 1930s included discussions of Faith and Order, Life and Work, and world mission. For Anglicans, ecumenism also meant discussions with particular churches as well as meetings of global scale. After the Lambeth Conference of 1920, Anglicans entered into extensive conversations with Roman Catholics, the Orthodox churches, and the Protestant churches in Britain. Breakthroughs were achieved, such as Orthodox acknowledgement of the validity of Anglican ordination in 1922. There were also Anglican concessions on the role of a state Church, which noted that the Church's integrity does not arise from its being part of the political establishment. These encounters brought closer an agreement on the need for Church unity but at the same time deepened appreciation for differences in doctrine and Church structure. Moderate Anglicans such as Randall Davidson, Archbishop of Canterbury, and Cosmo Lang, Archbishop of York, hoped for a union which might incorporate episcopacy, but not all Anglicans endorsed that ideal which eluded realization.[108]

Incorporation of key features of Church structure into ecumenical union became the Anglican priniciple. Anglicans readily participated in Life and Work discussions, as evinced by the role of F. T. Woods, Bishop of Winchester, who preached at the Stockholm Conference of 1925. Woods called for the "establishment of the sovereignty of Jesus Christ through the whole range of human affairs," believing the churches must bring the Kingdom of God to bear upon the world's needs. He depicted public service as the foremost mark of the churches' mission.[109] But Faith and Order discussions attracted wider Anglican participation, with Charles Brent and William Temple offering key statements at the Lausanne Faith and Order Conference in 1927. Attention to Church order became the Anglican means of ecumenical work, for cooperative social work seemed possible only when Church identity was secure.

In the period between the world wars, Anglican ecumenical intention achieved a fruitful balance between the preservation of order and the creation of cooperative endeavors. A host of voices encouraged ecumenical conversation and insisted that episcopacy and the sacraments offered the meeting ground for Church union. Though a few Anglo-Catholics feared the surrender of the Church's apostolicity, a consensus which balanced Church order with mission predominated in Anglican thinking.[110] The key exponent here was William Temple, who helped to fuse the Faith and Order and Life and Work conferences into the World Council of Churches in the late 1930s. He laid mutual stress upon social mission and the Church's apostolic character. Under his influence, ecumenism centered upon the search for mutuality in mission with appreciation for divergences in belief and Church structure.

That quintessentially Anglican balance held fast because there was pervasive Anglican interest in clarifying the Church's mission. Ecumenical gatherings articulated concerns which gave Anglicans the sense of leading a global movement of Christian faith with sensitivity to the relation between Christian mission and its cultural forms. By the 1920s in Britain and the United States, mainstream Church leaders were rethinking the purpose of Christian mission. A prominent opinion was that mission had been accommodated to Western cultural ambitions. Instead the missionary must acknowledge the integrity of all cultures, though it was less easy to agree about the difficult theological problem of the distinctiveness of the Christian religion.[111]

Anglicans responded to this issue at the International Missionary Council in Jerusalem in 1928. The Bishop of Salisbury, St. Clair

Alfred Donaldson, argued that missionary work entailed being co-creators with God of a new social world. Mission must be ecumenical because through reunion of the Churches the stigmas of European influence and modernization might be overcome. William Temple argued that Christianity acts as a principle of change in society which refuses to acquiesce to cultural influences.[112] That position relieved Anglicans of the association between Christianity and Western culture. In 1942, Gerald Broomfield, Secretary of the Universities' Mission to Central Africa (UMCA) argued that the integrity of Christian mission lay in the Church. It should be possible, for instance, "to distinguish between those who are members of it, and those who are not." The Church possessed visible marks delineating it from society, namely, its ministry and sacraments, which secured the Church in society without identifying it with particular cultures. These forms became important as the Church was threatened by nationalism in the mission field.[113]

THE END OF THE MISSIONARY ERA

Hensley Henson described Christianity's superiority to other religions in terms of its "unique genius of assimilation." Not bound to "any specific economic system," Christianity possesses an "amazing power of adaptation to circumstance" which has been the basis of ecclesiastical development, but which is limited by "the original and essential principles" of Christ's life. Civilization and Christianity must not be confused, although "a perfect civilization and a rightly apprehended Christianity would harmonize."[114] Most Anglicans trusted that the Church's "genius of assimilation" affirmed its ability to guide social development. Such intention played a prominent role in Anglican missionary work in the nineteenth century and after the First World War. But the ability of Anglican missionaries to guide social development was eroded because nationalism threatened missionary control of Church growth.

The idea that the Church could assimilate diverse cultural forms proved fragile. In the Victorian age the Church seemed able to adopt indigenous cultural forms without surrender of its Catholic features or loss of missionary oversight. However, mission suffered from association with notions of Western superiority and a mistrust of indigenous peoples. Anglican missionaries believed their goal to be a cultural modernization which safeguarded ecclesiastical identity. They presumed such a process demanded their oversight and could not foresee their withdrawal from the mission field. A tension emerged between the impulse to adapt the Church to indigenous culture and a concern to distinguish the Church from society, that is, between the particular form of the Church and its universal message. As missionaries sought an indigenous Church, however, they unwittingly abetted the rise of national self-consciousness. In South Africa the black activist Sol Plaatje, first General Secretary of the African National Congress, was educated for a civil service job in mission schools, including an Anglican one. Plaatje's training equipped him not merely to function in the existing society but to envision a new one.[115]

Means of assimilation

Anglicans sought means of assimilating nationalist movements to the Church and of adapting them to missionary oversight.[116] At the start of the twentieth century an opportunity to assimilate a nationalist movement fell into the laps of South African Anglicans. On August 21, 1900, the bishops of the Church of the Province of South Africa (CPSA) considered a request from James Mata Dwane, leader of an Ethiopian-style religious group, who petitioned the Church to unite with his movement in a way that would preserve their identity. The Ethiopian leaders felt that Anglican orders would legitimize their ministry, while, for the CPSA, there was the puzzling challenge of how to incorporate this kind of nationalist sentiment.[117] Ethiopian movements appeared in South Africa about 1890 as religious expressions of black independence from white domination. Unlike Zionist groups, which concerned themselves with ecstatic utterance and "prophecy," Ethiopians hoped to legitimize their aspiration for racial autonomy through church organization.[118]

Anglican missionaries had worked for eventual forms of black self-control, but most bishops felt that the Ethiopians were unprepared for autonomy. However, Archbishop William West Jones, expressing a degree of sensitivity unusual for that time, considered the Ethiopians might have their own bishop and assume the status of a missionary order within the Church's structure. Jones commissioned Bishop C. E. Cornish of Grahamstown to investigate the group, and Cornish advised that the incorporation of the Ethiopians was an opportunity for the Church to "control" this movement. In reply the Ethiopians relented on their initial demands. Dwane would not immediately become a bishop, nor would lay members of the movement be received *en masse* into the Anglican Church. Instead, Anglican missionaries would instruct the Ethiopians in preparation for confirmation. Ethiopian clergy would be trained for ordination as any other candidates for holy orders. As they filtered into the Church, the Ethiopians would constitute an order which would be supervised by a Provincial appointed by the bishops and a chapter appointed by the Provincial. The local diocesan bishop retained the right to visit the order, but a bishop exclusively for the Order was foreseen. The Compact was enacted and Dwane made a profession of faith to Jones on August 26, 1900.[119]

At first the Ethiopians seemed to fit smoothly into their Anglican niche. Dwane was ordained a deacon, and several lay catechists were commissioned. Large numbers from the movement were confirmed, and several Anglican clergy, notably W. M. Cameron, gained trust with its leaders. In 1904, however, Cameron was succeeded by E. C. West, who took an authoritarian approach to dealing with the order. Dwane felt his role being usurped, and urged Ethiopians to disavow Anglican authority.[120] This issue laid bare tensions within the Ethiopian movement itself as well as within the Anglican Church. Although the movement had ten thousand members when Dwane approached the Church, fewer than two thousand ultimately followed him into Anglicanism. Eventually Anglican and Ethiopian leaders reached a compromise which preserved their Compact. The Order was exempted from the jurisdiction of parochial and missionary clergy, but agreed to acknowledge the diocesan bishop. W. M. Cameron became Coadjutor Bishop of Cape Town in 1907 and was appointed as acting Provincial of the group, and Dwane, in 1911, became a priest, sealing the Order's incorporation.

In most cases the Church struggled to adjust its life to nationalism. Church leaders in Japan considered the concept of "self-support" as a pivotal means of adjustment to that society at the beginning of the twentieth century. For Bishop John McKim of Tokyo, self-support meant the consecration of Japanese bishops, for which he stipulated that a diocese must achieve financial autonomy. In 1902, McKim doubted that it was "safe to give the first generation of Christians in a heathen land complete autonomy as a Church. The old traditions and habits have a strong influence and the intense nationalism of the Japanese is such that it . . . would lead them to organize a Church quite different from that of the Catholic church throughout the world." McKim's fears were realistic because of the surge of nationalism and xenophobia prevalent in Japan since the late 1880s. Civil authorities judged religions by their contribution to national ideology, thus intensifying the challenge missionaries faced in their work.[121]

Anglican missionaries had aspired to being Japan's modernizing agents and initially applauded the growing interest in civic reform. The turn to ideology, however, increased pressure on the foreign missionaries to evolve a truly Japanese Church. Their response was to move Japanese men into leadership roles such as school headmasters. Sharing leadership portended the advance of Japanese men into the episcopate, however, and this gave the missionaries pause. A Japanese episcopate meant surrender of missionary control, a step which few ·dared to contemplate. One missionary, Henry St. George Tucker, later Presiding Bishop of the Episcopal Church, encouraged self-support and the development of a Japanese episcopate. "Japan as a nation can be won for Christ only by Japanese," he insisted. "An independent, self-supporting, self-led Japanese Church is the agency through which alone Christianity can be carried to the great mass of the people of the country." At first, Tucker hesitated at the thought that missionaries might be left without a role in Japan. But he resigned as Bishop of Kyoto in 1923 and returned to the United States, believing the time had come for indigenous leadership.[122]

Late in 1923 John Naide was consecrated Bishop of Osaka, and Joseph Motoda Bishop of Tokyo. But the achievement of Japanese bishops was to provide a symbolic step toward Japanese leadership rather than a literal one. Missionaries other than Tucker showed no inclination to disengage from their work in favor of a truly indigenous hierarchy. In fact, following an earthquake which flattened Tokyo in 1923, the need for relief work persuaded missionaries that their guidance was necessary. "With self-support and the gradual establishment of independent dioceses throughout Japan the need for ordained missionaries becomes even more evident," wrote Bishop Charles Reifsnider in 1925.[123] But, events in Japan and elsewhere were to challenge his perception.

The irresistible force of circumstances

Since their arrival in China in large numbers early in the nineteenth century, Christian missionaries had been viewed with suspicion. To most Chinese people this Western religion seemed an offshoot of Buddhism with an individualistic emphasis, a critical view of Chinese culture, a promise of dire consequences for those who failed to convert, and a close tie to Western culture's intrusion. Fortunately Christian missionaries also gained admiration for their promotion of education, philanthropy, and morality. Missionary schools and hospitals filled a void in Chinese life and helped to attract 100,000 converts by 1900. This constituted a tiny percentage of the population, but was a sufficiently large number to encourage missionaries in their belief that they could bring about the emergence of a modern China.[124]

"It is the duty of the Church, because of her greater moral and spiritual experience, to take the lead in abolishing social misery and poverty which is so deadening to the spiritual life," the Diocese of Anking, China newsletter declared early in 1922. Anking Anglicans shared the Protestant hope that the Church's ministries would inspire forms of social development; however, this hope proved futile.[125] Sensitive missionaries already acknowledged the realities of the situation in China. Late in 1924, Mildred S. Capron, editor of the Anking newsletters, reported on her tour through inland areas of China. It was "a wonderful privilege to see Chinese people in their own homes and natural surroundings, such a change from viewing them thru the glasses of our little western settlement here, where they try to do the foreign thing or affect the foreign idea . . . and I return from such trips feeling very humble. No more do I criticise the Chinese for their anti-foreign feeling. I would be anti-foreign too if I were a Chinese, and saw us as many of them do." The Chinese could not yet perceive that the fundamental message of Christianity was distinct from the disposable Western garb in which it was clothed. She lamented that the Chinese people feared the loss of their culture to Western influences, for missionaries understood that Western culture "seems so shallow in comparison to theirs, and so devoid of the richness that theirs possesses." She looked forward to "the time . . . when our Christian Message will be stripped of its foreign raiment, and will stand out in all its beauty. These people will then know that our Christ is their Christ as well, not merely a western deity." Thus the recent, "strong wave of anti-foreignism will bear good fruit."[126]

The immediate fruit of anti-foreign sentiment must have left a bitter taste in Capron's mouth. During the 1920s a nationalist revolt tore through large segments of China as the struggle for political hegemony opened between nationalist and Communist forces. Both sides agreed that China must be rid of foreign influence. The result was civil unrest and a violent xenophobia which had dire consequences for missionaries.[127] In January, 1927, Bishop D. T. Huntington of Anking concluded that "it may be that we shall have to change very radically our whole mission policy." Diocesan institutions considered elevating Chinese men to the roles of school principal and business manager, and professed support for Chinese nationalism. Control of Church property could be transferred from missionaries to Chinese boards, and Chinese clergy and laity might assume financial oversight of Church treasuries. This rush to implement Chinese leadership proved inadequate. Early in 1927, Anking missionaries took refuge in Shanghai when anti-foreign sentiment and fighting between nationalist factions consumed their region. When most returned by mid 1928, the goal of "self-support" became their top priority.[128]

"Self-support" proved incomplete in Japan. In 1931 a Japanese branch of the Brotherhood of St. Andrew was formed with the intention of imparting the ideal of Christian citizenship to young Japanese men and "breaking down the barriers of national mistrust and selfishness." Brotherhood leaders epitomized the missionary view of the 1930s that the Church could create a sense of the nation which opposed secularism and promoted international cooperation. In July, 1933, Paul Rusch, Associate Secretary of the Brotherhood, noted that there were twenty-six chapters in five of the Church's ten dioceses. Rusch feared, however, that missionaries would misread the Brotherhood's growth as confirmation of their indispensability. He hoped his colleagues would realize that the

Christian Church has to be Japanese in Japan and it has to be geared into Japanese life and not forever directed and controlled by a lot of foreign missionaries who still think in terms of their own colleges of 30 and 40 years ago, or the sailing ships they came over on. The man who has his ear to the ground today in Japan is discovering things that throw aside all the ideas of ten or twenty years ago.[129]

Rusch understood that the missionary role had become obsolete and that the Church should be led by the Japanese.

Most missionaries in Japan believed shared Church leadership was an adequate response to nationalism. Although one Episcopal missionary, J. Kenneth Morris, decried the Japanese invasion of China in 1936 and protested that the missionary days were over, most could not envision the Church without them. Bishop Shirley Nichols of Kyoto proposed in 1938 a twenty-year plan toward Japanese leadership. But his hope was dashed in 1939, when the Religious Organizations Law pressured all Protestants to join a union Church, and by early 1941 all missionaries were expelled from Japan.[130] Numerous Anglican congregations affiliated with the union Church, though many others resisted. During the war, Japanese Anglicans segmented into factions which either accommodated their faith to the national emergency or maintained their faith and suffered opprobrium. The Church was sustained during this crisis by Bishop Shinji Sasaki, who resisted cultural conformity. Yet Sasaki had joined with other Japanese bishops in 1940 to announce that "we must sever our connections with European and American Christianity and must now live Christianity in the Japanese spirit."[131]

Japan was an extreme example of a pervasive trend. By 1937 nationalist forces in Burma threatened British influence and demanded the expulsion of foreigners. In the Church of Uganda in 1941, the Mukono Crisis challenged white leadership to contain the "Balakole" revival, the eruption of a charismatic subgroup within the Church. The Church successfully incorporated this grassroots phenomenon by bringing leaders of the Balakole into the Church's ministry in a rare instance of visionary Church policy.[132]

The eruption of new forms

"The Church of England is evolving into the Church of India," an Indian delegate to a provincial synod declared late in 1912. He had ample justification for such confidence. The Indian Church had begun to create an autonomous structure and to designate its own leadership. The end of 1912 witnessed the consecration of V. S. Azariah, the first Indian bishop. Agitation for an Indian Church structure continued for some time because such a proposal required approval from the imperial power. That was secured when Royal Assent was given to the Indian Church Bill in December, 1927, and the Indian Church assumed governance of its own affairs.[133]

However, the creation of a national Church for Indian Anglicans had scarcely begun. On the subcontinent, denominational differences seemed a Western contrivance which confounded Christianity's truth. Bishop Azariah pointed out that a union Church, joining the witness of various Christian branches into one body, would become the most effective form of mission in India. In 1919, Azariah met leaders of the South India United Church – a merger of Presbyterians and Congregationalists. They prayed for the union of Christians, a sentiment Azariah took to the Lambeth Conference of 1920.[134] Azariah bore a deep impression of the nationalism rising throughout India and of the fecundity of the union Church meeting. He sensed the need for an Indian Church as the only appropriate form of mission. Azariah's outlook received broad support within India and throughout the Anglican communion. Ecumenism, and the idea of unity, had a magical appeal, and English bishops in India such as E. J. Palmer, Bishop of Bombay from 1908 to 1929, lent influential assistance. Palmer was an Anglo-Catholic who persuaded many of his colleagues that a union Church need not sacrifice episcopacy, which was the principal Anglican fear of ecumenical possibilities.[135] In 1930 the Indian Church gave four southern dioceses – Madras, Tinnevelly, Travancore and Cochin, and Dornakal – permission to enter a united Church of South India.

In an age when Church forms were seen to be the crucial factor in religious expression, it was not easy to broach the possibility of institutional merger. Careful theological delineation took place, so that points of doctrine crucial to the participants were not jettisoned. Anglicans wished to preserve episcopacy, if not apostolic succession, and pondered ways to incorporate Protestant clergy who had not been episcopally ordained. Protestants feared the imposition of the idea of apostolic succession and pressed for recognition of their ministries. What prevailed was not a particular formula for union but agreement on the need for a South Indian Church. After meetings in Bangalore in 1928 and Madras in 1929, a Scheme was published. It accepted the episcopate as the Church's basis but without a theory of apostolic succession and with acceptance of Protestant ordinations.[136] Nevertheless the Scheme needed clarification of synodical authority in relation to the authority of bishops. Informed by the American Episcopal Church's experience, the south Indian participants determined that there could be a legislative balance between the right of elected lay representatives to decide Church business and the prerogative of bishops to resolve matters of doctrine. Meanwhile opposition to the united Church included Indian nationalists who rebuked the effort as being a Western initiative, and Anglo-Catholics who feared the compromise of apostolic order. But the Scheme advanced because a wide swath of Indian and Western Church opinion sought a truly Indian Church. Anglicans, epitomized by William Temple, viewed such union as the realization of Anglican intention for unity. The Church of South India was officially organized on September 17, 1947, as India itself became independent.[137]

The Church of South India preceded the organization of united Churches in north India and Pakistan. These unions were rare instances of careful adaptation of Church structures to nationalistic circumstances through creation of indigenous forms. More often, sudden social upheaval compelled Church leaders to make dramatic, unplanned changes in Church life. From Kunming, China, on June 4, 1943, Bishop R. O. Hall of Hong Kong wrote advising his friend William Temple of a momentous decision. Though removed from his occupied see, Hall remained diocesan and pondered the Hong Kong Church's needs under war's exigencies. Hall told Temple that he had given permission to Deaconess Lei Tim-Oi to celebrate the Lord's Supper for a congregation in Macao. Her leadership of this congregation on the Portuguese island adjacent to Hong Kong had proven exceptional and Hall hoped the next Lambeth Conference would consider the possibility of ordaining women to the priesthood, a matter which had been discussed in prewar England. However, he could not wait for formal decisions. In January, 1944 he managed to arrange a meeting with Lei Tim-Oi at Xing Xing, where, in a packed church, he ordained her priest. Writing to Temple two days later, Hall still seemed spellbound by the occasion. "I have had an amazing feeling of quiet conviction about this – as if it was how God wanted it to happen rather than a formal regularisation first." He cautioned that "my reason was not theoretical views of the equality of men and women but the needs of my people for the sacraments – and the manifest gift of the personal charisma."[138]

Hall naturally sought to deflect criticism of his action, which he knew implied the equality of the sexes. He had reached this extraordinary measure by his concern to maintain the Hong Kong Church's ministry amid the unusual circumstances created by war. Throughout his episcopate, which lasted from 1932 to 1966, Hall saw his task to be the building of a new society, and he placed the Church in the forefront of social work.[139] In the 1950s he encouraged the construction of new parishes and he stressed the Church's sacramental life. But he also taught the Hong Kong Church to build schools, clinics, and social service agencies. He encouraged exploration of both traditional Chinese beliefs and Communism, hoping the Church would stand at the intersection of society and spirituality. The vigor of the Church's social ministry formed the basis of its integrity.

A consensus that the Church must build a new social order guided Anglicans after the Second World War. That task elicited impressive witness as Anglicans modified Church structures for the sake of response to social change. But circumstances confused Anglican identity and fragmented the post-liberal consensus, as a crisis of belief and an erosion of institutional confidence would settle in over the Western world like smog. Confidence in the character of the Church's mission and ministry, that careful balance of community and order, would vanish in postwar gloom.

CHAPTER EIGHT

The search for the authentic Church

THE COURSE OF MODERNITY

The Anglican achievement

By 1945, what had once been the Church of England had evolved into the Anglican Communion. These autonomous bodies shared a theology and worship which linked them to the see of Canterbury and created structures to govern their internal affairs and to mediate among themselves. Anglicans achieved a balance between the demands of ministering to the world and the necessity of distinguishing the Church from it. Although the tension between order and community proved endemic to modernity, Anglicans seemed able to surmount it. In 1945 the challenge Anglicans felt centered more on how to rebuild the world than on how to define the Church and its mission. Geoffrey Fisher, the Archbishop of Canterbury, in a sermon broadcast on the BBC late in 1946, depicted the Church as the answer to the world's problems. The Church

is not so united as it should be, but in a real sense it is one. It is not so effective as it should be . . . but it *is* the Church Militant . . . In every country it is operating . . . to teach men to live by their duty to God and to their fellow-men. *There* is something for you to set against the sandy and sludgy footings of the world – the Church of Christ, built on the living rock of Christian doctrine.[1]

The new Presiding Bishop of the Episcopal Church, Henry Knox Sherrill, shared Fisher's conviction but cautioned that "we must beware of contenting ourselves with an easy-going complacency under the guise of Christian faith and hope. There are deep reasons for belief in God's ultimate victory but this should not be confused with the failure to face the realities of our own inadequacy and blindness." Sherrill explained that the denominations faced considerable challenges from social disarray. Worse, it was "evident that the Church all too often simply accepts and reflects the standards, or the lack of standards, of the community. Thus we see in the Church the weaknesses and the limitation so evident at the present time in our total culture."[2]

Stephen Toulmin exposes "the hidden agenda of modernity" as the hope of ordering society in accordance with the reasonable structure of the cosmos. The result was a devaluation of affect and an emphasis upon a static, hierarchical society. Modernity's supreme social product was the nation, and the expansion of Western influence into imperial conquest enhanced the legitimacy of Western society by suggesting it embodied cosmic order and even, perhaps, a divine plan. Western society was understood as a set of institutions legitimated by reason, by reference to nature, and by tendentious use of "tradition," a concept signifying precedent. Yet this scheme was never complete and, by the late eighteenth century, which heralded the age of revolution, it began to disintegrate. By the early twentieth century Western confidence in reason, in order, and in the nation had been eroded severely.[3]

Toulmin sees it as curious that between 1920 and 1960 the modern world did not collapse as some figures, notably Oswald Spengler, anticipated. During those decades the Western world revived a reliance upon objectivity and national identity, an Indian summer of modernity. Despite evidence of the irrational, belief in rational order persisted. *Cosmopolis*, Toulmin's title for his book, signifies the modern intention to marry social to cosmic order in accordance with reason.[4] Yet modernity has proven "to be enigmatic at its core." The development of modernity has produced increasing awareness of life's irrational aspects, and of local cultures rather than national forms. Efforts to incorporate the irrational into rational forms have placed immense stress upon institutional self-understanding as the assumptions of the modern social edifice have become untenable.[5]

As Sherrill suspected, the Church shared the weaknesses of its cultural locus. The Church of England was a product of the rise of the modern world, an arm of a modern nation, integral to political arrangements, pivotal to the functioning of society. This assumption persisted, and arguments about the Church's identity proved to be intramural clashes about the proper ordering of a national Church. Sporadic protests against the Church's alignment with the nation suggested the presence of countercurrents within the Church, but did not sway Anglicans from their national course. In the period from the age of revolution at the end of the eighteenth century to 1978, the date of a notable Lambeth Conference, Anglicanism underwent impressive change. By 1945 the Church had become global and had absorbed non-English, non-Western cultural influences in limited ways. Its organizations in Britain had adapted impressively to accommodate the social changes inherent in industrial order. Anglican theologians had posed a new theological and liturgical basis for Church life in the broad school known as Liberal Catholicism. Despite prominent forms of dissent, such as Evangelicalism and Anglo-Catholicism, Liberal Catholicism represented an impressive Anglican achievement. Vague in many ways, Liberal Catholicism nevertheless embodied a consensus and an ethos. It conveyed the pervasive sense that Anglicans could be both modern and traditional, balancing the adaptation of their Church to modern circumstance with adherence to traditional forms. As Toulmin suggests, tradition was used by Anglicans as a construct to legitimate their adaptation to modernity.[6] Anglicanism became an institution governed by rational criteria of success.

If the Church in England, and in the British colonial context, illustrated the encounter between religious establishment and modernity, the American environment demonstrated Anglican response to the breakdown of formal establishment. There, far more than in Britain, the Church adapted its organization to new social and political forms and amalgamated into mainstream Protestant life. Jon Butler describes how religious groups in colonial America rejected the framework of state authority and emerged as independent denominations when American political independence was secured. The denominations sought ways to cooperate with one another in an informal establishment which believed the United States possessed a divinely appointed destiny. Leaders of the mainstream Protestant churches, including the Episcopal Church, encompassed the legitimate range of American religious experience. Later, groups such as the Disciples of Christ and the larger Lutheran bodies would enter this mainstream, and Catholics and Jews would defer to its style of civility. In the 1950s, Will Herberg, in his book, *Protestant–Catholic–Jew*, presented a coherent view of this American religious establishment at its zenith.[7] Herberg expressed the pervasive confidence that mainstream religion and modern civility had fused naturally and finally into one social order.

The American Protestant establishment represented a consensus that religious life and experience should be structured in particular patterns for the sake of the nation's identity. From the religious perspective the American task was to subdue disorder through moral betterment and social organization, a goal with expansive horizons. Mainstream Protestants believed they could realize their national destiny through increasing degrees of organization and exploratory ecumenical forms. By the 1920s Church and interchurch structures in America had become complex, a Protestant phalanx, utilizing all the resources of America's expanding corporate sector to guide the nation's spiritual life.

A vivid illustration of how the American establishment functioned can be gleaned from the life of Henry Knox Sherrill. Beginning with his undergraduate education at Yale University and moving through his call as Rector of Trinity Church, Boston, Sherrill's career developed in establishment circles. With his election as Bishop of Massachusetts in 1930, and as Presiding Bishop of the Episcopal Church in 1946, Sherrill emerged as one of the establishment's chief spokesman. He sat on the Yale University Corporation with major figures such as Senator Robert Taft and Secretary of State Dean Acheson. Using his clout in financial circles, he created the Episcopal Church Foundation, which funds church-building programs. He became one of the founders, and first President of, the National Council of Churches, the major, postwar, interchurch body. He even met privately with President Harry Truman in the early 1950s to express Protestant opposition to Truman's interest in appointing an American ambassador to the Vatican. Sherrill put it to Truman that the Protestant mainstream could mobilize the American Congress against the scheme. He was later to admit, however, that the proposal came to naught because the political moment was not right.[8]

Sherrill's social nexus demonstrates how religious identity for Anglicans became entangled with modern society. In the late 1960s Episcopalian and sociologist Gibson Winter began a study of modern religious identity by saying that "religion has emerged in the United States as a major organizational enterprise." Measures of religious vitality centered upon membership statistics and budgetary health. The "organizational revolution," which seemed inherently secular, contributed to the enhanced power of religious groups, and to the assumption that religion, like all forms of modern life, functioned best as a complex, corporate structure. Though only America fell within

Winter's purview, he would have found confirmation of his view throughout British domains. The essence of the Anglican response to modernity was the elaboration of ecclesiastical structure.[9]

A significant countercurrent persisted as Anglicans maintained a feeling of disjuncture between their faith and modern life. After the First World War a profound sense of caution overcame Victorian optimism and Anglicans became reluctant to accept modernity uncritically, although they remained hopeful of redeeming it. Meanwhile Evangelicals and Anglo-Catholics alike feared that modernity would overrun the Church's sacred beliefs and forms. Throughout the development of modern Anglicanism these groups encouraged distance between the Church and its social environment. This emphasis upon securing the boundary between Church and culture increased. Even in the 1950s, when the Anglican place in religion's mainstream was secure, some thoughtful Church figures, including Henry Knox Sherrill, stressed that the Church must guard the distinctiveness of its faith and worship. For the Church to be the "meeting place between God and man," its distinctive identity was the key to its integrity as a social institution.[10] Although Anglicans had made a profound adjustment to modern circumstances, this transition was merely the initiatory phase of modernity's impact upon the Church. The greater challenge posed by modernity lay in the question of ecclesiastical identity which was engulfing Anglicans. By the 1950s this question had become unavoidable, inspiring a variety of Anglican searches for means to define the Church's nature. The irony of modernity which I sense is that Anglicans often turned to images of ancient Christian tradition to resolve a modern problem.

The paradox of the fifties

Theological ferment

Though Anglican identity seemed to be secured by ecclesiastical life, profound hesitation lingered about the suitability of institutional criteria for theological truth and about the Church's social locus. Such concern emerged as Episcopalians concluded that reaffirming their belief would enhance their mission. The Church produced a series of books summarizing Anglican belief and stressing the Church's institutional authority. Authors James A. Pike and W. Norman Pittenger in 1951 asserted that "certain *dogmas*, or permanently necessary Christian assertions were made by the Church," not foisted "on us, in an arbitrary and dictatorial manner. It presents them as essential because it sees that they are statements of the very stuff of the Christian revelation." The life of faith, they emphasized, "cannot be understood apart from the Church."[11]

Pike and Pittenger reflected the era's trust in institutional life to incarnate Christian faith. They spoke confidently of the Anglican view of religious authority as "a way of understanding and evaluating all truth." Anglicanism they described as an *ethos*, a "spirit" which incorporated apostolic Christianity and Scripture into "the most adequate world-view," for modern people. Anglicanism transformed the personal need for faith into a living expression of tradition. The Church could be the meeting ground between the divine and the human, because Anglicanism balanced the historic and the modern, the corporate and the personal dimensions of Christian experience in its institutional forms.[12] This idealized understanding of Anglicanism revealed the hopes of the fifties. For example, in 1957, Pittenger reiterated his confidence in the Church's ability to be both historic and modern, grounded in belief and tradition yet adaptable, at the same time, to modern circumstances. The Church holds the key to personal and social wholeness in modern social circumstances. In its liturgy the Church brings people together to share the reality of the Kingdom of God. "When the world is really itself, as God intends it to be, it is a Liturgy, or public manifestation of God." The Church embodies "the right relationship . . . between God and His creation."[13]

Beneath the surface assurance of the decade lay turbulent undercurrents. Like Pike, Pittenger was searching for a contemporary mode to express a traditional faith, and rethinking the Church's presentation of Christian faith. Pittenger cautioned against uncritical surrender of the Church to the world. However, "there is a kind of 'offense' in much of our presentation of Christianity which is neither integral to the central assertions of the Christian message itself, nor necessary in making its imperatives vivid and compelling to modern men." "No Christian, certainly, would wish to assert that *all* of the presuppositions and the total structure of thinking of modern people can be right." However, throughout Christian history "it has been considered essential that the Christian message should be understood and presented in the light of the secular truth of the time." In order to serve the world, the Church must adapt its idiom.[14]

Hints of a new Anglican approach to modernity appeared in Pittenger's work. His *Christ in the Haunted Wood* addressed the

"bewilderment, confusion, frustration, meaninglessness, purposeless-
ness, loneliness, and nihilism" cited by Bishop Roger Blanchard in the
book's foreword as characteristic of modern colleges and universities.
Pittenger perceived great anxiety among the younger generation, the
product of a pervasive secularism which the Christian faith needed to
address. Accordingly the Gospel must be presented in a manner that
redeemed life from futility. Pittenger believed that Christianity is "a
declaration of God's mighty act in redeeming sinful man," a faith
which could become one's own only in the fellowship of the Church's
worship.[15] This apparently traditional affirmation actually set the
stage for the emerging pattern of Anglican thought. Pittenger
responded to modern restiveness by linking the Church's belief to a
specific understanding of humanity. He argued that human experience must be taken seriously by the Church because "we were
created by God to find fulfillment, ultimately in Him and proximately
with our fellowmen in community." The idea that the Church might
be the means of human fulfillment was an idea whose influence
increased. The hope of human salvation led to a search for earthly
fellowship, a social realization of the person's spiritual capabilities.[16]

Pike also believed the Gospel must be expressed in a contemporary
idiom and addressed issues of Christian ethics. He accepted human
experience as the basis of religion and he argued for the Gospel's
suitability in supplying meaning for life. Pike believed that God
intends people to find freedom and creativity through the realization
of redemptive interpersonal relationships. The Gospel commends a
way of life which is not the product of obedience to immutable moral
laws, but of an emphasis on the search for human possibility. "The
simplest conclusion to draw is that the particular commandments and
rules are not binding but that there is only one rule: the fulfillment of
one's vocation toward God."[17] Pike viewed sin not as a series of errors
but as an underlying condition. "Sin is separation. It involves
separation from God, from one's fellow men, and from one's own true
self." Sin resulted not from personal failure, but arose in a distorted
social environment which individuals must rise above morally.
Christianity promised that "a man [would] be able to accept
himself," break with the past, and form relationships in which
fulfillment became possible. Redeemed from sin, human beings
became co-creators with God of a new social world.[18]

As modern Anglicans increasingly did, Pike led a discussion of faith
inexorably to consideration of worship. In the modern world

Anglicanism has shifted away from its establishment heritage toward being a religious ethos rooted in a distinctive form of worship. Pike encouraged this sensibility by arguing that worship reminds participants of their fellowship with God and affords a model for the Christian life. Christianity, this viewpoint held, turns upon adherence to the search for fellowship, not upon obedience to legalistic forms. Indeed, for Pike, it was important to depict the Church as a human community, following a human Lord, who taught his followers to challenge political and social norms. Living in a sinful world, Pike emphasized, Christians often cannot keep to the moral law, but must choose the least of several evils. On occasion, for instance, divorce may be preferable to continuation of a marriage in which hope of true fellowship no longer exists. Though marriage is a sacrament, and a principle of social stability, the Church seeks human fulfillment, not adherence to forms. Indeed the Church must challenge political and social forms which subvert the possibility of personal fulfillment in redemptive community. The Church must initiate social "ferment" in the hope of a better world and "as witness to the fact that the Christian's citizenship is in heaven and that he is on earth a colonist" seeking conformity between the world and "our true native land."[19]

Though they portended the new shape of belief among Episcopalians, Pike's views seemed daring in the fifties. Pike himself gained something of a gadfly reputation as he assumed higher roles in Church life. Dean of New York's Cathedral of St. John the Divine, he subsequently became Bishop of California. Charged with heresy in 1966 by several fellow bishops in an inconclusive but arresting controversy, he resigned his episcopate and, at the time of his mysterious death in the Israeli desert in 1969, became known for his interest in paranormal phenomena, including efforts to communicate with a dead son. Pike's behavior was an extreme manifestation of the conviction which arose suddenly throughout much of the Episcopal Church that the Gospel must be expressed in terms of contemporary experience. This was not an entirely unprecedented trend. It represented the revival of historic Anglican liberalism, with its stress upon the humanity of faith. The truly new feature of the fifties was a sense of social anxiety. Secular life had been shaken by two major wars and by the dual threats of Communism and nuclear weapons. The individual seemed helpless before overwhelming social forces which made inherited Christian norms irrelevant. An impulse to revise the faith along humanistic lines gathered pace among Episcopalians.

In 1944, Albert T. Mollegen of the Virginia Theological Seminary began meeting biweekly with eight to ten couples to discuss the place of Christianity in the modern world. Before long four groups of couples were meeting, and eventually an annual series of classes taught by seminary faculty for lay people emerged. A student of the noted theologian Paul Tillich, Mollegen believed that modernity had fostered a climate in which people felt abandoned by all sources of meaning. Secular promises of goodness in the world had evaporated, and religious meaning seemed lost in antiquated rhetoric. Mollegen posed the Gospel as the inauguration of a relationship with God and with other persons. Amid the moral and spiritual rubble of the world "a new community of the Holy Spirit – the Church itself – is created by what God does to mankind in and through Christ." The way to resolve despair and meaninglessness lies in the Church, a new form of human community which foreshadows God's eternal Kingdom.[20]

In response to a sense of anxiety Episcopalians posed new theological criteria for Church programs. In 1947 Presiding Bishop Sherrill appointed John Heuss to develop a national Episcopal program of Christian education. Heuss' department inspired the series of books known as the Church's Teaching Series and organized Parish Life Conferences to train lay parish leadership. Under Heuss and David R. Hunter, his successor, the Church developed by 1955 the Seabury Series, a comprehensive curriculum of Christian education. The philosophy of this program stressed "relationship theology" and "redemptive fellowship." Seabury's designers believed that Christian education must address human "needs," as means of gaining access to a spiritual basis for life. Reflecting the current existential philosophy, Seabury theorists located Christianity's truth in its ability to shape human relationships, for the encounter between persons suggested the nature of the human experience of the divine. Thus the initiative for experiencing God lay with the human search for meaning; God became the respondent and human beings the initiators.[21]

Liturgical ferment
During the 1930s the continental Liturgical movement which had reached Britain created scarcely a ripple in the Episcopal Church. After the Second World War, however, energetic liturgical discussion began among Episcopalians. Prayer Book revision had been set in motion in 1928 when the Church created a Standing Liturgical Commission to guide further change. In 1950 that body set in motion the process needed to create a new Book of Common Prayer when it

published the first of a series of Prayer Book Studies. Prayer Book Studies I reviewed Baptism and Confirmation, while number II examined the Liturgical Lectionary. Questions concerning the relation of Confirmation to Baptism and the timing of Baptism motivated the Commission's call for further study. As the tide of liturgical renewal surged over into the next generation, questions concerning Baptism and Confirmation remained prominent. Liturgical reformers were concerned that Confirmation occur at a moment of personal development when conscious faith affirmation was feasible, minimizing the rite's potential for rote response.[22]

Christian initiation dramatized the boundary between the Church and the world, the life of faith versus secular values and assumptions. An important consensus emerged among some leading Episcopal bishops and theologians in the United States that they must steer the Church toward liturgical revision. They were convinced that the Church's rites must be distinctively Christian, untainted by secular associations, and that under their leadership the Church could recover its authenticity as a worshiping community, diminishing its reliance upon social establishment. In search of secure rootage for this transition, the liturgical designers sought precedent in apostolic Church patterns. In surveying the history of Christian initiation, for instance, Prayer Book Studies I adverted to the *Apostolic Tradition* of Hippolytus, a key document from the pre-Nicene era, before the Church was reconciled to the Roman Empire. Hippolytus became a key reference point as liturgical renewal progressed, for his work symbolized a pure Church unsullied by secular influences.[23]

The search for liturgical renewal, and for distance between the Church and the world, soon focused upon eucharistic theology and practice. In 1956 leaders of the Associated Parishes, a movement seeking renewal of parish life, called for uniformity in celebrating the Eucharist. The authors urged that church interiors be redesigned so the celebrant could face worshipers from behind the altar rather than turn away from the congregation when presiding at the Eucharist. Facing the people revived apostolic practice and enhanced the Church's teaching role. It included the congregation in the action at the altar, creating a vital corporate sense. "The rite is clearly visualized in its essential character as the holy Supper of the Lord," an anticipation of "the Messianic Feast in the Kingdom of God." The human search for meaning receives a "sincerity of expression and dignity of gesture."[24]

Discussion of the Eucharist proceeded at a series of pivotal conferences on liturgical renewal. At Grace Church, Madison, Wisconsin (in May, 1958) and at St. Paul's Church, San Antonio, Texas (in November, 1959) the liturgical future of the Episcopal Church was mapped out. Church leaders called for a new emphasis on the Eucharist and diminished the role of Morning Prayer, which had been the Sunday norm for much of the Church. Beneath this emphasis lay more than simply an infatuation with the Liturgical movement's recovery of early Christian experience. Liturgical planners understood they were charting strategies to create a new consensus about Episcopal identity. They emphasized that the Church's reality lies in its corporate ministry of clergy and laity grounded in apostolic precedent. They viewed the Eucharist as symbolic of a transition from an inauthentic Church, defined by culturally determined customs, to the authentic Church of Christ.[25]

The lineaments of this vision of the authentic Church could be seen among conference participants. W. O. Cross of the University of the South, speaking at San Antonio, argued that the Eucharist possesses distinctive ethical and social implications. It encourages a view of the Church as a fellowship, "a communal, social enterprise within which men are of one blood in the Mystical Body of Christ." Such a view is "catastrophic for a social order based upon self-seeking, enlightened self-interest, isolated individualism, and the raw brutalities that under some conditions sweep from the profit motive." Similarly, at Madison, Wisconsin, Presiding Bishop Arthur Carl Lichtenberger emphasized that Baptism created a new social order, distinct from the world. Baptism and the Eucharist called attention to the inequalities of the world, notably discrimination against women and minorities. He suggested that the Church must embody hope of a new and different world.[26]

The most influential voice in awakening liturgical renewal was Massey Hamilton Shepherd of the Church Divinity School of the Pacific, who reiterated the new principles of worship which he absorbed from the Liturgical movement. Shepherd was a key figure on the Standing Liturgical Commission, the Associated Parishes, and at liturgical conferences. He wrote the book on worship in the Church's Teaching Series and became the great visionary of a new theology of the Church.[27] By the end of the fifties Shepherd and other renewal advocates dared to call for Prayer Book revision. They cited not only the spate of new scholarship, but the signs of revision among Anglicans globally. However, they recognized the need for a procedure to implement revision, unlike previous occasions when revision had been dictated by the decisions of Church commissions without regard for participation from the wider Church. In light of the Liturgical movement's emphasis upon the laity, the Commission encouraged a new method of Prayer Book revision called "trial use," which had already been used in South Africa, India, Canada, Wales, and the West Indies. It allowed for liturgical proposals to be scrutinized by the entire Church, and for local experience to be incorporated into the framework of Church life.[28] Liturgical ferment revealed that some Anglicans were desperate to enhance the Church's distinctive mission.

Reconsideration of belief and worship encouraged new forms of social ministry. In the 1950s, the Episcopal Church first confronted the reality of racial discrimination in American life. Late in 1952, the Dean and seven faculty members of the School of Theology of the University of the South resigned because of its refusal to admit black students. A majority of the student body transferred to other seminaries, and James A. Pike refused the offer of an honorary degree in 1953. Eventually pressure from throughout the Episcopal Church forced the University to change its policy. The Episcopal Church also changed the site of its General Convention in 1955 from Houston to Honolulu because black delegates were offered only separate housing in the Texas city. Episcopalians were moving toward a positive effort to remodel culture.[29]

In Britain the horror of war had sunk in fully and the task of rebuilding society inspired new assaults on social problems. Opposition to nuclear weapons led, in 1958, to the creation of the Campaign for Nuclear Disarmament under Anglican aegis. Although the coronation of Queen Elizabeth II in 1953 was resplendent with Anglican pageantry, the decade was marked by a growing distance between Church and society. A fear of being identified with the nation resulted in a new emphasis by the Church upon parish life and worship, and produced an unfocused sense that the Church must overcome the social class-locus of its past.[30]

THE ASSAULT ON ESTABLISHMENT

During the fifties Anglicanism seemed to be integral to the Western world's establishment in both formal and informal ways; yet, this role was belied by ferment within the Church as Anglicans began to revise their social teachings. The impact of this revision fell first outside the

Western world, notably in South Africa, where Anglicans responded to an extreme nationalism in a way that was indicative of a new outlook. Rejecting the political establishment, Anglicans located Church identity in indigenous forms which upheld apostolic ideals. The idea that Anglicanism was demarcated by its sacramental life guided the Church's move away from establishment and encouraged Anglicans to believe that their social witness could inspire the proper sort of national identity.

Agony in South Africa

On Sunday, May 8, 1955, at the Cathedral of St. Mary and All Saints in Salisbury, Rhodesia, an elaborate Eucharist marked the formation of the Province of Central Africa. Anglicans in what are now the nations of Zimbabwe, Zambia, and Malawi became autonomous, subsequent to having been joined to the Church of the Province of South Africa. Although the celebrant at this event was the Archbishop of Canterbury, Geoffrey Fisher, the key figure in the event was Geoffrey Hare Clayton, the Archbishop of Cape Town. Chubby, English, and staunchly Anglo-Catholic, Clayton, who was the preacher on this occasion, realized that he stood on the cusp of history, and shared his vision with the congregation. "There is inevitably an element of sadness in what we are doing to-day. I am more conscious of it than you can be. It is the bringing to an end of something that was good in order that there may be a bringing of something that is better." Clayton extolled the virtue of being a self-governing province in a global union of autonomous Church bodies. Anglicanism paralleled the British Commonwealth, in which colonies became self-governing states in a loose-knit structure.

The new province's task was "to win for Jesus Christ all the multitudes who have not accepted Him" and to create "a real unity." "You are a multi-racial province. Christ came to break down barriers. In His name it is for you to create a union of hearts." Generally Anglicans must "show the truth that as men come closer to our Lord they inevitably come closer to each other . . . The Church must be one kraal for everybody. The unity of the Church must be the expression of mutual love and mutual respect." In regard to secular authority "you have to aim at being its conscience." "It is not your duty to be popular. It is your duty to be faithful . . . You do not exist to preach the Gospel of the Federation of Central Africa but to preach the Gospel to the Federation.''[31] Clayton had a clear sense of the meaning of preaching the Gospel to society. He died suddenly on the day after Ash Wednesday in March, 1957, when he led South African bishops in signing a letter of protest to the South African government. Clayton and his colleagues decried the proposal of new laws restricting the movements of non-white people. Such laws infringed parish boundaries, making multiracial parish life problematic. The bishops declared that "the Church cannot recognize the right of an official of a secular government to determine whether or where a member of the Church of any race . . . shall discharge his religious duty of participation in public worship or to give instructions to the minister of any congregation as to whom he shall admit to membership of that congregation." Putting it bluntly the bishops stated "that if the Bill were to become law in its present form we should ourselves be unable to obey it or counsel our clergy and people to do so."[32]

The Church which had valued its role in upholding secular authority had precipitated an extraordinary confrontation. Yet tension had built up gradually during Clayton's episcopate, which began in 1934 with his consecration as Bishop of Johannesburg. Clayton entered an Anglican province where all bishops were white and all but one British, and where black and white clergy and people saw little of one another. This troubled the sense of social mission he brought to his see. "The Church was formed for the express purpose of interfering, or . . . meddling with the world," he declared in his first charge to the Diocese of Johannesburg.[33] South Africa certainly gave Clayton much with which to meddle. Racial prejudice was already deeply ingrained, but Clayton recognized that there was a steady stream of black people joining the Anglican Church. He set about expanding the church's schools and clinics and enhancing the status of black clergy. He reiterated that racial distinctions did not affect one's character as a child of God, and he realized that the future of the Anglican Church lay in its ability to include non-Europeans. The Church must minister to all people as fellow heirs of God's Kingdom.[34]

As Clayton expanded the Church's ministry "the imperfections of the old order, and especially in South Africa, began to weigh heavily upon him." During the Second World War he stressed that Anglicanism was the Church of a universal Gospel which upheld those who felt bound by conscience not to fight in a war. Anglicans must stand for a new social order which enshrines the freedom and dignity of the individual. But in 1948 the electoral victory of the National Party began the legal institutionalization of the racial scheme known as apartheid. In the same year Clayton was elected Archbishop of Cape Town and became Metropolitan of the Church in South Africa.[35] Clayton's elevation brought him, and Anglicans generally, into confrontation with the South African government and revealed the new social critique sweeping through the Church. In his address to the Cape Diocesan Synod on November 7, 1951, Clayton insisted that whatever "in the organization and general set-up of the country which is contrary to the mind of Christ . . . against that we should make our protest." The source of apartheid was "an arrogant and exclusive national spirit," he added in 1953. "There is a wrong, but there is also a right nationalism. There is and can be nothing final about nationalism in itself . . . But there is something final about Christ. There is the true and Christian nationalism," for in God's Kingdom "nationalism is transcended."[36]

In 1950 Clayton foresaw "that the future of the Anglican Church in this Province will be mainly with non-Europeans." "We are a multi-racial Church. The very aspect of this Synod shows that we draw men of diverse races into the one Church and give them their voice in its administration and government." Later he added that "whatever be our historical origin, our destiny is not to be merely British . . . We claim to stand for the Catholic Faith of Christ, the Faith once for all delivered to the saints . . . We must not be content always to deliver that message in an English dress." Flushed with this ideal, and pained by the cruelty inflicted upon the growing sector of his Church, Clayton became an opponent of apartheid,[37] and moved toward advocacy of a selective violation of the apartheid laws. However, his protest was outflanked from within his own church. In 1946 Anglican priest Michael Scott began active protest against legislation restricting property ownership by Asian people in South Africa. Feeling Scott had gone too far, Clayton threatened to withdraw his salary and license to function as a priest. Yet Scott continued his campaign as the government began to usurp land belonging to black people, and in 1950 Scott was deported. His mantle was picked up by Trevor Huddleston, an English priest of the Community of the Resurrection, who ministered in the townships burgeoning near South Africa's cities. Black people were shunted into such areas to keep them as an urban labor pool living under degrading conditions. Huddleston built his ministry in such areas and developed trust among the people he served. He became a zealous advocate of confrontive protest, seeking to dramatize the evils of apartheid.[38]

Huddleston's zeal ran afoul of Clayton's sense of prerogative. Huddleston valued the Catholic features of the Church as much as Clayton did; however, Huddleston viewed the Church as a grassroots, localized form of Catholicism in the manner of F. D. Maurice, while Clayton stressed its authority and hierarchy. Even as a bishop in England and Tanzania, and as Archbishop of the Indian Ocean, Huddleston continually stood for an indigenous, local Catholicism, a Church rooted in the circumstances of its people, not aloof and authoritarian. While in South Africa, he clashed emotionally with Clayton, and the gap widened as Huddleston befriended Oliver Tambo and other leaders of the African National Congress. Huddleston felt moved to a level of political activism which Clayton believed was outside the legitimate prerogative of the Church.[39]

This was a fundamental divide which was becoming apparent in modern Anglicanism. Was the Church entrusted to a hierarchical structure, or was it inherent in its relationship to people and culture, apart from its English sensibility? This tension appeared in South Africa as a large proportion of the white membership disputed the tack of active opposition to apartheid. However, the Church resisted the potential for divisiveness because its non-European membership was becoming the Church's majority. Furthermore the spirit of protest infused the Church's hierarchy. Ambrose Reeves, Clayton's successor as Bishop of Johannesburg, supported Huddleston to a far greater extent than Clayton did. Reeves' sentiment signified the changing outlook of the South African Church's leadership. Clayton's successor at Cape Town, Joost De Blank, proved to be both a resolute Anglo-Catholic and an opponent of apartheid who envisioned an Anglicanism that was truly African and also multiracial.[40]

By the 1960s a sense of crisis gripped South Africa and its Church. The horrors of apartheid were dramatized brutally in March, 1960, when police at Sharpeville killed 69 black people and wounded 186 in response to a peaceful protest against racial pass laws. South African Churches planned to coordinate their resistance to apartheid, and Anglican Bishop Bill Burnett of Bloemfontein drafted his Church's analysis in November, 1960. Burnett cited Clayton and the Lambeth Conference in 1958 to condemn discrimination of any kind and to call for equal opportunity for all persons in the development of their country. This was especially important in Africa, where, from the Christian perspective, racial cooperation held the key to the continent's future. "The Christian must judge every social system by its effect on human personality," Burnett insisted. From that point of view the Church must oppose apartheid and accommodate all people, holding out hope for a just society in the process.[41]

Burnett, a future Archbishop of Cape Town, believed that the Church must incorporate non-English people of all races. In June, 1965, he proposed that Anglicans develop a mission to Afrikaners. "If we are true to our calling as Catholics we will acknowledge our missionary responsibility towards all men." He acknowledged there were formidable barriers of culture and religion between Afrikaners and Anglicans. Nevertheless he urged the Church to groom Afrikaner clergy and to print Afrikaans language materials. In his view, the future course of society, and the power of the Gospel, could surmount great racial divides.[42] Although Burnett's proposal was in vain, its being put forward at all pointed to the change in the character of South African Anglicanism. The Church was disengaging from its strictly English and colonial identity and adopting indigenous guise. It was becoming a localized Catholicism of English descent committed to building a multiracial society in anticipation of God's Kingdom. Burnett himself subsequently experienced a religious awakening and helped to foster an influential charismatic renewal movement in the Anglo-Catholic South African Church. The authority of the Spirit, and the persistence of a Catholic theology of Anglican worship, gave the Church reference points which afforded it a coherent identity.

The end of empire

The loss of colonial identity became the primary feature of Anglican life during the 1950s and 1960s. South Africa represented the tensions Anglicans experienced as the British Empire contracted. The independence of India in 1947 began the process of spawning new nations in Asia and Africa from what had been major outposts of empire. Anglicans recognized the approach of independence as the logical end of their work. By the end of the Second World War they understood that a new political moment was at hand, and they positioned the Church well for this development. The Church's schools helped to groom future national leaders, and increasing numbers of indigenous clergy abetted a process of training for national leadership. The Church's synodical structures, though often moribund, gave a theoretical basis for self-governance. Anglicans encouraged peaceful transitions of power which were achieved in many instances. In some cases, notably Zimbabwe, Anglicans such as Bishop Kenneth Skelton supported majority rule during the years of white supremacist rule and civil upheaval. Skelton's position reflected the successful shift within the Church to a largely non-European membership. By 1962, for example, there were sixteen country mission districts and four urban parishes in the Diocese of Mashonaland, ministering primarily to Africans, and all but six were directed by African priests. Black Church members outnumbered white ones by a ratio of ten to one in the diocese.

In the two Zimbabwean dioceses in 1963 African priests outnumbered white ones by 112 to 71. Furthermore African suffragan bishops were consecrated in Zambia and Malawi in 1964 and 1965, and they became diocesan bishops in 1970 and 1971. In Zimbabwe, Patrick Murindagomo became the first African bishop in 1973 as suffragan for Mashonaland. By 1980 new dioceses were created at Gweru and Mutare and new African bishops consecrated. In Zambia, the Church's majority shifted from rural to urban congregations, and the percentage of whites fell below 10 percent of the Church's membership.[43] These changes meant that Anglicans retained historic forms of ministry and worship while making this ethos familiar to local cultures. Indigenous leadership was followed by deepening reliance upon translations of the Bible and Prayer Book, and use of local music to accompany worship. The importance of worship and music increased as means of identifying the Church and assuring its authentically local character.

While worship and leadership demarcated the Church, its social ministries remained vital to its identity. Though no longer the established Church, Anglicans continued to think in terms of social guardianship – ameliorating society's ills, and educating future social leaders. In Hong Kong, for example, Anglicans developed the territory's most extensive education system. Behind such work lay the essence of the Church's blossoming identity. As Bishop Henry Okullu of Maseno South, Kenya, explained, the Church's influence can assure the achievement of a particular kind of national life. For Anglicans this meant concern for creation of a sense of social wholeness. Indigenous ministries and worship preserved the Church's distinctiveness and offered Anglicans a social ideal.[44]

Witness for civil rights

As identification with the establishment of the past became anathema, Anglicans began active opposition against the forms of racial domination which remained in their host societies. In South Africa, the experience of Gonville ffrench-Beytagh, who became Dean of the Cathedral in Johannesburg in 1965, shows the deepening Anglican witness against apartheid. Early in his tenure ffrench-Beytagh began to call attention to the degradation inflicted by apartheid and to insist that cathedral functions were equally available to all races. Eventually he was tried and convicted for inciting violence, but had his conviction overturned by South Africa's Supreme Court in April, 1972.[45] Protest became integral to the life of the South African Church. As a result the Church developed relative coherence in its identity through the sense of a national task. In the United States by the 1960s a powerful witness against racial discrimination and for civil rights arose among an influential segment of the Episcopal Church. Organized in 1958, the Episcopal Society for Cultural and Racial Unity for twelve years confronted the Church with the reality of racism in its midst and joined demonstrations for civil rights in the American South. The late fifties and early sixties were a moment of convergence when black and white civil rights advocates could work together. ESCRU propelled the Episcopal Church toward a reconsideration of itself and of its role in society.[46]

Though black people were an important minority among Episcopalians, they had played little part in the Church's leadership. That changed as John M. Burgess became the first black diocesan bishop in Massachusetts in 1970 and John T. Walker acceded to the see of Washington, D.C. in 1977. Other black clergy and laity moved into diocesan and national Church positions without opposition or even great notice. Episcopalians were not ruffled by the shifting composition of their Church's leadership; but many white Episcopalians were troubled by social activism for the sake of civil rights. Episcopalians supported peaceful change through restrained procedures, not public demonstrations or civil disobedience. The Bishop of Alabama bemoaned civil disobedience in 1960 as "just another name for lawlessness, [which] at this particular time is playing with dynamite."[47] Alabama, of course, was one of the targets of fervent activism by the early 1960s. In the spring of 1963, Dr. Martin Luther King, Jr., leader of the civil rights movement, was arrested in Birmingham, Alabama, but turned his jail term into a witness for peaceful confrontation. From the Birmingham jail he sent letters calling for change and bemoaning white churches and clergy which failed to consider the implications of their faith. Episcopal Bishop C. C. Jones Carpenter of Alabama had been an opponent of segregation, risking his reputation to witness against discrimination. Nevertheless Carpenter urged King to desist from his campaign of civil disobedience, however peaceful its intention. Thus Carpenter illustrated the chasm appearing among Episcopalians, many of whom could not countenance activism.[48]

The civil rights movement inspired black hope, and fueled white fears, but the Church's leaders resolutely supported the drive for racial equality. For Presiding Bishop, the General Convention of 1964 elected John E. Hines, Bishop of Texas, a zealous advocate of social justice. Yet his devotion was severely tested as polarization became the overriding characteristic of the movement for justice. In the late 1960s many black Americans began to question their reliance upon peaceful protest and their alliance with white America. A call for Black Power arose, symbolizing the black demand for economic and political self-control. This stance, which implied racial separativeness, critiqued American life as pervasively racist.[49] After riots in ghetto areas of Newark and Detroit in 1967, Bishop Hines resolved that Episcopalians must endorse black empowerment tangibly to dramatize the willingness of white America to abandon racism. At the General Convention of 1967 Hines called for a program by which the Church would identify with oppressed people. The institutional adjustment of the Church, he hoped, represented the transformation of America itself, toward a just society.[50] A fund of $3 million annually from Church funds was designated for a program to combat the effects of racism.

The General Convention Special Program endorsed the goal of a "genuinely open" society, a sign that Episcopalians believed they could appeal to black nationalism and awaken American justice. In 1969, at a special General Convention, the Church gave $200,000 to the controversial Black Economic Development Conference, which had demanded "reparations" from white denominations. The demands expanded as American Indians and Hispanics began to call for recognition by the Episcopal Church.[51] Although Bishop Hines determined to stay the course, one American Indian active in Church leadership charged that the Episcopal Church lacked "a consistent and relevant theology." That suspicion filtered among many Episcopalians, and a backlash developed as many parishes protested that the Episcopal Church had betrayed the trust of its white constituency. By the end of the 1960s, Church leaders and clergy often held divergent social views from those of laity and a few local clergy. A profound polarization loomed and staff positions were cut at Church headquarters as funding shrank. Worse, the gulf within the Church widened as the basis of its belief became problematic.[52]

THE LOSS OF COHERENCE

The crisis of belief

As was the case in race relations, Anglicans increasingly divided among themselves over social issues. While divorce remained abhorrent, the Church of England in 1966 received the report of a commission chaired by Bishop Mortimer of Exeter which recommended that divorce be morally allowable in cases where a marriage had irretrievably broken down. Reforms of the divorce law followed with encouragement from Michael Ramsey, the Archbishop of Canterbury, though remarriage after divorce remained problematic within the Church. In the United States, Episcopalians adopted procedures which legitimated the possibility of remarriage in the Church after divorce by permission of the local bishop. Archbishop Ramsey also encouraged relaxation of the Church's condemnation of homosexuality and suggested that abortion was a legitimate moral option in certain circumstances. He also articulated the Church of England's stance against capital punishment. Thus Ramsey, like John Hines, provoked both Church and society into refashioning their moral views.[53] During his tenure at Canterbury from 1961 to 1974 he expanded ecumenical relations and traveled widely to unite the global communion. Energetic bishops were a feature of the Church's life in the 1960s, notably the scholarly Ian Ramsey of Durham, who died before he could be considered for the see of Canterbury. The character of the bishops' social views reflected a deep-seated hope of inspiring the renewal of faith and attaining social justice. But modernity's advance shook the foundations of the Church.

In the 1950s Anglicans relished the breadth which allowed the

Church to tolerate theological doubts. In that spirit some Church leaders began in the 1960s to ask their own questions about traditional Christian convictions, notably Bishop John A. T. Robinson of the Church of England, who burst into the public eye in 1960 when he defended the publication of an unexpurgated edition of D. H. Lawrence's *Lady Chatterley's Lover*. A court case ensued to prevent publication, but Robinson defended the supposedly salacious work because it "put sex in the context of tender human relationship." Robinson was encouraged that human sexuality should be widely discussed, because such honesty encouraged healthy relationships. Robinson testified on behalf of Penguin Books, the publisher, which was acquitted of the obscenity charge.[54]

Robinson was publicly rebuked by Archbishop Fisher for defending what Fisher himself regarded as pornography. The furor over this matter was but a gentle breeze, however, compared with the storm which broke over a book Robinson published in 1963. *Honest to God* emerged out of Robinson's conviction that the Church and its faith had become irrelevant to modern experience. The fault lay in Christian belief's antiquated forms of expression. Robinson felt that the first priority of the times was reinterpretation of the idea of God itself. Thus Robinson defined himself as a radical, one who wished to address the root issue. He also considered himself a humanist, one who believed that Christianity encouraged a particular quality of life in the present world, rather than an anticipation of a world to come.[55]

In May, 1963, Archbishop Ramsey's response set the tone for the controversy which erupted. Ramsey affirmed the breadth of Anglicanism which encouraged individual expression and energetic inquiry. However, he disassociated himself from Robinson's belief that the Bible and the creeds did not permit belief in a personal God, and he expressed grave concern that such sentiments, coming as they did from a bishop in a highly public fashion, caused profound dismay to Christian people. Robinson replied that he intended to address the multitudes beyond the Church who found its faith problematic in the context of modern life. He also declared his personal trust in the Bible, the creeds, and the Catholic tradition of Anglicanism. Nevertheless Robinson had achieved international notoriety, and his subsequent books attracted immediate attention because he appeared to seek a contemporary sense of God, and to revamp Christian ethical norms in a humanistic direction.[56]

A sense of the beginning of an Anglican assault upon inherited conceptions of God, and an urge to shed moralism and guilt for an ethic of personal fulfillment, spread. Some Anglicans decided that the Gospel could be purged of outdated presumptions and expressed in the secular terms appropriate for the age. They took their cues from the theological works of Paul Tillich and Rudolf Bultmann, who posed a new sense of God's nature and "demythologized" the Bible of premodern references. In 1963, Episcopal theologian Paul Van Buren published *The Secular Meaning of the Gospel* to much less of a fanfare than Robinson had received. Nevertheless Van Buren declared that transcendental references in Christian faith had no empirical meaning. Christian faith must be expressed in terms which refer to immediate experience, where verification becomes possible. Drawing upon Ian Ramsey's work, Van Buren concluded that the language of biblical Christianity could be revised to vitalize ancient experience for the people of the twentieth century.[57]

Robinson and Van Buren unwittingly became contributors to what was designated the "Death of God" theology. The Anglican agenda centered upon revision of the manner in which Christian convictions had traditionally been presented, and attention to the Church as the context in which Christian references made sense. Theodore O. Wedel noted in 1962 that the Church's laity were theologically and biblically illiterate because "the communication of the thought world of the Bible presents difficulties in our time." Beneath the mythological references found in the Bible, however, lay a record of faith experience. By uncovering the human layer in the Bible one revealed that the Word was not a call to withdrawal inside the Church, but rather a drama of cosmic dimensions to be played out in the world. Wedel argued that Christianity is a "worldly holiness or holy worldliness," a religion which addresses the ills of this world and demolishes the idea of a secular world apart from the realm of faith. The Church becomes the "training ground," the "home base" for an assault on the world.[58]

Few Anglican theologians were to challenge the basis of Christian belief as centrally as did Robinson and Van Buren. Most, like Wedel, encouraged the reorientation of the Church's belief so that it might adopt the language of personal experience and human community as its primary references. The importance of psychological categories revealed the goal of rearticulating Christian conviction itself; not merely realigning the Church with modern society, but abetting the search for a dynamic theology of experience. Norman Pittenger returned to the fray armed with insights derived from process theology, convinced that belief included psychological, physical, and social meanings which Christian assertions must take steps to incorporate. Belief in God, he affirmed, "makes sense to us because it provides each man with a purpose that can become an integrating factor in his conscious life." Within the Church, where a context of meaning is disclosed, life's purpose is seen as an unfolding process linking collective memory, immediate experience, and shared hope. The Church thus affords a unity and a dynamism which give life meaning.[59]

Moderate Anglo-Catholics such as Austin Farrer were not perturbed by theological rumblings. Farrer felt he could reorient the reference point of belief to human needs so long as the Church's historic worship and ministry remained its basis. E. L. Mascall also reverted to the catholicity of Anglican worship and ministry as a shelter from the storm. The Church, he insisted, must not be seen as a human community, but as the body commissioned by Christ to bear his Spirit into the world.[60] Unfortunately for Farrer and Mascall, even these assumptions about the Church's nature became problematic. In the late twentieth century, the crisis of belief foreshadowed the Church's loss of coherence as ecclesiastical identity proved vulnerable to social forces. Assessing the Church's "suburban captivity," Gibson Winter realized that not only older forms of belief, but prior forms of Church life were no longer possible. The city was a destructive context for traditional communal bonds, creating an exodus of the middle class to the suburbs, where mainstream churches sought a new locus. As modernity deepened, it challenged the churches to find new forms of belief and new norms of community. It became clear to some that the Church must not simply refashion its beliefs, or address the needs of racial minorities. Modernity created for Anglicans a crisis of ecclesiastical identity which required a new sense of the Church as a human community.[61]

In the 1960s the public role of American religion lost the congruence it once enjoyed because the "symbolic connection between values and behaviour" became "unglued."[62] As Anglicans sensed this reality, they responded by seeking a new sense of the Church's nature which retained their habitual hope of being a model for society. The essence of the Church's nature has always been embodied in its worship, so, as the crisis of belief intensified, Prayer Book revision assumed more importance as the epitome of the

Church's response to modernity. The idea of "trial use" produced a draft eucharistic liturgy in 1967 – *The Liturgy of the Lord's Supper* – and more elaborate Prayer Book proposals appeared in the form of *Services for Trial Use* in 1970 and the *Authorized Services* of 1973. A *Draft Proposed Book of Common Prayer* appeared early in 1976 in anticipation of a vote on Prayer Book revision at the General Convention of 1976. That Convention approved the proposed Book and set the stage for a final vote on Prayer Book revision at the Convention of 1979.[63] Throughout the Anglican Communion, alternative Prayer Books appeared by the early 1970s.

Prayer Book revision revealed the Anglican search for a modern form of their Church. Advocates of Prayer Book revision defended it as a process which began with the liturgical scholarship of Frere, Hebert, Dix, and Shepherd. But revision revealed the assumption that the Church must change because the world had changed. The city had become the setting of belief in a scientific context, where unquestioned authority and inherited orthodoxy could not withstand erosion. The modern world promoted a shared authority which evolved from relationships whose mutualities required symbols, actions, and unstructured human encounters. The church must respect the profound distinctiveness of persons and cultures, but seek humanity's completion in the realization of its fundamental unity. Church language must be contemporary and its form variable, yet its references must be historic and transcendent. Prayer Book revision attempted to embrace the modern tension between community and order, by placing eucharistic emphasis in a familiar idiom.[64] It was a planned, institutional redefinition in a cultural context where institutional initiative was rapidly becoming irrelevant.

The conflagration of the Spirit

On April 3, 1960, during his Palm Sunday sermon, Dennis Bennett, Rector of St. Mark's Church, Van Nuys, California, announced that he and a small group of parishioners had prayed for and received Baptism in the Holy Spirit. Bennett's announcement caused consternation in his congregation, and he soon resigned to become Vicar of St. Luke's Church, Seattle, Washington, which was a small, struggling congregation. Soon that parish grew rapidly and gave evidence that Bennett's apparently local conflict actually marked an historic upheaval in American religious life. Bennett's declaration marked the birth of the charismatic and renewal movements among mainstream American Protestants. Bennett dramatized the mainstream's turn away from its historic presumptions about its role as the religious basis for American life in search of affective criteria for religious integrity. Among Episcopalians there soon were other instances of parish renewal organized along charismatic lines. In Houston, Graham Pulkingham revived an inner-city parish much like Bennett's. Everett "Terry" Fullam brought dramatic growth to St. Paul's, Darien, Connecticut through an emphasis upon the gifts of the Spirit and conservative Bible teaching. In England, parish clergy such as John Gunstone and Michael Green led a similar movement, and in Singapore, Bishop Chiu Ban It experienced conversion at a Billy Graham Crusade and led his diocese in a widespread experience of the Spirit's gifts.[65]

There had not been such an outburst among Anglicans since the Evangelicalism of the eighteenth century. The twentieth-century version had many conscious parallels with its distinguished predecessor. That upheaval began in religious affect as John Wesley had a sense of conversion which inspired a life-time of work to awaken public faith and reform the Church. Anglican Evangelicals dedicated themselves to instilling vitality into parish life and inspiring a moral revolution in society. As Evangelicals settled on a party identity within the Church, their identity became linked to a moralistic biblical theology and a suspicion of Liberal Catholic ideas. Spontaneous conversion and speaking in tongues found little place among Anglicans who prized the decorum of Prayer Book worship. Religious emotion belonged among poor Americans outside mainstream religion. Bennett's announcement signaled the revamping of mainstream religion and the relocation of Anglican identity.

From the time of the first eruption among Anglicans, charismatic renewal was a diverse movement. It included outright Pentecostals who valued immediate apprehension of the Spirit and it awakened new life within the Evangelical party. A renewal movement came about as some Anglicans dedicated themselves to recovery of the Church's vitality and their loose fellowship led to new groups such as Episcopal Renewal Ministries. Often from the late 1970s on there was support for the agenda of the "New Right" on issues such as abortion and prayer in public schools. Renewal comprised a miasma of movements which were linked out of common concerns for a more vital faith. Anglican charismatics and renewal advocates shared the desire to refocus the Church's nature and authority. They intended to revitalize the Church from the grassroots level up by stressing the personal basis of Christian faith. Renewal posed an understanding of religious authority as immediate and personal, and sought to recover an authentic Church life beneath prescribed liturgies and hierarchical organizations. Its deepest imprint came as small-group experience became characteristic of parish life. Anglicans turned to intimate forms for prayer, Bible study, and parish renewal. The small-group trend also manifested itself in a concern for spirituality. Guided by the writings of Morton Kelsey, Tilden Edwards, and Kenneth Leech, and attracted by the Cursillo movement and other kinds of spiritual retreat, Episcopalians discovered ancient tools for building a modern Church.[66]

Michael Green's *Evangelism in the Early Church* illustrated that through reliance upon affect and small groups, contemporary Christianity recovered the vitality characteristic of the first-century Church. For Anglicans who traditionally upheld episcopacy as the guarantee of the Church's apostolic character, this was somewhat ironic. For the sake of reviving the Church's vitality, however, proponents of renewal recast the nature of its apostolicity in terms of religious affect and fellowship rather than external forms alone.[67] During the 1970s the emphasis Anglicans laid upon affect widened into a new interest in psychology. Many clergy and laity studied Transactional Analysis or the writings of Carl Jung or Carl Rogers in search both of new ways to convey their faith and of how to relate to one another. An emphasis upon the religious priority of personal experience over adherence to form and precedent took hold. No evidence of this new insight was more dramatic than the movement of the ordination of women to the priesthood. Its emergence could be seen in the life of Pauli Murray, a middle-aged, black activist, lawyer, and academic who, in 1966, felt she could no longer tolerate the limited roles available to women in her parish.[68]

Murray at first merely wanted women to have opportunities to serve as acolytes or lectors, and she voiced her hope to parish committees. By 1970, as women entered Episcopal seminaries and expressed calls to the ordained ministry, Murray began to consider her own vocation. It crystallized when she ministered to a close friend dying of cancer in 1973. No priest was available at the last, so Murray prayed and read Scripture with her friend, then designed a memorial service. The priest who officiated asked if she had considered ordination, and a course of action appeared. Murray resigned her teaching position, entered seminary in the fall of 1973, and, in 1977, became a priest.[69] Her path illustrates the experience of increasing numbers of women, whose call emerged as a vocation born of ministry in their own communities. The integrity of women's call made it as impossible for the Church to ignore as it was difficult to incorporate.

The movement for the ordination of women in the United States inevitably became political with the formation of the Episcopal Women's Caucus in 1970, a lobby which encouraged the expansion of opportunities for women in the Church with special focus on the priesthood. Aware of precedent in Hong Kong, and similar movements in Canada and New Zealand, Episcopal women hoped the General Convention of 1973 would permit them to be ordained. By the opening of Convention, the majority of the Church's bishops supported the ordination of women and twenty-seven dioceses added their endorsement. There were ninety-seven women deacons hoping for permission to advance, forty-two of whom had been ordained since the General Convention of 1970 approved the role of deacon for women. But resistance stiffened and the Convention's vote fell short of the required majority for passage.[70] But the groundswell of hope for priesthood increased among women and encompassed a diverse set of personal calls which coalesced into a common sense of possibility. The movement typified modern Anglican experience, in which religious authority shifted to powerful forms of local and personal experience. Anglicanism had become a modern construct, the effort to encompass globally myriads of local forms for the sake of achieving a modern Catholicism. The ordination of women was a natural outgrowth of modern Anglican life.

Final approval for the ordination of women took place in an atmosphere of protest. In July, 1974 three retired bishops and one active bishop defied Church canon law to ordain eleven women deacons to the priesthood in Philadelphia. This service brought discussion of women's ordination, and the agony of modernity, to an emotional pitch. Anglicans prized their ability to incorporate diversity, but found that encompassing modern experience challenged the basis of the Church's identity. Polarization emerged as some Anglicans hoped the Church would authorize women priests while others feared the corruption of the Catholic nature of Anglican ministry for the sake of accommodating the Church to culture. This division hardened after the General Convention of 1976 approved the ordination of women as priests. It became clear that no insuperable barriers prohibited the consecration of women as bishops.[71]

Reaction and fragmentation

The movement for the ordination of women elicited an articulate rationale in terms of Anglican identity. Reginald H. Fuller argued that early Christian experience revealed an "emergent Catholicism" which laid down principles for future development rather than unalterable forms of Church life. Frederick H. Borsch interpreted the essence of Christ's ministry not as a male legacy but as servanthood. Generally advocates for the ordination of women insisted that the limitation of the priesthood to men reflected a cultural phenomenon, while opening this office to women suggested a completion or wholeness of the ministry inaugurated by Christ.[72] As the ordination of women became fact, homosexual Episcopalians hoped not simply for ordination but for legitimation by the Church of their lifestyle. In 1974 a group of gay Episcopalians founded Integrity, a support group which by 1976 had twenty-six chapters, most meeting in parish churches for worship and discussion. The organization itself elicited concern among many Episcopalians because it sought open acceptance for a sexual orientation that historically had been judged immoral and encouraged homosexual persons to pressure the Church for ordination. Episcopalians acknowledged that there were homosexual clergy who had been discreet about their orientation. In the 1970s, however, discretion became a vice, and homosexual persons spoke of living openly and seeking ordination. In 1975 Bishop Paul Moore ordained Ellen Barrett, one of Integrity's first co-presidents, as a deacon, and in 1977 admitted her to the priesthood. The ordination created a national furor which led the Church's House of Bishops to disapprove of the ordination of admittedly homosexual persons. The Bishops acknowledged that study was needed, and few Episcopalians felt that a satisfactory resolution had been reached.[73]

Revision of the Church's Prayer Book, the ordination of women, and the surfacing of homosexual aspirations were unrelated issues which arose contemporaneously. By the late 1970s the Episcopal Church stood on Anglicanism's frontier with the modern world, compelling the Lambeth Conference of 1978 to address these issues. To those who pressed the Church for change, its leadership seemed stodgy; other Episcopalians, however, were distraught by the changes

which had occurred in the Church's life and concluded, as Paul
Seabury, a collateral descendant of the first Episcopal bishop, did in
1978, that Episcopalians had abandoned their historic faith to
embrace the trendy social activism of the moment. Seabury cited the
opening of prominent parishes to militant groups and the relaxation
of graceful forms of prayer in favor of hip jargon. Episcopal priest
Malcolm Boyd's bestseller of 1965 – *Are You Running with me, Jesus?* –
encapsulated the trends many feared, especially when Boyd later
admitted to being homosexual.[74]

In the 1960s and 1970s a few Episcopalians actually broke with the
Church in order to sustain what they believed was a legitimate
Anglicanism. Before the bombshells of Prayer Book revision, the
ordination of women, and the legitimation of homosexuality burst
upon the Church, several groups had already separated themselves.
The Reformed Episcopal Church's example in the nineteenth century
was not matched until 1962, when the Southern Episcopal Church,
with eleven parishes, organized to protest against political radicalism
among Episcopalians, notably alliance with the National Council of
Churches and the World Council of Churches. More visible, the
Anglican Orthodox Church, formed by James P. Dees at Statesville,
North Carolina, in 1963, denounced the supposed departure of the
Episcopal Church's leadership from "orthodox" Christian doctrines
such as the Virgin Birth and Christ's bodily resurrection. Dees
condemned the National Council of Churches because it encouraged
"co-existence with Russia, the abolition of loyalty security laws,
recognition of Red China [and] forced racial integration."[75]

Dees, who received consecration to the episcopate in 1964 by the
primate of the Holy Ukranian Autocephalic Orthodox Church,
sought alliance with overseas splinter churches, and founded a
seminary. He claimed to supervise thirty-five congregations and
200,000 members who endorsed his conservative theology and far
right political agenda. Dees condemned homosexuality, the ordination of women, civil rights activism, and liberal theology and
supported fringe political groups. Some of his followers joined the
American Episcopal Church, formed in 1968 at Mobile, Alabama.
This body organized congregations in the South and West of the
United States, later attracting members from the Old Episcopal
Church, founded in 1972 at Mesa, Arizona by Jack Capers Adam, a
former alligator wrestler and owner of a small zoo.[76]

Such tiny, unstable groups became spawning grounds for the

reactionary movements which broke upon the Church in the mid 1970s. The Fellowship of Concerned Churchmen, organized in 1973, attracted members of the American Church Union (an Anglo-Catholic group), the Society for the Preservation of the Book of Common Prayer (founded in 1971), The *Christian Challenge* magazine, and the *Certain Trumpet* newsletter. These clusters had maintained opposition to various trends in the Episcopal Church's life, from participation in the National Council of Churches, to the eruption of social activism, to proposals to revise the Prayer Book and to ordain women. They found sympathetic Anglicans in Australia, Britain, and New Zealand who shared their view of orthodox Christian belief and Catholic practice. Similar calls came from new groups such as the Coalition for the Apostolic Ministry, which appeared in 1972, and Episcopalians United, formed in 1975.[77]

The force of such conservative protest within the Church became strident. At the Philadelphia ordination in 1974, DeWitt Mallary spoke for the Committee for the Apostolic Ministry, denouncing the service as a violation of Church law and Catholic custom.[78] The new coalitions did not initially intend to separate from the Church, but to mount a last-ditch defense of traditional Church practice as they understood it and opposition to what appeared to be accommodation of the Church to cultural whims. This was no mere defense of orthodoxy or a countercultural instinct, but a sign of modernity's pervasive influence. Modern circumstances challenged the Church's forms and beliefs; no heretical conspiracy tampered recklessly with the Church's doctrine. Anglicans could not agree among themselves about the implications of modernity, and lost the hope of a coherent identity.

The tempo of protest quickened after the Episcopal Church's General Convention of 1976 approved the ordination of women to the priesthood and the first reading of the proposed Prayer Book. At Chicago, in December, 1976, Bishop Charles Gaskell of Milwaukee and Stanley Atkins of Eau Claire brought together a number of interested persons, and especially the Coalition for the Apostolic Ministry, to form the Evangelical and Catholic Mission. This "fellowship of orthodox churchmen who intend to work within the structure of the Episcopal Church" hoped to be a meeting ground for all opposition to recent changes in the Church and to return the Church "to the faith that was once delivered to the saints and from which the Church has grievously strayed." The ECM and the

Fellowship of Concerned Churchmen reached formal agreement on goals in June, 1977, illustrating the search for a means to differ with the Episcopal Church while remaining within it.[79] In September, 1977 in St. Louis, the Fellowship sponsored a convention at which more than 1,700 persons heard their principles reaffirmed and considered proposals for a continuing Church structure.

A powerful spirit of reaction opposed the Church's adaptation to the modern world. After the meeting at St. Louis, the reactionary impulse bifurcated into groups which chose to remain with the Church, such as the ECM, and others which concluded that what they regarded as the pure faith of Anglicanism must be preserved by separation into new ecclesiastical structures. For example, the Anglican Catholic Church, consisting of ten dioceses, 100 parishes, and 6,500 members organized in October, 1978 under James O. Mote, who, as Rector of St. Mary's Church, Denver, led that parish to renounce the Episcopal Church. Subsequently three dioceses and an entirely separate Church – the United Episcopal Church – broke with Mote's group. The leading splinter group became the American Episcopal Church under Bishop Anthony F. M. Clavier; it had had seventy-four parishes and 5,000 members.[80]

Such dissident groups firmly believed the Episcopal Church had sacrificed its theological integrity, and they trumpeted statistics which demonstrated membership loss. Church membership shrank from over 3.6 million in 1966 to barely 3 million in 1983. Groups such as the ECM, which remained within the Church, concurred that the Church was in jeopardy, and shrugged off moves by Anglicans globally to revise their Prayer Books and, in some instances, to ordain women. They further ignored the preponderance of Anglican theological commitment to liberal theological trends. Anglican dissidents viewed their Church through sectarian lenses, feeling that this extreme perspective was necessary to preserve the Church's purity from modernity's assaults. Their sense of mission may have been grandiose and futile, but their perception spoke volumes about the nature of the Anglican dilemma. Modernity tampered with the Church and rendered its identity uncertain.

Ironically mission became a major theme as many Anglicans shared the perception that the Church must assert itself and its faith. The Lambeth Conference of 1968 initiated two notable forms of inter-Anglican cooperation. It affirmed the concept of Mutual Responsibility and Interdependence (MRI), the idea of a comprehensive study of Anglican needs and resources, and urged Anglicans to develop a common commitment to mission. MRI inspired the creation of an Overseas Development Fund which made grants to assist Church growth globally. The Conference also established the Anglican Consultative Council, with clergy and lay representatives from throughout the Anglican Communion. This was the Church's first, continuing body of a global nature, meeting every two years in various parts of the world. At its Dublin meeting in July, 1973, the ACC upheld the concept of MRI as the basis of its understanding of Anglican partnership. Also in 1973, the Council reviewed the progress of liturgical change among Anglicans, noting that most of the Church's branches were in various stages of liturgical transformation.[81]

New forms of cooperation abounded as Anglicans also pursued new ecumenical endeavors. Despite the failure of Anglican–Methodist unity talks in Britain in 1972, Anglicans were heartened by discussions with Rome, including meetings with the Pope by Archbishops Ramsey and Coggan. An Anglican–Orthodox Doctrinal Commission gave hope of new accords with Eastern Christianity. In the United States, Episcopalians joined the Consultation on Church Union (COCU), an ecumenical Protestant structure in anticipation of some form of Christian reunion. Episcopalians also encouraged other Anglicans to join as Partners in Mission, a program of intra-Anglican partnership and cooperation. Venture in Mission (VIM) appeared as Presiding Bishop John Allin called the Church in 1977 to refocus its energy on proclaiming the Christian faith. VIM raised more than $170 million for new programs which would extend the Church's ministry. It was evidence that Anglicans sensed they possessed a common perspective and mission.[82]

Anglicans also gave evidence that the Church had become indigenous in diverse cultures. By the 1970s there were signs of growth in Latin America as Anglicans in tiny numbers found niches for their ministry. In Francophone nations such as Haiti and Zaire there also were signs of growth, increasing the conviction that Anglicanism was not bound to Western culture but represented a way to unite a Catholic Christianity with local authority and cultural integrity. The Anglican sense of identity was given powerful expression in the person of Desmond Tutu in South Africa, who eventually became Archbishop of Cape Town and who, in 1984, was awarded the Nobel Prize for Peace. In China, Bishop K. H. Ting represented the Anglican ability to adapt to novel social circumstances as he became a leader in the Three Self Movement, China's continuing Church structure.

There were several ironies in the Anglican situation of the late twentieth century. First, Anglicanism exhibited dynamism in Africa and Asia which seemed lacking in its British and American counterparts. The Church's ability to become a prominent social force outside the Western world attested to the Anglican commitment to nation building and to the flexibility of Anglican forms of authority and Church life. Moreover, throughout the Anglican world, a sense of a global Church was solidified by new forms of consultation and mission. But in Britain and North America its public role and institutional shape became uncertain. A crisis of identity deepened as a profusion of subgroups dramatized the Anglican plight. The modern transformation of Anglicanism from the English religious establishment to a global, grassroots, liturgical communion initially appeared to have succeeded. But the transfer of authority provoked a loss of reliance upon hierarchical order and a turn to popular opinion in search of definitive forms of Church life and worship. Anglicans agreed that their Church possessed a Catholic nature, an English heritage, and an inclination to absorb modern social and intellectual currents. However, they lacked means to resolve differing perceptions of these ideals. There seemed to be no definitive Anglicanism as the twentieth century waned.

In response to modernity Anglicans began to view themselves as a liturgical fellowship which aspired to a particular quality of social life. Yet the advance of modern circumstances severely challenged the Anglican ability to respond in a way which preserved their own coherence. The search for authentic forms of religious life led Anglicans away from inherited expressions of belief and from historic, institutional configurations. Modernity upheld the integrity of cultural forms and the authority of personal and local experience. The deepening of local influences upon the Church brought forth a profusion of new religious forms, all claiming historic precedent and religious validity, which shattered the unity of Anglican identity. The modern question became one of mediating between diverse forms of Anglican experience. Crises of belief and social experience revealed that the Church which prized its ability to incorporate diversity could find no definitive means to encompass modern experience while retaining a sense of itself. Modernity had proven to be both Anglicanism's glory and its frustration, a paradox without apparent means of resolution.

Notes

I THE DAWN OF MODERNITY

1 Frank Weston, *The Fullness of Christ*. London: Longmans, Green, 1916, viiif.
2 A. E. J. Rawlinson, *The Church of England and the Church of Christ*. London: Longmans, Green, 1930, 4, 31, 77, 88.
3 Paul Avis, *Anglicanism and the Christian Church*. Minneapolis: Fortress, 1989, 5f.
4 *Ibid.*, 7–11. Italics in the original.
5 P. E. More and F. L. Cross, *Anglicanism*. London: SPCK, 1935. Cited in Stephen Sykes and John Booty, eds., *The Study of Anglicanism*. London: SPCK, 1988, xiii.
6 Martin E. Marty, *Modern American Religion. Volume I. The Irony of it All, 1893–1919*. Chicago and London: University of Chicago Press, 1986, 11, 8.
7 Jaroslav Pelikan, *The Vindication of Tradition*. New Haven and London: Yale University Press, 1984, 5. Edward Shils, *Tradition*. Chicago and London: University of Chicago Press, 1981, 3, 13.
8 Edward Farley, *Ecclesial Reflection*. Philadelphia: Fortress, 1982, 177, 193.
9 S. N. Eisenstadt, *Tradition, Change, and Modernity*. New York: John Wiley, 1973, 5, 9. Farley, 193.
10 Eisenstadt, 171.
11 Stephen Sykes, *The Integrity of Anglicanism*. London: Mowbray, 1978.
12 John R. H. Moorman, *A History of the Church in England*. Third edition. Wilton, Connecticut: Morehouse-Barlow, 1980. Henry R. McAdoo, *The Spirit of Anglicanism*. New York: Charles Scribner's Sons, 1965. Stephen Neill, *Anglicanism*. Fourth edition. New York: Oxford University Press, 1977.
13 John Pobee, "Newer Dioceses of the Anglican Communion," in Sykes and Booty, 399. A. G. Dickens for one sees the English Reformation as the birth of Anglicanism. See his *The English Reformation*. New York: Schocken, 1969. On the other hand, G. R. Elton places the English Reformation in the context of Tudor political reform. See his *Reform and Reformation 1509–1558*. Cambridge, Mass.: Harvard University Press, 1977.

14 Henry Chadwick, "Tradition, Fathers, and Councils," in Sykes and Booty, 93. Avis, 42.
15 Paul Avis, "What is Anglicanism?," in Sykes and Booty, 416.
16 Avis, *Anglicanism and the Christian Church*, 48f.
17 Robert S. Bosher, *The Making of the Restoration Settlement: The Influence of the Laudians, 1649–1662*. London: Dacre, 1951.
18 I. M. Green, *The Re-Establishment of the Church of England, 1660–1663*. Oxford: Oxford University Press, 1978.
19 John Marshall, "The Ecclesiology of the Latitude-men, 1660–1689: Stillingfleet, Tillotson and 'Hobbism.'" *Journal of Ecclesiastical History*, 36, 3 (July, 1985), 412.
20 J. R. Jones, *The Revolution of 1688 in England*. New York: Norton, 1972.
21 Geoffrey Holmes, *Politics, Religion and Society in England, 1679–1742*. London and Ronceverte: Hambledon, 1986, 2.
22 George Every, *The High Church Party, 1688–1718*. London: SPCK, 1956. F. A. Clarke, *Thomas Ken*. London: Methuen, 1896.
23 G. V. Bennett, "King William III and the Episcopate," in G. V. Bennett and J. D. Walsh, eds., *Essays in Modern English Church History in Memory of Norman Sykes*. London: Adam & Charles Black, 1966, 104–131.
24 Avis, *Anglicanism and the Christian Church*, 111–116, 128.
25 Geoffrey Holmes and W. A. Speck, eds., *The Divided Society: Parties and Politics in England, 1694–1716*. New York: St. Martin's Press, 1968, 50.
26 Dudley W. R. Bahlman, *The Moral Revolution of 1688*. New Haven: Yale University Press, 1957.
27 Norman Sykes, "Queen Anne and the Episcopate." *English Historical Review*, 50, 199 (July, 1935), 433–464.
28 Holmes, 13.
29 Norman Sykes, *From Sheldon to Secker*. Cambridge: Cambridge University Press, 1959, 45.
30 G. V. Bennett, *The Tory Crisis in Church and State, 1688–1730*. Oxford: Clarendon Press, 1975.
31 Norman Sykes, *William Wake*. Cambridge: Cambridge University Press, 1957, 89f.
32 *Ibid.*, 97. G. V. Bennett, *White Kennett*. London: SPCK 1957.
33 Holmes, 197.
34 Geoffrey Holmes, "The Achievement of Stability: The Social Context of Politics from the 1680s to the Age of Walpole," in John Cannon, ed., *The Whig Ascendancy*. New York: St. Martin's Press, 1981, 1–27.
35 H. T. Dickinson, "Whiggism in the Eighteenth Century," in Cannon, 28–50. H. T. Dickinson, *Liberty and Property: Political Ideology in Eighteenth-Century Britain*. London: Weidenfeld & Nicolson, 1977.
36 J. C. D. Clark, *English Society, 1688–1832*. Cambridge: Cambridge University Press, 1985.
37 Arthur Warne, *Church and Society in Eighteenth-Century Devon*. New York: Augustus M. Kelley, 1969, 129–165.
38 Norman Sykes, *Church and State in England in the Eighteenth Century*. The

Birkbeck Lectures, 1931–3. New York: Octagon, 1975.

39 F. C. Mather, "Georgian Churchmanship Reconsidered: Some Variations in Anglican Public Worship, 1714–1830." *Journal of Ecclesiastical History*, 36, 2 (April, 1985), 255–283.

40 A recent illustration of the tendency to fault the Hanoverian age and its established Church can be found in David Lyle Jeffrey's introduction to his edited volume of English spiritual writings. Jeffrey contrasts the Tory, High Church tradition as "committed to the inner life of piety" with the Church as "a spiritually flightless bird" which "attempted to make its own heaven on an increasingly muddy earth." The Church's "muddiness" was partly intellectual and partly moral, a participation of established religion in the age's debauchery. Few bishops "were true shepherds; most were indolent and many entirely dissolute." The result was "the nearly complete corruption of its administrative hierarchy" and "a wholesale neglect of spiritual life at the parish level." Unfortunately Jeffrey failed to engage the revisionist tradition of interpreting the age which began with Norman Sykes, and he maintained a caricature which neglected the admirable figures and the spiritual integrity of establishment religion. See David Lyle Jeffrey, ed., *A Burning and a Shining Light: English Spirituality in the Age of Wesley*. Grand Rapids: Eerdmans, 1987, 3–6.

41 Basil Williams, *The Whig Supremacy, 1714–1760*. Oxford: Clarendon Press, 1939, 87–89.

42 Norman Sykes, *Edmund Gibson*. Oxford: Oxford University Press, 1926, 65–69, 181f.

43 Williams, 84. William Warburton, *The Alliance Between Church and State*. London, 1736.

44 Williams, 87–93. Italics in the original. R. W. Greaves, "The Working of the Alliance: A Comment on Warburton," in Walsh, 163–180.

45 Greaves, 178f.

46 Michael R. Watts, *The Dissenters*. Oxford: Clarendon Press, 1978.

47 *Ibid.*, 369.

48 Donald Davie, *A Gathered Church*. New York: Oxford University Press, 1978. Italics in the original.

49 Linda Colley, *In Defiance of Oligarchy: The Tory Party, 1714–1760*. Cambridge: Cambridge University Press, 1982, 7, 85f., 100.

50 Robert Hole, *Pulpits, Politics and Public Order in England, 1760–1832*. Cambridge: Cambridge University Press, 1989, 12f., 73f.

2 NEW VISIONS OF ESTABLISHMENT

1 Edmund Burke, *Reflections on the Revolution in France*, in *Edmund Burke: Selected Works*. Ed. W. J. Bate. New York: The Modern Library, 1960, 401.

2 Edmund Burke, "Speech on the Petition of the Unitarians," May 11, 1792. Cited in Sykes, *Church and State*, 379.

3 I have summarized the relationship between extra-parliamentary politics and religious mobilization in my unpublished dissertation. See William L. Sachs, "Improving the Time: The World-View of Activist Evangelicalism in England, 1785–1833," University of Chicago Ph.D., 1981.

4 The achievement is discussed clearly by Norman Gash in *Aristocracy and People: Britain, 1815–1865*. Cambridge, Mass.: Harvard University Press, 1979, 135–155.

5 *Ibid.*

6 G. F. A. Best, *Temporal Pillars*. Cambridge: Cambridge University Press, 1964, 148ff. Richard Brent, *Liberal Anglican Politics: Whiggery, Religion, and Reform, 1830–1841*. Oxford: Clarendon Press, 1987, 3.

7 An informative, comprehensive study of Coleridge as a Christian writer is that of J. Robert Barth, *Coleridge and Christian Doctrine*. Cambridge, Mass.: Harvard University Press, 1969. A clear sense of Coleridge in the context of his time emerges in Bernard M. G. Reardon, *Religious Thought in the Victorian Age*. London: Longman, 1980, 60–89.

8 Barth, 18f.

9 Reardon, 69.

10 *Ibid.*, 77.

11 *Ibid.*, 82.

12 Reardon, 85.

13 Samuel Taylor Coleridge, *On the Constitution of the Church and State According to the Idea of Each*. London: J. M. Dent & Sons, 1972, 15.

14 *Ibid.*, 21.

15 *Ibid.*, 31.

16 *Ibid.*, 34.

17 Peter Allen, "S. T. Coleridge's *Church and State* and the Idea of an Intellectual Establishment." *Journal of the History of Ideas*, 46, 1 (January–March, 1985), 90.

18 *Ibid.*, 91.

19 *Ibid.*, 95.

20 *Ibid.*, 100.

21 Coleridge, 101.

22 Reardon, 43. Brent, 145–163.

23 Brent, 154–168.

24 *Ibid.* Reardon, 52.

25 Thomas Arnold, "Christian Politics," in *Miscellaneous Works*. New York: D. Appleton, 1845, 448.

26 *Ibid.*, 453.

27 *Ibid.*, 459.

28 *Ibid.*, 464.

29 *Ibid.*, 468.

30 *Ibid.*, 470.

31 *Ibid.*, 474.

32 Arnold, "National Church Establishments," in *Miscellaneous Works*, 497.
33 Arnold, "Principles of Church Reform," in *Miscellaneous Works*, 5.
34 *Ibid.*, 112.
35 W. E. H. Lecky, "The History of the Evangelical Movement." *The Nineteenth Century*, 6 (August, 1879), 280–292.
36 Thomas Haweis, *Evangelical Principles and Practice*. London: E. Dilly, 1763, 271. George Whitefield, *The Great Duty of Charity Recommended, Particularly to All Who Profess Christianity*. London: C. Whitefield, 1740, 5, 22. Thomas Scott, *Essays on the Most Important Subjects in Religion*. London: D. Jacques, 1794, 255. Harold Lindstrom, *Wesley and Sanctification*. Stockholm: Nya Bokforlags Aktiebologet, 1946. John Wesley, *A Plain Account of Christian Perfection*. New York: T. Mason and G. Lane, 1837. See also Boyd Hilton, *The Age of Atonement: The Influence of Evangelicalism on Social and Economic Thought, 1785–1865*. Oxford: Clarendon Press, 1988.
37 Brent, 126f. Abraham D. Kriegel, "A Convergence of Ethics: Saints and Whigs in British Antislavery." *Journal of British Studies*, 26, 4 (October, 1987), 423–450. Also, Roger Anstey, *The Atlantic Slave Trade and British Abolition, 1760–1810*. Atlantic Highlands, N.J.: Humanities Press, 1975.
38 Sachs, "Improving the Time."
39 See P. J. Marshall and Glyndwr Williams, *The Great Map of Mankind: Perceptions of New Worlds in the Age of Enlightenment*. Cambridge, Mass.: Harvard University Press, 1982. David Kopf, *British Orientalism and the Bengal Renaissance*. Berkeley and Los Angeles: University of California Press, 1969. Philip D. Curtin, *The Image of Africa: British Ideas and Action, 1780–1850*. 2 vols. Madison: University of Wisconsin Press, 1964.
40 Curtin, vol. 1, 64, 68, 253f.
41 *Ibid.*, 95–102.
42 James W. St. G. Walker, *The Black Loyalists: The Search for a Promised Land in Nova Scotia and Sierra Leone, 1783–1870*. New York: Holmes & Meier, 1976.
43 Eugene Stock, *The History of the Church Missionary Society*, vol. 1. London: Church Missionary Society, 1899, 62f. Josiah Pratt, ed., *Eclectic Notes*. London: James Nisbet & Co., 1856.
44 Stock, 72.
45 *Proceedings of the Society for Missions to Africa and the East*, 2 (1806–1809). London: C. Whittingham, 1809, 74–90.
46 *CMS Proceedings*, 3 (1810), 20.
47 *Ibid.*, 4 (1814), 251, 253.
48 *Ibid.* (1822), 61.
49 Curtin, vol. 1, 264.
50 *Ibid.*
51 Stephen H. Tyng, *A Memoir of the Rev. W. A. B. Johnson*. New York: Robert Carter & Brothers, 1853, 52.
52 Walker, 345. In Sierra Leone the CMS found more response among the indigenous peoples than among the Nova Scotia émigrés for whom their

work had been intended. The Nova Scotians had fallen under the influence of a more fervent Evangelical style, and developed their own unique religious life which resisted even Baptist and Methodist influence. Ultimately the Anglican position in Sierra Leone came to rest with those émigrés who cherished a sense of being a social and religious elite – the Creoles – and with certain of the neighboring tribes.

53 Ross Border, *Church and State in Australia, 1788–1872*. London: SPCK, 1962, 16f.

54 *Ibid.*, 22–29. Robert Hughes, *The Fatal Shore: The Epic of Australia's Founding*. New York: Alfred Knopf, 1987, 187–191, 245–249.

55 *CMS Proceedings*, 3 (1810), 73. Border, 37.

56 Thomas Blanshard, John Owen, Robert Carr, and David Browne to the Rt. Honourable Earl Cornwallis, Calcutta, June 20, 1788, Fulham Papers 434, Lambeth Palace Archives, London.

57 M. E. Gibbs, *The Anglican Church in India, 1600–1970*. Delhi: ISPCK, 1972, 32. Hugh Pearson, *Memoirs of the Life and Writings of the Rev. Claudius Buchanan, D.D.* Philadelphia: George & Bylington, 1837.

58 Ainslie Thomas Embree, *Charles Grant and British Rule in India*. London: George Allen & Unwin, 1962, 154.

59 Gibbs, 51. Sachs, "Improving the Time."

60 Hans Cnattingius, *Bishops and Societies: A Study of Anglican Colonial and Missionary Expansion, 1698–1850*. London: SPCK, 1952, 68.

61 Charles Daubeny, *A Guide to the Church*. Third edition. London: F. C. and J. Rivington, 1830, p. xxvi.

62 *Ibid.*, 7.

63 A. B. Webster, *Joshua Watson: The Story of a Layman, 1771–1855*. London: SPCK, 1954.

64 *The Life of Reginald Heber, D.D., by his Widow*. New York: Protestant Episcopal Press, 1830, 161.

65 Stock, 183. Gibbs, 87.

66 Gibbs, 109. Josiah Bateman, *The Life of Daniel Wilson, D.D.* Boston: Gould and Lincoln, 1860, 348.

67 Bateman, 400.

68 John Frederick Woolverton, *Colonial Anglicanism in North America*. Detroit: Wayne State University Press, 1984, 17.

69 *Ibid.*, 16.

70 *Ibid.*, 52.

71 By the eve of the American Revolution a variety of legal measures existed to give Anglican clergy in Virginia greater security against the whims of capricious, powerful laity. After 1720, for instance, vestries had difficulty ejecting clergy from their livings. See Joan Gundersen, "The Myth of the Independent Virginia Vestry," *Historical Magazine of the Episcopal Church*, 44 (June, 1975), 133–141. A subsequent statute of Virginia's General Assembly, in 1749, gave a minister legal tenure in his parish. Cf. Rhys Isaac, *The Transformation of Virginia*. Chapel Hill: University of North Carolina Press, 1982, 145.

72 Woolverton, 76.

73 *Ibid.*, 83f.

74 *Ibid.*, 92.

75 S. Charles Bolton, *Southern Anglicanism: The Church of England in Colonial South Carolina*. Westport: Greenwood Press, 1982, 25, 43. Parke Rouse, Jr., *James Blair of Virginia*. Chapel Hill: University of North Carolina Press, 1971.

76 *Ibid.*, 44.

77 *Ibid.*, 59–64.

78 *Ibid.*, 147.

79 *Ibid.*, 123.

80 James Thayer Addison, *The Episcopal Church in the United States, 1789–1931*. Hamden: Archon Books, 1969, 45.

81 Woolverton, 32.

82 On Inglis, see Judith Fingard, *The Anglican Design in Loyalist Nova Scotia, 1783–1816*. London: SPCK, 1972. Also, John Wolfe Lydekker, *The Life and Letters of Charles Inglis*. London: SPCK, 1936. On Mayhew and the controversy over an American bishop, see Martin E. Marty, *Pilgrims in their Own Land*. Boston: Little, Brown & Co., 1984, 134.

83 Frederick V. Mills, Sr., *Bishops by Ballot*. New York: Oxford University Press, 1978, 41ff.

84 Isaac, 163f.

85 *Ibid.*, 284. Jan Lewis, *The Pursuit of Happiness*. Cambridge: Cambridge University Press, 1985, 57.

86 Mills, 157–181.

87 *Ibid.*, 184. William White, *The Case of the Protestant Episcopal Churches in the United States Considered*. Ed. Richard G. Salomon. Philadelphia: Church Historical Society, 1954.

88 *Ibid.*, 185.

89 Mills, 186.

90 Mills, 212.

91 *Ibid.*, 258.

92 *Ibid.*, 275.

93 William Wilson Manross, *The Episcopal Church in the United States, 1800–1840*. New York: AMS Press, Inc., 1967, 75, 180ff. Henry Caswall, *America and the American Church*. New York: Arno Press, 1969, 55, 64.

94 James Elliott Lindsley, *This Planted Vine: A Narrative History of the Episcopal Diocese of New York*. New York: Harper & Row, 1984, 100.

95 Addison, 89.

96 *Ibid.*, 114f.

97 Robert Bruce Mullin, *Episcopal Vision/American Reality: High Church Theology and Social Thought in Evangelical America*. New Haven and London: Yale University Press, 1986, xv.

98 Lindsley, 116.

99 Mullin, 73.

100 *Ibid.*, 54, 71.

101 F. D. Maurice, *The Kingdom of Christ*, vol. I. London: SCM, 1958, 43. W. Merlin Davies, *An Introduction to F. D. Maurice's Theology*. London: SPCK, 1964, 22.
102 Reardon, 167.
103 Maurice, vol. I, 13, 15. Reardon, 167.
104 Maurice, vol. I, 20.
105 *Ibid.*, 220f.
106 *Ibid.*, 228. Frank Mauldin McClain, *Maurice: Man and Moralist*. London: SPCK, 1972, 94.
107 Maurice, vol. I, 230.
108 *Ibid.*, 233. McClain, 119f.
109 Maurice, vol. II, 186. McClain, 142.
110 McClain, 143. Maurice, vol. II, 203.
111 Maurice, vol. II, 233, 257.
112 *Ibid.*, 258. Frederick Denison Maurice, *Theological Essays*. London: James Clarke, 1957, 276f.
113 *The Kingdom of Christ*, vol. II, 271.
114 *Ibid.*, 360.
115 McClain, 143f.
116 Frederick Denison Maurice, *The Religions of the World*. The Boyle lectures, 1846. Fifth edition. London: Macmillan, 1877, 9.

3 THE ADJUSTMENT OF CHURCH AND STATE

1 Charles James Blomfield, *A Charge Delivered to the Clergy of his Diocese*. London: B. Fellowes, 1830, 7.
2 *Ibid.*, 9.
3 Brent, 125.
4 *Ibid.*, 138.
5 *Ibid.*, 138f.
6 Donald Read, *Peel and the Victorians*. Oxford: Basil Blackwell, 1987, 133, 65.
7 *Ibid.*, 71. See P. J. Welch, "Blomfield and Peel: A Study in Co-operation between Church and State, 1841–1856." *Journal of Ecclesiastical History*, 12, 1 (April, 1961), 71–84.
8 Norman Gash, *Peel*. London and New York: Longmans, 1976, 157.
9 Read, 138–140. Peter Stansky, *Gladstone: A Progress in Politics*. Boston: Little, Brown & Co., 1979, 34ff.
10 Perry Butler, *Gladstone: Church, State, and Tractarianism*. Oxford: Clarendon Press, 1982, 37.
11 *Ibid.*, 47.
12 *Ibid.*, 77. Italics in the original. W. E. Gladstone, *The State in its Relations with the Church*. Fourth edition. Vol. I. London: John Murray, 1841, 6.
13 Gladstone, 9.
14 *Ibid.*, 86. Butler, 79.
15 Gladstone, 265.

16 W. E. Gladstone, *Church Principles Considered in their Results*. London: John Murray, 1840, 25.

17 *Ibid.*, 32, 33.

18 Butler, 85.

19 *Ibid.*, 98f.

20 *Ibid.*, 105. Stansky, 45.

21 G. I. T. Machin, *Politics and the Churches in Great Britain, 1832 to 1868*. Oxford: Clarendon Press, 1977, 32–36.

22 *Ibid.*, 42, 56, 275, 285, 337.

23 *Ibid.*, 18f.

24 J. P. Ellens, "Lord John Russell and the Church Rate Conflict: The Struggle for a Broad Church, 1834–1868." *Journal of British Studies*, 26, 2 (April, 1987), 236, 240.

25 *Ibid.*, 242.

26 Machin, 258.

27 Ellens, 243.

28 *Ibid.*

29 *Ibid.*, 245–253.

30 Machin, 306–319.

31 *Ibid.*, 337–343.

32 *Ibid.*, 161–163.

33 D. G. Paz, *The Politics of Working-Class Education in Britain, 1830–50*. Manchester: Manchester University Press, 1980, 11–13.

34 Machin, 64. Paz, 4.

35 Paz, 22.

36 *Ibid.*, 63.

37 *Ibid.*

38 *Ibid.*, 82.

39 Ian D. C. Newbould, "The Whigs, the Church, and Education, 1839." *Journal of British Studies*, 26, 3 (July, 1987), 332–346.

40 Machin, 151ff.

41 Best, 297f.

42 Kenneth A. Thompson, *Bureaucracy and Church Reform*. Oxford: Clarendon Press, 1970, 1.

43 Best, 298. Philip Ziegler, *Melbourne*. New York: Atheneum, 1982.

44 Best, 302f.

45 T. C. Hansard, *Parliamentary Debates*, third series. Vol. 32, March 8 to April 20, 1836. London: T. C. Hansard, 1836, 126, 127. Hereafter the *Parliamentary Debates* will be referred to by the customary appellation, Hansard.

46 *Ibid.*, 128, 160, 161.

47 *Ibid.*, 135f.

48 *Ibid.*, 162f.

49 Best, 305f.

50 Hansard, vol. 55, June 23 to August 11, 1840, 1116.

51 *Ibid.*, 1135, 1137.

52 *Ibid.*, 1138, 1144.

53 Machin, 182.

54 *Ibid.*, 17.

55 Charles James Blomfield, *The Uses of a Standing Ministry and an Established Church*. Two sermons. London: B. Fellowes, 1834, 9, 25. See also Blomfield, *Proposals for the Creation of a Fund to be Applied to the Building and Endowment of Additional Churches*. London: B. Fellowes, 1836.

56 Charles James Blomfield, *A Charge Delivered to the Clergy of the Diocese of London*. London: B. Fellowes, 1846, 35f., 41, 45.

57 Horace Mann, "Report on the Census of Religious Worship," in Richard J. Helmstadter and Paul T. Phillips, eds., *Religion in Victorian Society*. Lanham: University Press of America, 1985, 155.

58 James Fraser, *A Charge Delivered at the Third Visitation of his Diocese*. Manchester: Thos. Roworth, 1880, 5, 20, 25.

59 Desmond Bowen, *The Idea of the Victorian Church*. Montreal: McGill, 1968, ix.

60 Brian Heeney, *Mission to the Middle Classes: The Woodard Schools, 1848–1891*. London: SPCK, 1969.

61 *Ibid.*, 22–30.

62 *Ibid.*, 41, 95.

63 Susan Pedersen, "Hannah More Meets Simple Simon: Tracts, Chapbooks, and Popular Culture in Late Eighteenth-Century England." *Journal of British Studies*, 25, 1 (January, 1986), 91f.

64 *Ibid.*, 109.

65 John Bird Sumner, *A Treatise on the Records of the Creation, and on the Moral Attributes of the Creator*. London: J. Hatchard, 1833, 33, 36f.

66 *Ibid.*, 344, 351.

67 James Phillips Kay, "The Moral and Physical Condition of the Working Classes Employed in the Cotton Manufacture in Manchester," in Helmstadter and Phillips, 140. *The Quarterly Review*, 57 (September–December, 1836). London: John Murray, 1836, 396, 435.

68 Hansard, 44, July 9 to August 16, 1838, 398.

69 Hansard, 55, June 23 to August 11, 1840, 1268, 1272f.

70 Geoffrey B. A. M. Finlayson, *The Seventh Earl of Shaftesbury, 1801–1885*. London: Eyre Methuen, 1981, 76, 125. David Roberts, *Paternalism in Early Victorian England*. New Brunswick, N.J.: Rutgers University Press, 1979.

71 Donald M. Lewis, *Lighten their Darkness: The Evangelical Mission to Working-Class London, 1828–1860*. Westport, Conn.: Greenwood Press, 1986, 36, 44, 110f.

72 Dennis Smith, *Conflict and Compromise: Class Formation in English Society, 1830–1914*. London: Routledge & Kegan Paul, 1982, 127.

73 *Ibid.*, 138f.

74 W. R. W. Stephens, *The Life and Letters of Walter Farquhar Hook*. Sixth edition. London: Richard Bentley, 1881, 210, 224, 233.

75 *Ibid.*, 252, 279, 372.

76 *Ibid.*, 381f.
77 John Ludlow, *The Autobiography of a Christian Socialist.* Ed. A. D. Murray. London: Frank Cass, 1981, 101–104.
78 *Ibid.*, 113.
79 "Politics for the People," in Helmstadter and Phillips, 121.
80 *Ibid.*, 124, 127.
81 Ludlow, 146.
82 Edward Norman, *The Victorian Christian Socialists.* Cambridge: Cambridge University Press, 1987, 6–10.
83 Ludlow, 188.
84 Peter Adams, *Fatal Necessity: British Intervention in New Zeland, 1830–1847.* Auckland: Auckland University Press, 1977.
85 J. Gallagher, "Fowell Buxton and the New African Policy, 1838–1842." *The Cambridge Historical Journal,* 10, 1 (1950), 46.
86 *Ibid.*, 47.
87 See Norris Pope, *Dickens and Charity.* New York: Columbia University Press, 1978, 100ff.
88 Gallagher, 55.
89 Anthony Grant, *The Past and Prospective Extension of the Gospel by Missions to the Heathen.* The Bampton lectures, 1843. London: Rivington, 1844, viif., xi.
90 *Ibid.*, xvi–xviii.
91 *Ibid.*, 231, 266.
92 E. B. Pusey, *The Church the Converter of the Heathen.* Oxford: J. H. Parker, 1838.
93 Samuel Wilberforce, *The Planting of Nations a Great Responsibility.* London: George Bell, 1852.
94 Samuel Wilberforce, "Upon South Africa, India, Etc.," in *Speeches on Missions.* Ed. Henry Rowley. London: William Wells Gardner, 1874, 137ff.
95 See Samuel Wilberforce, *A History of the Protestant Episcopal Church.* London: James Burns, 1844.
96 Charles James Blomfield, *The Church in Africa.* London: B. Fellowes, 1852, 2f., 6f., 8.
97 *Ibid.*, 18f.
98 *Ibid.*, 20.
99 Border, 85.
100 Alfred Blomfield, *A Memoir of Charles James Blomfield, D.D.*, vol. 1. London: John Murray, 1863, 281f.
101 *Ibid.*, 283.
102 *Ibid.*, 284f. *Proceedings of the Colonial Bishoprics Fund.* London: Rivington, 1841, 3, 7, 12.
103 Clara Burdett Patterson, *Angela Burdett-Coutts and the Victorians.* London: John Murray, 1953, 206.
104 *Journal of the General Convention of the Protestant Episcopal Church.* New York: Protestant Episcopal Press, 1835, 66.

105 William Croswell Doane, *The Life and Writings of George Washington Doane*. Vol. II. Sermon VII: "The Missionary Bishop." New York: D. Appleton, 1860, 399.
106 *Ibid.*, 407.
107 *Ibid.*, 409–411.
108 James Thayer Addison, *The Episcopal Church in the United States, 1789–1931*. Hamden: Archon Books, 1969, 142–144.
109 Geoffrey Rowell, *The Vision Glorious*. Oxford: Oxford University Press, 1983, 163.
110 David Livingstone, *Dr. Livingstone's Cambridge Lectures*. Ed. William Monk. Cambridge: Deighton, Bell & Co., 1858, 21, 36f., 47.
111 Owen Chadwick, *Mackenzie's Grave*. London: Hodder & Stoughton, 1959, 14. Harvey Goodwin, *Memoir of Bishop Mackenzie*. Second edition. Cambridge: Deighton, Bell & Co., 1865, 189.
112 Goodwin, 188. Chadwick, 20.

4 THE STRUGGLE TO DEFINE THE CHURCH AND ITS BELIEF

1 Eugene R. Fairweather, ed., *The Oxford Movement*. New York: Oxford University Press, 1964, 37. John Henry Newman, *Apologia Pro Vita Sua*. Ed. David DeLaura. New York: Norton, 1968, 41.
2 John Keble, "National Apostasy," in Fairweather, 39–42.
3 *Ibid.*, 44.
4 Newman, *Apologia*, 21.
5 *Ibid.*, 26.
6 *Ibid.*, 33.
7 *Ibid.*, 37.
8 *Tracts for the Times*, vol. I. New York: AMS, 1969, iii.
9 *Ibid.*, "Thoughts on the Ministerial Commission," 1; "The Catholic Church," 3.
10 *Ibid.*, "Adherence to the Apostolical Succession the Safest Course," 5; "The Episcopal Church Apostolical;" "The Visible Church," 5.
11 John Keble, *The Life of the Right Reverend Father in God, Thomas Wilson, D.D.* Oxford: John Henry Parker, 1863.
12 Richard Hurrell Froude, *Remains*, vol. I. Derby: Henry Mozley, 1839, 185, 272.
13 *Ibid.*, 270–303.
14 Charles Pettit McIlvaine, *Oxford Divinity Compared with that of the Roman and Anglican Churches*. Philadelphia: Joseph Whetham & Son, 1841, 14.
15 John Henry Newman, *The Via Media of the Anglican Church*, vol. I. London: Longmans, 1891. Owen Chadwick suggests that the first use of the term "Anglicanism" is in H. J. Rose's review of Newman's book. Actually the term had been used occasionally to refer to the Church of England or to the English nation. In Newman's hands "Anglican" acquired a precise, modern meaning from which Rose derived his understanding. See Owen Chadwick, *The Victorian Church*, part I.

London: Adam and Charles Black, 1971, 171, n. 2. I acknowledge the insights of Dr. Peter Gorday on this point and in my treatment of Tractarianism.

16 Newman, *Apologia*, 89, 91, 95.

17 Newman, *An Essay on the Development of Christian Doctrine*. London: Longmans, 1900, 372.

18 *Ibid.*, 372.

19 Chadwick, 251–253. Peter Toon, *Evangelical Theology, 1833–1856*. Atlanta: John Knox Press, 1979, 86f.

20 Chadwick, 263.

21 Neil Batt and Michael Roe, "Conflict within the Church of England in Tasmania, 1850–1858." *Journal of Religious History*, 4, 1 (June, 1966), 39–62. George E. DeMille, *The Catholic Movement in the American Episcopal Church*. Philadelphia: Church Historical Society, 1941, 67, 92.

22 F. D. Maurice, *The Epistle to the Hebrews*. London: John W. Parker, 1846, xxxiii.

23 *Ibid.*, xxxv–xxxviii.

24 *Ibid.*, xxxviii.

25 *Ibid.*, lvii, lxi, lxxiii.

26 *Ibid.*, lxxvii.

27 *Ibid.*, xcvii.

28 E. B. Pusey, *An Eirenicon*. Oxford: Parker, 1865, 10.

29 *Ibid.*, 37, 39.

30 *Ibid.*, 46f., 49.

31 Pusey, "Scriptural Views of Holy Baptism," in Fairweather, 208.

32 David Jasper, "Pusey's 'Lectures on Types and Prophecies of the Old Testament,'" in Perry Butler, ed., *Pusey Rediscovered*. London: SPCK, 1983, 54, 61. Geoffrey Rowell, *The Vision Glorious*. Oxford: Oxford University Press, 1983, 77.

33 E. B. Pusey, *A Letter to the Right Reverend Father in God, Richard Lord Bishop of Oxford*. Oxford: Parker, 1839, 128, 133.

34 E. B. Pusey, *The Holy Eucharist a Comfort to the Penitent*. Oxford: Parker, 1843, 4, 9, 14.

35 E. B. Pusey, *Appendices*. Oxford: Parker, 1838, 6, 21.

36 E. B. Pusey, *The Rule of Faith, as Maintained by the Fathers, and the Church of England*. Oxford: Parker, 1851, 7.

37 *Ibid.*, 40.

38 J. M. Neale, *A Few Words of Hope on the Present Crisis of the English Church*. London: Joseph Masters, 1850, 8, 19.

39 J. M. Neale, *Confession and Absolution*. London: Joseph Masters, 1854, 5, 11.

40 *Ibid.*, 17.

41 J. M. Neale, *Deaconesses and Early Sisterhoods*. London: Joseph Masters, 1869.

42 *The Claims of the Camden Society*. Cambridge: W. P. Grant, 1842, 5.

43 *Ibid.*, 13. *Church Enlargement and Church Arrangement*. Cambridge:

Cambridge University Press, 1843. *A Few Hints on the Practical Study of Ecclesiastical Antiquities.* Second edition. Cambridge: Cambridge University Press, 1840. Rowell, 101, *Thoughts on the Proposed Dissolution of the Cambridge Camden Society.* London: Francis & John Rivington, 1845.

44 Reardon, *Religious Thought in the Victorian Age*, 257.

45 *Ibid.*, 287, 290.

46 Pietro Corsi, *Science and Religion: Baden Powell and the Anglican Debate, 1800–1860.* Cambridge: Cambridge University Press, 1988, 59.

47 *Ibid.*, 47, 191.

48 Reardon, 47, 223–242.

49 *Ibid.*, 293.

50 *Ibid.*, 327f. *Essays and Reviews.* Ninth edition. London: Longmans, 1861, 145–206,.

51 *Essays and Reviews*, 151, 159.

52 Reardon, 323–331.

53 *Ibid.*, 336.

54 *Essays and Reviews*, 337.

55 *Ibid.*, 339. Reardon, 337f.

56 *Replies to Essays and Reviews.* Oxford and London: Parker, 1862, xi, xiv.

57 *Ibid.*, 138, 151, 191.

58 Jeff Guy, *The Heretic.* Johannesburg: Ravan Press, 1983, 45.

59 *Ibid.*, 72.

60 *Ibid.*, 74.

61 John William Colenso, *The Pentateuch and Book of Joshua Critically Examined.* London: Longmans, 1870, 17.

62 Guy, 137.

63 Randall Thomas Davidson and William Benham, *Life of Archibald Campbell Tait*, vol. i. London: Macmillan, 1891, 275.

64 *Ibid.*

65 Benjamin Jowett, *Sermons on Faith and Doctrine.* Ed. W. H. Fremantle. London: John Murray, 1901, 53.

66 *Ibid.*, 117, 135, 142. Cf. Frederick Temple, *The Relations Between Religion and Science.* The Bampton lectures. London: Macmillan, 1884. Benjamin Jowett, *College Sermons.* Ed. W. H. Fremantle. New York: Macmillan, 1895, 75.

67 Jowett, *College Sermons*, 14, 22. *Sermons on Faith and Doctrine*, 33.

68 *Sermons on Faith and Doctrine*, 91. Peter Hinchliff, *Benjamin Jowett and the Christian Religion.* Oxford: Clarendon Press, 1987, 133.

69 Benjamin Jowett, *Sermons Biographical & Miscellaneous.* Ed. W. H. Fremantle. New York: Dutton, 1899, 144, 149f.

70 Rowland E. Prothero, *The Life and Correspondence of Arthur Penrhyn Stanley*, vol. ii. New York: Charles Scribner's Sons, 1894, 109, 164.

71 A. P. Stanley, *Christian Institutions.* New York: Charles Scribner's Sons, 1881, v.

72 Jowett, *Sermons Biographical & Miscellaneous*, 216f. Hinchliff, 159f. Reardon, 306f.

73 W. H. Fremantle, *Christian Ordinances and Social Progress*. The William Belden Noble lectures. Boston and New York: Houghton, Mifflin, 1901, vif.

74 *Ibid.*, ixf.

75 *Ibid.*, xi.

76 *Ibid.*, xiii. W. H. Fremantle, *Natural Christianity*. London and New York: Harper & Brothers, 1911, 7.

77 F. J. A. Hort, *The Way the Truth the Life*. London: Macmillan, 1922, 3, 5, 17.

78 *Ibid.*, 26f., 33.

79 *Ibid.*, 49, 76.

80 B. F. Westcott, *Lessons from Work*. London: Macmillan, 1901, 4.

81 *Ibid.*, 7, 15.

82 *Ibid.*, 16f.

83 *Ibid.*, 22.

84 *Ibid.*, 28f., 33, 43.

85 *Ibid.*, 45ff., 52.

86 *Ibid.*, 53.

87 Charles Gore, ed., *Lux Mundi*. New York: John Lowell, 1889, viif.

88 *Ibid.*, ix.

89 Westcott, 134, 158f.

90 *Ibid.*, 180f.

91 Reardon, 434f. Henry Scott Holland, "Faith," in *Lux Mundi*, 7, 11f.

92 Holland, 24.

93 See Jon Alexander, OP, ed., *William Porcher DuBose: Selected Writings*. New York: Paulist, 1988.

94 *Ibid.*, 23–26.

95 *Ibid.*, 28ff., 85, 107.

96 *Ibid.*, 121, 129.

97 Charles Gore, "The Holy Spirit and Inspiration," in *Lux Mundi*, 263, 272.

98 E. S. Talbot, "Preparation in History for Christ," *Lux Mundi*, 110f., 113.

99 J. R. Illingworth, "The Incarnation and Development," *Lux Mundi*, 172, 176.

100 R. C. Moberly, "The Incarnation as the Basis of Dogma," *Lux Mundi*, 204ff.

101 See John Seely, *Ecce Homo*. Ninth edition. London: Macmillan, 1868. Charles Gore, *The Incarnation*. The Bampton lectures. London: John Murray, 1891, 85.

102 Gore, *The Incarnation*, 87, 127.

103 *Ibid.*, 129, 157.

104 *Ibid.*, 183ff.

105 B. F. Westcott, *The Incarnation and Common Life*. London: Macmillan, 1893, vii, 12, 41ff. B. F. Westcott, *Christus Consummator*. Fourth edition. London: Macmillan, 1906, 44, 55, 102, 118f., 136.

106 R. C. Moberly, *Atonement and Personality*. New York: Longmans, Green, & Co., 1910.

107 *Ibid.*, xiii, 70f.

108 *Ibid.*, 125f., 275.

109 Reardon, 442.

110 *Ibid.*, 453.

111 Hastings Rashdall, *Doctrine and Development*. London: Methuen, 1898. Reardon, 459. Hastings Rashdall, *The Idea of Atonement in Christian Theology*. The Bampton lectures for 1915. London: Macmillan, 1925, vii.

112 Rashdall, *The Idea of Atonement*, 11f., 454.

113 *Ibid.*, 82, 335.

114 *Ibid.*, 236–239, 273–275.

115 Charles Gore, *The Mission of the Church*. London: John Murray, 1892, 8–11.

116 *Ibid.*, 28, 36f.

117 Charles Gore, *The Church and the Ministry*. Fourth edition, revised. London: Longmans, Green, & Co., 1900. F. J. A. Hort, *The Christian Ecclesia*. London: Macmillan, 1900, 29–31.

118 Hort, 39, 85.

119 *Ibid.*, 167, 229f.

120 Gore, *The Church and the Ministry*, x, 7, 9.

121 *Ibid.*, 58, 64f., 153.

122 R. C. Moberly, *Ministerial Priesthood*. New York: Longmans, Green & Co., 1916, xxv, xxviii.

123 J. B. Lightfoot, *The Christian Ministry*. London: Macmillan, 1901, 31, 41, 75, 83.

124 Reardon, 460. Hinchliff, 169. Francis J. Hall, *The Kenotic Theory*. New York: Longmans, Green, & Co., 1898.

5 THE CHURCH AND EMPIRE

1 John Seeley, *The Expansion of England*. Ed. John Gross. Chicago and London: University of Chicago Press, 1971, 12.

2 J. A. Hobson, *Imperialism*. Ann Arbor: University of Michigan Press, 1972. See also E. J. Hobsbawm, *The Age of Empire, 1875–1914*. New York: Pantheon, 1987, 66. M. E. Chamberlain, "Imperialism and Social Reform," in C. C. Eldridge, ed., *British Imperialism in the Nineteenth Century*. London: Macmillan, 1984, 162.

3 Paul Kennedy, "Continuity and Discontinuity in British Imperialism, 1815–1914," in Eldridge, 25. See also J. A. Gallagher and R. E. Robinson, "The Imperialism of Free Trade," *Economic History Review*, second series, 6 (1953), 1–15. Michael W. Doyle, *Empires*. Ithaca and London: Cornell University Press, 1986, 143.

4 Peter Burroughs, "Colonial Self-government," in Eldridge, 40.

5 John P. Halstead, *The Second British Empire: Trade, Philanthropy, and Good*

Government, 1820–1890. London and Westport: Greenwood Press, 1983, 13–15.

6 Robert S. Smith, *The Lagos Consulate, 1851–1861*. London and Basingstoke: Macmillan, 1978, 20f.

7 J. F. Ade Ajayi, *Christian Missions in Nigeria, 1841–1891*. London: Longmans, 1965, 79. Modupe Oduyoye, "The Planting of Christianity in Yorubaland, 1842–1888," in Ogbu Kalu, ed., *Christianity in West Africa: The Nigerian Story*. Ibadan: Daystar Press, 1978, 257f.

8 Oduyoye, 263f.

9 Ajayi, 57ff.

10 *Ibid.*

11 *Ibid.*, 84f.

12 *Ibid.*, 61f., 66.

13 Smith, 20.

14 Edmund Patrick Thurman Crampton, "Christianity in Northern Nigeria," in Kalu, 20. Jesse Page, *The Black Bishop*. London: Hodder & Stoughton, 1908, 139f., 142.

15 Crampton, 22.

16 Andrew Porter, "'Commerce and Christianity': The Rise and Fall of a Nineteenth-Century Missionary Slogan," *Historical Journal*, 28, 3 (1985), 597–621.

17 *Ibid.*

18 Cited in Page, 147.

19 M. A. Laird, *Missionaries and Education in Bengal, 1793–1837*. Oxford: Clarendon Press, 1972, 63.

20 *Ibid.*, 52–54. Cf. David Kopf, *British Orientalism and the Bengal Renaissance*. Berkeley and Los Angeles: University of California Press, 1969.

21 Laird, 230ff. See also John Clive, *Macaulay: The Making of the Historian*. New York: Alfred A. Knopf, 1973, 342–400.

22 Clive, 409.

23 The most recent narrative is Christopher Hibbert, *The Great Mutiny*. New York: Viking, 1978.

24 Michael Edwards, *British India, 1772–1947*. New York: Taplinger, 1967, 176.

25 S. Gopal, *British Policy in India, 1858–1905*. Cambridge: Cambridge University Press, 1965, 2f. See also Bernard S. Cohn, "Representing Authority in Victorian India," in Eric Hobsbawm and Terence Ranger, eds., *The Invention of Tradition*. Cambridge: Cambridge University Press, 1983, 165–209.

26 Frances Maria Milman, *Memoir of the Right Rev. Robert Milman, D.D.* London: John Murray, 1879, 23, 40f.

27 *Ibid.*, 41.

28 *Ibid.*, 48f.

29 *Ibid.*, 51, 80.

30 Gibbs, 278ff. *The Story of the Cawnpore Mission*. (Author's name is not supplied.) London: SPG, 1909, 109.

31 W. G. Beasley, *The Modern History of Japan*. London: Weidenfeld & Nicolson, 1984, 98, 111, 134–139, 150f.

32 Channing Moore Williams to R. B. Doane, March 19, 1874, in the Japan Records, 1859–1953, of the Domestic and Foreign Missionary Society Records in the Archives of the Episcopal Church, Austin, Texas, Record Group 71, Box 22. I wish to express gratitude to the Archives, Dr. V. Nelle Bellamy, Archivist, for permission to quote from these records. A larger treatment of the development of the Church in Japan is found in my article, "'Self-Support': The Episcopal Mission and Nationalism in Japan," in *Church History* (December, 1989). On the Church's sudden growth in Japan, see also Henry St. George Tucker, *The History of the Episcopal Church in Japan*. New York: Charles Scribner's Sons, 1938, 88, 94. For another missionary perspective on Church development, see Arthur Morris, Annual Report, July 10, 1873, Japan Records of the Episcopal Church (hereafter, JR), Box 14.

33 Williams, Annual Report, June 30, 1880, JR, Box 23.

34 Williams, "The Japan Mission during the Past Three Years," September 8, 1883, JR, Box 23.

35 Henry D. Page, JR, Box 15. Williams, JR, Box 23.

36 John McKim, "The Spread of Christianity in Japan," *The Spirit of Missions*, 69, 9 (September, 1904), 653.

37 *Ibid.*, 654.

38 D. M. Schreuder, *The Scramble for Southern Africa, 1877–1895*. Cambridge: Cambridge University Press, 1980.

39 Samwiri Rubaraza Karugire, "The Arrival of the European Missionaries," in A. D. Tom Tuma and Phares Mutibwa, *A Century of Christianity in Uganda, 1877–1977*. Nairobi: Afropress, 1977, 3–6.

40 Alfred R. Tucker, *Eighteen Years in Uganda & East Africa*. Westport, Conn.: Negro Universities Press, 1970, 47.

41 *Ibid.*, 49.

42 *The Diaries of Lord Lugard*. Ed. Margery Perham and Mary Bull. London: Faber & Faber, 1959. Vol. II, 56, and vol. III, 49.

43 Tucker, 54.

44 Holger Bernt Hansen, *Mission, Church and State in a Colonial Setting: Uganda, 1890–1925*. London: Heinemann, 1984, 33, 55.

45 Gordon Martel, *Imperial Diplomacy: Rosebery and the Failure of Foreign Policy*. Kingston and Montreal: McGill–Queen's University Press, 1986, 81.

46 Tucker, 89.

47 "West African Native Independent Bishoprics," reprinted in *The Jubilee Volume of the Sierra Leone Native Church*. London: Furnival Press, 1917, 103.

48 Loh Keng Aun, *Fifty Years of the Anglican Church in Singapore Island, 1909–1959*. Singapore: University of Singapore, 1963, 5, 7, 15.

49 Charles H. Brent, "With God in the Philippine Islands," *The Spirit of Missions*, 68, 2 (February, 1903), 82. Also, Charles H. Brent, "The

Church in the Philippine Islands," *The Spirit of Missions*, 68, 9 (September, 1903), 635.

50 *Journal of the Fourth Annual Convocation of the Missionary District of the Philippine Islands* (Manila, 1907), 42.

51 *Rangoon Diocesan Association Quarter Paper*, 4, 2 (June, 1906), 64f. (Hereafter, the *Paper* shall be cited as *Rangoon*.)

52 *Ibid.*, 79f.

53 Craig Alan Lockard, *From Kampung to City: A Social History of Kuching, Malaysia, 1820–1970*. Ohio University Southeast Asia Series No. 75. Athens, Ohio, 1987, 102.

54 See Robert A. Huttenback, *Racism and Empire*. Ithaca and London: Cornell University Press, 1976. Douglas A. Lorimer, *Colour, Class and the Victorians*. New York: Holmes & Meier, 1978.

55 *Rangoon*, 4, 1 (March, 1906), 12.

56 *Ibid.*, 4, 2 (June, 1906), 66f.

57 R. M. Heanley, *A Memoir of Edward Steere*. London: George Bell & Sons, 1888, 130. John Widdicombe, *In the Lesuto*. London: SPCK, 1895, 66.

58 John Henry Hopkins, *The American Citizen: His Rights and Duties*. New York: Pudney & Russell, 1857, 85.

59 *Jubilee of the Diocese of Toronto*. Toronto: Rowsell & Hutchison, 1890, 20, 23, 25.

60 Henry Codman Potter, *The Scholar and the State*. New York: The Century Co., 1897, 202, 206.

61 William Lawrence, "The Mission of the Church to the Privileged Classes," in *Five Lectures upon the Church*. New Haven: Tuttle, Morehouse, Taylor, 1897, 6. Harold C. Martin, *Outstanding Marble and Brass*. New York: Church Hymnal Corporation, 1986, 65.

62 Samwiri Rubaraza Karugire, "The Arrival of the European Missionaries," in Tuma and Mutibwa, 1. Kenton J. Clymer, *Protestant Missionaries in the Philippines, 1898–1916*. Urbana and Chicago: University of Illinois Press, 1986, 17.

63 *Rangoon*, 5, 2 (June, 1909), 49. Charlotte Mary Yonge, *Life of John Coleridge Patteson*, vol. 1. London: Macmillan, 1875, 129. Ellen Maples, *Chauncy Maples*. London: Longmans, 1897, 57.

64 *Journal of the Thirteenth Annual Convocation of the Church in the Missionary District of Cuba*. Havana: Echemendia, 1919, 20.

65 *Ibid.*, 19, 20f.

66 On the nature of public religion in the United States, see Martin E. Marty, *Religion and Republic*. Boston: Beacon Press, 1987, 53–71. I argue that Marty's criteria for a public religion transcend the American context and can be applied to Anglican missionary intentions.

67 Stock, *The History of the Church Missionary Society*, vol. III (1899), 153. *The Story of the Cawnpore Mission*, 112.

68 A. D. Tom Tuma, *Building a Ugandan Church*. Nairobi: Kenya Literature Bureau, 1980, 71, 83, 88. Deogratias M. Byabazaire, *The Contribution of the Christian Churches to the Development of Western Uganda*,

1894–1974. Frankfurt: Peter Lang, 1979, 8of.

69 Byabazaire, 89, 110.

70 Tuma, *Building a Ugandan Church*, 112–115.

71 See the series of articles on "Railway Mission" in *Railroader: National Railways of Zimbabwe House Journal*, 3, 8, 9, 10 (August–October, 1986). *Rangoon*, 5, 3 (September, 1909), 89.

72 *Rangoon*, 5, 3, 81. *Journal of the Missionary District of Cuba* (1919), 19.

73 W. H. Fremantle, *The World as the Subject of Redemption*. The William Belden Noble lectures. New York: E. & J. B. Young, 1885, 1f. Paul T. Phillips, "The Concept of a National Church in Late Nineteenth-Century England and America." *Journal of Religious History*, 14, 1 (June, 1986), 26.

74 Fremantle, *The World*, 4, 19, 32, 37f., 44.

75 Phillips, 29f. William Reed Huntington, *The Church Idea: An Essay Towards Unity*. Second edition. New York: Hurd and Houghton, 1872. *A National Church*. New York, 1898.

76 Huntington, *The Church Idea*, 42, 47, 96. As approved by the American House of Bishops at Chicago in 1886, the Quadrilateral adopted Huntington's criteria – the Bible, the Nicene creed, the sacraments of Baptism and the Lord's Supper, and the Historic Episcopate as marks of the Church and the basis for Christian reunion. The Quadrilateral gave ecumenical endeavor by Anglicans a basis and an impetus. See J. Robert Wright, ed., *Quadrilateral at One Hundred*. Cincinnati: Forward Movement, 1988.

77 Eliphalet N. Potter, *Education and Unity*. Bethlehem, Pa.: Times, 1890, 13, 28.

78 Bishop Charles Brent of the Philippines articulated the connection between unity and the missionary's social responsibility. See Brent, "The Realization of Christian Unity," in *The Inspiration of Responsibility*. Reprint of the 1915 edition. Freeport, New York: Books for Libraries, 1966, 76ff.

79 Potter, "The Significance of the American Cathedral," in *The Scholar and the State*, 325, 327.

80 J. J. Willis, *The Church in Uganda*. Second impression. London: Longmans, Green & Co., 1914, 8f.

81 *Ibid.*, 16, 18f.

82 W. G. Peel and J. J. Willis, *Steps towards Reunion*. London: Longmans, Green & Co., 1914, 6.

83 *Ibid.*, 20, 7.

84 Frank Weston, *Ecclesia Anglicana: For What does she Stand?* London: Longmans, Green & Co., 1913, 1of.

85 R. T. Davidson, *Kikuyu*. London: Macmillan, 1915, 8f., 23.

86 Charles Gore, *The Basis of Anglican Fellowship*. Fifth impression. London: Mowbray, 1914, 7–9.

87 *Ibid.*, 9.

88 *Ibid.*, 32f., 36.

89 *Ibid.*, 43.
90 H. M. Gwatkin, *The Bishop of Oxford's Open Letter: An Open Letter in Reply.* London: Longmans, Green & Co., 1914, 7. J. F. Bethune-Baker, *The Miracle of Christianity.* London: Longmans, Green & Co., 1914.
91 Charles Gore, *Crisis in Church and Nation.* London: A. R. Mowbray, 1915.
92 Charles Gore, *Christianity Applied to the Life of Men and of Nations.* The Essex Hall lecture. Introduction by R. H. Tawney. London: John Murray, reprint, 1940, 7f., 22.
93 H. W. Tucker, *Memoir of the Life and Episcopate of George Augustus Selwyn, D.D.*, vol. I. New York: Pott, Young, & Co., 1879, 158. See also Fred D. Schneider, "The Anglican Quest for Authority: Convocation and the Imperial Factor, 1850–60," *The Journal of Religious History*, 9, 2 (December, 1976), 141.
94 Tucker, vol. II (1879), 89f.
95 *Ibid.* Cf. G. A. Wood, "Church and State in New Zealand in the 1850s," *Journal of Religious History*, 8, 3 (June, 1975), 255–270.
96 Tucker, vol. II, 91f., 100f., 108.
97 *Ibid.*, 110.
98 Border, 127, 138.
99 *Ibid.*, 159, 163.
100 *Ibid.*, 171f.
101 *Ibid.*, 174f. G. P. Shaw, *Patriarch and Prophet: William Grant Broughton, 1788–1853.* Melbourne: Melbourne University Press, 1978, 235–237.
102 E. D. Daw, "Synodical Government for the Church of England in N.S.W.: The First Attempt," *The Journal of Religious History*, 6, 2 (December, 1970), 156–159. William Cowper, *Episcopate of the Right Reverend Frederic Barker.* London: Hatchards, 1888, 113–116.
103 Daw, 170f. Cowper, 118.
104 Border, 183. Schneider, 142.
105 Philip Carrington, *The Anglican Church in Canada.* Toronto: Collins, 1963, 113–119.
106 Francis Fulford, *An Address Delivered in the Chapel of the General Theological Seminary.* New York: Church Depository, 1852, 2. John Irwin Cooper, *The Blessed Communion.* Montreal: Diocese of Montreal, 1960.
107 Francis Fulford, *A Letter to the Bishops, Clergy, and Laity of the United Church of England and Ireland in the Province of Canada.* Montreal: John Lowell, 1864, 8.
108 George J. Mountain, *A Letter Addressed to the Clergy and Laity of the Diocese of Quebec.* Quebec: The Mercury Office, 1858, 3f.
109 *Ibid.*, 15.
110 Peter Hinchliff, *The Anglican Church in South Africa.* London: Darton, Longman & Todd, 1963, 18. Charles Gray, *The Life of Robert Gray*, vol. I. London: Rivingtons, 1876, 155.
111 Gray, vol. I, 212.
112 *Ibid.*, 259, 341.
113 *Ibid.*, 349.

114 Schneider, 143–153. Eric Waldram Kemp, *Counsel and Consent*. London: SPCK, 1961, 175–185.
115 Gray, vol. I, 512.
116 Hinchliff, *The Anglican Church*, 91.
117 Gray, vol. II, 105, 147.
118 Hinchliff, *The Anglican Church*, 100.
119 William Redmond Curtis, *The Lambeth Conferences*. New York: Columbia University Press, 1942, 79f.
120 Alan M. G. Stephenson, *The First Lambeth Conference*. London: SPCK, 1967, 167.
121 *Ibid.*, 188.
122 *Ibid.*, 88–97.
123 *Ibid.*, 210f. Alan M. G. Stephenson, *Anglicanism and the Lambeth Conferences*. London: SPCK, 1978, 32f.
124 Curtis, 141f.
125 *Ibid.*, 151f.
126 Randall T. Davidson, *The Five Lambeth Conferences*. London: SPCK, 1920. 59f.
127 *Ibid.*, 63f.
128 Curtis, 169–171.
129 *Ibid.*, 202.
130 *Ibid.*, 204.
131 Randall Thomas Davidson and William Benham, *Life of Archibald Campbell Tait*, vol. II. London: Macmillan, 1891, 365.
132 *Ibid.*, 367.
133 *Ibid.*, 373–375.
134 Davidson, *The Five Lambeth Conferences*, 152.
135 Stephenson, *Anglicanism and the Lambeth Conferences*, 85–87. As J. Robert Wright observes, Huntington's original four points underwent rewording at the American General Convention and at Lambeth. See J. Robert Wright, "Heritage and Vision: The Chicago–Lambeth Quadrilateral," in Wright, ed., *Quadrilateral at One Hundred*. Cincinnati: Forward Movement, 1988.

6 ANGLICANISM CONFRONTS CULTURAL DIVERSITY

1 The term "popular religion" advances the distinction denoted in the history of religions by "folk religion" or "little tradition" as opposed to "elite" religion or "great" tradition. The category describes a level of religious life apart from that expressed in canonical writings, definitive doctrines, or magisterial hierarchies. Popular religion generally highlights local levels of practice, reflecting variety within a larger tradition. Often ritual demarcates popular religion as a category reflecting practice rather than theory. In this study, popular religion also suggests the idea of "party," that is, of subgroups of particular ideological stamp with a sense of definitive boundaries within the larger ecclesiastical

tradition. A helpful summary of the category is found in Catherine Bell, "Religion and Chinese Culture: Toward an Assessment of 'Popular Religion,'" *History of Religions*, 29, 1 (August, 1989), 35–57.

2 Marty, *Modern American Religion. Volume I*, 282–284. Richard T. Ely, *Social Aspects of Christianity and Other Essays*. New York: Thomas Y. Crowell, 1889, 137.

3 G. I. T. Machin, *Politics and the Churches in Great Britain, 1869 to 1921*. Oxford: Clarendon Press, 1987.

4 J. G. Rogers, "Social Aspects of Disestablishment," *The Nineteenth Century*, 1 (May, 1877), 437, 441, 447.

5 A. H. Mackonochie, "Disestablishment and Disendowment," *The Nineteenth Century*, 1 (June, 1877), 686f., 689, 692.

6 *Ibid.*, 696.

7 J. P. Parry, *Democracy and Religion: Gladstone and the Liberal Party, 1867–1875*. Cambridge: Cambridge University Press, 1986, 34.

8 Machin, *Politics and Churches, 1869 to 1921*, 279.

9 Parry, 150.

10 *Ibid.*, 152, 188f.

11 Machin, *Politics and Churches, 1869 to 1921*, 317.

12 Stewart D. Headlam, "Christian Socialism," *Fabian Tracts*, no. 42, 1884–93. Mendeln, Liechtenstein: Kraus-Thomson, 1969, 4.

13 *Ibid.*, 3.

14 *Ibid.*, 4ff.

15 *Ibid.*, 7.

16 Norman, 102. Peter d'A. Jones, *The Christian Socialist Revival, 1877–1914*. Princeton: Princeton University Press, 1968, 101.

17 Jones, 48, 101.

18 M. B. Reckitt, *Maurice to Temple*. London: Faber, 1947, 135. Jones, 160. Bernard Kent Markwell, "The Anglican Left: Radical Social Reformers in the Church of England and the Protestant Episcopal Church, 1846–1954." University of Chicago Ph.D. thesis, 1977.

19 Markwell, 117.

20 Jones, 126–129.

21 Donald Gray, *Earth and Altar*. Alcuin Club Collections, no. 68. Norwich: Canterbury Press, 1986, 116–119.

22 Jones, 145f.

23 See William L. Sachs, "Stewart Headlam and the Fabian Society," *Historical Magazine of the Protestant Episcopal Church* (June, 1976).

24 Norman, 107–111.

25 Gray, 92f.

26 Cited in Markwell, 136.

27 B. F. Hilton, *The Age of Atonement: The Influence of Evangelicalism on Social and Economic Thought, 1795–1865*. Oxford: Clarendon Press, 1988.

28 *Ibid.*, 289–303.

29 Norman, 162f.

30 *Ibid.*, 168. Westcott, 52.

31 Westcott, 311.
32 *Ibid.*, 56.
33 Hilton, 321. Markwell, 147.
34 Henry Scott Holland, *God's City and the Coming of the Kingdom*. London: Longmans, Green, 1900, 6f., 13, 16.
35 *Ibid.*, 123f., 127, 129.
36 *Ibid.*, 89, 97.
37 Hilton, 322.
38 Wilfrid Richmond, *Christian Economics*. New York: E. P. Dutton, 1888, vii.
39 *Ibid.*, 26, 8, 67, 34.
40 *Ibid.*, 71f.
41 Ely, 60, 79, 97, 104.
42 Charles Gore, "Christianity and Socialism" *The Church and Human Society*. Pan-Anglican Congress Papers, vol. II, section A. London: SPCK, 1908, 2f., 6.
43 Jones, 225–228.
44 G. P. H. Pawson, *Edward Keble Talbot: His Community and his Friends*. London: SPCK, 1954, 39.
45 Jones, 239f. Gray, 95.
46 Jones, 248. Gray, 98.
47 Markwell, 166–180.
48 *Ibid.*, 203, 221f.
49 *Ibid.*, 237.
50 Vida D. Scudder, *The Church and the Hour*. New York: E. P. Dutton, 1917, 3f.
51 *Ibid.*, 14, 26f.
52 *Ibid.*, 28f., 35f.
53 Markwell, 284, 290f.
54 Phillips Brooks, *The Law of Growth*. New York: E. P. Dutton, 1910, 20–24.
55 *Ibid.*, 106, 165.
56 F. D. Huntington, *Human Society*. New York: Thomas Whittaker, 1925, 272.
57 *Ibid.*, 273.
58 John A. Dix and Leicester C. Lewis, eds., *A History of the Parish of Trinity Church in the City of New York*, part V. New York: Columbia University Press, 1950, 123.
59 *Ibid.*, 115.
60 See James Obelkevich, "Religion and Rural Society in South Lindsey, 1825–75," Columbia University Ph.D. thesis, 1971.
61 Timothy L. Smith, *Revivalism and Social Reform*. Gloucester, Mass.: Peter Smith, 1976, 69.
62 William Wilson Manross, *The Episcopal Church in the United States, 1800–1840*. New York: AMS, 1967, 144.
63 *Ibid.*, 156–158.
64 See Peter J. Jagger, *Clouded Witness*. Allison Park, Pa.: Pickwick, 1982.

65 Anthony Russell, *The Clerical Profession*. London: SPCK, 1981, 33.
66 *Ibid.*, 37, 39.
67 Standish Meacham, *Lord Bishop: The Life of Samuel Wilberforce, 1805–1873.* Cambridge, Mass.: Harvard University Press, 1970, 105–107.
68 William Meade, *Lectures on the Pastoral Office.* New York: Stanford and Swords, 1849, 13, 21, 27.
69 Richard G. Becker, "The Social Thought of William Augustus Muhlenberg," *Historical Magazine of the Protestant Episcopal Church*, 27, 4 (December, 1958), 314, 317. See also W. A. Muhlenberg, *Evangelical Catholic Papers.* Compiled by Anne Ayres. Second series. Suffolk County, N.Y.: St. Johnland Press, 1877.
70 William P. Haugaard, "The Missionary Vision of James Lloyd Breck in Minnesota," *Historical Magazine of the Protestant Episcopal Church*, 54, 3 (September, 1985), 241f. James C. Ransom, "The Associate Mission: An Experimental Ministry of the Episcopal Church in Omaha, 1891–1902," *Nebraska History*, 61, 4 (winter, 1980), 449, 455f.
71 Standish Meachem, *Toynbee Hall and Social Reform, 1880–1914.* New Haven and London: Yale University Press, 1987.
72 DeMille, 134f. Martin L. Smith, SSJE, ed., *Benson of Cowley.* Oxford: Oxford University Press, 1980. Timothy L. Smith, 32.
73 Mary Sudman Donovan, *A Different Call: Women's Ministries in the Episcopal Church, 1850–1920.* Wilton, Conn.: Morehouse-Barlow, 1986, 57ff. Miss Nellie G. Eddy, journal entry, April 4, 1876, Japan Records of the Episcopal Church, RG 71, Box 4.
74 Donovan, 7, 120. Brian Heeney, *The Women's Movement in the Church of England, 1850–1930.* Oxford: Clarendon Press, 1988, 43. In a few instances women even founded new parishes, ultimately having to turn leadership over to men. See Joan R. Gundersen, "The Local Parish as a Female Institution: The Experience of All Saints Episcopal Church in Frontier Minnesota." *Church History*, 55, 3 (September, 1986), 307–322. Gundersen's work enhances the meaning of the feminization of religion in the late nineteenth century, for she shows women's initiative broadening in an unprecedented way.
75 Donovan, 66–73.
76 Heeney, 5, 16.
77 *Ibid.*, 89ff.
78 *Ibid.*, 96ff.
79 *Ibid.*, 124.
80 Owanah Anderson, *Jamestown Commitment: The Episcopal Church and the American Indian.* Cincinnati, Ohio: Forward Movement, 1988, 39.
81 *Ibid.*, 47.
82 *Ibid.*, 48, 55f.
83 Virginia Driving Hawk Sneve, *That They may have Life: The Episcopal Church in South Dakota, 1859–1976.* New York: Seabury, 1977, 10. David M. Dean, *Breaking Trail: Hudson Stuck of Texas and Alaska.* Athens, Ohio: Ohio University Press, 1988.

84 Sneve, 74–76.

85 J. Carleton Hayden, "After the War: The Mission and Growth of the Episcopal Church among Blacks in the South, 1865–1877," *Historical Magazine of the Protestant Episcopal Church*, 42, 4 (December, 1973), 403ff.

86 "A Unique Sunday-School," *The Spirit of Missions* (February, 1879), 65. *Journal of the Ninety-Fifth Annual Council of the Protestant Episcopal Church in Virginia*. May 21–24, 1890. Richmond: Wm. Ellis Jones, 1890, 43.

87 *Journal of the 106th Annual Council of the Protestant Episcopal Church in Virginia*. May 15–17, 1901. Richmond: Wm. Ellis Jones, 1901, 78. Samuel H. Bishop, "The Church and the City Negro," *The Spirit of Missions*, 76, 4 (April, 1911), 297–299.

88 "A Wonderful Work among the Plantation Negroes," *The Spirit of Missions* (March, 1879), 105. *Journal of the Eighty-first Annual Convention of the Protestant Episcopal Church in the Diocese of Georgia*. May 13–15, 1903. Macon, Ga.: J. W. Burke, 1903, 91.

89 Samuel H. Bishop, "The Negro and the Church," *The Spirit of Missions*, 75, 6 (June, 1910), 438.

90 C. K. Nelson, "High Ground, Right Thinking," in *The United Negro: His Problems and his Progress*. Ed. I. Garland Penn and J. W. E. Bowen. Atlanta: D. E. Luther, 1902, 3.

91 John Kershaw, *The Issue in South Carolina*. New York: Baum & Geddes, 1887, 386, 405.

92 Nigel Yates, *The Oxford Movement and Parish Life: St. Saviour's, Leeds, 1839–1929*. Borthwick Paper no. 48. York: University of York, 1975, 3, 6–10.

93 Rowell, 119ff.

94 Davidson and Benham, vol. I, 218f., 220f.

95 *Ibid.*, 412.

96 *Ibid.*, vol. II, 191, 201.

97 James Bentley, *Ritualism and Politics in Victorian Britain*. Oxford: Oxford University Press, 1978.

98 *Ibid.*, 86f.

99 *Ibid.*, 96–100.

100 Davidson and Benham, 101. Bentley, 102.

101 Rowell, 152.

102 Bentley, 119. Rowell, 155f.

103 James DeKoven, "The Church of the Living God," in *Sermons Preached on Various Occasions*. New York: D. Appleton, 1880, 47f.

104 John Henry Hopkins, *The Law of Ritualism*. New York: Hurd and Houghton, 1866. Robert Bruce Mullin, "Ritualism, Anti-Romanism, and the Law in John Henry Hopkins." *Historical Magazine of the Protestant Episcopal Church*, 50, 4 (December, 1981), 377–390.

105 DeMille, 125.

106 John M. Kinney, "'The Fond du Lac Circus:' The Consecration of Reginald Heber Weller," *Historical Magazine of the Protestant Episcopal*

Church, 38, 1 (March, 1969), 3–24. See also Charles Grafton, *A Journey Godward*. Milwaukee: The Young Churchman, 1910. Also see Annie Darling Price, *A History of the Formation and Growth of the Reformed Episcopal Church, 1873–1902*. Philadelphia: James Armstrong, 1902.

107 Max Warren, ed. *To Apply the Gospel: Selections from the Writings of Henry Venn*. Grand Rapids, Mich.: Eerdmans, 1971, 28, 60.

108 Wilbert R. Shenk, *Henry Venn – Missionary Statesman*. Maryknoll, N.Y.: Orbis, 1983, 30.

109 *Ibid.*, 34.

110 Ajayi, 183.

111 *Ibid.*, 187.

112 *Ibid.*, 214–224.

113 *Ibid.*, 233. E. A. Ayandele, *African Historical Studies*. London: Frank Cass, 1979, 141.

114 Ajayi, 235f.

115 Roland Allen, *The Spontaneous Expansion of the Church*. Grand Rapids, Mich.: Eerdmans, 1962, 1f., 19, 26.

116 David M. Paton, ed., *The Ministry of the Spirit: Selected Writings of Roland Allen*. London: World Dominion Press, 1960, 26f., 42, 46. Roland Allen, *Essential Missionary Principles*. New York and Chicago: Fleming H. Revell, 1913, 20f., 24f.

117 Allen, *Essential Missionary Principles*, 27.

118 *Ibid.*, 88f.

119 George Longridge, *A History of the Oxford Mission to Calcutta*. London and Oxford: Mowbray, 1910, 61, 63, 77f.

120 T. O. Beidelman, *Colonial Evangelism*. Bloomington: Indiana University Press, 1982, 23, 101f. Robert W. Strayer, *The Making of Mission Communities in East Africa*. London: Heinemann, 1978.

121 Beidelman, 27, 131f., 135.

122 A. E. M. Anderson-Morshead, *The History of the Universities' Mission to Central Africa*, vol. I. London: UMCA, 1955. Gerald Broomfield, *Towards Freedom*. London: UMCA, 1957.

123 Weston, vii.

124 H. Maynard Smith, *Frank Bishop of Zanzibar*. London: SPCK, 1926, 59.

125 *Ibid.*, 130.

126 Alban Winter, CR, "Till Darkness Fell." Typescript in possession of the Archives, Church of the Province of South Africa, University of the Witwatersrand, Johannesburg. Hereafter the Archives shall be designated as CPSA.

127 *Ibid.*, 8.

128 *Ibid.*, 49.

129 *Ibid.*, 49. See also Karen Tranberg Hansen, *Distant Companions*. Ithaca and London: Cornell University Press, 1989.

130 "Short Summary of the Proceedings of the First Conference of Women Missionaries of the Church of the Province of South Africa," Bloemfontein, July 1–4, 1913. CPSA, AB226f.

131 James Arthur Muller, *Apostle of China.* New York and Milwaukee: Morehouse, 1937, 45, 63f.
132 Ruth Edgecombe, ed., *Bringing Forth Light: Five Tracts on Bishop Colenso's Zulu Mission.* Pietermaritzburg: University of Natal, 1982, xiv.
133 J. W. Colenso, "Church Missions among the Heathen," in Edgecombe, 16.
134 Edgecombe, xvi.
135 Marian S. Benham, *Henry Callaway.* London: Macmillan & Co., 1896, 41f.
136 *Ibid.*, 53, 57.
137 *Ibid.*, 79, 81.
138 *Ibid.*, 88, 117, 142.
139 Henry Callaway, "A Fragment on Comparative Religion," n.p., 1874.
140 Hugh Tinker, *The Ordeal of Love: C. F. Andrews and India.* Delhi: Oxford University Press, 1978, 8.
141 *Ibid.*, 18.
142 Cf. David McI. Gracie, ed., *Gandhi and Charlie: The Story of a Friendship.* Cambridge, Mass.: Cowley, 1989.

7 THE CRISIS OF CHURCH AND CULTURE

1 Winston Churchill, "Liberalism and Socialism," in *Winston S. Churchill: His Complete Speeches, 1897–1963.* Ed. Robert Rhodes James. Vol. 1. New York and London: Chelsea House, 1974, 671.
2 Modris Eksteins, *Rites of Spring: The Great War and the Birth of the Modern Age.* New York: Anchor Books, Doubleday, 1989, 129.
3 George Dangerfield, *The Strange Death of Liberal England, 1910–1914.* New York: G. P. Putnam, 1961, 74–138.
4 Robert H. Wiebe, *The Search for Order.* New York: Hill and Wang, 1967, 55. F. M. L. Thompson, *The Rise of Respectable Society.* Cambridge, Mass.: Harvard University Press, 1988, 360–1.
5 Jeffrey Cox, *The English Church in a Secular Society.* New York: Oxford University Press, 1982, 5, 93, 14.
6 *Ibid.*, 210.
7 Robert Rhodes James, *The British Revolution, 1880–1939.* New York: Alfred A. Knopf, 1977, 356. Eksteins, 177. Machin, *Politics and Churches, 1869 to 1921*, 310.
8 James, 359f. See also Susan Pedersen, "Gender, Welfare, and Citizenship in Britain during the Great War," *The American Historical Review*, 95, 4 (October, 1990), 983–1006.
9 J. M. Bourne, *Britain and the Great War, 1914–1918.* London: Edward Arnold, 1989, 209, 227.
10 Oswald Spengler, *The Decline of the West.* New York: Alfred A. Knopf, 1937, 39.
11 Harry F. Ward, "How can Civilization be Saved?," *The Christian Century*, 41, 37 (September 11, 1924), 1162, 1176.

12 H. R. L. Sheppard, *The Impatience of a Parson*. Garden City, N.Y.: Doubleday, 1928, 2.

13 Alan Wilkinson, *The Church of England and the First World War*. London: SPCK, 1978, 34f.

14 *Ibid.*, 15f., 25.

15 *Ibid.*, 37f., 45, 66. As evidence of the increased pastoral role for the Church in English society, Adrian Hastings notes that though marriages performed by the Church of England declined from 74 percent of all marriages in England in 1874 to 59 percent by 1919, the percentage of Anglican baptisms among all births in England rose from 62 percent in 1885 to 70 per cent in 1917. Large increases occurred in the number of confirmations and Easter communions during the same period. I also conclude from these statistics that thanks to the infusion of Anglo-Catholic ideas, worship had become pivotal to the Church's ministry. See Adrian Hastings, *A History of English Christianity, 1920–1990*. Third edition. Philadelphia: Trinity Press, 1991, 35f.

16 Cited in F. A. Iremonger, *William Temple*. Oxford: Oxford University Press, 1948, 205.

17 Wilkinson, 78.

18 Iremonger, 221.

19 Wilkinson, 83, 131, 140f. Machin, *Politics and Churches, 1869 to 1921*, 232, 318. Hastings, 62.

20 Wilkinson, 161.

21 *Journal of the General Convention of the Protestant Episcopal Church* (St. Louis, October 11–27, 1916), 401–403.

22 *Ibid.*, 486f.

23 William Temple, *Church and Nation*. London: Macmillan, 1915, xii.

24 *Ibid.*, 20, 29–31.

25 *Ibid.*, 94.

26 Leicester C. Lewis, "Troeltsch vs. Ritschl: A Study in Epochs," *Anglican Theological Review*, 1, 1 (May, 1918), 42f. Dickinson S. Miller, "The Problem of Evil in the Present State of the World," *Anglican Theological Review*, 1, 1 (May, 1918), 3, 4.

27 *Journal of the General Convention* (1916), 503.

28 Roderick Phillips, *Putting Asunder: A History of Divorce in Western Society*. Cambridge: Cambridge University Press, 1988, 517.

29 *Journal of the General Convention of the Protestant Episcopal Church* (1922), 697, 701.

30 *Ibid.*, 701, 703.

31 *Ibid.*, 71, 545.

32 *Encyclical Letter. Conference of Bishops of the Anglican Communion*. London: SPCK, 1920, 108–111.

33 Randle Manwaring, *From Controversy to Co-Existence: Evangelicals in the Church of England, 1914–1980*. Cambridge: Cambridge University Press, 1985, 17, 35.

34 Francis J. Hall, "This Miserable and Naughty World," *Anglican*

Theological Review, 3, 2 (October, 1920), 97–113.

35 Ernst Troeltsch, *Protestantism and Progress*. Philadelphia: Fortress Press, 1986, 45.

36 James, 398, 414–416.

37 Gerald Studdert-Kennedy, *Dog-Collar Democracy: The Industrial Christian Fellowship, 1919–1929*. London: Macmillan, 1982, 3f., 21.

38 *Ibid.*, 37, 49, 63.

39 *Ibid.*, 75–83, 93.

40 William Temple, *Christ in His Church*. London: Macmillan, 1925, 29. E. R. Norman, *Church and Society in England, 1770–1970*. Oxford: Clarendon Press, 1976, 280, 281, 283.

41 William Temple, 10, 54, 71.

42 Arthur Michael Ramsey, *An Era in Anglican Theology: From Gore to Temple*. New York: Charles Scribner's Sons, 1960, 46, 50f.

43 Alan M. Suggate, *William Temple and Christian Social Ethics Today*. Edinburgh: T. & T. Clark, 1987, 48. William Temple, *The Nature of Personality*. London: Macmillan, 1911, 60f.

44 William Temple, *Personal Religion and the Life of Fellowship*. London: Longmans, 1926, 28, 22f.

45 *Ibid.*, 28f.

46 *Ibid.*, 66–68. William Temple, *Essays in Christian Politics and Kindred Subjects*. London: Longmans, 1927.

47 William Temple, *Essays*, 119.

48 *Ibid.*, 7, 5f.

49 Iremonger, 335. Norman, 285. Suggate, 38.

50 Troeltsch, 46.

51 W. R. Inge, *Lay Thoughts of a Dean*. New York and London: G. P. Putnam, 1926, 323. H. C. Ackerman, "Saul: A Psychotherapeutic Analysis," *Anglican Theological Review*, 3, 2 (October, 1920), 114f., 121.

52 H. Stuart Hughes, *Consciousness and Society*. New York: Vintage Books, 1958, 112, 116f.

53 James Thayer Addison, *The Episcopal Church in the United States, 1789–1931*. Hamden: Archon, 1969, 313.

54 Elwood Worcester, Samuel McComb, and Isador H. Coriat, *Religion and Medicine: The Moral Control of Nervous Disorders*. New York: Moffat, Yard & Co., 1908, 6f.

55 *Ibid.*, 350, 371.

56 Angus Dun, "The Psychology of Religious Practices," *Anglican Theological Review*, 8, 3 (January, 1926), 218f.

57 *Ibid.*, 222f.

58 Inge, 323. W. R. Inge, *Christian Mysticism*. The Bampton lectures, 1899. London: Methuen, 1899, 5.

59 W. R. Inge, *Faith and its Psychology*. New York: Scribner, 1910.

60 Evelyn Underhill, *The Mystic Way*. London: J. M. Dent, 1913.

61 Evelyn Underhill, *The Life of the Spirit and the Life of To-Day*. New York: E. P. Dutton, 1922, 168f.

62 Samuel M. Shoemaker, Jr., *The Conversion of the Church*. New York: Fleming H. Revell, 1932, 7f.

63 Herbert Hensley Henson, *The Group Movement*. Second edition. Oxford: Oxford University Press, 1933, 17.

64 *Ibid.*, 17, 29.

65 Cf. Frederic Hood, "The Group Movement," *Church Quarterly Review*, 116, 232 (July, 1933), 230–243. H. A. Hodges, "The Meaning of Moral Rearmament," *Theology*, 38, 227 (May, 1939), 322–332.

66 Inge, *Lay Thoughts*, 302–304.

67 Wilfred L. Knox, *The Catholic Movement in the Church of England*. New York: Edwin S. Gorham, 1923, 236.

68 Gray, 24, 28f.

69 *Ibid.*, 159f., 164–173.

70 W. H. Frere, *Some Principles of Liturgical Reform*. London: John Murray, 1911, 3f., 91.

71 Cf. *Walter Howard Frere: His Correspondence on Liturgical Revision and Construction*. Ed. Ronald C. D. Jasper. Alcuin Club Collections no. 39. London: SPCK, 1954.

72 "The Reconstruction of Worship," in *Walter Howard Frere: A Collection of his Papers on Liturgical and Historical Subjects*. Ed. J. H. Arnold and E. G. P. Wyatt. Alcuin Club Collections no. 35. London: Oxford University Press, 1940, 72, 76.

73 Cited in Gray, 57. See also Kenneth Hylson-Smith, *Evangelicals in the Church of England, 1734–1984*. Edinburgh: T. & T. Clark, 1988, 233ff. Also, Manwaring, 35. Evangelicals generally opposed ritualism and Anglo-Catholicism and feared loss of the Church's connection to the state. Rightly they suspected that liturgical change served to distance the Church from its establishment heritage.

74 W. R. Inge, *Labels & Libels*. New York: Harper, 1929, 42.

75 Gray, 199.

76 A. G. Hebert, *Liturgy and Society: The Function of the Church in the Modern World*. London: Faber & Faber, 1935, 8.

77 *Ibid.*, 11–13.

78 *Ibid.*, 51, 113, 131, 159.

79 On the sense of confusion about Anglican identity and liturgical practice in the 1930s, see Frederick C. Grant, "Mass or Holy Communion," *Anglican Theological Review*, 15, 1 (January, 1935), 27–38. On the Parish Communion see the volume edited by A. G. Hebert, *The Parish Communion*. London: SPCK, 1937. Hebert's own essay, "The Parish Communion in its Spiritual Aspect, with a note on the Fast before Communion" (pp. 1–30), reiterates the argument of *Liturgy and Society*, with particular interest in the centrality of the Eucharist in the Church's liturgy.

80 Gregory Dix, "The Idea of 'The Church' in the Primitive Liturgies," in Hebert, ed., *The Parish Communion*, 95–144.

81 As illustrations of the new sense of the Church as corporate and

liturgical, see L. S. Hunter, "The Worship of God and the Life of the People," *Theology*, 38, 223 (January, 1939), and John Drewett, "Corporate Worship as the Expression of Community," *Theology*, 39, 229 (July, 1939).

82 See the review of recent works on healing in Douglas McLaren, *The Church Quarterly Review*, 117, 234 (January, 1934), 209–237.

83 Roland Allen, "The Priesthood of the Church," *The Church Quarterly Review*, 115, 230 (January, 1933), 234–244. Charles Raven, *Women and the Ministry*. Garden City, N.Y.: Doubleday, 1929, On the debate over women's ordination in the 1930s see Mrs. W. C. Roberts and Lord Hugh Cecil, "The Ordination of Women to the Priesthood," *The Church Quarterly Review*, 117, 233 (October, 1933), 1–24.

84 William Temple, "Theology To-day," *Theology*, 39, 233 (November, 1939), 326–333.

85 E. L. Mascall, "The Future of Anglican Theology," *Theology*, 39, 234 (December, 1939), 406–412.

86 W. Norman Pittenger, "The Christian Apologetic of James Franklin Bethune-Baker," *Anglican Theological Review*, 37, 4 (October, 1955), 260–277. See also J. F. Bethune-Baker, *Nestorius and his Teaching*. Cambridge: Cambridge University Press, 1908.

87 Charles E. Raven, *Jesus and the Gospel of Love*. London: Hodder & Stoughton, 1931, 7.

88 William Temple, *Mens Creatrix*. London: Macmillan, 1917, 175.

89 Suggate, 199.

90 *Ibid.*, 60. William Temple, *Nature, Man and God*. The Gifford lectures. London: Macmillan, 1956, 422.

91 Suggate, 60. William Temple, *Nature, Man and God*, 341, 486.

92 William Temple, *Christianity and the State*. London: Macmillan, 1929, 174. William Temple, *A Conditional Justification of War*. London: Hodder & Stoughton, 1940. William Temple, *The Hope of a New World*. New York: Macmillan, 1942, 77. William Temple, *Thoughts in War-Time*. London: Macmillan, 1940. William Temple, *Citizen and Churchman*. London: Eyre & Spottiswoode, 1941, 101.

93 On Temple's later social principles, see his *Christianity and Social Order*. London: SCM, 1942. Also see his *Nazi Massacres of the Jews*. London: Victor Gollancz, 1943.

94 James R. Cochrane, *Servants of Power: The Role of English-Speaking Churches in South Africa, 1903–1930*. Johannesburg: Ravan, 1987, 139. Joan Mansfield, "The Christian Social Order Movement, 1943–51." *Journal of Religious History*, 15, 1 (June, 1988), 109–127.

95 W. R. Inge, *Christian Ethics and Modern Problems*. London: Hodder & Stoughton, 1932, 21, 35.

96 *Ibid.*, 383, 397f.

97 K. E. Kirk, *Marriage and Divorce*. London: Centenary, 1933.

98 K. E. Kirk, *Some Principles of Moral Theology*. Second impression. London: Longmans, Green, 1921, 7, 106. K. E. Kirk, *The Vision of God*.

London: Longmans, 1931. K. E. Kirk, *The Crisis of Christian Rationalism*. London: Longmans, 1936, 116.

99 K. E, Kirk, *Conscience and its Problems*. London: Longmans, 1927, xiv, 63.

100 Alonzo Potter, ed., *Memorial Papers*. Philadelphia: E. H. Butler, 1857, 30.

101 Herbert Symonds, *Lectures on Christian Unity*. Toronto: William Briggs, 1899, 16, 29f.

102 H. Hensley Henson, *Godly Union and Concord*. London: John Murray, 1902, 160.

103 Kenneth Scott Latourette, "Ecumenical Bearings of the Missionary Movement and the International Missionary Council," in Ruth Rouse and Stephen Neill, eds., *A History of the Ecumenical Movement, 1517–1948*. Second edition. London: SPCK, 1967.

104 *Ibid.*, 361. Tissington Tatlow, "The World Conference on Faith and Order," in Rouse and Neill, 407–410.

105 C. P. Anderson, *The Work of the Church on Behalf of Unity*. The Hale Memorial Sermon, Western Theological Seminary, Chicago. Milwaukee: The Young Churchman, 1917. William T. Manning, *The Call to Unity*. The Bedell lectures, Kenyon College. N.Y.: Macmillan, 1920.

106 Charles A. Briggs, "The Historic Episcopate as a Basis of Reunion," in *Church Reunion Discussed on the Basis of the Lambeth Propositions of 1888*. New York: The Church Review, 1890.

107 M. C. Bickersteth, *Unity and Holiness*. London: Mowbray, 1914.

108 G. K. A. Bell, *Christian Unity: The Anglican Position*. London: Hodder & Stoughton, 1948, 95. G. K. A. Bell and W. L. Robertson, eds., *The Church of England and the Free Churches*. Oxford: Oxford University Press, 1925. H. Paul Douglass, *A Decade of Objective Progress in Church Unity, 1927–1936*. New York and London: Harper, 1937.

109 G. K. A. Bell, ed., *The Stockholm Conference, 1925*. Oxford: Oxford University Press, 1926, 39.

110 For a moderate Anglican position on reunion, see Arthur C. Headlam, *The Doctrine of the Church and Christian Reunion*. The Bampton lectures, 1920. London: John Murray, 1920. Also, H. L. Goudge, *The Church of England and Reunion*. London: SPCK, 1938. On Anglo-Catholic concern, see Francis J. Hall, "The Anglican Movement for Reunion," *Anglican Theological Review*, 8, 2 (October, 1925), 97–113. On liberal hopes, see *Christ and Unity*. The Cromer Convention. London: SPCK, 1938.

111 On the changes in missionary philosophy, see William R. Hutchison, *Errand to the World*. Chicago and London: University of Chicago Press, 1987, 150–165.

112 St. Clair Alfred Donaldson, "The New World," *Addresses on General Subjects*, vol. VIII. Jerusalem Meeting of the International Missionary Council. New York: International Missionary Council, 1928. William Temple, "A Statement of the Case for Evangelization," *The Christian Life and Message in Relation to Non-Christian Systems of Thought and Life*, vol. I. New York: International Missionary Council, 1928.

113 Gerald Webb Broomfield, *Revelation and Reunion*. London: SPCK, 1942, 105.

114 Herbert Hensley Henson, *Christian Morality*. The Gifford lectures. Oxford: Clarendon Press, 1936, 150f.

115 Andrew F. Walls, "The Gospel as the Prisoner and Liberator of Culture." *Missionalia*, 10, 3 (1982), 93–105. Lamin Sanneh, *Translating the Message: The Missionary Impact on Culture*. Maryknoll, N.Y.: Orbis, 1989. Brian Willan, *Sol Plaatje*. Berkeley: University of California Press, 1984.

116 Peter Alter, *Nationalism*. London: Edward Arnold, 1985, 9.

117 Michael H. M. Wood, *A Father in God: The Episcopate of William West Jones, D.D.* London: Macmillan, 1913, 324.

118 T. D. Verryn, "History of the Formative Years of the Order of Ethiopia." Unpublished B.D. thesis, 6, 14.

119 *Ibid.*, 40, 46–49.

120 Wood, 328. Verryn, 73.

121 John McKim to John Wood, September 5, 1902, JR, Box 43. Cited in my article, "'Self-Support': The Episcopal Mission and Nationalism in Japan." *Church History*, 58, 4 (December, 1989), 497. On nationalism in Japan, see Carol Gluck, *Japan's Modern Myths*. Princeton: Princeton University Press, 1985. On state Shinto and nationalism, see Helen Hardacre, *Shinto and the State, 1868–1988*. Princeton: Princeton University Press, 1989. Also, Minor L. Rogers and Ann T. Rogers, "The Honganji: Guardian of the State (1868–1945)." *Japanese Journal of Religious Studies*, 17, 1 (March, 1990), 3–28.

122 Henry St. George Tucker, "How to Win Japan." *The Spirit of Missions*, 77 (October, 1912), 768.

123 Charles Reifsnider to J. Wood, January 15, 1925, JR, Box 123.

124 John King Fairbank, *The Great Chinese Revolution: 1800–1985*. New York: Harper & Row, 1986, 125–127.

125 *District of Anking Newsletter*, 2, 1 and 2 (January–February, 1922), 4.

126 Mildred S. Capron, "Reflections from Wandering Inland." *Ibid.*, 4, 8 (November, 1924), 32.

127 Fairbank, 204ff.

128 *Anking Newsletter*, 7, 4 (January, 1927), 42. Also, 7, 5 (February, 1927), 56 and 7, 6–8 (March–June, 1927), 78–87.

129 P. Rusch to J. Wood, July 24, 1933, June 25, 1934, JR, Box 127.

130 J. Kenneth Morris to J. Wood, May 25, 1937, JR, Box 147. Shirley H. Nichols to J. Wood, December 16, 1938 and December 5, 1939, JR, Box 149. Shigeyoshi Murakami, *Japanese Religion in the Modern Century*. Trans. H. Byron Earhart. Tokyo: University of Tokyo Press, 1980, 101–102.

131 John Mitsuru Oe, "Church and State in Japan, 1940–1945." *Anglican and Episcopal History*, 59, 2 (June, 1990), 202–223. Y. Naide, Y. Matsui, S. Sasaki, S. Yanagiwara, and H. Yashiro to John Wood, December 2, 1940, JR, Box 147.

132 Albert D. Moscotti, *British Policy and the Nationalist Movement in Burma, 1917–1937*. Asian Studies at Hawaii no. 11. Honolulu: University of Hawaii Press, 1974. Kevin Ward, "'Obedient Rebels': The Mukono Crisis of 1941." *Journal of Religion in Africa*, 19, 3 (October, 1989), 194–227.

133 Gibbs, 340, 343, 355.

134 *Ibid.*, 373. Bengt Sundkler, *Church of South India: The Movement towards Union, 1900–1947*. Greenwich, Conn.: Seabury, 1954, 91ff.

135 Sundkler, 115.

136 *Ibid.*, 169.

137 Gibbs, 382.

138 David M. Paton, *R.O.: The Life and Times of Bishop Ronald Hall of Hong Kong*. Diocese of Hong Kong and Macao. Gloucester: Alan Sutton, 1985, 128f.

139 *Ibid.*, 176ff.

8 THE SEARCH FOR THE AUTHENTIC CHURCH

1 Geoffrey Francis Fisher, "Address in a Service Broadcast from the Old Palace, Canterbury, on the Last Sunday in 1946," in *Redeeming the Situation*. London: SPCK, 1948, 9.

2 Henry Knox Sherill, *The Church's Ministry in Our Time*. New York: Charles Scribner's Sons, 1949, 28, 46.

3 Stephen Toulmin, *Cosmopolis: The Hidden Agenda of Modernity*. New York: The Free Press, 1990, 109, 140.

4 *Ibid.*, 152f.

5 Anthony Giddens, *The Consequences of Modernity*. The Raymond Fred West Memorial lectures at Stanford University. Stanford, California: Stanford University Press, 1990, 49.

6 See Kenneth A. Thompson, *Bureaucracy and Church Reform: The Organizational Response of the Church of England to Social Change, 1800–1965*. Oxford: Clarendon Press, 1970.

7 Jon Butler, *Awash in a Sea of Faith: Christianizing the American People*. Cambridge, Mass. and London: Harvard University Press, 1990. Will Herberg, *Protestant–Catholic–Jew: An Essay in American Religious Sociology*. Garden City, N.Y.: Doubleday, 1955.

8 Henry Knox Sherrill, *Among Friends*. Boston: Little, Brown, 1962, 298–300.

9 Gibson Winter, *Religious Identity*. New York: Macmillan, 1968, 1.

10 Sherrill, *The Church's Ministry in Our Time*, 64.

11 James A. Pike and W. Norman Pittenger, *The Faith of the Church*, vol. III, *The Church's Teaching*. Greenwich, Conn.: Seabury Press, 1951, 14, 24.

12 *Ibid.*, 18, 29.

13 W. Norman Pittenger, *The Episcopalian Way of Life*. Englewood Cliffs, N.J.: Prentice-Hall, 1957, 81, 154f.

14 W. Norman Pittenger, *Rethinking the Christian Message*. Greenwich, Conn.: Seabury Press, 1956, 15, 21, 57.

15 W. Norman Pittenger, *Christ in the Haunted Wood*. Greenwich, Conn.: Seabury Press, 1953, v, 38.

16 *Ibid.*, 107.

17 James A. Pike, *Doing the Truth*. Garden City, N.Y.: Doubleday, 1955, 36f., 57.

18 *Ibid.*, 72, 83, 86.

19 *Ibid.*, 132.

20 Albert T. Mollegen, *Christianity and Modern Man*. Indianapolis: Bobbs-Merrill, 1961, 139, 144.

21 David E. Sumner, *The Episcopal Church's History, 1945–1985*. Wilton, Conn.: Morehouse-Barlow, 1987, 75–81. Dorothy L. Braun, "A History of the Origin and Development of the Seabury Series of the Protestant Episcopal Church." Ph.D. dissertation, New York University, 1960. William Bedford Williamson, "A Review of the Historical and Philosophical Foundations of the Seabury Series for Christian Education in the Protestant Episcopal Church in the United States of America." Ed.D. dissertation, Temple University, 1966, 8, 113.

22 Prayer Book Studies, I: *Baptism and Confirmation*; II: *The Liturgical Lectionary*. New York: The Church Pension Fund, 1950, v, vi.

23 *Ibid.*, 6.

24 *Before the Holy Table*. Greenwich, Conn.: Seabury Press, 1956, 6.

25 Massey Hamilton Shepherd, Jr., ed., *The Liturgical Renewal of the Church*. New York: Oxford University Press, 1960. Massey Hamilton Shepherd, Jr., ed., *The Eucharist & Liturgical Renewal*. New York: Oxford University Press, 1960.

26 Shepherd, *The Eucharist & Liturgical Renewal*, 72f. Shepherd, *The Liturgical Renewal of the Church*, 109.

27 Cf. Massey Hamilton Shepherd, Jr., *The Living Liturgy*. New York: Oxford University Press, 1946. Also, Massey H. Shepherd, Jr., *The Worship of the Church*. The Church's Teaching Series, vol. IV. Greenwich, Conn.: Seabury Press, 1952.

28 Prayer Book Studies, XV: *The Problem and Method of Prayer Book Revision*. New York: The Church Pension Fund, 1961, 4, 8.

29 Sumner, 35f.

30 Paul A. Welsby, *A History of the Church of England, 1945–1980*. Oxford: Oxford University Press, 1984, 26, 34.

31 Geoffrey Clayton Papers, AB381f., May 8, 1955, Archives of the Church of the Province of South Africa, University of the Witwatersrand, Johannesburg. Hereafter referred to as CPSA.

32 Cited in Alan Paton, *Apartheid and the Archbishop*. London: Jonathan Cape, 1973, 279ff.

33 Quoted in Paton, 52.

34 *Ibid.*, 67.

35 *Ibid.*, 101, 90.

36 C. T. Wood, ed., *Where we Stand: Archbishop Clayton's Charges*. Cape Town: Oxford University Press, 1960, 19, 28.

37 *Ibid.*, 10, 13, 20.

38 Paton, 151–155. Cf. Trevor Huddleston, *Naught for your Comfort*. London: Collins, 1956. Also, Deborah Duncan Honoré, ed., *Trevor Huddleston*. Oxford: Oxford University Press, 1988.

39 Paton, 236–240. Cf. Francis Meli, *South Africa Belongs to us: A History of the ANC*. Harare: Zimbabwe Publishing House, 1988, 124, 187.

40 John S. Peart-Binns, *Archbishop Joost De Blank: Scourge of Apartheid*. London: MBW, 1987, 111, 139.

41 B. B. Burnett, "Memorandum from the Church of the Province of South Africa." Cottlesloe Conference. November, 1960. CPSA, fAB 421, 25.

42 Bill Burnett, "C.P.S.A. and Afrikanerdom." Confidential memorandum. June, 1965. CPSA, fAB 896.

43 John Weller and Jane Linden, *Mainstream Christianity to 1980 in Malawi, Zambia and Zimbabwe*. Gweru: Mambo Press, 1984, 75. Personal correspondence with the Rev. Denys Whitehead, Livingstone, Zambia. October, 1986.

44 Henry Okullu, *Church and State in Nation Building and Human Development*. Nairobi: Uzima Press, 1984.

45 Gonville ffrench-Beytagh, *Encountering Darkness*. New York: Seabury Press, 1973.

46 Sumner, 38f. John L. Kater, Jr., "Dwelling Together in Unity: Church, Theology, and Race 1950–1965." *Anglican Theological Review*, 58, 3 (October, 1976), 444–457.

47 Cited in Kater, 451.

48 Taylor Branch, *Parting the Waters: America in the King Years, 1954–1963*. New York: Simon & Schuster, 1988, 741f.

49 Sumner, 42. John L. Kater, Jr., "Experiment in Freedom: The Episcopal Church and the Black Power Movement." *Historical Magazine of the Protestant Episcopal Church*, 48, 1 (March, 1979), 67–82.

50 Sumner, 47.

51 Kater, "Experiment," 75. Sumner, 53.

52 Vine Deloria, Jr., "GCSP: The Demons at Work." *Historical Magazine of the Protestant Episcopal Church*, 48, 1 (March, 1979), 83–92. Sumner, 53. Jeffrey K. Hadden, *The Gathering Storm in the Churches*. Garden City, N.Y.: Doubleday, 1969.

53 Norman, 411–13. Owen Chadwick, *Michael Ramsey: A Life*. Oxford: Clarendon Press, 1990, 145–159.

54 Eric James, *A Life of Bishop John A. T. Robinson*. Grand Rapids, Mich.: Eerdmans, 1987, 96.

55 *Ibid.*, 113f.

56 *Ibid.*, 116–122.

57 Robert J. Page, *New Directions in Anglican Theology*. New York: Seabury Press, 1965, 150. Paul Van Buren, *The Secular Meaning of the Gospel*. New York: Macmillan, 1963.

58 Theodore O. Wedel, *The Gospel in a Strange, New World*. Philadelphia: Westminster Press, 1963, 16, 39, 82.

59 Norman Pittenger, *The Christian Church as Social Process*. Philadelphia: Westminster, 1971, 11, 67. Norman Pittenger, *God in Process*. London: SCM, 1967.

60 Austin Farrer, *The End of Man*. London: SPCK, 1973. E. L. Mascall, *Theology and the Future*. New York: Morehouse-Barlow, 1968.

61 Gibson Winter, *The Suburban Captivity of the Churches*. New York: Macmillan, 1962.

62 Robert Wuthnow, *The Restructuring of American Religion*. Princeton: Princeton University Press, 1988, 147.

63 Sumner, 111–113.

64 Alfred R. Shands and H. Barry Evans, *How & Why: An Introduction to the Three New Trial Eucharists and the Daily Office of the Episcopal Church*. New York: Seabury Press, 1971. Charles P. Price, *Introducing the Proposed Book*. New York: The Church Pension Fund, 1976.

65 Sumner, 120ff. Joseph W. Trigg and William L. Sachs, *Of One Body: Renewal Movements in the Church*. Atlanta: John Knox Press, 1986, 35.

66 Sumner, 124. Trigg and Sachs, 152.

67 Trigg and Sachs, 143. Michael Green, *Evangelism in the Early Church*. Grand Rapids, Mich.: Eerdmans, 1970.

68 Pauli Murray, *Song in a Weary Throat*. New York: Harper & Row, 1987, 369f.

69 *Ibid.*, 425, 434.

70 Sumner, 21.

71 *Ibid.*, 23–28.

72 Reginald H. Fuller, "Pro and Con: The Ordination of Women in the New Testament," 8, and Frederick H. Borsch, "The Authority of the Ministry," 18, in *Toward a New Theology of Ordination: Essays on the Ordination of Women*. Ed. Marianne H. Micks and Charles P. Price. Somerville, Mass.: Green, Hadden & Co., 1976.

73 Sumner, 65f.

74 Paul Seabury, "Trendier than Thou." *Harper's*, 257, 1541 (October, 1978), 39–52.

75 Donald S. Armentrout, "Episcopal Splinter Groups." Unpublished study. Sewanee, Tenn.: University of the South, 1985, 7, 9.

76 *Ibid.*, 13, 12.

77 *Ibid.*, 21f.

78 *Ibid.*, 33.

79 *Ibid.*, 41, 44.

80 Sumner, 160.

81 Welsby, 183. *Partners in Mission*. London: SPCK, 1973.

82 Welsby, 269–272. Sumner, 168.

Index

Abeokuta, 166–168
abortion, 323, 328
Act for the Regulation of Public Worship (1874), 237–238
Act of Supremacy of 1534, 9
Act of Uniformity of 1662, 11, 12
Adam, Jack Capers, 332
Addington, Henry, Viscount Sidmouth, 37
Africa, 51–52, 109, 118–119, 164; see also individual countries
African National Congress, 294, 318
Afro-Americans, 230, 234–236
  episcopate, 262–263
Akassa, 168
Akitoye, King of Lagos, 168
Alaska, 233
Allen, Roland, 243–245, 283
Allin, John, 335
Althorp, Lord, see Spencer, John Charles, Viscount Althorp
America, see United States
American Episcopal Church, 332, 334
American Indians, 51, 64, 225, 229, 232–234, 322
American Protestant establishment, 305–306
Anderson, Charles P., 291
Andrews, Charles Freer, 253–254
Andros, Edmund, 63
Anglican Catholic Church, 334
Anglican Consultative Council, 335
Anglican Orthodox Church, 332
Anglo-Catholic movement, 120–136, 236–240, 267
  and charismatic movement, 319
  and ecumenical movement, 292, 300
  and foreign missions, 188, 204, 247
  anti-Erastianism, 84–85, 97
  distinction between Church and world, 288–289, 291–292, 307, 326
  liturgy and sacraments, 211, 227, 236–240

popular appeal, 211, 236
Anne, Queen of England, 16, 18
Anstey, Roger, 49
anti-Erastianism, 18
anti-slavery movement, 34, 36, 49–51, 102, 166
architecture of churches, 63, 135, 187, 226
Arinori, Mori, 174
Armstrong, John, 197
Arnold, Thomas, 37, 43–47, 77, 84, 229
Ashley, William J., 186
Ashley Cooper, Anthony, seventh Earl of Shaftesbury, 100–102, 107
Astor, John Jacob, 225
Astor, William Waldorf, 225
Atkins, Stanley, 333
atonement, 157–159, 217, 270
Atterbury, Francis, 18–20
Australia, 55, 164–165, 258
  Christian Socialism in, 287
  Church and state in, 128, 193–195
  episcopate in, 115
  see also Roman Catholicism in Australia
Avis, Paul 2
Ayres, Anne, 228
Ázaraiah, V. S., 299–300

Badagry, 166
Balakole revival, 299
Baldwin, Maurice, 181–182
Barker, Frederic, 194–195, 206
Barnett, Samuel, 229
Barrett, Ellen, 331
Barth, Karl, 284
Baxter, Richard, 11
Beecroft, John, 168
Bell, Andrew, 54
Bennett, Dennis, 327–328
Benson, Edward, 239
Benson, Richard Meux, 230, 236
Bentinck, William, 170
Bergson, Henri, 272–273

Berkeley, George, 24–25, 64
Bethune-Baker, J. F., 189–190, 284
Bible, *see* Scripture
Bickersteth, Edward, 54
Birks, A. R., 180
Black Power, 322
Blair, James, 62
Blanchard, Roger, 309
Bliss, William Dwight Porter, 223
Blomfield, Charles James, 75–76, 84
  and Church and state, 75–76, 78, 84,
    88–90
  and missions, 75–76, 102, 112–116
  and the Ecclesiastical Commission, 90–91,
    93–95, 198
  Newman's opinion of, 123
Book of Common Prayer, 2, 125–126, 238
  in the United States, 226, 280
  of 1549 and 1552, 9
  of 1662, 11, 135
  proposed revision of 1927, 279–281
  revision by Provinces, 206, 334
  revision through trial use (United States),
    311–314, 326–327, 331–332
  translations, 56, 113, 166, 174, 233, 249,
    320
Boone, William J., 118
Borsch, Frederick H., 331
Bosher, Robert, 12
Boyd, Malcolm, 332
Bradlaugh, Charles, 136, 216
Brahmo Samaj, 170
Bray, Thomas, 62
Breck, James Lloyd, 229, 232
Brent, Charles H., 179, 290–292
Briggs, Charles, 291
Bright, John, 105
Broad Church movement, 77, 84, 147, 202,
  204, 227
Brooks, Phillips, 224–225
Broomfield, Gerald, 293
Brougham, Henry, 36, 87
Broughton, William Grant, 114, 193–194
Brown, Daniel, 64
Browne, David, 56
Buchanan, Claudius, 53, 56
Buchman, Frank, 277–278
Buganda, 176
Bull, George, 18
Bull, Paul, 222
Bultmann, Rudolf, 325
Burdett-Coutts, Angela, 115
Burgess, John M., 321
Burke, Edmund, 32–33, 80
Burma, *see* Myanmar
Burnet, Gilbert, 16–17

Burnett, Bill, 318–319
Burton, Edward, 120
Butler, Jon, 305
Butler, Joseph, 24, 43
Buxton, Thomas Fowell, 49, 102, 108–110,
  118, 166

Callaway, Henry, 250–253
Cambridge Mission to India, 253
Cambridge Platonists, 13
Camden Society, 226
Cameron, W. M., 295
Canada, 66, 165, 204, 258
  Book of Common Prayer revision by
    "trial use", 314
  Church and state, 195–197
  episcopate in, 114–115
  ordination of women 330
  synods, 195–197
Cannon, Harriet Starr, 229
capital punishment, 323
Capron, Mildred S., 297
Carey, William, 56, 169
Carlyle, Thomas, 101
Carpenter, C. C. Jones, 322
Carter, Bishop, of Pretoria, South Africa,
  248
caste, 59, 170
Catholic Association, 34–35
Catholic Emancipation, 35
Central Africa, Province of, 315
Central African Mission, 119
Ceylon, *see* Sri Lanka
Chadwick, Henry, 9
Chadwick, Owen, 119
Chambers, Robert, 137
charismatic movement, 327–329
Charles II, King of England, 11
Chartism, 106
Chicago–Lambeth Quadrilateral, *see*
  Lambeth Quadrilateral
child labor, 100–101
Chillingworth, William, 13
China, 118, 244, 271, 335–336
  Anglican Church and Chinese culture,
    249–250, 296–298
  Book of Common Prayer revision, 280
  nationalism, 297–298
  ordination of women, 301–302
Chiu Ban It, 328
Christian Social Order Movement
  (CSOM), 287
Christian Social Union (CSU), 216, 219,
  221–222, 253, 268
Christian Socialism, 105–108, 215–224
  Australia, 287

Headlam's revival of, 212–221
influence of, and later revivals of,
   221–224, 229, 231, 253, 260, 268, 289
Christianity and commerce, 118, 166–169,
   247
Church, R. W., 134
Church and state, 2; *see also* Australia,
   Canada, Ireland, New Zealand, South
   Africa, Uganda, United States, and
   Wales
   in England, 32–47, 73, 75–90, 209–212,
   260–261, 269
Church Association for the Advancement of
   the Interests of Labor (CAIL), 223
Church Defence Institution, 209
Church Fathers, 9, 14, 18, 122, 134, 159,
   161, 282
Church League for Women's Suffrage, 232
Church Missionary Society (CMS), 52–60,
   102, 110, 184–185
   and Henry Venn, 119, 167–168, 241–242
   in India, 53, 56–57, 172, 184
   in Japan, 173
   in Kenya, 246
   in New Zealand, 55–56
   in Nigeria, 166–169, 242–243
   in Sierra Leone, 53–55, 242
   in Uganda, 176, 178, 184–185
Church of South India, 300–301
Church of the Province of South Africa
   (CPSA), *see* South Africa
church rates, 82–86
Church Reform League, 209, 261
Church Reform Union, 209
Church Socialist League (CSL), 222–223
Churchill, Winston, 255
Clapham Sect, 37, 49–54, 57–58, 98, 102,
   108
   influence of, 76, 166
Clarendon Code, 12–13, 15
Clark, J. C. D., 22
Clarkson, Thomas, 49
Clavier, Anthony F. M., 334
Clay, William, 85
Clayton, Geoffrey Hare, 315–318
Clegg, Thomas, 167
clerisy, 41–42
Clough, Arthur Hugh, 136
Cobden, Richard, 105
Coggan, J. F. Donald, Archbishop, 335
Colenso, John William, 142–144, 176,
   198–202, 204, 250–252
Coleridge, Samuel Taylor, 37–43, 46–47,
   71, 80, 84
commissaries, 62–63
Communism, 298, 302, 310

Community of St. John Baptist, 229
Community of St. Mary, 229
Community of the Resurrection, 221–222,
   229, 248–249, 262
Community of the Sacred Passion of Jesus,
   248
Compton, Henry, 62
Conference on Christian Politics,
   Economics, and Citizenship (COPEC),
   271
confession, auricular, 211
Connecticut, 61, 64–65, 67
Conservative Party (Tory)
   in the eighteenth century, 24, 28–29
   in the nineteenth century, 36–37, 77–80,
   84–86, 88–89, 92, 101, 110, 170, 238
   in the twentieth century, 256
   origin and early development of Tories,
   15–16, 18, 20–21
Consultation on Church Union (COCU),
   335
Convocation
   and colonial synods, 198–202, 205
   and liturgical reform, 278–279
   and ritualists, 237
   and women, 231–232
   condemnation of liberal theology, 141
   reestablishment of (1689–1714), 17–21
   reestablishment of (nineteenth century),
   93, 210, 261
Cooper, Anthony Ashley, *see* Ashley Cooper,
   Anthony
Copleston, Edward, 43
Cornish, C. E., 294
Cornwallis, Charles, second Earl of, 56
Cory, Archdeacon, 183
Cotterill, Henry, Bishop of Grahamstown,
   203–204
Cram, Ralph, 187
Cranmer, Thomas, 9, 66
Creighton, Louise, 231
Creighton, Mandell, 261
Cross, W. O., 313
Crowther, Josiah, 168, 243
Crowther, Samuel Ajayi, 110, 168–169,
   242–243
Cuba, 183–185
culture, Christianity and, 208, 255–302,
   303–307, 336
Cummins, George David, 240
Cunningham, William, 268
Custer, George, 233
Cutler, Timothy, 64

Dakota Indians, 232–234
Dakota Territory, 225, 233

Dale, R. W., 158
Dangerfield, George, 256
Darwin, Charles, 138
Daubeny, Charles, 57–58
Davidson, Randall, 188, 259, 262, 291
Davis, William, 54
deaconesses, 231
Dearmer, Percy, 222, 279–280
"Death of God" theology, 325
De Blank, Joost, 318
De Blanquière, Peter Boyle, 195
Declaration of Breda, 11
Dees, James P., 332
Deism, 17, 136
DeKoven, James, 239–240
Derby, fifteenth Earl of, *see* Stanley, Edward Henry
Dickens, Charles, 109
discipline, Church, 124
Disraeli, Benjamin, 85–86, 101, 170–171, 238
Dissenters, 27–28, 46, 58
    alliance with Liberal Party, 28, 80–81, 88, 118, 211
    Evangelical cooperation, 50, 87, 89
    in the American colonies, 63
    rights of, 30, 33–37, 82–84, 86
divorce, 264–266, 288, 310, 322
Dix, Gregory, 282, 326
Dix, Morgan, 225
Doane, George Washington, 116–118
Doddridge, Philip, 27
Donaldson, F. Lewis, 217, 268
Donaldson, St. Clair Alfred, 292–293
Drexel, Anthoy J., 182
DuBose, William Porcher, 153–154
Dun, Angus, 274–275
Dwane, James Mata, 294–295

East India Company, 53, 56–57, 169
Ecclesiastical Commission, 82, 90–94, 96, 198
Eclectic Society, 52–53, 55
Ecumenical movement, 289–293, 300–301, 323
Eddy, Nellie G., 230
Edward VI, King of England, 9
Edwards, Jonathan, 48
Edwards, Tilden, 329
Eisenstadt, S. N., 5–6
Eliot, George, 136
Elizabeth I, Queen of England, 9
Ely, Richard, 208–209, 221
Emery, Julia Chester 231
Emery, Mary Abbot, 231
empire, 52, 109–111, 164–208, 246, 256

and racial superiority, 243, 250, 252
decline and end of, 258, 299, 319–321
Enabling Bill (1919), 261
Enmegahbowh, 232
episcopacy, 14, 189
    apostolic unity, 12, 18, 46, 122–124, 160
    in ecumenical conversations, 292, 300
    missionary, 111, 114–119, 242
    native, 113, 179, 242–243, 295–296, 299, 320
    see also Afro-Americans, Episcopal Church (USA), India
Episcopal Church (USA), 223–226, 228, 305–306, 310–314, 331–335
    Afro-Americans in, 234–236
    American Indian missions in, 225–226, 232–234
    and ecumenical movement, 290–291, 335
    and modern society, 310–311, 331–335
    Anglo-Catholic Party in, 128–129, 239–240
    charismatic movement in, 328
    episcopate, 64–67
    liturgical renewal in, 311–314, 331–334
    Low Church party in, 226
    marriage and divorce policy of, 264–266, 323
    missionary bishops in, 116–118
    model for autonomous provincial synods, 112, 196, 204, 300
    organizing of, 37, 65–69
    social mission of, 223–224, 262, 321
    women in, 230–332, 341–334
Erastians, 13, 15–16, 19, 23, 46, 84, 86, 89, 197, 238
Essays and Reviews, 139–143, 202
Ethiopian movements, 294–295
Eucharist
    interpretations of, 133, 146, 240
    weekly, 24, 104, 278–279, 281–282
Evangelical and Catholic Mission (ECM), 333–334
Evangelical party, 28–30, 47–50, 150, 269, 305
    and reform of the Church, 90
    anti-liberalism, 138, 147, 217, 266, 307
    Lambeth Conference of 1867, 202–204
    "Low-Church" views, 128, 135, 237, 280
    missions and social concerns of, 33–34, 48–60, 97–104, 108–110, 120, 147, 170, 241
    political activity of, 34, 48, 78, 84, 123

Fabian Society, 213, 216, 224, 229
Faith and Order movement, 290–292
Farrer, Austin, 326

Fellowship of Concerned Churchmen, 333–334
Feuerbach, Ludwig, 136
ffrench-Beytach, Gonville, 321
Figgis, John Neville, 222, 259
First World War, 258–268, 278, 307
Fisher, Geoffrey, 303, 315, 324
Fletcher, John, 29
Fond du Lac, 240
Forty-two Articles (1553), 9
Fraser, James, 95–96
Freedmen's Commission (of Episcopal Church, USA), 230, 234
Fremantle, W. H., 146–147, 186
Frere, W. H., 222, 268, 278–281, 327
Freud, Sigmund, 273
Froude, Richard Hurrell, 122–124
Fulford, Francis, 196, 201, 203–204
Fullam, Everett "Terry," 328
Fuller, Reginald H., 331
Fyfe, Bishop of Burma, 185

Gallagher, J. A., 164
Gandhi, Mohandas, 253–254
Garden, Alexander, 29, 62–63
Gaskell, Charles, 333
geology, 137
George, Henry, 214–215, 223
Georgia, 61, 234–235
Germany, 262, 265, 287
Ghost Dance, 233
Gibson, Edmund, 25
Gladstone, William Ewart, 79–81, 84–86, 88, 128, 178, 192, 209, 238
Glorious Revolution (1689), 14–16
Goodwin, C. W., 140
Gore, Charles,
   social views of, 212, 216–217, 221–222, 259, 261, 268–269
   theological views of, 152, 154, 156–157, 160–61, 188–189
Gorham, G. C., 128
Goulburn, E. M., 141
Grafton, Charles, 230, 236, 240
Graham, James, 89
Grant, Anthony, 110–111
Grant, Charles, 49, 57
Grant, Charles, the younger (Lord Glenelg), 108
Grant, Ulysses S., 232
Gray, Robert, 119, 142, 197–204
Great Ejection, 11
Green, I. M., 12
Green, Michael, 328–329
Green, Sidney F., 239
Green, T. H., 146, 153, 229

Grey, Charles, second Earl Grey, 36
Grey, George, 85, 250
Groser, John, 261
Guild of St. Matthew, 214–216, 222
Gunstone, John, 328
Gwatkin, H. M., 189

Hackney Phalanx, 37, 57–58, 69, 87, 93–94, 111, 147
Haiti, 335
Hales, John, 13
Hall, Francis J., 162, 267
Hall, Joseph, 10
Hall, R. O., 301
Hammond, Henry, 10
Hampden, Renn Dickson, 43, 138
Hanbury, Robert, 102
Hancock, Thomas, 216
Hannington, James, 177
Hardcastle, J. A., 85–86
Hare, William Hobart, 225, 232–233
Harnack, Adolf von, 6, 158
Harris, Townsend, 175
Hartwig, Peter, 53
Haweis, Thomas, 48
Hawkins, Edward, 43, 122
Headlam, Stewart, 212–216, 218, 238
Heber, Reginald, 58
Herbert, A. G., 281–282, 327
Hennell, Charles, 136
Henry VIII, King of England, 9
Henson, Herbert Hensley, 259–261, 277, 280, 290, 293
Hepburn, J. C., 173
Heurtley, C. A., 141
Heuss, John, 311
High Church party
   1714–1833, 24, 37, 43, 46, 78
   after 1833, 84, 90, 93, 147
   before 1714, 10, 13–21
   in missions, 57–60
   in the colonies, 114, 202
   in United States, 64, 69
   popular appeal, 103–104, 212
Hill, Francis, 248–249
Hilton, Boyd, 49
Hines, John E., 322–323
Hinman, Samuel, 232
Hispanics (USA), 322
Hoadly, Benjamin, 23, 66
Hoare, Henry, 85, 198–199
Hobart, John Henry, 37, 69
Hobson, John, 164
Hodson, George, 102
Holland, Henry Scott, 153, 216, 218–220, 260

Holocaust, 287
homosexuality, 216, 323, 331–332
Hong Kong, 164, 301, 320, 330
Hook, Walter Farquhar, 103–105, 236
Hooker, Richard, 10, 14, 44, 46, 66, 79
Hooper, George, 18
Hopkins, John Henry, 181, 201, 226, 239
Hort, F. J. A., 148–149, 160–161
Howard, George, Viscount Morpeth, 77
Howley, William, 89–90, 92, 115
Huddleston, Trevor, 317–318
Hughes, Thomas, 106–107
Hulse, Hiram Richard, 183, 185
Hunter, David R., 311
Huntington, D. T., 298
Huntington, Frederick Dan, 225–226
Huntington, James O. S., 223
Huntington, William Reed, 186, 206
Hutton, Thomas, 167
Huxley, Thomas, 136, 138
Hyde, Edward, Earl of Clarendon, 12

Igbebe, 168
Illingworth, J. R., 155, 216
Imperial British East African (IBEA)
    Company, 177–178
Incarnation
    and Eucharist, 132, 282
    and mission, 228, 245, 262, 285–286
    Liberal Catholic view of, 149–151, 153,
        155–157, 161–162, 217–219
    Temple, William, view of, 269–270
India
    and British Empire, 164–165, 169–172,
        319
    Book of Common Prayer, revision of, 314
    episcopate in, 57–60, 114, 169
    mission to, 18, 50–51, 53–54, 56–57, 184,
        245, 253–254
    nationalism, 171, 300
    self-governing Church in, 299–301
India Mutiny of 1857, 169–170
Indian Church Bill (1927), 299
Indian National Congress, 171
Industrial Christian Fellowship (ICF),
    268–269
industrialization, 208
    in Britain, 32, 95, 98, 101, 219, 221,
        226–227, 236, 258
    in South Africa, 248
Inge, W. R., 272, 275, 278, 280–281,
    287–288
Inglis, Charles, 64, 114
Inglis, Robert, 92–93
Integrity, 331
International Missionary Council, 292–293

Ireland
    Church and state, 209, 212, 257
    Church of Ireland, 77, 82, 120, 202, 209,
        257
    Home Rule 79, 209, 256
Irish policy, 35
Islam, 248
    in Uganda, 176–177, 185
Ives, Levi Silliman, 129, 229

James, William, 272–274, 282
James II, King of England, 14
Japan, 118, 165, 172–176, 230, 271, 280,
    295–296, 298–299
    nationalism, 175, 295–296, 298–299
Jefferson, Thomas, 65
Jenyns, Soame, 30
Jewel, John, 9–10
Johnson, Edward Ralph, 172
Johnson, James, 243
Johnson, Nathaniel, 63
Johnson, Richard, 55
Johnson, Samuel, 64
Johnson, T. S., 242
Johnson, W. A. B., 54
Johnston, Mercer G., 179–180
Jones, Harold S., 233–234
Jones, William (orientalist), 170
Jones, William West (Archbishop of CPSA),
    294–295
Jowett, Benjamin, 140, 144–146
Jung, Carl G., 273, 329

Kaguru nation, 246
Karen nation, 185
Karugire, Samwiri Rubaraza, 182
Kay, James, 99–100
Keble, John, 120–124, 128
Keith, George, 62
Kelsey, Morton, 329
Kemper, Jackson, 68, 116–117, 232
Ken, Thomas, 16
Kennedy, G. A. Studdert, 261, 268–269
Kennett, White, 20
kenosis, 156, 162
Kenya, 176, 187, 246
Kikuyu controversy, 187–189, 247, 291
King, Edward, 239
King, Martin Luther, Jr., 322
Kingsley, Charles, 106–107, 213, 221
Kirk, K. E., 288–289
Knight, Arthur, 181, 185
Knight, Eleanor, 180–181
Knox Alexander, 57
Knox, Wilfred, 278
Krapf, Johan, 176

Labour Party, 211–212, 238, 255–256
Lagos, 168
Laird, Macgregor, 168
Lamb, William, second Viscount
   Melbourne, 90–92
Lambeth Conference, 301
   of 1867, 201–205
   of 1878, 205–206
   of 1888, 206
   of 1897, 206
   of 1908, 206–207, 221
   of 1920, 265–266, 291, 300
   of 1968, 334
   of 1978, 305, 331
Lambeth Quadrilateral, 186–189, 206,
   290–291
Lang, Cosmo, 291
Latin America, 335
Latitudinarianism, 13, 15–16
Laud, William, 10, 12, 46
Law, William, 28
Lawrence, William, 182
League of the Kingdom of God, 223
Leech, Kenneth, 329
Lei Tim-Oi, 301
Leslie, Charles, 16
Lewes, George Henry, 136
Lewis, John Travers, 201
Lewis, Leicester C., 263–264
Liberal Catholicism, 147–263, 188,
   216–217, 221, 225, 266–268, 305
Liberal Party (Whig)
   in the eighteenth century, 21–28, 31
   in the nineteenth century, 36–37, 44,
      49–50, 76–90, 97, 102, 110, 123, 171,
      209, 238
   in the twentieth century, 255–257
   origin and early development as Whigs,
      15–16, 18, 20–21
liberal political philosophy, 36–37, 41, 47
liberal theology, 6–7, 38, 120, 256–257
   collapse of (c. 1920s), 267, 281–284,
      288–289
   in missions, 252–253
   of Arnold, Thomas, 43–47
   of *Essays and Reviews*, 137–147
   of Liberal Catholicism, 147–163
   opposition to, 126
   revival of (c. 1960s), 310, 332–334
Liberation Society, 86, 210
Lichtenberger, Arthur Carl, 313
Liddell, Robert, 237
Liddon, Henry Parry, 162, 212, 236
"Life and Liberty," 260–261, 280
Life and Work movement, 291–292
Liggins, John, 173

Lightfoot, J. B., 161–162
liturgical renewal, 278–283, 311–314
Livingstone, David, 109, 118–119, 247
Lloyd George, David, 258
Locke, John, 15, 17
London City Mission (LCM), 102
London Missionary Society, 118
Long, William, 198
Longley, C. T., 201–202, 204
Low Church party, 17–21
   in USA, 68, 226
Lowder, Charles, 236–237
Ludlow, John Malcolm, 105–107, 213
Lugard, Frederick, 177–178
Lux Mundi, 151–156, 162, 216
Lyell, Charles, 137

Macao, 301
Macaulay, T. B., 170
Macaulay, Zachary, 49, 54
McComb, Samuel, 273–274
Machin, G. I. T. 83–84, 211
McIlvaine, Charles, 125
Mackenzie, Charles Frederick 119, 247
McKim, John, 175, 295–296
Mackonochie, Alexander H., 210–211, 236
Macrorie, W. K., 200
Madison, James, 65
Malawi, 315, 320
Malaysia, 60, 180
Mallary, DeWitt, 333
Mann, Horace, 95
Manning, Henry, 128
Manning, William T., 290–291
Mansel, H. L., 138
Maori nation, 55–56, 183
Maples, Chauncy, 183
marriage, 264–266, 288, 310, 323
Marsden, Samul, 55–56
Marty, Martin, 4, 208
Martyn, Henry, 56
Maryland, 61–62, 65, 67, 69
Masakazu, Tai, 174
Mascall, E. L., 284, 326
Masih, Abdul, 58–59
Massachusetts, 63, 67–68
Mathison, G. F., 88
Maurice, Frederick Denison, 70–74,
   105–108, 129–131
   comparison to, 132, 138
   influence of, 33, 149, 213–215, 217–218,
      223–224, 250–251, 268, 318
Maynooth, 78–79, 81
Mazizini, 247
Meade, William, 228
Meiji Restoration, 173

Melanesia, 183
Melbourne, second Viscount, *see* Lamb,
    William
Methodism, 29, 30
Middleton, Thomas Fanshawe, 57–58
Mill, John Stuart, 136
Miller, Dickinson S., 264
Miller, John Cale, 103
Milman, Robert, 171–172
Milnor, James, 68
Minnesota, 229, 232
miracles, 5
mission
    American Indian, 225–226, 229, 232–236
    domestic, 94, 96–108, 225–226
    foreign, 33, 50–57, 108–119, 191, 221;
        and native culture, 167–170, 172–177,
        180–182, 184, 188, 199, 240–254,
        293–302, 318, 320; autonomous
        Provinces, 165, 315–316; church
        planting, 59, 165–169, 173, 177,
        241–248, 293; educational missions,
        53–54, 58, 167–177, 180, 184, 197, 243,
        245–246, 248–249, 297, 301, 320;
        indigenous ministry, 58, 168, 172, 174,
        184, 241–245, 247–248, 294–301, 318,
        320; industrial education, 167–169,
        171; medical missions, 184, 246, 297,
        301; policy, 142–143, 165–175,
        184–185, 240–254, 291, 293–302;
        women, 176, 230–231, 246, 249, 252,
        301
    of the Church, 1–2, 45, 75–76, 78, 86, 95,
        185–187, 189, 191–192, 194, 197,
        201–202, 205, 260, 266, 270, 281,
        292–293, 307, 325, 334
    social, 45–46, 48–50, 70, 74, 98–108,
        261–262, 265, 268, 271, 281, 289–92,
        297, 301–302, 314, 316, 320
Moberly, R. C., 155, 157–158, 161–162, 270
modernity, 4, 5, 31, 48, 60, 120, 133, 151,
    187, 208–209, 214, 218–219, 282,
    303–314, 326–327, 330, 333–336
Mohawk Indians, 64
Moll, W. E., 222
Mollegen, Albert T., 310–311
Moore, John, 53
Moore, Paul, 331
More, Hannah, 49, 98–99
Morgan, J. Pierpont, 182
Morpeth, Viscount, *see* Howard, George
Morris, Arthur R., 174
Morris, J. Kenneth, 298
Mortimer, Bishop, of Essex, 323
Moseley, Thomas, 103
Mote, James O., 334

Motoda, Joseph, 296
Mott, John R., 290
Mountain, G. J., 195–197
Muhlenberg, William Augustus, 228, 290
Mukuno Crisis, 299
Murindagomo, Patrick, 320
Murray, Charles Knight, 90
Murray, Pauli, 329–330
Mutual Responsibility and Interdependence
    (MRI), 334–335
Mwanga, King of Buganda, 177
Myanmar (Burma), 60, 180, 185, 299
    nationalism, 299
mysticism, 275–276

Naide, John, 296
National Council of Churches (USA), 306,
    332–333
National Mission of Repentance and Hope
    (1916), 259–260, 280
nationalism, 258, 293; *see also* China, India,
    Japan, Myanmar, Uganda
Neale, John Mason, 134–135
Nelson, C. K., 235
New England, 62–64; *see also* individual
    states
New Jersey, 65, 69
New South Wales, 195
New York, 61, 67–69
New Zealand, 55–56, 109, 115–116, 165,
    191–193, 258, 330
    Church and state, 191–193
Newman, John Henry, 2–3, 5, 121–123,
    125–131, 162
Newton, John, 48
Nichols, Shirley, 299
Niebuhr, Reinhold, 285
Niger expedition, 109–110, 166
Nigeria, 164–169, 242–243
Niobrara Convocation, 232–233
Nippon Sei Ko Kai, 174
Nobori, Kanai, 174
Noel, Conrad, 222, 260
Noetics, 43, 137
Nonconformists, 18, 209–210
Non-Jurors, 16, 24
Norman, E. R., 269
North Carolina, 61
Nova Scotia, 52, 196
nuclear weapons, 310, 314

O'Connell, Daniel, 34–35
Okullu, Henry, 320–321
Old Episcopal Church, 332
O'Neill, Simeon Wilberforce, 230
opium, 171, 265

Order of the Holy Cross, 223, 228
Orthodox churches, 91, 335
Otey, James, 118
Ottawa Indians, 232
Oxford Group movement, 276–278
Oxford movement, *see* Tractarian
    movement

Page, Henry, 175
Paine, Thomas, 30
Pakistan, 301
Paley, William, 30, 43
Palmer, E. J., 300
Palmerstone, third Viscount, *see* Temple,
    Henry John
Pan-Anglican Congress (1908), 221, 231
Pankhurst, Emmeline, 256
Parish Communion, *see* Eucharist, weekly
Parkes, Harry, 175
Parliament
before 1714, 11–12, 15, 17–20
    in eighteenth century, 23, 25, 31
    in nineteenth century, aetheist in House
        of Commons, 216
    in nineteenth century, Church and state,
        34–36, 77–81, 85–86, 90, 92–93, 120,
        124, 210, 237–238
    in nineteenth century, education, 86–90
    in nineteenth century, reforms, 34, 49–50,
        100
    in nineteenth century, the Empire, 57,
        109, 167–168, 170
    in twentieth century, 257, 260–261,
        279–280, 287
patristics, *see* Church Fathers
Patteson, John Coleridge, 183
Pattison, Mark, 140
Peel, Robert, 36, 77–78, 81, 84, 89–90
Peel, W. G., 187–188
Pelikan, Jaroslav, 4
Pennsylvania, 65, 67, 69
Pepple, King of Bonny, 168
Percival, John, 259
Perry, Charles, 193–194
Perry, Matthew, Commodore 173
Philippines, 179–180, 182
Phillpotts, Henry, 84, 93, 128
Pike, James A., 307–310, 314
Pious Clause, 57
Pittenger, Norman, 307–309, 325–326
Plaatje, Sol, 294
Pobee, John 9
Polk, Leonidas, K., 118, 234
polygamy, 142–143, 199, 206, 241, 246–247,
    250, 252
Ponca Indians, 233

poor relief, 22–23, 103
Portal, Gerald, 178
Porteous, Beilby, 53
post-liberal theology, 284, 302
Potter, Eliphalet N., 186
Potter, Henry Codman, 182, 186
Powell, Baden, 137–139, 141
Pratt, Josiah, 54
Primrose, Archibald John, fourth Earl of
    Rosebery, 178
professionalization of the clergy, 227
Providence, 22, 29, 49, 76
Provoost, Samuel, 67
Prynne, George Rundle, 236
psychology, 272–276, 282, 285, 288, 329
Pulkingham, Graham, 328
Puritans
    in America, 63–65
    in England, 10–15
Pusey, Edward Bouverie, 3, 111–112, 122,
    128, 131–134, 145, 162, 236

racial justice
    South Africa, 287, 316–319, 321
    United States, 262–263, 314, 321–322
racial supremacy, 180–182, 242–243, 252
Raikes, Robert, 98
Ramsey, Ian, 323
Ramsey, Michael, 323–324, 335
Rashdall, Hastings, 158–159, 162
Raven, Charles, 283–285
Rawlinson, E. J., 1
Reason, 39, 304; *see also*
    Scripture–Tradition–Reason
Reeves, Ambrose, 318
Reform Bill of 1832, 35–36, 48, 77, 82–83
Reformation, 8–11
Reformed Episcopal Church, 240
Reichart, Theophilus, 59
Reifsnider, Charles, 296
religious experience, 272, 288
religious orders, 135, 221, 223, 228–230,
    236, 248–249, 262
Religious Organization Law (Japan, 1939),
    299
Renner, Melchior, 53
Resurrection, 5
Rhodes, Cecil, 176
Rice, Spring, 77
Richmond, Wilfrid, 218, 220–221
Ripon, first Earl of, *see* Robinson, Frederick
    John
Risdale, C. J., 238
Robinson, Frederick John, first Earl of
    Ripon, 171
Robinson, John A. T., 324–325

Robinson, R. E., 164
Roebuck, J. A., 87
Rogers, Carl, 329
Romaine, William, 29
Roman Catholicism, 14–15, 34, 36, 78,
    126–128, 173
  dialogue with Anglicans, 291, 335
  in Australia, 195
  in Uganda, 176–178, 185
Rose, Hugh James, 122–123, 141
Rosebery, fourth Earl of, *see* Primrose,
    Archibald John
Roy, Ram Mohan, 170
Royden, Maude, 231
Ruatara, 56
Rusch, Paul, 298
Russell, James S., 234
Russell, John, Lord, 36, 44, 76–77, 83–85,
    89, 92–93, 109
Ryder, Henry, 53, 102

Sacheverell, Henry, 18, 20
Sancroft, William, 13–14, 16
sanctification, 48
Santee Sioux, 232
Sarawak, 180
Sarson, George, 216
Sarum Missal, 279
Sasaki, Shinji, 299
Savoy Conference of 1661, 11
Schereschewsky, Samuel Isaac Joseph, 249
Schleiermacher, F. D. E., 153
Scott, Michael, 317
Scott, Thomas, 48
Scripture
  authority of, 9, 10, 22, 39–40, 43–44, 72,
    80, 122, 129, 131, 150, 189, 199, 203,
    288–289, 308
  biblical criticism, 139–141, 143, 148, 150,
    152
  translation of, 56, 113, 166, 233, 249, 320
  see also Scripture–Tradition–Reason
Scripture Readers' Association, 102
Scripture–Tradition–Reason, 4, 10, 11
Scudder, Vida Dutton, 223–224
Seabury, Paul, 332
Seabury, Samuel, 37, 67
Second World War, 283, 286–287, 299, 301,
    303
secularism, 257, 269, 288, 298
Seeley, John, 164
"self-governing, self-supporting, and self-
    extending," 184, 241–244, 295–296,
    298–299, 320
Selwyn, George Augustus, 116, 191–192,
    194, 203–206

Shaftesbury, seventh Earl of, *see* Ashley
    Cooper, Anthony
Sharp, Granville, 49, 51
Shaw, Alexander Croft, 173
Sheldon, Gilbert, 11–12
Shepherd, Massey Hamilton, 312, 327
Sheppard, H. R. L. ("Dick"), 259–260
Shepstone, Theophilus, 250
Sherrill, Henry Knox, 303–304, 306–307,
    311
Shils, Edward, 4
Shoemaker, Samuel, 276
Shore, John, Lord Teignmouth, 49
Short, Bishop of Adelaide, 194
Shoshone-Bannock Indians, 233
Shuttleworth, H. C. 222
Sidmouth, Viscount, *see* Addington,
    Henry
Sierra Leone, 51–55, 113, 164, 179, 242
Simeon, Charles, 52, 76
Singapore, 60, 179, 328
Sioux Indians, *see* Dakota Indians
Sisterhood of St. Margaret, 229
Sisterhood of the Holy Communion, 229
Sisterhood of the Holy Nativity, 229
Skelton, Kenneth, 320
skepticism, 136–137, 209
Skinner, John, 67
slave trade, 109, 166, 168
slavery, 63, 167
Smeathman, Henry, 51
Smith, Sydney, 36
social gospel, 208, 212
socialism, 150–151, 206, 208–224, 238, 247,
    255; *see also* Christian Socialism
Society for the Promotion of Christian
    Knowledge (SPCK), 17, 50, 52, 58, 62,
    169
Society for the Propagation of the Gospel
    (SPG), 17–18, 52, 112, 201
  in India, 18, 50, 58, 60, 169, 172
  in Japan, 173
  in North America, 18, 50–51, 62, 64
  in South Africa, 197
Society of St. John the Evangelist (Cowley
    Fathers), 230, 262
Society of the Holy Cross, 236
Society of the Sacred Mission, Kelham, 262,
    281
South Africa, 60
  and Empire, 176, 258
  apartheid, 287, 314–319, 321, 335
  as a foreign mission field, 119, 181, 222,
    248–253
  Book of Common Prayer, revision of, 280
  Church and state, 197–201, 250–251

Colenso, Callaway, and the Zulu Mission,
142–143, 199–200, 250–253
episcopate in, 115
Ethiopian Church, 294–295
see also racial justice, South Africa
South Carolina, 29, 61–63, 235–236
South Dakota, 233–234
South India United Church, 300
Southern Episcopal Church, 332
Southey, Robert, 101
Spencer, Herbert, 138
Spencer, John Charles, Viscount Althorp,
76, 82–83, 87
Spengler, Oswald, 258–259, 304
Spooner, William, 102
Sri Lanka, 60
Standing Liturgical Commission (USA),
311, 313
Stanley, Arthur Penrhyn, 145–146
Stanley, Edward Henry, fifteenth Earl of
Derby, 84
Stanley, Henry, 176
Steere, Edward, 181, 247
Stephen, James, 49
Stephen, James, the younger, 108
Stillingfleet, Edward, 13
Strachan, Bishop, of Toronto, 195
Strauss, D. F., 136
Stuart, Edward, 237
Stuck, Hudson, 233
Sumner, C. R., 102
Sumner, J. B., 99
Sunday school, 68–69, 98
Swahili language, 247
Sykes, Norman, 19, 23
Sykes, Stephen, 2, 7
Symes, John Elliotson, 216
Symonds, Herbert, 186, 290
synods, 190–201

Tait, A. C., 143–144, 202, 204–206,
237–238
Talbot, E. S., 155, 280
Tambo, Oliver, 318
Tawney, R. H., 190, 268
Taylor, Jeremy, 10
Temple, Frederick, 139, 141, 144
Temple, Henry John, third Viscount
Palmerstone, 168
Temple, William, 232, 260–261, 263,
268–272, 283–287, 292–293, 301
Test and Corporation Acts, 30, 33, 35
Thirwall, Connop, Bishop, of St. David's,
202
Thirty-nine Articles, 9, 126
Thompson, F. M. L., 256–257

Thornton, Henry, 49, 76
Three Self Movement (China), 336
Tillich, Paul, 325
Tillotson, John, 13
Ting, K. H., 335–336
Tokugawa shogunate, 173
Toland, John, 17
toleration, 15
Tooth, Arthur, 238–239
Tory, *see* Conservative Party
Toulmin, Stephen, 304–305
Townsend, Henry, 166–168, 242–243
Tozer, William G., 247
Tractarian movement, 2–3, 6, 121–129
and missions, 197–199, 208
as a political force, 80, 84, 86, 88, 93, 198,
202–203
criticism of, 146–147
criticism of liberalism, 138
influence of, 148, 150, 224, 227, 229, 239
Tradition, 5, 122, 131, 289, 308; *see also*
Scripture–Tradition–Reason
Transactional Analysis, 329
Transvaal, 176
Travers, Walter, 10
Tevelyan, Charles, 170
Troeltsch, Ernst, 267, 272
Truman, Harry, 306
Tucker, Alfred, R., 177–178
Tucker, Henry St. George, 296
Tutu, Desmond, 335
Tyrell, Bishop of Newcastle, 194–195

Uganda, 165–166, 176–179, 184–185, 299
Church and state, 176–179
nationalism, 299
see also Islam, in Uganda; Roman
Catholicism, in Uganda
Underhill, Evelyn, 275–276
Understanding (as used by Coleridge), 39
United States, 46, 259, 305;
as English colonies, 18, 28–29, 33, 50,
60–65
Church and state, 65–69
see also Episcopal Church (USA); racial
justice, United States
unity, 218, 285, 286, 289
unity of the Church, 186, 204; *see also*
Ecumenical movement
Universities Mission to Central Africa
(UMCA), 247, 293
Upjohn, Richard, 226
Ussher, James, Archbishop of Dublin, 66

Van Buren, Paul, 325
Venn, Henry (1725–1797), 29

Venn, Henry (1796–1873), 167–168, 240–243
Venture in Mission (VIM), 335
Verinder, Frederick, 215
vernacular, use of, 170, 233
vestments, 134, 211, 226, 238, 279
vestries, 61–62
via media, 8, 10, 125–126
Victoria, Queen of England, 171
Vidal, Owen Emeric, 113
Virginia, 61–63, 65, 67, 234

Wake, William, 19–20
Wakefield, Edward Gibbon, 109
Wales
　Church and state, 212, 257–258
　Church in Wales, 257–58, 314
Walker, J. M. Stanhope, 261
Walker, John T., 321
Warburton, William, 25–27, 44
Watson, Joshua, 57–58, 79, 87
Watson, Richard, 36–37
Watts, Isaac, 27–28
Weber, Max, 5
Wedel, Theodore O., 325
Weller, Reginald Heber, 240
Wellesley, Arthur, first Duke of Wellington, 36
Wellington, first Duke of, *see* Wellesley, Arthur
Welsh, William, 232
Wesley, John, 28–29, 48–49
West, E. C., 295
West Indies, 50, 88, 114–115, 314
Westcott, Brooke Foss, 149–152, 157, 217–218, 253, 261
Weston, Frank, 1, 188, 247–248
Whately, Richard, 43
Whig, *see* Liberal Party
Whipple, Henry, 232– 233
White, James, 168
White, William, 37, 66–67
Whitefield, George, 29, 48, 63, 65
Whitgift, John, 46, 66
Whittingham, William, 201
Whittle Francis, 234
Widdcombe, John, 181
Widdrington, Percy, 222–223

Wilberforce, Henry, 128
Wilberforce, Robert Isaac, 122, 128
Wilberforce, Samuel, 84, 112, 118, 138, 140–141, 198–200, 202, 227–228
Wilberforce, William, 49, 51, 53, 55, 57, 76, 79, 98, 100
Wilde, Oscar, 216
Wilkes, John, 30
William and Mary, King and Queen of England, 15–16
Williams, Channing Moore, 118, 173–175
Williams, Rowland, 139, 141
Willis, J. J., 187–188
Wilson, Daniel, 59–60, 76, 170
Wilson, H. H., 170
Wilson, Henry Bristow, 139, 141
Wilson, Thomas, 124
Winnington-Ingram, A. F., 259
Winter, Gibson, 306–307, 326
Wodehouse, Thomas, 214
women, 228–232, 262
　ordination, 2, 232, 282, 301, 329–334
　suffrage, 231–232, 256
Women's Auxiliary to the Episcopal Church's Board of Missions, 231
Woodard, Nathaniel, 97
Woods, F. T., 292
Worcester, Elwood, 273–274
Wordsworth, Christopher, 37, 57, 85
World Council of Churches, 290, 292, 332
World Missionary Conference (Edinburgh, 1910), 290
Worthington, George, 229
Wyvill, Christopher, 34, 49

Xavier, Francis, 173

Yale College, 64
Yates, Richard, 37
Yokoyama, Isaac, 174
Yoruba nation, 166–167, 243

Zaire, 335
Zambia, 315, 320
Zanzibar, 247
Zimbabwe, 185, 315, 320
Zulu nation, 142, 199–200, 250–252